HISTORY OF BUDDHISM
(CHOS-HBYUNG)

HISTORY OF BUDDHISM

(CHOS-HBYUNG)

II. PART

THE HISTORY OF BUDDHISM IN INDIA AND TIBET

BU-STON

TRANSLATOR

E. OBERMILLER

IN TWO PART'S

PART - II

GYAN

Published by

Gyan Publishing House
5, Ansari Road
Daryaganj, New Delhi-110002
Phone: 011-47034999, 9811692060
E-mail: books@gyanbooks.com

Distribution Network
gyanbooks.com
India, USA, Canada, UK, Australia

ISBN: 978-93-6920-009-2 (Set)
978-93-6920-353-6 (HB)
First Published, 1931

2nd Impression 2025

Printed at: Gyan Press, Delhi.

THE MODERN BUDDHIST (Part.II)
Author: BU-STON, Translator: E. OBERMILLER

History of Buddhism

(Chos-ḥbyung)

by

Bu-ston

II. Part

The History of Buddhism in India and Tibet

Translated from Tibetan by

Dr. E. Obermiller

The History of Buddhism in India and Tibet

by

Bu-ston

Translated from Tibetan by

Dr. E. Obermiller

Introduction

The present volume contains the translation of the 2d Part of Bu-ton's History of Buddhism, i. e. of the historical part proper. The latter begins with the Life of the Buddha and ends with an account of the work carried out by the Tibetan Lotsavas and Indian Paṇḍits of Bu-ton's own period and immediately before him (XII and XIII Cent.), viz. the translation of the Buddhist kanonical texts and exegetical treatises from the Sanskrit. We have here, just as in the 1st Part, numerous quotations from both *sūtra* and *çāstra*. Owing to this it becomes possible to get a clear aspect of the principal sources from which Bu-ton has compiled his History, and which have likewise later on served as a basis for the work of Tārānātha. —

Bu-ton's History of Buddhism proper is divided into the following principal parts: —

I. The Life of the Buddha Çākyamuni, the narrative of the so-called 12 Acts of the Buddha *(mdzad-pa bcu-gñis)*, or rather of the 12 principal events in his life. The account of the first eleven, ending with the first "Swinging of the Wheel of the Doctrine" *(chos-kyi ḥkhor-lo bskor-ba = dharma-cakra-pravartana)* represents a summary of the *Lalita-vistara-sūtra* and contains numerous verses from it. Then, after a short indication of the Second and the Third Swingings (i. e. of the Scripture of the intermediate and the later period), there follows the story of the Buddha's attainment of Nirvāṇa. It is taken from the *Vinaya-kṣudraka* (tib. *Ḥdul-ba-phran-tshegs*, Kangyur ḤDUL, XI), being a summary of the corresponding part of the latter.

II. The Rehearsals of the Buddhist Scripture. This part begins with the account of the first Rehearsal (Mahākāçyapa, Ānanda, Upāli), of the death of Kāçyapa and Ānanda, and of the second Rehearsal (Yaças, Kubjita, Revata, etc.). The only source here is likewise the *Vinaya-kṣudraka*, the corresponding text of which is rendered in an abridged form, all the verses being quoted at full length. As concerns the 3d Rehearsal and the 18 Sects, the texts referred to on this subject are: —

1. The *Nikāya-bheda-upadarçana-saṁgraha* of Vinītadeva (Tg. MDO. XC.).
2. The *Bhikṣu-varṣāgra-pṛcchā* of Padmākaraghoṣa (Ibid).
3. The *Prabhāvatī* of Çākyaprabha. (Tg. MDO. LXXXIX.)
4. The *Tarkajvālā* of Bhāvaviveka. (Tg. MDO. XIX.)

The latter work, though not directly mentioned, represents the principal source. Some passages of it are fully contained in Bu-ton's text. —

III. The different theories concerning the time of duration of the Buddhist Doctrine. Here we have quotations from the *Karuṇā-puṇḍarīka*, from Vasubandhu's Commentary on the *Akṣayamati-nirdeça-sūtra* (Tg. MDO. XXXV.), the Commentary on the *Vajracchedikā* (Tg. MDO. XVI), the Commentary on the 3 *Prajñāpāramitā-Sūtras* (Tg. MDO. XIV), etc. We have likewise the chronological calculations of the Sa-skya Paṇḍita and others concerning the time that has passed since the death of the Buddha.

IV. The "prophecies" concerning the persons that have furthered the spread of Buddhism. The most important are those contained in the *Lankāvatāra*, the *Mahā-karuṇā-puṇḍarīka* (Kg. MDO. VI), and the *Mañjuçrī-mūla-tantra*. (Kg. RGYUD. XI. Narthaṅ edition, or XII. Derge edition) A separate prophecy referring to the Tantric Ācāryas, that of the *Kālacakra-uttaratantra* (Kg. RG YUD. I) and the *Mahākāla-tantra-rāja* (Kg. RGYUD. V), is given at the end of this part. It is especially the *Mañjuçrī-mūla-tantra* which is to be regarded as a source of the greatest importance, not only for the History of Buddhism, but for the historiography of India in general. The most interesting is that part of it which refers to the Indian kings, — Açoka, Vira-sena, Nanda, Candragupta, etc. Noteworthy is the passage concerning Pāṇini who is spoken of as the friend of the king Nanda. — A detailed analysis of the historically important parts of all these texts will be published by me before long. —

V. The biographies of the celebrated Buddhist teachers, viz. Nāgārjuna, Āryadeva, Candragomin, Candrakīrti, Āryāsanga, Vasubandhu, Sthiramati, Dignāga, Dharmakīrti, Haribhadra, Çāntideva, etc. Each of these is followed by a list of the works composed by the teacher in question. An Indication of the volumes of the Tangyur (Sūtra and Tantra) in which the works are contained is always given in the notes.

VI. A short summary of the history of the grammatical literature, or rather of the legends referring to it, viz. the stories about Bṛhaspati, Pāṇini, Sarvavarman *(alias* Çarvavarman, Saptavarman, or Īçvaravarman), etc. After that comes an enumeration of the kanonical texts (Sūtra and Tantra) wh'ch have been lost or have not been translated into Tibetan. —

VII. Prophecies of an apocalyptic character foretelling the disappearance of the Buddhist Doctrine. Among these, that of the *Candragarbha-paripṛcchā* is quoted at full length with a very few abbreviations. This prophecy is treated in the Kangyur as a separate work (Kg. MDO. XXXII). In this place the text of the Lhasa block-print of Bu-ton's History contains a great number of mistakes in the proper names, which are sometimes quite illegible (e. g. Akandradha instead of Agnidatta!). A correct rendering of these names has been made possible with the help of the Derge (Sde-dge) edition of the Kangyur.

VIII. The History of Buddhism in Tibet. It begins with the genealogy of the early legendary Tibetan kings, commencing with Ña-ṭhi-tsen-po. Next come the legends about Tho-tho-ri-ñen-tsen and Sroṅ-tsen-gam-po. These are followed by a more detailed account concerning the spread of Buddhism in Tibet during the reign of Ṭhi-sroṅ-de-tsen, viz. the activity of Çāntirakṣita (called the "Ācārya Bodhisattva"), the selection of the first 7 Tibetan monks *[Sad-mi mi bdun]*, the dispute between the adherents of Kamalaçīla and of the Chinese Hva-çaṅ Mahāyāna (the Tsen-min and the Tön-mün), etc. Then we have a brief account of the reign of Ral-pa-can, of the persecution by Laṅ-dar-ma, and of the restauration of the Church by the 10 monks of Ü and Tsaṅ, an indication of the monasteries and monastic sections founded by the said monks and their pupils and, finally, a narrative of the events that followed, viz. the arrival of Dīpaṁkaraçrījñāna (Atīça) in Tibet and the subsequent propagation of Buddhism. In particular we have an enumeration of the texts translated by some of the Lotsavas from the Sanskrit. It may be noted that, with very few exceptions, the texts mentioned belong to the Tantric parts of the Kangyur and Tangyur. Here ends the history proper. It is followed by a list containing the names of all the Paṇḍits and Lotsavas who have acted in Tibet, beginning with Çāntirakṣita and Padmasaṁbhava. With it ends the 3d Chapter *(leḥu)* of Bu-ton's text: "The History of the Doctrine in Tibet".

The last part is a systematical Index of all the Buddhist literature which has been translated from the Sanskrit by the Lotsavas and Paṇḍits. It is divided into 1. Sūtra Scripture (including the Vinaya, Prajñāpāramitā, Avataṁsaka, Ratnakūṭa, and Sūtra sections of the Kangyur), 2. Sūtra Exegesis, 3. Tantra Scripture, and 4. Tantra Exegesis. This Index, as well as the list of the Lotsavas and Paṇḍits, arranged in the alphabetical order, will form a separate 3d part which is to contain numerous other Indices and Appendices besides.

The part now published, similar to the first, includes a great number of smaller chapters and subdivisions. The system according to which these have been designated, is the same as in the first part, and is directly connected with the latter. A full table of the contents is given at the end. —

I may now be permitted to express my deepest gratitude to my revered teacher Professor Th. Stcherbatsky and Professor M. Walleser whose kind attention has made it possible for this work to appear in press. My deepest thanks are likewise due to the Tshan-ñid Lama Chö-ḍag (Chos-grags = Dharmakīrti) Vañchenu, now Abbot of the Kijinge Monastery, for his kind assistance in my study of this part of Bu-ton's text during the summer of 1927, in Transbaikalia. —

E. Obermiller.

The Life of the Buddha

(Description of the 12 acts of the Buddha)[1].

1 and 2. [The Existence of the Bodhisattva in the Form of Çvetaketu and his Descent from the Abode of Tuṣita.]

Twelve years before the Bodhisattva was to enter (his mother's) womb, the sons of the gods belonging to the Pure Region[2], having miraculously assumed the form of Brāhmaṇas, proclaimed aloud that if (the Bodhisattva) would be conceived in the womb, — in the way that is to be described below, — he would become a universal monarch[3] or a Buddha, endowed with the characteristic features and marks (of the super-man)[4]. And (other similar gods) addressed the Pratyekabuddhas (in Jambudvīpa) as follows: — In 12 years the Bodhisattva will become conceived in the womb; therefore you must abandon this land (since there is nothing more for you to do here)[5]. — This was heard by the Pratyekabuddha Mātanga[6] who was abiding on the hill Golāngulaparivartana[7], near Rājagṛha, and he passed away into Nirvāṇa, having left his footprints on a stone. At Vārāṇasī, 500 Pratyekabuddhas gave themselves up to the element of fire[8]. And, after (they were consumed and) had passed away, their ashes fell (on the earth). Thencefrom that place received the name of Ṛṣipatana, —"the place where the Sages fell".

---

[1]) The following narrative of the 12 acts of the Buddha is a summary of the contents of the Lalita-vistara-sūtra (tib. Rgya-cher-rol-paḥi-mdo).

[2]) Tib. *gnas-gtsaṅ-maḥi lhaḥi-bu-rnams* = *çuddha-āvāsa-kāyikā devaputrāḥ*.

[3]) *ḥkhor-los-bsgyur-rgyal* = *cakravarti-rāja*.

[4]) *skyes-bu-chen-poḥi mtshan* = *mahā-puruṣa-lakṣaṇa* and *dpe-byad* = *anuvyañjana*.

[5]) Lalita-vistara 18. 12 — *riñcata mārṣā buddha-kṣetram. ito dvādaça-vatsare bodhisattvo mātuḥ kukṣim avakramiṣyati*.

[6]) Glaṅ-po.

[7]) Mjug-ma-bsgyur-baḥi ri. Lal.-vist. 18. 14 sqq.

[8]) *meḥi khams-la žugs* = *tejo-dhātuṁ samāpadya*. Lal.-vist. 18. 20 sqq.

Now (the Bodhisattva residing in the abode of Tuṣita) [62 a.], having reflected over the meaning of the words of exhortation (which he had heard from the sounds of celestial music), became engaged in 4 kinds of contemplation,[9]) viz. that his future life was to dure a 100 years (1), that Jambudvīpa was to be the continent (in which he would appear) (2), that Central India[10]) was to be the country (where he would be born) (3), and that his caste was to be the royal one[11]) (4). Otherwise, in accordance with Scripture, he contemplated 5 points: — his caste, descent, native country, duration of life, and the woman (that would be his spouse). Having contemplated the world (of his future existence) in these 4 or 5 aspects, he commenced his descent into the human world. He said to the gods (of Tuṣita)[12]): — O friends, there are 108 media for the perception of the Truth, which the Bodhisattva, departing for a future existence, has to demonstrate. O friends, faith[13]) is a means for the perception of the Truth. It is necessary, in order that the thoughts might never become diverted from the Truth[14]). The serenity (of the mind) is a means for the perception of the Truth, since (in order to obtain such a perception), the mind that was agitated and turbid must become pure and serene[15]). — (So he continued) up to: — The position of one who is consecrated for Buddhahood) is a medium for the perception of the Truth. This state dures from the time of (the Bodhisattva's) entering the womb[16]) and up to that of his making manifest the great Nirvāṇa. —

When, from the high region of Tuṣita,
The Leader, the Lion of Men made his departure,
He spoke to the gods the following words: —
O friends, cease to lead a careless life[17])!

---

[9]) Lal.-vist. 19. 6 sqq. — *catvāri mahāvilokitāni vilokayati sma.*

[10]) *yul-dbus = madhya-deça.*

[11]) Or that of the Kṣatriyas. — tib. *rgyal-rigs.*

[12]) Lal.-vist. 31. 10 sqq. — *aṣṭottaram idaṁ mārṣā dharmāloka-mukham-çatam.* [13]) *dad-pa = çraddhā.*

[14]) Lal.-vist. 31. 12—13 — *çraddhā mārṣā dharmāloka-mukham abhedya-āçayatāyai saṁvartate.*

[15]) Ibid. — *prasādo dharmāloka-mukham avila-citta-prasādanatāyai saṁvartate.* [16]) *mnal-du-ḥjug-pa = garbha-avakrānti.*

[17]) Lal.-vist. 36. 14—15. —

Tuṣita-vara-bhavana-nilayād yadā cyavati nāyakaḥ puruṣa-siṁhaḥ /
āmantrayate devān pramādam akhilaṁ visarjayata //

Having delivered these and similar sermons, he placed the diadem of precious jewels on the head of Maitreya[18]) and said: — O friends, I am now departing for Jambudvīpa in order to become a Buddha. Henceforth Maitreya shall expound the Doctrine to you[19]). As he uttered these words, the gods became full of grief and spoke: —

O Highest of beings, if thou shalt not reside here,
This abode of Tuṣita will lose all its splendour[19a]).

And: O Bodhisattva, now (the living beings in) that continent of Jambudvīpa are deceived by the 18 (heretical) teachers who are: Pūraṇa Kāçyapa[20]), Maskarī Goçalīputra[21]), Sañjayī Vairatīputra[22]), Ajita Keçakambala[23]), Kakuda Kātyāyana[24]), and Nirgrantha Jñātiputra[24a]), — the 6 dialectitians [62 b.], by the Brāhmaṇa[25])†, the Brāhmaṇa[26])†, the Brāhmaṇa Bhadraka[27]), the Brāhmaṇa Brahmāyuḥ[28]), the Brāhmaṇa Padmagarbha[29]), and the Brāhmaṇa Lohita[30]), — the 6 reciters (of Brāhmaṇical Scripture), and by Udraka Rāmaputra[31]), Ārāḍa-Kālāma[32]), the Parivrājaka Subhadra[33]), the Brāhmaṇa's son Sañjayaka,[34]) the anchorite Araṇa[35]), and Kāçyapa with the tresses[36]), — the 6 meditators. — It is therefore not the time for thee to go there. Thus they entreated him, but he replied: —

The sound of the conch-shell cannot be confounded with other sounds,
The light of the sun cannot be matched by any other kind of light.

---

[18]) Ma-pham-pa = Ajita.

[19]) Lal.-vist. 39. 1—2. — *ayaṁ Maitreyo bodhisattvo yuṣmākaṁ dharmaṁ deçayiṣyati.*

[19a]) Ibid. 38. 20. *idaṁ khalu satpuruṣa Tuṣita-bhavanaṁ tvayā vihīnaṁ na bhrājiṣyate.*

[20]) Ḥod-sruṅs-rdzogs-byed.

[21]) Kun-tu-rgyu Gnag-lhas-kyi-bu.

[22]) Smra-ḥdod-kyi bu-moḥi bu Yaṅ-dag-rgyal-ba-can.

[23]) Mi-pham skraḥi-lva-ba-can.

[24]) Kā-tyaḥi-bu Nog-can.

[24a]) Gcer-bu-pa Gñen-gyi-bu. [25]) Rgyus(?rgyas)-rgyal = Puṣkara (?).

[26]) Rnas-brdeg (?Rna-dregs = Karṇadarpaṇa). [27]) Bzaṅ-ldan.

[28]) Tshaṅs-paḥi.-tshe [29]) Padmaḥi-sñiṅ-po. [30]) Dmar-po.

[31]) Raṅs-byed-kyi-bu Lhag-spyod.

[32]) Sgyu-rtsal-çes-kyi-bu Riṅ-ḥphur.

[33]) Kun-tu-rgyu Rab-bzaṅ. Cf. below.

[34]) Bram-zeḥi-khyeḥu Kun-rgyal.

[35]) Draṅ-sroṅ Ñon-moṅs-med. [36]) Lhar-rgyas Ḥod-sruṅs-ral-pa-can.

Similarly (my Doctrine) cannot be confounded with the teachings (of all these heretics).
And I alone have the power of vanquishing them.
One single lion terrifies many multitudes of beasts,
A single thunderbolt can shatter the summits of many rocks,
Indra, though single, defeats the numerous chiefs of the Asuras,
And the sun alone disperses the dense mass of darkness.

Thereafter he asked the gods: — In what form am I to go? Some (of the gods) replied that he should assume the form of Brahma, others said that it would be suitable for him to descend in the shape of Indra or some other (god). But the Devaputra Agratejas declared, that, according to the Vedas, it would be the most suitable (for the Bodhisattva) to descend in the form of an elephant. Thereupon the Bodhisattva departed. —

3. [*The Entrance into the Womb.*]

In the palace of the king Çuddhodana[37]) there appeared 18 miraculous signs (foretelling his birth). Thereafter, when winter had passed away, in the first month of spring, when the full moon was in the 16th lunar constellation[38]), and when the stars foretold good luck, at the time when the queen-mother was observing the Poṣadha[39]) fast, [63 a.] he entered her womb through her right side in the form of an elephant. (And she had a dream of which she spoke as follows): —

I felt that, covered with a golden net, with a red crest on the head,
With 6 tusks of exceeding whiteness,
Resembling in colour a conch-shell, snow, or silver,
An elephant entered my womb. —
And, (after the elephant had entered), my body and mind
Became possessed of the most delightful state of ease
Which had never been experienced, heard of or felt before;
As if I were absorbed in concentrated trance[40]).

---

[37]) Zas-gtsan.

[38]) Lal.-vist. 54. 18. — *çiçira-kāla-vinirgate vaiçākha-māse viçākha-nakṣatra-anugate.*

[39]) Gso-sbyon.

[40]) Lal.-vist. 55. 7—10. — *hima-rajata-nibhaç ca ṣaḍ-viṣāṇaḥ sucaraṇa cārubhujaḥ surakta-çirṣaḥ / udaram upagato gaja-pradhāno lalita-gatir dṛḍha-*

(The queen) asked the Brāhmaṇas the meaning of this dream, and they foretold that a son endowed with exclusive properties was to be born who, if he remained residing in the royal palace, would become a universal monarch, and, if he were to lead a monastic life, would attain the state of a Buddha[41]). Thereafter, having blessed the womb as the precious dwelling enjoyed by the Bodhisattva[42]), the latter enjoyed therein for 10 months the purest felicity and, (during that time), converted 3.600.000.000 living beings, gods and men. At that time the flowers opened their leaves and expanded, and other miraculous signs, 32 in number, were to be seen.[43])

4. [The Birth of the Bodhisattva.]

And once, when the mother was abiding in the Lumbinī garden, she seized with her hand the stem of a fig-tree, and (at that moment) the Bodhisattva came out of her right side without causing pain to her and clothed[44]). The gods strewed flowers (before him), Brahma and Indra deposited him on a sheet of Benares linen, and Nanda[45]) and Upananda[46]) offered to wash his body[47]). (The Bodhisattva said): — Behold me, o Kauçika![48]) And, turning to the east: — I shall be antecedent to all that is virtuous![49]) — To the south: — I shall be worthy to receive gifts from gods and men![50]) — To the west: — I shall become the highest and the most preeminent in this world. [63 b.] This is my last birth. I shall now put an end to (the sufferings of) birth, old age, and death[51]). Turning to the north (he exclaimed): — I shall become the highest amongst all living beings![52]) — Looking downward: — I shall

---

vajra-gātra-saṁdhiḥ / na ca mama sukha jātu evaṁrūpaṁ dṛṣṭam api çrutaṁ nā'pi cā'nubhūtaṁ / kāya-sukha-citta-saukhya-bhāvā yathariva (sic) dhyāna-samāhitā abhūvan //

[41]) Lal.-vist. 57. 9—22.

[42]) *ratna-vyūho bodhisattva-paribhogaḥ.*

[43]) Lal.-vist. 73. 11—12. — *daça-māsa-kukṣi-gatena bodhisattvena ṣaṭ-triṁçan-nayutāni deva-manuṣyāṇāṁ paripācitāny abhūvan*; and ibid. 76. 9. sqq. — *rājñaḥ Çuddhodanasya gṛhodyāne dvātriṁçat pūrva-nimittāni prādurabhūvan.*

[44]) Ibid. 82. 14—83. 11. [45]) Dgaḥ-bo. [46]) Ñer-dgaḥ.

[47]) Lal.-vist. 83. 21—22. [48]) I. e. Indra.

[49]) Lal.-vist. 84. 16—17. — *pūrvaṁgamo bhaviṣyāmi sarveṣāṁ kuçala-mūlānāṁ dharmāṇām.*

[50]) Ibid. 84. 20—21. — *dakṣiṇīyo bhaviṣyāmi deva-manuṣyāṇām.*

[51]) Ibid. 85. 1—2. — *iyaṁ me paçcimā jātiḥ / kariṣyāmi jāti-jarā-maraṇa-duḥkhasya antam.*

[52]) Ibid. 85. 2—3. — *anuttaro bhaviṣyāmi sarva-sattvānām.*

vanquish the Evil One and his hosts and shall grant bliss to the denizens of Hell by letting the rain that appeases the hellish fire descend from the great clouds of the Doctrine![53]) And looking upward: — I shall be looked up to by all the living beings! —[54]) Thus spoke he and made 7 steps in each direction. And under his feet there sprung forth lotuses.

At that time all the different countries were full of lucky omens that were to be perceived everywhere. In the 4 great realms four tributary sovereigns and, likewise, 500 men belonging to families of high rank, 800 noble women, Yaçovatī[55]) and the rest, 500 servants, Chandaka[56]) etc., 10 000 male foals, Kaṇṭhaka[57]) etc., 10 000 female foals, and 10 000 oxen were born. In the midst of an island there grew a Bodhi tree, 500 gardens sprung forth and 500 treasures miraculously appeared. Owing to all these circumstances, the prince received the name of Sarvārthasiddha, — he who conveys the accomplishment of all the desired aims and objects[58]).

After that (the Bodhisattva) went to the temple to worship the tutelary deity, and there he subdued and pacified the Çākyas that were using rough obusive language. Henceforth he received the surname of Çākyamuni, — the mighty one amongst the Çākyas. Then, as he received the homage of Çākyavardhana,(?)[59]) or as he was worshipped by the gods, he came to be called Devātideva, — "the god of gods" or "he who is higher than the gods".

7 days after, his mother died and was reborn in the region of the 33 gods. Her death was not caused by (the birth of) the Bodhisattva, but as she saw that her son was to depart (from home in order to lead a monastic life), the mother's heart broke (from grief) and her life thus ended[60]).

In another Sūtra (we have the following account): — Agnidattaputra[61]), the grandson of the sage Araṇa[62]), abiding on the mountain Ādhāra (?)[63]). came to know about (the birth of the Bodhisattva). (Having beheld a vision) he asked: — O, teacher,

---

[53]) Ibid. 85. 4—5. *nihaniṣyāmi māraṁ ca māra-senāṁ ca / sarva-nairayikāṇāṁ ca niraya-agni-pratighātāya mahā-dharma-megha-vṛṣṭiṁ varṣiṣyāmi*

[54]) Ibid. 85. 7. — *ullokanīyo bhaviṣyāmi sarva-sattvānām /*

[55]) Grags-ldan-ma. [56]) Ḥdun-pa. [57]) Sdags-ldan.

[58]) Don-thams-cad-grub-pa.

[59]) Ça-kya-ḥphel. [60]) Lal.-vist. 98. 3—9.

[61]) Mes-sbyin-gyi-bu. [62]) Ñon-moṅs-med. [63]) Kun-ḥdzin.

what does this mean, that the sun simultaneously appears in all the different regions. — Indeed, the mountain [64 a.] with all its caverns is illuminated by one stream of light. — The teacher replied: — The rays of the sun are sharp and piercing, but the rays of the light, that issues from the one child (that has been born), produce a (pleasant) cool feeling if they reach the body. (Such is this light) and it certainly comes from the Bodhisattva. Thereafter Araṇa went to Kapilavastu[64]) and said (to the king Çuddhodana): —

O great king, we who are here
Wish to behold your son.
We are desirous to see him, the Lord,
Who is the Highest and the Leader of the World.

And, as (the Bodhisattva), though sleeping, beheld him, the teacher said: —

Horses that belong to a good breed
Sleep only a quarter of the night.
In a like way, sleep does not long abide
On the eyelids of those who are desirous of fulfilling a great aim.

And: — How is it that the soothsayers have foretold (that the prince is to become) a universal monarch? —

O sovereign, the minds of the learned are mistaken;
In the age of strife[65]) no universal monarch appears.
But he, the treasury of the highest virtuous elements,
Is to become a Buddha, free from all that is sinful.

The young prince was thereafter entrusted to the care of Mahāprajāpatī[66]) Gautamī, and 32 nurses were appointed to him, — 8 who nursed him in their lap[67]), 8 who fed him with their breast[68]), 8 who played with him,[69]) and 8 who wiped off the impurities from his body[70]). Thus cherished, he grew up.

All these miraculous events came to be known by the sage

---

[64]) Ser-skya.
[65]) *rtsod-paḥi dus* = *kaliyuga.*
[66]) Skye-dguḥi-bdag-mo.
[67]) *paṅ-na ḥtsho-baḥi ma-ma* = *anga-dhātrī.*
[68]) *nu-ma-bsnun-pa* = *kṣīra-dhātrī.*
[69]) *rtsen-paḥi ma-ma* = *krīḍā-dhātrī.*
[70]) *dri-ma-ḥphyi-ba* = *mala-dhātrī.* Lal.-vist. 110. 13—19.

Asita[71]) — endowed with the 5 supernatural faculties[72]) who was abiding on the Himālaya. (This sage), with his nephew Naradatta[73]), miraculously (descended from his abode) and came to the city of Kapilavastu[74]). Having beheld the characteristic marks (of the youth), he understood of what kind they were. And, astonishment and grief having arisen in him, he bowed to the Bodhisattva's feet, circumambulated him, and, shedding tears, uttered his prophecy: —

> I perceive the characteristic features of this youth who has been born. [64 b.]
> He is adorned by the 32 marks (of the super-man),
> Therefore there are only two things possible and no other: —
> If he remains at home, he will become a universal monarch,
> And if he departs from home and becomes a homeless ascetic,
> He will attain Enlightenment here in this world
> And become a leader who is independent from others.
> (But I know that) he is not to abide at home,
> For his private parts that are concealed[75]) and the crown of his head
> Cannot be seen by all[76]). —

But (asked the king), why doest thou weep? —
(The sage replied) —[77]):

> O sovereign, having met with this Highest of Beings, the treasury of virtue,
> I shall die without attaining my aim.
> I have not come to quiescence and perceive all that is sinful in me;
> Therefore my mind is greatly suffering, and I weep. —

Having said this, he departed to his abode.

When the Bodhisattva had grown older, he, with 10 000 other

---

[71]) Nag-po. [72]) *mṅon-çes* = *abhijñā*.

[73]) Sic. acc. to Lal.-vist., but tib. Mes-byin = Agnidatta.

[74]) Lal.-vist. 101. 1—5.

[75]) *ḥdoms-kyi sbo-ba spubs-su-nub-pa* = *koça-gata-vasti-guhya*.

[76]) Sic. acc. to tib. — *gsaṅ-baḥi-gnas-mchog spubs-su-nub-pa daṅ spyi-gtsug ḥgro-ba kun-gyis mi-mthoṅ-bas*. But Lal.-vist. 105. 9. sqq. and 106. 8. sqq. — *nārhati Sarvārthasiddhaḥ kumāro' gāram adhyāvasitum. tat kasya hetoḥ? sa hi mahārāja Sarvārthasiddhaḥ kumāro dvātriṁçatā mahā-puruṣa-lakṣaṇaiḥ samanvāgataḥ*.

[77]) Lal.-vist. 104. 3—105. 5.

youths of the Çākya clan entered the school of the teacher Viçvāmitra[78]) who taught the art of writing. (The Bodhisattva) asked: — O teacher, which of the 64 kinds of writing, Brāhmī[79]) and the rest, must I study?[80]). The teacher was greatly astonished and said[81]) —:

Most wonderful is this purest of living beings:
He is proficient in all the different sciences, but still
Adapting himself to the worldly usage,
He has come to my school of writing.
Of these different kinds of writing
Of which I do not know even the name,
All are known to him. But nevertheless
He has entered my school of writing. —

Once the youth descended into the garden, and there in the shade of a Jambu tree, he became absorbed in mystic meditation[82]), beginning with the first degree and ending with the fourth[83]). Owing to the (power of this his meditative trance), 5 heretical sages, endowed with miraculous powers became incapable of moving in the skies. Full of awe they worshipped the Bodhisattva and circumambulated him[84]). At that time the shadows of the other trees were constantly changing their direction, but that (of the Jambu tree under which the Bodhisattva was sitting) remained immovable [65 a.] (Upon seing this) his father was greatly astonished and worshipped him, saying[85]): —

O Lord, at the time when thou wert born,
And now, when thou, O Glorious, art practising meditation,
These two times, O Leader and Protector,
My salutation was and is due to thee. —

---

[78]) Kun-gyi-bçes-gñen. [79]) *tshaṅs-paḥi yi-ge.*

[80]) Lal.-vist. 125. 18—20. sqq. — *katamāṁ me bho upādhyāya lipiṁ çikṣāpayasi: brāhmī-kharoṣṭī-puṣkarasārim* etc.

[81]) Ibid. 126. 15—18. — *āçcaryaṁ çuddhasattvasya loke lokānuvartino /*
çikṣitaḥ sarva-çāstreṣu lipi-çālām upāgataḥ //
yeṣām ahaṁ nāmadheyaṁ lipīnāṁ na prajānami (sic!) /
tatrai'ṣa çiṣitasanto lipi-çālām upāgataḥ //

[82]) *bsam-gtan = dhyāna.*

[83]) Lal.-vist. 128. 15—129. 11. [84]) Ibid. 129. 12—14 sqq.

[85]) Ibid. 132. 16—17. —
yadā cā' si mune jato yadā dhyāyasi cā'rciman /
eka-dvir api te nātha pādau vande vināyaka. //

5. [The Acts of Dexterity performed by the Bodhisattva.]

Thereafter, the eldermen of the Çākyas said to the king: — O Sovereign, the sooth-sayers have foretold that the youth, if he is to remain in the palace, will become a universal monarch. As this is so, he must take a worthy princess for his wife. — To this the king replied: — You must look where you find a maiden worthy of the youth[86]). — Then each of the 500 Çākya eldermen said that his daughter was the worthiest. The king then told them to ask the youth himself. The latter, having been questioned, said, that in 7 days he would give an answer[87]). And such were the thoughts that came to him:[88]) —

I know that the evil caused by desire has no end,
That it is the source of strife, enmity, grief, and suffering,
Is like a poisonous plant that causes fear,
Like fire or like the edge of a sword.
I have no desire of the objects of sensual pleasure,
And it is not suitable for me to abide in a circle of women;
With a mind, pacified through the bliss of mystic meditation and concentrated trance,
I shall do better to abide silently in the forest. —

But, as he again reflected over the matter, (he changed his intention) owing to his Wisdom and Commiseration. — And such were the words he uttered[89]) —:

The lotus-flowers grow amidst an impure mire,
A king receives homage amongst ordinary people.
At the time when the Bodhisattvas become possessed

---

[86]) Lal.-vist. 137. 5—6. [87]) Ibid. 137. 10—12.

[88]) Ibid. 137. 13—17. —
vidita mama ananta-kāma-doṣāḥ sarana-savaira-saçoka-duḥkha-mūlāḥ /
bhayakara-viṣapatra-saṁnikūçāḥ jvalana-nibhā asidhāra-tulyarūpāḥ /
kāma-guṇi (sic) *na me'sti chanda-rāgo na ca ahu çobhami istrigāra-madhye* /
yannu ahu vane vaseya tuṣṇīṁ dhyāna-samādhi-sukhena çānta-cittaḥ //

[89]) Ibid. 137. 21—138. 6. —
saṁkīrṇi panki padumāni vivṛddhimanti /
ākīrṇa rāja nara-madhyi labhāti pūjāṁ /
yada Bodhisattva parivāra-balaṁ labhante /
tada sattva-koṭi-nayutāny amṛte vinenti //
ye cā'pi pūrvaka abhūd vidu-Bodhisattvāḥ /
sarvebhi bhārya-suta darçita istri-gārāḥ /
na ca rāga-rakta na ca dhyāna-sukhebhi bhraṣṭāḥ /
hantā'nuçikṣayi ahaṁ pi guṇeṣu teṣām /

Of the highest congregation (of followers)[90],
They lead millions of living beings to the state of immortality.
The wise Bodhisattvas who have appeared before (me)
Have all of them manifested themselves
As having wives, children, and followers.
Now, they were not possessed of desire,
And have not been deprived
Of the bliss of concentrated trance. [65 b.]
I must likewise become possessed of these their virtues[91]).

Having thought so, he wrote down all the virtuous qualities of a woman and said: — Such (a wife) do I wish for myself. Then the king said to his chief household priest[92]): — Go thou and get a maiden with whom all these virtuous qualities are to be found. —

She may be of the royal race, or the daughter of a Brāhmaṇa,
She may be of the Vaiçya[93]) or of the Çūdra[94]) caste;
This is quite the same. Bring us only such a maiden
With whom all these virtues do exist.
My son is not to be surprised by high birth and descent;
Virtue, truthfulness and righteousness, —
In these alone his mind finds pleasure[95]).

Thereafter, that Brāhmaṇa went through all the different countries and came to see Gopā[96]) the daughter of the Çākya Daṇḍapāṇi[97]). He gave to her the letter (of the prince) and she said with a smile: — O Brāhmaṇa, I am possessed of all these qualities. Therefore, the prince of noble appearance can become my husband. Tell the youth that, if he wishes (to wed me), he must not delay. He ought not to live with an ordinary being of low degree[98]). —

---

[90]) Tib. *ḥkhor-mchog* = *parivāra-varaṁ*; the Lal.-vist. has *parivāra-balaṁ*.

[91]) I. e. of the preceding Bodhisattvas.

[92]) *mdun-na-ḥdon* = *purohita*.

[93]) *rjeḥu-rigs*. [94]) *dmaṅs-rigs*.

[95]) Lal.-vist. 140. 2—5. —
brāhmaṇiṁ kṣatriyāṁ kanyāṁ vaiçyāṁ çūdrīṁ tathaiva ca /
yasyā ete guṇā santi tāṁ me kanyāṁ pravedaya //
na kulena na gotreṇa kumāro mama vismitaḥ /
guṇe satye ca dharme ca tatrā'sya ramate manaḥ //

[96]) Sa-ḥtsho-ma.

[97]) Lag-na-be-con-can.

[98]) Lal.-vist. 140. 21—141. 4. —

All this the chief priest repeated to the king. The latter said: — These women are great in telling lies; they are therefore not to be relied upon. Let, after 7 days, all the maidens assemble in the hall, and the youth shall give them presents that are agreeable to them. (That maiden) on whom the youth shall fix his eyes, is to become his wife[99]).

After 7 days had passed away, the youth descended into the hall and offered diverse precious ornaments to the maidens that came, but they could not support the lustre of the Bodhisattva's beauty and speedily departed. Last of all came Gopā, and, as the ornaments had been, all of them, given away, she said with a smile: — What fault have I committed, that thou despisest me? — I do not despise thee, — said the youth, but thou hast come too late[100]) [66 a.]. Thus spoke he and presented her a ring worth many hundreds and thousands. She then departed, and those that had witnessed (all this in secret),[101]) said to the king: —The youth has fixed his eyes on Gopā and they have conversed with each other for a short time[102]). —The king then sent a messenger to the Çākya Daṇḍapāṇi, praying him to give his daughter in marriage to the prince. But Daṇḍapāṇi said: — The youth has grown up amidst the pleasures of palace-life and is not skilled in arts and sports. According to the usage of my family, I may give my daughter only to one who knows the different arts. How can I give her in marriage to one who is not skilled in them?[103]) This was repeated to the king who, having been thus twice offended, sat and pondered deeply. The youth heard about this and said to the king: — What has happened? — Is it not proper that thou shouldst tell me? — And the king told him all. The youth then proposed that a match in all the different arts and sports should be fought. The king was delighted and ordered to announce, by the sound of bells, that such a match was to take place. And, after 7 days, 500 youths of the Çākya tribe assembled in order to join in the match, and Gopā was declared to be the prize of him who would win[104].) It was proclaimed that she was to belong

---

[99]) Ibid. 141. 11—12. — *tatra yasyāṁ dārikāyāṁ kumārasya cakṣur abhiniveksyati kumārasya vārayiṣyāmi iti* /

[100]) Lal.-vist. 142. 14, 15. — *nā'haṁ tvāṁ vimānayāmi api tu khalu punas tvam atipaçcād āgatā* /

[101]) *bya-ra-ba = guhya-puruṣa.* [102]) Lal.-vist. 142. 20—22.

[103]) Ibid. 143. 4—7. [104]) Ibid. 144. 6—9.

to him who would be victorious in swordsmanship, in shooting and wrestling. And first of all came Devadatta[105]); he encountered an elephant that was led (into the city for the Bodhisattva), and, full of envy and pride, struck it with the palm of his hand and killed it. Thereafter, the youth Sundarananda[106]) came and (seing the body of the elephant), flung it out of the gates of the city. But last of all came the Bodhisattva, uplifted the elephant's body with his great toe and hurled it a mile far beyond 7 walls and 7 trenches. And at the place, where the elephant's body fell, a great pit was dug up (and up to this day) it is called "the elephant's pit"[107]).

Thereafter the teacher Viçvāmitra having been appointed as a judge, [66. b.] a match in the skill of writing took place, and the Bodhisattva was victorious in the contest. After that there was a match in the skill of counting in which the teacher Arjuna[108]) of the Çākya clan was the judge. Here the Bodhisattva likewise gained the prize, having vanquished all the others. Arjuna himself did not know the numbers higher than that which is called ***akṣobhya***[109]), whereas the Bodhisattva knew them all up to that which bears the name of ***agrasāra***[110]). Then the Bodhisattva proved superior (to the rest) in leaping, swimming, and in the foot-race. Thereupon Nanda and Ānanda both came to match their strength (with that of the Bodhisattva), but (the latter) only touched them with his hand and they instantly fell down. Next came Devadatta, and the Bodhisattva seized him with his right hand, turned him round in the air and then threw him on the ground, without however doing harm to his body. Then all the Çākya youths rushed upon him, but the Bodhisattva only touched them with his hand and they all fell down.

The contest in shooting next took place. The target, an iron drum, was hit by Ānanda at the distance of 4 miles,[111]) by Devadatta —within the reach of 8 miles, by Sundarananda, — from beyond 12 miles, and by Daṇḍapāṇi — at the distance of 2 yo-

---

105) Lhas-byin. 106) Mdzes-dgaḥ-bo.

107) Ibid. 145. 4—7....... ***yat sāṁpratam hasti-gartā ity abhidhīyate*** /

108) Srid-sgrub.

109) ***mi-ḥkhrugs-pa.*** Cf. Vol. I. Note 1118.

110) ***sñiṅ-po-mchog.*** Lal.-vist. 146. 9—149. 2.

111) Ibid. 154. 6. sqq.; ***rgyaṅ-grags = kroça.***

janas.[112]) So far each of them could shoot, but not at a greater distance. But the Bodhisattva planted the iron drum at the distance of 20 miles, behind it 7 Tala trees and, beyond them, — the figure of a wild boar made of iron. He then brought from the temple the bow of his grandfather Siṁhahanu[113]) and bent it, drawing in one leg and stretching out the other. Off sped the arrow, piercing the iron drum, the 7 Tala stems and the iron figure of the wild boar. And, having hit the ground, it disappeared. At that place there appeared (a pit) resembling a well which is known thencefrom as "the well of the arrow"[114]). (Thereafter) the Bodhisattva likewise showed his superiority in all the other arts, as palmistry[115]), riding an elephant, and so on up to the preparation of incense-sticks. [67. a.] And Daṇḍapāṇi gave his daughter in marriage to him[116]).

6. [The Life of the Bodhisattva in the circle of noble women.]

The Bodhisattva, in order to act in accordance with the worldly custom, caused Gopā to be crowned (as the chief princess) amongst 84 000 noble women. And in their company he led a life full of bliss and enjoyment.

Thereafter, some of the gods, Nāgas etc.[117]) beheld him and thought as follows: — If this highest of men will abide amidst the circle of noble women for a long time, the living beings who are to be the receptacles of his Doctrine, will be no more existing and he will not depart (from home to lead a religious life)[118]). And, full of reverence, they thought: — He must depart from home, become a Buddha and expound his Doctrine. — And the Buddhas, the Lords (abiding in the regions situated in the 10 quarters of the sky)[119]) summoned him by the following verse that issued from the sounds of celestial music[120]):

---

[112]) *dpag-tshad.* [113]) Seṅ-geḥi-za-ḥgram.

[114]) Lal.-vist. 155. 19, 20. — *yatra ca pradeçe sa iṣur bhūmi-talaṁ bhittvā praviṣṭas tasmin pradeçe kūpaḥ saṁvṛttaḥ / yad adyatve' pi çara-kūpa ity abhidhīyate /* [115]) *lag-rtsis.* [116]) Lal-vist. 157. 3—5.

[117]) Ibid. 160. 3, 4. sqq. *deva-nāga-yakṣa-asura-garuḍa-kiṁnara-mahoraga-Çakra-Brahma-lokapālānām.*

[118]) Sic. acc. to tib., but Lal.-vist. 160. 8—9. *tāni dharma-bhājanāni sarvāṇy antarhitāni bhaviṣyanti / bodhisattvaç ca paçcād abhiniṣkramya anuttarāṁ samyaksaṁbodhim abhisaṁbhotsyate //*

[119]) Lal.-vist. 161. 12, 13. sqq. — *daça-dig-loka-dhātu-sthitair buddhair bhagavadbhiḥ.* [120]) Ibid. 161. 17—20. sqq.

Long before, having perceived the living beings
Enduring a hundred different kinds of suffering,
Thou hast uttered the following entreaty:
"May I become the refuge, the protector and the shelter,
The benefactor and the friend of all that lives! —"
O, hero of virtue, remember now thy previous life
And thy vow of helping the living beings.
The time and the hour for thee have come; —
Depart thou, O great Sage, from thy home.

And from the sounds of the musical instruments, played by the noble women of his retinue he heard the following words which were preceded by a narrative of his previous births[121]): —

The 3 spheres of the world are subjected to the suffering of decrepitude and illness,
And, being without a refuge, are consumed by the fire of death.
The living beings are ignorant of the means of deliverance from this Phenomenal Life,
Being like bees that have fallen into a water-pot.
The 3 spheres of the world are non-enduring, being like clouds in autumn,
The birth and death of a living being appear like a pantomime on the stage,
And the duration of life is short, like that of lightning in the skies. [67. b.]
It flows speedily, like a stream, descending from a mountain.

And[122]): —

Remember thou thy previous life
And grant thou the vision of the Truth,
Free from defilement and immaculate,
And the sublime light of the Highest Divine Wisdom to the living beings
Who are obscured by the gloom of ignorance and infatuation.

Upon hearing all this the Bodhisattva got rid of his intoxication and directed his mind toward Supreme Enlightenment. Thereupon, 3 200 000 Devaputras likewise summoned him, saying[123]): —

[121]) Ibid. 173. 11—14.
[122]) Ibid. 179. 3—4.
[123]) Ibid. 183. 21—184. 2.

The change of existence, most wonderful[124]),
And this thy birth have been demonstrated by thee, O Lion of men,
And thou hast likewise made manifest
Thy life in the circle of noble women[125]).
Thou hast thus acted in conformity with the worldly custom,
Having become familiar with the worldly properties,
And hast brought to maturity a multitude of gods and men.
But at present thou must think, how to depart from home,
For the time to do this has now come. —

And further on[126]): —

O thou, sweet-voiced and soft-voiced, —
Remember thou the prophecy of Dīpaṁkara,
And let thy voice of a Buddha be heard,
True, right, and free from error. —

At that time the king beheld in a dream that the Bodhisattva was departing (from home). When he awakened, he asked the eunuch whether the Bodhisattva was still abiding (in the palace). The answer was: — He is here. — The king thought: — This is a sign, that the Bodhisattva is to become an ascetic. — And, in order to make the Bodhisattva still more attached (to his present worldly life), he caused three palaces to be built for him, — a cool one for summer-time, one suitable for the rainy season, and a warm one for the winter[127]). And in each of these palaces 500 men accompanied the Bodhisattva when he ascended and descended the staircase, and half a yojana far was heard their watch-word: — The prince is not to go out unnoticed! —

Now, the sooth-sayers had all of them foretold, that (the Bodhisattva, would depart by the royal gates[128]). And the king ordered many massive door-planks to be made. 500 men were

---

[124]) tib. *çin-tu-brtan* (?) for *atiyaçāḥ*.

[125]) Or the harem — *btsun-moḥi-ḥkhor* = *antaḥpura*.

[126]) Lal.-Vist. 185.15, 16. — *mañju-ruta mañju-ghoṣa smarāhi Dīpaṁkarasya vyākaraṇaṁ* /
bhūtaṁ tathā avitathā jina-ghoṣa-rutam udīrehi //

[127]) Ibid. 186. 9, 10. sqq. — *tato rājñā Çuddhodanena kumārasya paribhogārthaṁ trayo yathartukā-prāsādāḥ kāritā abhūvan / graiṣmiko vārṣiko haimāntikaç ca* /

[128]) *bkra-çis-kyi chab-sgo* = *mangala-dvāra*.

appointed to open and shut these doors, and their watch-word was to be heard [68. a.] half a yojana far[129]).

Thereafter, the Bodhisattva said to (his charioteer) Chandaka[130]): — Prepare for me a chariot to go to the garden. — And Chandaka told this to the king. The latter gave the order that (on the way) the prince was to be kept far from all disagreeable sights and that he should see only pleasant and delightful objects[131]).

Then the Bodhisattva went out through the eastern gate, and saw there a man, subjected to the suffering of old age. This apparition was produced by the Devaputras through the incitation of the Bodhisattva himself[132]). The latter asked Chandaka:[133]) —

> O, charioteer, who is this man, feeble and helpless?
> His flesh and blood have dried up, he has but skin and sinews,
> His hair is white, his teeth are scarce, his body meager,
> He walks painfully and reeling and leans upon a staff. —

The charioteer replied:[134]) —

> This man, O Prince, is overcome by old age,
> His senses are weakened, he is greatly suffering,
> And his strength and energy are gone.
> He is disrespected by his friends and has no protector,
> Is unfit for action and cast out like a withered tree. —

The Bodhisattva then said[135]): —

> Tell me, is this a characteristic of this man only,
> Or does the whole of the living world undergo such a state?
> Tell me quickly, how is the state of things,
> And having heard, I shall duly reflect over the sense. —

---

129) Lal.-vist. 186. 17—19.

130) Ḥdun-pa.

131) — *mā kumāraḥ pratikūlaṁ paçyed* etc. Lal.-Vist. 187. 3—11.

132) Ibid. 187. 21. sqq. — *bodhisattvasya eva anubhāvena çuddha-āvāsa-kāyikair devaputraiḥ.* Ibid. 188. 5—9. — *kiṁ sārathe puruṣa durbala alpasthāmo / ucchuṣka-māṁsa-rudhira-tvaca-snāyu-naddhaḥ / çvetaṁçiro virala-danta kṛṣāṅga-rūpo / ālambya-daṇḍa vrajate asukhaṁ skhalantaḥ //*

134) Ibid. 188. 11—14. — *eṣo hi deva puruṣo jarayā' bhibhūtaḥ / kṣīṇen-driyaḥ suduḥkhito bala-vīrya-hīnaḥ / bandhū-janena paribhūta anāthabhūtaḥ / kāryā' samartha apaviddhu vaneva dāruḥ //*

135) Ibid. 16—19. — *kula-dharma-eṣa oyam asya hitaṁ bhaṇāhi / athavā' pi sarva-jagato' sya iyaṁ hy avasthā / çīghraṁ bhaṇāhi vacanaṁ yatha-bhūtam etat / çrutvā tathā' rtham iha yoniça cintayiṣye //*

The charioteer answered[136]): —

> O Prince, this is neither the property of his race, nor of his country only.
> With all the living beings, youth gives way to decrepitude;
> Thy father and mother and the host of thy relatives likewise
> Cannot be delivered from the suffering of old age. —
> No other way exists for the living beings! —

To this the Bodhisattva said[137]):

> O Charioteer, fie on the minds of the stupid living beings,
> They are infatuated with the pride of youth and have no look for (the coming) old age!
> I will go back, turn round the chariot quickly [68. b.]
> I too will be subjected to old age; what use is there
> For me to be merry and amuse myself? —

So saying, he returned to the city.

Then he went out by the southern gate and, seeing a sick person, asked[138]):

> O, charioteer, who is that man whose body is stiff and pallid,
> Who is deprived of all the senses and breathing hard,
> Whose members have all withered, whose belly
> Is swollen, and who, perfectly exhausted, sits
> In his own urine and ordure, an object of disgust? —

The charioteer replied[139]):

> This man, O Prince, is severely ill,
> And, full of the fear, caused by this illness, is near to death;
> He has not the bright appearance of the healthy, his strength is gone,

---

136) Ibid. 188. 21—189. 2. — *nai'tasya deva kula-dharma na rāṣṭra-dharmaḥ / sarve jagasya jara yauvanu dharṣayāti / tubhyaṁ pi mātṛ-pitṛ-bāndhava-jñāti-saṁgho / jarayā amukta na hi anya gatir janasya //*

137) Ibid. 189. 4—7. — *dhik sārathe abudha-bāla-janasya-buddhiḥ / yad yauvanena mada-matta jarāṁ na paçyet / āvartayā' çu mi rathaṁ punar ahaṁ pravekṣye / kiṁ mahya krīḍa-ratibhir jarayā' çritasya //*

138) Ibid. 189. 14—17. *kiṁ sārathe puruṣa ruṣya-vivarṇa-gātraḥ / sarvendriyebhi vikalo guru-praçvasantaḥ / sarvāṅga-çuṣka udarākula-kṛcchra-prāpto / mūtre purīṣi svaki tiṣṭhati kutsanīye //*

139) Ibid. 19—22. — *eṣo hi deva puruṣo paramaṁ gilāno / vyādhībhayam upagato maraṇānta-prāptaḥ / ārogya-teja-rahito bala-viprahīno / atrāṇa-dvīpa-çaraṇo hy aparāyaṇaç ca.*

And he has neither protector, nor refuge, nor shelter, nor
help. —

The Bodhisattva said[140]):

The state of health is (ephemere) like enjoyment in a dream,
And (on the contrary) the terror of illness is so great!
How can a wise man, having seen this state (of illness),
Indulge in pleasures or have the notion of something as
being blissful? —

(And, as before he returned to the city.)

Then, as he went out through the western gate, he saw a dead body and asked again[141]):

Who, O charioteer, is that man,
Whom they carry there on a bier, surrounding him,
Tearing out their hair and nails and scattering dust on
their heads,
Uttering various sounds of lamentation and beating their
breasts? —

The charioteer answered[142]):

This man, O Prince, has died here in Jambudvīpa,
Henceforth he shall no more see his parents, his wife and
children,
He has left his wealth, his home, and the circle of his friends,
He is now in another world and shall no more see those
whom he knew. —

The Bodhisattva said[143]):

Fie on the youth that is overpowered by decrepitude!
Fie on the health that is overpowered by illness!
Worthless for a sage is life that has no long duration, [69. a.]

---

140) Ibid. 190. 2—5. — *ārogyatā ca bhavate yatha svapna-krīḍā / vyādhībhayaṁ ca imam īdṛçu ghora-rūpaṁ / ko nāma vijñapuruṣo ima dṛṣṭva vasthāṁ* (sic) / *krīḍā-ratiṁ ca janayec chubha-saṁjñatāṁ ca //*

141) Ibid. 190. 14—17. — *kiṁ sārathe puruṣa mañca-parigṛhīto / uddhūta-keça-nakha pāṁçu çire kṣipanti / paricārayitva viharanty uras tāḍayanto / nānā-vilāpa-vacanāni udīrayantaḥ //*

142) Ibid. 190. 19—22. — *eṣo hi deva puruṣo mṛtu Jambudvīpe / na hi bhūyu mātṛpitṛ-drakṣyati putra-dārān / apahāya bhoga-gṛha-mitra-jñāti-saṁghaṁ para-loka-prāptu na hi drakṣyati bhūyu jñātiṁ //*

143) Ibid. 191. 2—9. *dhig yauvanena jarayā samabhidrutena / ārogya dhig vividha-vyādhi-parāhṛtena / dhig jīvitena viduṣā nacira-sthitena / dhik paṇḍitasya puruṣasya rati-prasaṅgaiḥ* etc.

And worthless is for the wise man the attachment to worldly pleasures!
O, that old age, illness, and death would not exist!
But great is the suffering that takes hold of the 5 groups of elements,
And what is there to say of old age, illness and death, which are persisting and continuous.
Enough, let us go back and reflect
Over the means how to attain Salvation. —

(And, having once more returned to the city, he again went out, this time) by the northern gate. There he saw a mendicant monk and asked[144]):

Who, O charioteer, is this man with a calm and tranquil mind,
Who goes with downcast eyes, looking only a *yuga*-length before himself,
Clad in a mantle of reddish hue and walking in perfect peace,
Bearing an alms-bowl and free from arrogance and conceit? —

The charioteer answered[145]):

This man, O Prince, is called a mendicant monk,
He has abandoned all desires and undergoes the strictest discipline,
He has embraced religious life and seeks quiescence for himself,
Is free from passion and hatred, and wanders, living on alms. —

To this the Bodhisattva said[146]):

Well hast thou spoken, this pleases me;
Religious life has been always praised by the wise. —
In it lies the welfare of oneself and other living beings,

---

[144]) Ibid. 191. 20—192. 2. — *kiṁ sārathe puruṣa çantā-praçānta-citto / notkṣipta-cakṣu vrajate yuga-mātra-darçī / kāṣāya-vastra-vasano supraçānta-cārī / pātraṁ gṛhītva na ca uddhatu unnato vā //*

[145]) Ibid. 192. 4—7. — *eṣo hi deva puruṣo iti bhikṣu nāma / apahāya kāma-ratayaḥ suvinīta-cārī / pravrajya-prāptu çamam ātmana eṣamāṇo / saṁrāga-doeṣa-vigato' nveti piṇḍa-caryām //*

[146]) Ibid. 192. 9—12. — *sādhū subhāṣitam idaṁ mama rocate ca / pravrajya nāma vidubhiḥ satataṁ praçastā / hitam ātmanaç ca para-sattva-hitaṁ ca yatra / sukha-jīvitaṁ sumadhuraṁ amṛtaṁ phalaṁ ca //*

And its result is a blissful existence, full of beatitude and immortality. —

Thereupon the Bodhisattva returned to his home.

7. [The Departure of the Bodhisattva from Home].[147])

The king, having seen and heard all this, (made arrangements) in order to guard (the Bodhisattva and prevent his departure). Walls were built, moats dug out, and massive doors were erected. At the crossing places of the roads[148]), going from each of the four gates of the city, strong detachments of troops were placed, in order to guard the passage. The harem received the order to sing and make music (uninterruptedly) and to arrange various mirthful plays. But at that time there appeared certain ominous signs foretelling the Bodhisattva's departure. — The birds ceased to sing, the lotus-flowers withered, the trees bloomed no more, the sound of the pipes and lutes suddenly broke up, and the drums, though they were beaten, ejected no sound. The king sat deeply pondering [69. b.] Gopā beheld in a dream that the earth trembled and many other visions, and the Bodhisattva himself had the following dream. — He saw that he was moving the waves of the ocean, that the whole of the earth was his couch and the mount Sumeru — his pillow, that a great light dispersed all darkness, and that an umbrella, arising from the ground, was spread over the 3 Spheres of the world. He saw, moreover, that animals black and white and birds of 4 different colours appeared, and became, all of them, of one colour, that he himself ascended a mountain consisting of impurities without becoming polluted, rescued many living beings that were carried by the waters of a stream, healed the sick and, finally, having seated himself on the slope of the mount Sumeru on a throne supported by lions, received the homage of the gods. —

Thereupon the Bodhisattva, thinking it unsuitable to depart without the leave of his father, went to the latter and said: — The time of my departure has come. I pray thee not to hinder me and not to be grieved. The king replied: I shall give thee everything that thou canst desire, if thou wouldst but remain in the palace. The Bodhisattva said: — Grant me perpetual youth,

---

[147]) *mṅon-par-ḥbyuṅ-ba* = *abhiniṣkramaṇa*.

[148]) Lal-vist. *bži-mdo* = *çṛṅgāṭaka*.

health, and immortality. — I have not the power to give thee these. Ask thou something else, — returned the king. Again the Bodhisattva said[149]):

> O King, if thou canst not grant me these 4 highest boons,
> The absence of the fear of old age, illness, death, and of all calamities,
> I pray thee then to hear another my wish, — make
> That there should be no repeated existence[150]),
> After this life has taken an end. —

After that the king said: — May thy desire be fulfilled, — whereupon the Bodhisattva returned to his abode.

And the king told all that to the Çākyas. The latter having agreed to guard the prince, 500 Çākya youths were placed at each of the 4 gates of the city. [70. a.] Each of these had 500 chariots under his command and each chariot was surrounded by 500 foot-soldiers. The eldermen of the Çākyas placed themselves at all the crossing places of 3 and 4 roads, and the king himself held watch[151]).

At that time, the Yakṣa chiefs and the 500 sons of Hāritī[152]), as they knew that the Bodhisattva was to depart that evening, exerted themselves in worshipping him. The 4 great guardian-kings thought of offering horses for his departure[153]), and the 33 gods likewise performed acts of worship. And the 4 great vows which the Bodhisattva had previously made, now appeared before his mind[154]). At the same time, Dharmacārin and other Deva-putras drew the attention (of the Bodhisattva) on the dissolute life of the harem and aroused in him the consciousness of its being disgusting like a cemetry. And after that he uttered the following words[155]):

> Alas! miserable are these creatures!
> How can one find pleasure in an assembly of she-devils?
> The foolish minds, obscured by the darkness of ignorance,
> Perceive the objects of sensual pleasure, unreal as they are
> As if they had some real value,

---

149) Ibid. 200. 4—11.
150) *Ñiṅ-mtshams-sbyor-ba = pratisaṁdhi.*
151) Lal.-vist. 200. 15—201. 10.
152) *Ḥphrog-maḥi bu lṅa-brgya = pañca Hārītī-putra-çatāni.*
153) Lal.-vist. 202. 13—15. 154) Ibid. 204. 13—205. 16.
155) Ibid. 206. 19—22.

And never can one obtain deliverance,
Being like an encaged bird.

And, having reflected over the subject in 32 ways[156]), he concentrated his mind upon the impurity (of the objects of sensual pleasure)[157]). Thereafter he went to the top of the palace and made there his salutations to all the Buddhas. And, as he looked about, he saw that Indra, the 4 guardian kings, the sun and the moon were likewise worshipping[158]). He beheld moreover that the asterism Puṣya had arisen, and said to Chandaka[159]):

This is a lucky omen for me that all my aims are to be attained.
This night my projects will be fulfilled;
Therefore, O Chandaka, do not delay, be quick
And get me a horse decorated with ornaments.

Chandaka asked: —Whither shalt thou go? —and the Bodhisattva replied: — I am departing (from this worldly life). [70. b.] Then Chandaka tried repeatedly to divert him, but (the Bodhisattva) spoke much of the evil[160]) caused by desire, and it was impossible to make him change his intention[161]). Then the Devaputras Çāntamati[162]) and Lalitavyūha[163]) made it impossible for the citizens of Kapilavastu to awake from their sleep and to utter a sound. Then the Bodhisattva said to Chandaka: — Bring me the horse![164]) And at that moment, Indra, the chief of the gods, and the 4 guardian kings likewise descended into Kapilavastu[165].) Chandaka then said that it was not the time to depart, but the Bodhisattva replied: —

"In pursuit of the welfare of all that lives,
I, having attained Enlightenment and the state
Where there is no old age, illness, and death,
Shall bring deliverance to the world[166])." —

---

[156]) Ibid. 207. 1—208. 6.

[157]) *mi-sdug-paḥi sgom-pa = açubha-bhāvanā.*

[158]) Ibid. 209. 12—210. 1.

[159]) Ibid. 210. 4—6. — *Chandaka capalu mā vilambahe / açva-rāja dada me alaṁkṛtaṁ / sarva-siddhi mama ete mangalā / artha-siddhi dhruvam adya bheṣyate //*

[160]) *ñes-dmigs = ādīnava.* [161]) Lal.-vist. 210. 6—217. 4.

[162]) Ži-baḥi-blo-gros. [163]) Brtse-ba-bkod-pa.

[164]) Lal.-vist. 217. 5—11. [165]) Ibid. 217. 12—15.

[166]) Ibid. 219. 3, 4.

Such was the vow I made long before,
And the time of fulfilling it has now come. —

The Devaputra Saṁcodaka[167]) then summoned him, saying[168]):

Rise speedily, O thou, endowed with highest power and energy,
Deliver the living beings, who are tormented by suffering;
The time of thy departure (from worldly life) has now come. —

Then Indra opened the royal gates, Chandaka, having decorated the horse Kaṇṭaka, brought it before the Bodhisattva who mounted. The 4 guardian-kings having lifted him up (to the saddle), themselves rose up to the skies. Brahma and Indra showed the way, a light, dispersing the gloom, appeared, and, with various sounds of music and hymns of praise, they passed the place where the armed men were encamped (and fast asleep)[169]).

When the Bodhisattva had arrived at the Perfectly Pure Sanctuary, he gave back to Chandaka the horse and the ornaments and bade him return. And at that place a monument was erected which was known as "The monument in memory of Chandaka's return"[170]). Thereafter, at the foot of the Perfectly Pure Sanctuary he cut off the locks on the crown of his head, and the gods seized these locks and carried them off (as an object of worship). And at that place a monument was likewise erected in memory of this[171]).

Then the Bodhisattva considered that the rich garment of Benares linen ill suited the custom of a monk, and that it would be right if he obtained a garment befitting one who has embraced religious life. [71. a.] And accordingly one of the gods of the Pure Region[172]), having assumed the form of a huntsman, offered him a garment of a reddish hue[173]). The Bodhisattva, in his turn gave him his clothes of Benares linen, and the Devaputra seized them with both hands, placed them on the crown of his head and

---

167) Yaṅ-dag-par-bskul-ba-po.

168) Lal.-vist. 220. 1—4.

169) Ibid. 222. 1—8.

170) Ibid. 225. 10—14. — *adyā' pi tac caityaṁ Chandaka-nivartanam iti jñāyate.*

171) Ibid. 225. 15—19. — *adyā' pi ca tac cūḍā-pratigrahaṇam iti jñāyate.*

172) *gnas-gtsaṅ-maḥi lha = çuddha-āvasikā devatā.*

173) *gos ṅur-smrig = kāṣāya-vastra.*

departed to the realm of the gods in order to worship (these relics). All this was seen by Chandaka who erected there a monument which is called "The monument in memory of (the Bodhisattva's having put on) the religious robes"[174]). At that moment (all the Devaputras) exclaimed aloud: — Siddhārtha has embraced religious life! — And this their exclamation was heard as far as Akaniṣṭha[175]).

Thereafter Chandaka brought home the horse and the ornaments, and, having related all that had happened, appeased the grief of the king and the harem[176]).

The Bodhisattva, having cut off the locks on the crown of his head and put on the reddish garments of an ascetic, assumed the character of a mendicant monk and went first to the abode of the Brāhmaṇa Raivata[177]) and other hermitages. Finally, he attained Vaiçalī[178]) and came to the place where Ārāḍa-Kālāma[179]) was teaching about the (mystic absorbtion in) the Sphere of Nothingness[180]) to his 300 pupils. The Bodhisattva expressed the wish to become likewise a pupil (of Ārāḍa) and, having undergone the necessary training, attained the state of the mind absorbed in the Sphere of Nothingness. He then said to Ārāḍa: — Have you attained only this degree of concentration? — Yes, — replied Ārāḍa. — The Bodhisattva said: — I too have attained it now. — To this Ārāḍa said: — What thou knowest — I know, and what I know—thou knowest. Accordingly, we shall teach the assembly of disciples both together! — Thereupon the Bodhisattva thought: — By this (degree of concentration only) deliverance is not to be attained. One must seek for something more efficient than this[181]). (Accordingly, he departed and) gradually made his way through Magadha. Finally he reached the mountain Pāṇḍava[182]) and rested there. Thereupon he entered Rājagṛha[183]) by the Tapoda[184]) gate. The citizens and their king Bimbisāra[185]), full of faith, [71. b.] offered him a part of the kingdom, but he refused.

---

[174]) Lal.-vist. 226. 6—13.

[175]) Ibid. 226. 14—227. 2.

[176]) Ibid. 237. 18—20. [177]) Sic acc. to Lal., Tib. Rigs-ldan.

[178]) Yańs-pa-can. [179]) Rgyu-rtsal-çes-kyi bu Rlń-ḥphur.

[180]) *ci-yań-med-paḥi skye-mched* = *ākiṁcanya-āyatana.*

[181]) Lal.-vist. 238. 14—239. 16.

[182]) Skya-bo. [183]) Rgyal-poḥi-khab.

[184]) Chu-dron-can-gyi sgo.

[185]) Gzugs-can-sñiń-po.

Thereafter he met Udraka Rāmaputra[186]) who was teaching to his 700 pupils about the concentration of mind in the sphere where there is neither consciousness nor unconsciousness[187]), and thought: —By such excercises of austerity I shall produce an elevated state of the mind and get rid of every kind of contemplation that is influenced by defiling agencies. Accordingly he declared that he would be one of the disciples (of Udraka) and soon attained the state of the mind absorbed in the sphere in which there is neither consciousness nor unconsciousness. Then, having spoken (with Udraka) as before (*with Ārāḍa-Kālāma*)[188]), *he left him saying:* — This is not conducive to Nirvāṇa. — From that time 5 disciples[189]) (who had studied with Udraka) followed the Bodhisattva. And, when they had arrived at the summit of the mountain Gayā, the Bodhisattva had a sudden flash of idea regarding 3 points of resemblance unknown and unheard of before, (referring to the ascetics and Brāhmanas who have not abandoned their desires)[190]). Then the Bodhisattva, having come to the shore of the river Nairañjanā, thought as follows: —(I have come into this world) at the time of the 5 kinds of degeneration[191]), amidst (living beings) who are devoted to teachings of a low order and think to attain purification by incorrect religious observances. In order (to be able to) remove these false views, I must begin the practice of the true form of penance and asceticism.

8. [The Practice of Asceticism.]

Accordingly, after that he abided for 6 years in the state of concentration called "the All-pervading"[192]) and during these 6 years underwent the most rigid austerity, feeding upon one grain of

---

[186]) Rańs-byed-kyi-bu Lhag-spyod.

[187]) *naiva-saṁjñā-nāsaṁjñā-āyatana.* The tib. has *srid-rtse* = *bhavāgra.*

[188]) Lal.-vist. 243. 15—245. 15.

[189]) Lṅa sde-bzań-po = Pañcakā bhadra-vārgīyāḥ.

[190]) Lal.-vist. 246. 10—247. 4. (First point of resemblance — *prathamā upamā*), 247. 5—11. (Second point of resemblance — *dvitīyā upamā*), 247. 12—22 (Third point of resemblance — *tṛtīyā upamā*). — *tisra upamāḥ pratibhānti sma / açruta-pūrvā anabhijñāta-pūrvāḥ /*

[191]) *sñigs-ma-lṅa* = *pañca-kaṣāya.* Cf. M. Vyutp. § 124.

[192]) *nam-mkhaḥ-khyab-kyi tiṅ-ṅe-ḥdzin* = *āsphāraka-samādhi* — *ākāçam āspharaṇam akaraṇam avikaraṇam tac ca sarvaṁ spharatī' ti hy ākāça-samaṁ tad dhyānaṁ teno' cyate āsphārakam iti* // Lal.-vist. 250. 19—20. The Lal. has *āsphānaka.*

the jujube, one grain of sesamum, and one grain of rice, and sat suspending his breath. At that time (as he was sitting there immovable), some of the Devaputras said to his mother Māyādevī[193]): Thy son is dead. She came (down) from the realm of the gods, saw the body of the Bodhisattva resembling a corpse and began to lament: — (O my son, said she), immediately after thou wert born, thou hast declared: — This is my last birth. — Now this thy promise has not been fulfilled and the prophecy of the sage Asita (regarding thy future Buddhahood) proves to be untrue. — The Bodhisattva replied[194]):

> May the sun, the moon, and the multitude of the stars fall on the ground,
> But I shall not die as I am now, an ordinary being.
> Therefore thou must not be grieved, for in a short time
> Thou shalt witness (my) Enlightenment and attainment of Buddhahood. —

Thus spoke he, and Māyādevī, delighted, returned to her abode. [72. a.]

(And, as he continued to sit without stirring), the village cowherds and others stuffed cotton into his ears, but he cast it out from his nose, etc.[195]) Then the Evil One, (approaching him), addressed him with pleasant-sounding words, saying: — Maintain, cherish thy life, etc. But, although he thus sought an opportunity (to lead the Bodhisattva into temptation), he found none[196]).

Then the Bodhisattva thought: — In order to get rid of the incorrect view, that through the practice of asceticism (alone) one can attain Salvation, I shall now take more substantial food[197]) and thereafter go to Bodhimaṇḍa[198]). And as he said this, the 5 disciples lost their faith in him and went off to Benares. After that the Bodhisattva got the rags[199]) in which the body of Rādhā[200]) the servant of Sujātā[201]) had been wrapped, washed it in a pond

---

[193]) Lha-mo Sgyu-ḥphrul-ma.

[194]) Lal-vist. 253. 18, 19 — *candrārka-tāragaṇa bhū pateta / pṛthagjano naiva ahaṁ mriyeyam / yasmān na çoko tvayi atra kāryo / na vai cirād drakṣyasi buddha-bodhim //*

[195]) Ibid. 257. 3—12. [196]) Ibid. 260. 17—263. 5.

[197]) *sas rags-pa = audārika-āhāra.*

[198]) Ibid. 263. 21—264. 3.

[199]) *pāṁsukūlika.* Cf. Childers, Pāli Dictionary, p. 325.

[200]) Grub-ma. [201]) Legs-skyes-mo.

dug out by the gods, on a flat stone put there by Indra. Then, having got tired, he resolved to get out of the pond. The Evil One (in order to hinder him) suddenly, by magical power, produced high rocks (on the banks of the pond). But the nymph of a tree caused the branches of the latter to bend down; the Bodhisattva grasped them and drew himself out. Then, at the foot of the Kakubha tree[202]), he stitched together the garment of rags and, having put over the cloths of reddish hue, presented to him by one of the gods of the Pure Region, entered the village (that was in the neighbourhood), in order to get some food. And, summoned by the gods, Sujātā prepared (food for him), having taken 7 times the cream from the milk of a thousand cows and cast into it fresh grains of rice. And, as in this food prepared by her, the Çrīvatsa[203]) and other lucky signs were to be seen, she became delighted, and the sooth-sayers prophecied that she would obtain the nectar of immortality. Then she invited the Bodhisattva to eat and, having filled a golden vessel with honey and with the broth of milk (she had prepared), she presented it to him[204]). And he, having accepted it, went to the bank of the Nairañjanā. There he deposited the food and his garments likewise and began to wash. The gods worshipped him and poured water (upon his body). His hair and beard were carried off by Sujātā (as relics). [72. b.] Thereafter he seated himself on a seat supported by lions which was presented to him by the Nāga maiden of that river, and took his meal. And (having eaten), he cast the golden vessel into the water, and it was carried away by Sāgara, the king of the Nāgas[205]). But Indra, having obtained it from him, brought it to the realm of the 33 gods, worshipped it there, and celebrated a feast in its honour[206]).

9. [The Victory over the Evil One.]

Then the Bodhisattva, having washed and taken his meal, grew full of strength and with superhuman energy set off toward the Bodhi tree, in order to vanquish Māra. The deities of the rain and wind moistened his path and strew flowers upon it. And all

---

[202]) *çiṅ sgrub-byed-kyi druṅ-du.* Lal.-vist. 267. 6—8.

[203]) *dpal-beḥu.* [204]) Lal.-vist. 268. 22, 22.

[205]) Kluḥi-rgyal-po Rgya-mtsho = Sāgara-Nāgarāja.

[206]) Lal.-vist. 270. 1—12..... *nītvā pātrī-yātrām nāma parvāṇi pravartitavān* /

the mountains and trees bent down (in the direction of Bodhimaṇḍa), and even the new-born infants showed him the way with their heads, as they slept with their faces turned in that direction[207]. And Brahma, the Powerful[208], the Lord of the 3000 worlds, summoned all who surrounded him to worship, as the Bodhisattva was to reach Bodhimaṇḍa that evening. Accordingly, inconceivable acts of worship were performed[209]. And from the body of the Bodhisattva there came forth a light, through which all suffering and turmoil was pacified and the spirits of the converts rendered pure. (Seeing this), Kālika the king of the Nāgas[210] likewise worshipped the Bodhisattva[211]. Thereafter the latter, seeing to the right side of the road a tuft of the Svastika grass[212], addressed it as follows[213]:

O give me quickly a bundle of grass,
To-day such grass will be of great use to me:
Having vanquished Māra and his hosts,
I shall attain Supreme Enlightenment and Quiescence.

And it presented him with a bundle of grass, green, soft, and pleasant to feel. Having taken it, he thrice walked round the Bodhi tree, spread the grass with the tops inward and the roots outwards, and, looking toward the east, sat down, erected himself, and, concentrating his mind, said[214]:

May, as long as I sit here, my body wither away,
May the skin, the bones and the flesh decay,
But until I have not attained Enlightenment
Which is hard to be secured even during many aeons, —
I shall not move from this spot. — [73 a.]

Such was the powerful oath he uttered.

At that time the gods, in order to protect the Bodhisattva, placed themselves at the 10 quarters of the skies. And the Bodhi-

---

207) Ibid. 273. 9—15.

208) Tshaṅs-pa dbaṅ-bsgyur = Brahmā vaçavartī.

209) Lal.-vist. 274. 16—278. 5.

210) Klu Nag-po. 211) Lal.-vist. 278. 20—281. 9. sqq.

212) *bkra-çis-rtsva brṅa-ba = svāstika-yāvasika.*

213) Lal.-vist. 287. 3—4. — *tṛṇu dehi mi svastika çīghraṁ / adya samārthu tṛṇaiḥ sumahantaḥ / sabalaṁ namuciṁ vihanitvā / bodhim anuttara-çānti spṛçiṣye.*

214) Lal.-vist. 289. 19—20. — *ihā' sane çuṣyatu me çarīraṁ / tvag-asthi-māṁsaṁ pralayaṁ ca yātu / aprāpya bodhiṁ bahu-kalpa-dullabhāṁ / naivāsanāt kāyam ataç caliṣyate //*

sattva caused a light to issue from his body, called "the light summoning the Bodhisattvas"[215]. This light was seen throughout innumerable regions, and many Bodhisattvas, having assembled, worshipped him[216]. Then he thought: — It is not proper for me to attain Enlightenment, without having made it known to Māra. — And, accordingly, he let a light called "the Destroyer of all the realms of Māra"[217] issue from his forehead. This light caused all the abodes of the Evil One to be seen, made them tremble, and darkened them. And the following words were to be heard[218]:

> The purest living being who has practised virtue during numerous aeons,
> The son of Çuddhodana, having renounced his royal power,
> Has departed (from home) in the wish of helping others and striving for the nectar of immortality,
> And has now come to the Bodhi tree. Take care, therefore now, (O Māra)! —

and so on.

And Māra, the Evil One, had 32 dreams, that his abode was covered with darkness and the like, and made this known to his adherents. Māra's son, Sārthavāha[219], tried to divert him (from going to encounter the Bodhisattva), but in vain. —

> In the forms of Yakṣas, vampires, and great serpents,
> Of cannibal demons, ghosts, and fiends,
> Terrifying, hideous and fierce, —
> Did Māra cunningly transform all his hosts[220].

But, although he beheld such and many other frightful forms, —

> The son of the Çākyas, having cognized
> That all the elements are relative and essentially unreal,

---

[215]) *byaṅ-chub-sems-dpaḥ bskul-ba žes-bya-baḥi ḥod.* = *bodhisattva-saṁcodanī nāma raçmi.*

[216]) Lal.-vist. 290. 5—299. 7.

[217]) *bdud-kyi-dkyil-ḥkhor thams-cad ḥjoms-par-byed-pa žes-bya-baḥi ḥod* = *sarva-māra-maṇḍala-vidhvaṁsana-karī-nāma raçmi.*

[218]) Lal.-vist. 300. 13—15. — *kalpogha-cīrṇa-carito hy atiçuddha-sattvaḥ / Çuddhodanasya tanayaḥ pratijahya rājyaṁ / so nirgato hitakaro hy amṛtābhilāṣī / bodhi-drumaṁ hy upagato' dya kuru prayatnam. //*

[219]) Ded-dpon.

[220]) Lal.-vist. 307. 18, 19. — *yakṣa-kumbhāṇḍa-mahoraga-rūpāḥ / rākṣasa-preta-piçācaka-rūpāḥ / yattaka loki virūpa-suraudrāḥ / sarvi ta nirmita tatra çaṭhebhiḥ //*

And being endowed with a mind (all-pervading and quiescent) like space,
Did not become deluded on seeing all the cunning of the Evil One's hosts[221]).

Thereafter Māra was persuaded by those of his adherents who stood to the right side and sympathized with the Bodhisattva, to abstain (from further contest). On the contrary those to the left who were hostile to him, urged (Māra to continue the strife). [73. b.] And Māra hurled various weapons at the Bodhisattva, but these were all transformed into flowers. Then the Evil One said: — How canst thou attain Salvation only by these thy merits? — The Bodhisattva replied: — Thou hast performed one unimpeded sacrifice[222]) and hast by the virtue of it become the Lord of the World of Desire. I, in my turn have made many unimpeded sacrifices. — The sacrifice performed by me, said Māra, was unimpeded and irreproachable. Thyself, thou art the witness of it. But for thy deeds there is no witness whatever; therefore all thou sayest is useless: thou art defeated. — To this the Bodhisattva said: — This earth is my witness. And, striking the earth with his right hand[223]): —

This earth is the support of all the living beings,
It is equal and it is impartial
With regard to all, that does and does not move.
May it bear evidence that I do not lie,
And may it be the witness before you.

And, as he said this, the earth trembled 6 times and out came Sthāvarā[224]) the goddess of the earth, showing half of her body and, folding her hands, said: — O highest of beings, so it is. As thou hast said, so is it, perfectly true. It is all evident and clear to me. But, O Lord, thou art thyself the highest witness (of the truth) for all the world, including the gods. — Thus spoke she and disappeared. —

---

[221]) Ibid. 308. 13, 14. — *çākya-sutas tu svabhāvam abhāvam / dharma pratītya-samutthita buddhvā / gaganopama-cittu suyukto / na bhramatc sabalaṁ çaṭha dṛṣṭvā //*

[222]) *gtan-pa-med-paḥi mchod-sbyin = nirargaḍa-yajña.*

[223]) Lal.-vist. 318. 18, 19. — *iyaṁ mahī sarva-jagat-pratiṣṭhā / apakṣa-pātā sacarā' caro samā / iyaṁ pramāṇā mama nāsti me mṛṣā / sākṣitvam asmin mama saṁprayacchatu //*

[224]) Brtan-ma.

And the Cunning One with his hosts,
Having heard this voice of the earth,
Like jackals hearing the lions roar
In the forest, and like ravens at the sound of a missile,
Fled with hearts full of wrath and fear[225]).

Thereafter the Evil One, disappointed, sent his own daughters to disturb (the Bodhisattva). These tried in 32 different ways to seduce him, by covering half of their faces etc. [74 a.] But (all these efforts) were unable to delude (the Bodhisattva), to the great distress of the Evil One[226]). Then Çrī[227]) and other tree-nymphs, 8 in number, praised the Bodhisattva in 16 different ways, saying: — Thou art beautiful, like the disc of the ascending autumn moon, — and so on[228]). In 16 forms likewise did these deities scorn Māra: — O Evil One, thou art feeble like an old elephant fallen into a mire, etc.[229]) And in 16 different ways did the gods try to divert Māra, but in vain. He again hurled different missiles (at the Bodhisattva) and showed many miraculous apparitions, but gained no ground by this. The host of demons dispersed in confusion, and for 7 days they could not meet together again. And many demons at that time made the Creative Effort for Supreme Enlightenment.

10. [The Attainment of Supreme Enlightenment.]

Thereafter the Bodhisattva became absorbed in the 4 degrees of trance[230]) and obtained the 3 kinds of Highest Knowledge. Then, from the last part of the night, before sunrise, and within the space of time of the beating of a drum he came to the cognition of the 12 members of the causal chain and the 4 Truths of the Saint. And after that, by the force of momentary Highest Wisdom[231]), he attained the full Enlightenment, grew to the height of 7 palm-

---

[225]) Lal.-vist. 319. 13—16. — *taṁ çrutvā medi-niravaṁ sa çaṭhaḥ sasainyaḥ / uttrasta bhinna-hṛdayo prapalāna sarve / çrutvai' va siṁha-naditaṁ vane hi çṛgālāḥ / kākū va loṣṭu-patane sahasā praṇaṣṭāḥ //*

[226]) Ibid. 320. 1—331. 19. [227]) Dpal-ldan.

[228]) Lal.-vist. 332. 3—4. — *upaçobhase tvaṁ viçuddha-sattva candra iva çukla-pakṣe / abhivirocase tvaṁ viçuddhabuddha sūrya iva prodayamānaḥ //*

[229]) Ibid. 333. 2. — *durbalas tvaṁ pāpīyan jīrṇa-gaja iva paṅka-magnaḥ //*

[230]) *bsam-gtan* = *dhyāna*.

[231]) *skad-cig gcig daṅ ldan-paḥi çes-rab-kyis* = *eka-citta-kṣaṇa-saṁyuktayā prajñayā*. Is the same as *eka-kṣaṇa-abhisaṁbodha*.

trees and made the following solemn utterance[232]): — "Finished is the course of my Path", — and so on[233]).

And the gods strewed flowers which covered his feet up to his knees and worshipped him. The world grew full of light, the earth trembled, and all the Buddhas in the 10 quarters of the sky became full of highest delight and saluted him, saying[234]):

Just as we have attained Enlightenment (before),
In the same way thou hast likewise come to Buddhahood,
(Being pure) like clarified butter and its essence. —

And the daughters of the gods likewise praised him. The Teacher in his turn made another solemn utterance[235]):

The fruit of virtue is bliss and the removal of all suffering,
The projects of a virtuous being meet with success.
[74 b.] Having vanquished Māra he attains Enlightment
And the cool quiescent essence of Nirvāṇa at an early date. —

And then, after the gods had again greatly praised him, he remained for a week, sitting immovably in a cross-legged posture and contemplated the Bodhi tree[236]). On the second week he made his journey through the 3000 thousands of worlds. On the third he again contemplated the Bodhi tree without shutting his eyes. And, on the fourth week he made another walk, not so long (as the first) to the eastern and the western (seas). Thereafter Māra, the Evil One, entreated him to depart into Nirvāṇa, but, as the Buddha declared that, before having accomplished the aim of all the converts, he would not pass away, Māra was again disappointed. His daughters, Rati[237]) and the rest approached the Buddha (in order to seduce him), but he transformed them into old hags. On the fifth week there was rainy and stormy weather, and at that time the Buddha abided in the realm of the Nāga king Mucilinda[238]). On the sixth week he went to the Nyagrodha-tree of Ajapāla[239]) and addressed the Parivrājakas[240]) as follows[241]):

---

[232]) *ched-du-brjod-pa = udāna.* [233]) Lal.-vist. 351. 1, 2.

[234]) Ibid. 353. 7, 8. — *bodhir yathāmanugatā bhavatā viçuddhā / tulyaḥ samo'si yatha sarpiṇi sarpa-maṇḍaiḥ //*

[235]) Ibid. 355. 19—22. — *puṇya-vipāku sukha sarva-duḥkhāpaneti / abhiprāyu sidhyati ca puṇyavato narasya / kṣipraṁ ca bodhi spṛçato vinihatya māraṁ / çāntūpatho gacchati ca nirvṛti*(sic)*-çīti-bhāvam //*

[236]) Ibid. 369. 9—11. [237]) Dgaḥ-ma. [238]) Btaṅ-bzuṅ.

[239]) Ra-skyoṅ. [240]) Kun-tu-rgyu.

[241]) Lal.-vist. 380. 16—19.

Blissful is the solitary life of him
Who has heard the Doctrine and perceived the Truth,
And full of uninterrupted bliss is the life
Of him who has subdued the animate beings,
But has not done harm to anybody, —

and so on. On the seventh week he abided at the foot of a sacred fig-tree.[242]). The merchants Trapuṣa[243]) and Bhallika[244]) offered him honey, rice-gruel, and sugar-cane, the bark of which had been taken off. But he thought: — It is not suitable to take (this food) with one's hands. With the previous Buddhas it was a bowl in which they accepted (the offerings). — And the 4 guardian kings offered him vessels made of gold etc., but he did not take them (knowing that the bowls of the former Buddhas had been made of stone). Accordingly, each of the 4 kings took one of the 4 vessels that were presented to Vaiçrāvaṇa[245]) by the deities of the Blue Region[246]), filled them with flowers, offered them and made their salutations. [75. a.] The Lord said[247]): —

Give the mendicant's bowl to the Buddha,
And thou shalt be thyself the vessel of the Highest Doctrine.
He who offers the bowl to such like me,
Will never be deprived of wisdom and memory.

Such and similar words he uttered, accepted (the 4 vessels) and pronounced a blessing by the force of which they were transformed into one. Then Trapuṣa and Bhallika prepared cream taken from the milk of a thousand cows, poured it into a trough made of precious stones and offered it to him. And (the Buddha), after having taken this meal, cast away the trough which was carried off by Brahma. Then the Teacher granted the following benediction to Trapuṣa and Bhallika[248]):

The blessing of the Divine bring fortune to all the countries,
And bring to accomplishment all the desired aims.
All your projects are to be fulfilled,
And everything will soon be favourable to you. —

---

242) *çiṅ sgrol-rgyuḥi druṅ-du = tārāyaṇa-mūle.*

243) Ga-gon. 244) Bzaṅ-po (? Bhadrika).

245) Rnam-sras.

246) *nīla-kāyika-devaputra.*

247) Lal.-vist. 384. 8, 9. — *upanāmayasva sugatasya bhājanaṁ / tvaṁ bheṣyase bhājanam agra-yāne / asmad-vidhebhyo hi pradāya bhājanaṁ / smṛtir matiç caiva na jātu hīyate //* 248) Ibid. 387. 12—391. 18.

This and the following he said and prophesied them to be the Buddhas known by the name of Madhusaṁbhava[249].

11. [The Swinging of the Wheel of the Doctrine.]

Thereafter the Teacher seated himself, intending to abide in silence and indifference, and said[250]:

> I have secured the cognition of the Truth, profound,
> Free from defilement, illuminating, eternal, and like nectar.
> But, if I should demonstrate it to others, they will not understand.
> Therefore I shall abide in solitude in the forest.

But then he thought[251]:

> Infinite is my Commiseration with regard to all that lives,
> And I must not hesitate when others pray me.
> These living beings are devoted to Brahma; so
> If he prays me I shall swing the Wheel of the Doctrine. —

Accordingly he caused a light to issue from his body, and Brahma, the crested[252], the lord of the 3000 worlds, came to know this, summoned his adherents and, with 6 800 000 other deities of the Brahmaloka entreated the Buddha with folded hands, saying[253]:

> Thou hast attained the sphere of Sublime Divine Wisdom,
> And, the rays of this Wisdom, expanding through the 10 quarters of the sky,
> Cause to open those lotuses who are the living beings.
> O Thou, sun of Sublime Speech, why dost Thou now remain indifferent? —

With such and similar words did he summon the Buddha. And, as the latter expressed his consent by silence [75 b.], Brahma departed, and the Buddha, in his turn, remained sitting as if he was quite indifferent (to Brahma's exhortation).

---

[249]) *Sbraṅ-rtsi-ḥbyuṅ-ba žes-paḥi rgyal-bar luṅ-bstan-no.* — Lal.-vist. 391. 22. — *Madhusaṁbhavā nāma jinā bhaviṣyatha* //

[250]) Ibid. 393. 1, 2. — *gambhīra çānto virajaḥ prabhāsvaraḥ / prāpto mi dharmo hy amrto' saṁskṛtaḥ / deçeya cā' haṁ na parasya jāne / yan nūna tūṣṇī pavane vaseyam* //

[251]) Ibid. 393. 13, 14.

[252]) Tshaṅs-pa gtsug-phud-can = Çikhī Mahābrahmā.

[253]) Lal.-vist. 394. 17, 18.

Thereupon Indra likewise entreated him saying[254]):

Thy mind has obtained complete deliverance
Like the full moon delivered from the jaws of Rahu,
I pray thee, rise up, Thou who hast conquered in battle,
And let the light of Thy Wisdom appear in the darkness of this world. —

Thus spoke he, but Buddha did not answer a word. Then Brahma again addressed him[255]):

O Great Sage, I pray Thee to expound the Doctrine, —
For there are such who are desirous (of hearing it). —

The Teacher replied[256]):

The living beings are fettered by the bonds of Desire,
And are carried by the stream (of Phenomenal Life).
I, in my turn, have come to the intuition of the Truth with great difficulty,
For this reason there is no use of teaching it. —

Again the Teacher gave up his mind to indifference. And various unlucky signs appeared: — The fire did not blaze forth, and so on[257]). (Having seen this), Brahma said[258]): —

In this country of Magadha an impure teaching,
Produced by defiled thoughts has been preached.
Therefore, O Sage, I pray Thee to admit us to the nectar,
And may the immaculate Doctrine of the Buddha be heard.

As he thus insisted, Buddha looked upon the living beings who were unsteady (as regards the means of deliverance) and gave his consent, saying[259]):

---

[254]) Ibid. 397. 1, 2. — *uttiṣṭha vijita-saṁgrāma prajñakārā timisrā vivara loke / cittaṁ hi te vimuktaṁ çaçir iva pūrṇo graha-vimuktaḥ //*

[255]) Ibid. 397. 11. *deçaya tvaṁ mune dharmaṁ ājñātāro bhaviṣyanti //*

[256]) Ibid. 397. 18, 19. — *anusrotaṁ pravāhyante kāmeṣu patitāḥ prajāḥ / kṛcchreṇa me' yaṁ saṁprāptam alaṁ tasmāt prakāçitum //*

[257]) Ibid. 398. 2—8.

[258]) Ibid. 398. 16, 17. — *vādo babhūva samalair vicintito dharmo' viçuddho Magadheṣu pūrvam / amṛtaṁ mune tad vivṛṇīṣva dvāraṁ çṛṇvanti dharmaṁ vimalena buddham //* Cf. Yaçomitra, Abhidharmakoça-vyākhyā, II. Koçasthāna, B. B. 16. 15—17. 4.

[259]) Ibid. 400. 18, 19. — *apāvṛtās teṣām amṛtasya dvārā / brahmanti satatam ye çrotavantaḥ / praviçanti çraddhā navihetha-saṁjñāḥ*, etc.

I shall admit to the nectar those of the living beings,
Who have ears to hear, are possessed of faith,
And always listen to the Doctrine, free from sinful thoughts.

Thereafter the deities of the Bodhi tree, Dharmaruci[260]), and others asked: — Where shalt thou turn the Wheel of the Doctrine? — He replied: — In Benares. — To this they said: — There are few people in that place and there is no shade; it will be better to preach elsewhere. — O ye, fair-faced, do not say so, — returned he. Then he reflected, as to who could be those disciples who were easy to convert, and to whom he was to teach the Doctrine first of all. And, knowing that Udraka had died a week before and Ārāḍa-Kālāma had likewise passed away 3 days ago, he resolved to teach the Doctrine to the 5 disciples. [76 a.] Accordingly, from Magadha, he went to Benares. And on the way he met a beggar[261]) who addressed him as follows: — Thy faculties are acute and Thy skin is pure; — from whom hast Thou learned to live in virtue? The Lord replied[262]):

There is none who could be my teacher, and none who could be equal to me.
I am the Unique Buddha, perfectly calm and free from defilement. —

Thereupon (the beggar) asked: — Doest thou call thyself an Arhat? — (The Lord) replied[263]):

I am the Arhat in this world, —
I am the Teacher, greater than whom there is none.
There is not a being that could be like me,
Including the gods, the Asuras and the Gandharvas. —

The beggar asked again: — Doest thou say that thou art a Buddha, one who is called "the Victorious"? — The Teacher said[264]):

"The Victorious"[265]) (the Buddhas) are those
Who like myself have come to the extirpation of defilement;

---

[260]) Chos-sred.

[261]) *ḥtsho-ba-pa = ājīvaka.*

[262]) Lal.-vist. 405. 20, 21. — *ācāryo na hi me kaçcit sadṛço me na vidyate / eko' ham asmi sambuddhaḥ çītī-bhūto nirāsravaḥ //*

[263]) Ibid. 406. 2, 3. — *aham evā' rahan loke çāstā hy aham anuttaraḥ / sa-devāsura-gandharve nāsti me pratipudgalaḥ //*

[264]) Ibid. 406. 6, 7. — *jinā hi sādṛçā jñeyā ye prāptā āsrava-kṣayam / jitā me pāpakā dharmās teno' paka jino hy aham //*

[265]) *rgyal-ba = jina.*

I have vanquished all that is sinful,
Therefore, O Upaka[266]), I am "the Victorious". —

Whither art thou going? — inquired the beggar. —

To Benares I intend to go;
Having come to that illustrious city,
I shall produce an unsurpassable light,
For the sake of the world that is like blind[267]).

The beggar said: — May it be so, — and departed to the south. The teacher in his turn, went northward, reached the mountains Gayā, Rohitavastu[268]), Uruvilvākalpa[269]) and Aṇāla[270]), went from there to the city called Sārathipura[271]), and finally came to the shores of the Ganges. There the ferryman asked him the passage-money. — I have none, — replied the teacher, rose up into the air and passed over the river. This came to be known by the king Bimbisāra who forbade after that to take any loan from the monks. Buddha then came to Benares, collected alms, took his meal, and then went to the place called Ṛṣipatana[272]). The 5 disciples (who had left him) saw him coming and said: — The ascetic Gautama who has slackened (in his austerities), has eaten plentifully, and has neglected the removal (of all that is worldly), is now coming here. [76 b.] No one need to rise up and to present him the religious robes and the bowl. If he wants, he may seat himself on the seat that is left. Such was the agreement they made[273]), but Ājñātakauṇḍinya did not approve it in his mind. The Teacher arrived, but the 5 were not able to fulfill their intention (of showing disrespect to him). They broke their agreement and rose up from their seats. — One went to meet the Teacher, another prepared the seat (for him) and water to wash his feet, etc. Welcome, they said, — pray to sit thyself on this seat. — The Teacher seated himself and spoke many a word to the 5 disciples that excited their joy[274]). The five said: — O long-lived Gautama, thy senses are

---

[266]) N̄er-ḥgro.

[267]) Lal.-vist. 406. 10, 11. — *Vārāṇasīṁ gamiṣyāmi gatvā vai Kāçinūṁ purīṁ / andhabhūtasya lokasya kartāsmy asadṛçāṁ prabhām //*

[268]) Lteṅ (?) [269]) Rgyas (?) [270]) Tsan-dan-la (?)

[271]) Groṅ-khyer Kha-lo-bsgyur.

[272]) Draṅ-sroṅ-ltuṅ-ba.

[273]) *ḥog-khrims bcas = kriyābandham akārṣuḥ.* Lal.-vist. 407. 18 sqq.

[274]) Ibid. 409, 1.

acute and thy skin (body) is pure[275]). Hast thou made manifest the special intuitive knowledge (of a Saint)? — (The Buddha replied): — You must not call the Buddha "long-lived". A long period of life-time does not bring happiness. — I have obtained the nectar, have become a Buddha, and am omniscient[276]). Have you not made just now a bad agreement (in order to show disrespect to me)? — And, as he spoke thus, they became monks (under his orders), fell to his feet, confessed their sins, and became full of reverence. After the Teacher had refreshed his body, he thought: — Where am I to turn the Wheel of the Doctrine? — And at that place there appeared 1000 seats made of the 7 kinds of jewels[277]). (The Teacher) circumambulated 3 of these (that had belonged to the previous Buddhas) and then seated himself on the 4th. And, after he had done this, a light issued from his body, illuminating the 3000 thousands of worlds. The earth trembled, and the living beings became purified. Thereupon the gods presented him a golden wheel with a 1000 spokes and prayed him to swing the Wheel of the Doctrine. During the first quarter of the night, he did not utter a word; then at midnight he spoke so as to gladden (the disciples). [77 a.] And, finally, from the last quarter of the night he began to preach (to the five): — O monks, there are 2 extremities which are to be avoided by him who has embraced religious life. These are: — The extremity of licence[278]) and that of self-torture[279]). The Buddha teaches the Doctrine as being the middle way[280]) shunning both these extremities. (This middle way) is the 8 fold Path of the Saint[281]). O monks, these are the 4 Truths (or cardinal principles)[282]) of a Saint. There is the uneasiness (of Phenomenal Life)[283]), there is the cause of it[284]), its Extinction,[285]), and the Path that leads to this Extinction[286]).

---

[275]) Ibid. 409. 2, 3. — *viprasannāni te āyuṣman Gautama indriyāṇi pariçuddhaç chavi-varṇaḥ* etc. [276]) Ibid. 409. 8, 9.

[277]) Ibid. 410. 6. — *sapta-ratna-mayam āsana-sahasraṁ prādurabhūt* /

[278]) *ḥdod-pa bsod-ñams-kyi mthaḥ* = *kāma-sukhallika-anuyoga-anta.*

[279]) *ṅal ži̇ṅ dub-paḥi mthaḥ* = *ātma-klamatha-anuyoga-anta.*

[280]) *dbu-maḥi lam* = *madhyama-pratipad.*

[281]) *ḥphags-paḥi lam yan-lag-brgyad* = *ārya-aṣṭāṅga-mārga.*

[282]) *ḥphags-paḥi bden-pa bži* = *catvāri ārya-satyāni.*

[283]) *sdug-bsṅal* = *duḥkha.*

[284]) *kun-ḥbyuṅ* = *samudaya.*

[285]) *ḥgog-pa* = *nirodha.*

[286]) *lam* = *mārga* or *nirodha-gāminī pratipad.*

— Then: — Phenomenal Existence is to be cognized[287]), its cause is to be removed[288]), and so on. And: — Phenomenal Existence is cognized, its cause is removed, — etc. In such a way he thrice entered upon the subject of the 4 Truths and turned the Wheel of the Doctrine in 12 ways[289]). The consequence was, that Kauṇḍinya became an Arhat and came to the full realization (i. e. the cognition) of the 3 Jewels. —

> Thus, in 12 forms did the Buddha swing the Wheel of the Doctrine,
> And Kauṇḍinya came to the full cognition
> And the realization of the 3 Jewels[290]).

In regard of this swinging of the Wheel of the Doctrine, we must distinguish 5 points, viz. the place (1), time (2), hearers (3), the Doctrine itself (4), and its aim (5). The first was Benares. The time was, according to some, 6 years and 6 months, according to Chimpa[291]) — 7 years, and according to Chag — 7 years without 2 months. The hearers were Kauṇḍinya, Açvajit[292]), Bāṣpa[293]) Mahānāman[294]), and Bhadrika[295]), — 5 men and a numerous assembly of gods. The Doctrine was that of the 4 Truths, repeated 3 times, thus representing the swinging of the Wheel in 12 forms. In the *Abhidharmakoça*[296]) it is said: —

> The Wheel of the Doctrine represents (the Teaching of) the Path of Illumination[297]).
> (The latter resembles a Wheel) by its swift movement, etc.
> And by its component parts[298]) likewise. — [77. b.]

Thus the Path of Illumination is called the "Wheel of the Doctrine", since it has a resemblance with a wheel by its swift movement, sweeping away, turning, subduing that which has not been subdued, fixing that which has been subdued, ascending and descending. The venerable Ghoṣaka[299]) says: — Of the eightfold Path

---

287) *sdug-bsṅal yoṅs-su-çes-par-bya = duḥkhaṁ parijñeyam.*

288) *kun-ḥbyuṅ spaṅ-bar-bya = samudayaḥ prahātavyaḥ.*

289) *triparivarta-dvādaçākāra-dharma-cakra-pravartana.* Cf. M. Vyutp. § 64.

290) Lal.-vist. 421. 1, 2. — *evaṁ hi dvādaçākāraṁ dharma-cakraṁ pravartitaṁ / Kauṇḍinyena ca ājñātaṁ nirvṛttā ratanās trayaḥ* (sic) //

291) Mchims-pa. 292) Rta-thul. 293) Rlaṅs-pa.

294) Miṅ-chen. 295) Bzaṅ-ldan.

296) Transbaikalian (Tsugol Monastery) edition, 89 b. 1—2.

297) *mthoṅ-lam = darçana-mārga.*

298) Lit. "its spokes". 299) Dbyaṅs-sgrog.

of the Saint, the correct view[300]), correct reflection[301]), correct exertion[392]), and recollection[303]) are the spokes (of the Wheel). Appropriate speech[304]), acts[305]), and means of livelihood[306]) are like the navel. Finally correct concentration is similar to the circumference of a wheel. Owing to all these points of resemblance (the 8 fold Path of the Saint) is called the Wheel of the Doctrine. We have it however usually said that the Path of Illumination is called the Wheel of the Doctrine. The realization of this Path in (the stream of elements) of Kaundinya, is spoken of as "the Swinging of the Wheel of the Doctrine". It has been repeated 3 times, viz. 1. "This is the uneasiness of Phenomenal Life", etc., 2. "Phenomenal Existence is to be fully cognized," etc., 3. "Phenomenal Existence has been fully cognized", etc. With regard to each of these 3 "repetitions" it has been said: — The vision (of this) has arisen, and the cognition, full apprehension, and analysis (of it) have been brought about[307]). —The Path free from impediments[308]), the Path of Deliverance[309]), and the Special Path[310]) have been demonstrated, as representing the 12 aspects of the Teaching. — But, may it be said, we shall have altogether 12 "repetitions" and 64 aspects. — There is no mistake in this, since the divisions in 3 and in 12 correspond to each other. According to the Vaibhāṣikas, the 3 repetitions or recurrences (of the Wheel) demonstrate the Paths of Illumination, Contemplation[311]), and the Ultimate Path[312]). But in such a case the swinging of the Wheel of the

---

[300]) *yaṅ-dag-paḥi lta-ba = samyag-dṛṣṭi.*

[301]) *yaṅ-dag-paḥi rtog-pa = samyak-saṁkalpa.*

[302]) *yaṅ-dag-paḥi-rtsol-ba = samyag-vyāyāma.*

[303]) *yaṅ-dag-paḥi dran-pa = samyak-smṛti.*

[304]) *yaṅ-dag-paḥi ṅag = samyag-vāk.*

[305]) *yaṅ-dag-paḥi las-mthaḥ = samyak-karmānta.*

[306]) *yaṅ-dag-paḥi ḥtsho-ba = samyag-ājīva.*

[307]) Lal.-vist. 417, 16, 17. *jñānam utpannaṁ cakṣur utpannaṁ vidyā utpannā medhā utpannā prajñā utpannā ālokaḥ prādurbhūtaḥ.*

[308]) *bar-chad-med-lam = ānantarya-mārga.*

[309]) *rnam-grol-lam = vimukti-mārga.*

[310]) *khyad-par-gyi lam = viçeṣa-mārga.* Cf. Yaçomitra, Abhidharmakoça-vyākhyā II Koçasthāna, B. B. 31. 20—32. 1. — ..... *ānantarya-mārga utpadyate / sa punar yena kleçān prajahāti / vimukti-mārgo' py ānantarya-mārgād anantaram utpadyate kleça-prahāṇa-prāpter avadhārakaḥ / viçeṣa-mārgas tata uccaṁ viçiṣṭo mārgaḥ / tena mārgeṇa nava-prakārāḥ kleçāḥ praheyāḥ /*

[311]) *sgom-lam = bhāvanā-mārga.*

[312]) *mi-slob-lam = açaikṣa-mārga.*

Doctrine could not consist of 3 recurrences and 12 forms, since the Path of Illumination alone would not represent these 3 recurrences and 12 forms. For this reason, just this division of the Doctrine[313]) is called "The Wheel of the Doctrine". The 3 recurrences are the 4 Truths of the Saint as repeated 3 times. The 12 forms (or aspects) are: — 1) — "This is Phenomenal Existence". 2) — "This is its cause." 3) — "This is the Extinction" (of Phenomenal Existence). 4) — "This is the Path leading to this Extinction." [78 a.] 5) "Phenomenal Existence is to be fully cognized." 6) — "Its cause is to be removed." 7) — "Extinction is to be realized." 8) — "The Path is to be made an object of Concentration." 9) — "Phenomenal Existence has been fully cognized." 10) — "Its cause has been removed." 11) — "Extinction is realized." 12) — "The Path has been made an object of Concentration[314])." The "Swinging" of the Wheel means introducing it or making it intelligible to the mind of another person. The aim attained (by this swinging) was as follows: — At the first recurrence, the Path of Illumination was realized in (the mind of) Kauṇḍinya and the numerous gods. At the second — Kauṇḍinya attained Arhatship and the Path of Illumination likewise became originated in (the minds of) the other 4 disciples. Finally, at the 3ᵈ swinging these 4 likewise became Arhats. This was the direct aim (attained). The indirect, or the special aim was: — To cause the converts, to abstain from views maintaining the reality of the Individual[315]) (as an independent whole) and, thereafter, to make them partake of the 4 Results of saintliness. —

As concerns the Teaching of the Intermediate Period[316]), "the Wheel of the Doctrine of Non-substantiality", — the place (where it was delivered) was the mountain Gṛdhrakūṭa[317]). The duration of time was, according to Ṭho-lo[318]) 30 years, according to Chimpa — 27 years, according to Chag — 31 years, and according to others — 12 years. The hearers were 1250 or 5000 monks, nuns, and male[319]) and female[320]) devotees of the laity and a multitude of myriads of Bodhisattvas. The Doctrine is that of Non-substantiality, that which is contained in the *Prajñāpāramitā* and the

---

313) *chos-kyi rnam-graṅs = dharma-paryāya.*

314) Cf. M. Vyutp. § 64. 315) *gaṅ-zag = pudgala.*

316) *madhya-cakra.* 317) Bya-rgod-phuṅ-po.

318) Khro-lo. 319) *dge-bsñen = upāsaka.*

320) *dge-bsñen-ma = upāsikā.*

Scripture of the Intermediate Period. According to Dharmamitra[321]), the *Prajñāpāramitā* contains a 2 fold subject-matter, viz. the essence of the Doctrine and the process of intuition (of the Truth)[322]). The first is exposed in the *Prajñā-hṛdaya*[323]) etc. These discourses demonstrate the Absolute Truth, i. e. the Non-substantiality (and Relativity) of all the elements of existence and the 3 Media of Deliverance[324]). The second is exposed in (the following Sūtras): — The most detailed of all is the *Çatasāhasrikā*[325]), the most detailed of the discourses of intermediate compass, — the *Pañcaviṁçatisāhasrikā*[326]), the intermediate of the intermediate, — the *Aṣṭādaçasāhasrikā*[327]), the most abridged of the intermediate, — the *Daçasāhasrikā*[328]), the most detailed of the abridged Sūtras, — i. e. the *Aṣṭasāhasrikā*[329]) and the most abridged of the abridged, [78 b.] — the *Ratna-guṇa-saṁcaya*[330]). These all have the same subject-matter which is the Teaching about the 8 forms of intuition (on the Path)[331]). There is a difference only in the verbal part, the latter being either diffused or abridged. So is it said in the commentary on the verse: —

> There is only a difference in the varieties of exposition,
> The abridged, etc.

The first 5 have been expounded simultaneously. Indeed, the inquirers[332]) are the same in all these Sūtras. Moreover in the part concerning the methods of purification of the Sphere of Buddhahood[333]), the prophecy granted to the goddess of the Ganges is everywhere the same. This latter fact is a decisive argument, for

---

321) Prasphuṭapadā, Tg. MDO. VIII.

322) *mṅon-rtogs* = *abhisamaya.*

323) Çer-sñiṅ (Çes-rab-sñiṅ-po), Kg. RGYUD. XII.

324) *rnam-thar-sgo-gsum* = *triṇi vimokṣa-mukhāni.* M. Vyutp. § 73.

325) Stoṅ-phrag-brgya-pa.

326) Ñi-khri-lṅa-stoṅ-pa. Is likewise known by the abridged title Ñi-Khri.

327) Khri-brgyad-stoṅ-pa.

328) Çes-rab-khri-pa.

329) Brgyad-stoṅ-pa.

330) Yon-tan-rin-po-che-sdud-pa. According to Tsoṅ-kha-pa's Gser-phreṅ this classification is not correct. The Saṁcaya cannot be regarded as an independent Sūtra, the most abridged of all, since it represents the 84th chapter of the Aṣṭādaça-sāhasrikā (Gser-phreṅ, Labraṅ edition, I, 7 a. 4, 5).

331) I. e. the 8 principal subjects of the Abhisamayālaṁkāra. Cf. vol. I. page 51, notes 509, 510, 511, 512, 513, 514, 515).

332) *žu-ba-po*, i. e. Subhūti, Çāriputra, Ānanda, etc.

333) *Žiṅ-dag-sbyor-ba* = *kṣetra-çuddhi-prayoga*, Abhisamayālaṁkāra IV. 61.

it is not proper that one and the same Buddha should foretell the attainment of Enlightenment by one and the same person again and again. But, may it be said, this disagrees with the fact, that several prophecies had been delivered with regard to Nāgārjuna. (To this we answer): — These prophecies were each of a different character. In some it was said that he would be the elucidator of the Doctrine, in others — that he would attain Buddhahood, etc. But the prophecy granted to the goddess of the Ganges is (only) that of future Buddhahood and is everywhere the same.

Now (may it likewise be said), in the introductory chapters[334]) it has been said that the hearers were half a hundred and thirteen, and afterwards we have it stated that their number was 5000. — This is contradictory. — (To this we say): — There is a difference here, viz. (in the first case) we have an enumeration of the different congregations, (and in the second) — of the individuals that were present.

In the *Catasāhasrikā* the chapter containing the questions of Maitreya[335]), that on Eternity, that which contains the sermon delivered to Dharmodgata, and the summary at the end — these 4 are absent; they have not been brought by Nāgārjuna from the realm of the Nāgas.

It has moreover been said: — Although it (the *Prajñāpāramitā*) has been delivered in one way, it has been differently understood in many different forms. Or, to speak otherwise, the Word is one and it has been communicated in one form, but it can be understood in different forms, so that everyone can apprehend it, (being convinced): — This is intended for me. Accordingly, in conformity with one's own faculty of understanding which can be weak, inter-

---

[334]) *gleṅ-gži = nidāna.*

[335]) This passage is noteworthy, since just this chapter containing the questions of Maitreya is evidently a later production, as it contains the teaching about the 3 aspects of Reality in accordance with the standpoint of the Yogācāra school. (*kalpitaṁ rūpam = parikalpita-lakṣaṇa, vikalpitaṁ rūpam = paratantra-lakṣaṇa* and *dharmatā-rūpam = pariniṣpanna-lakṣaṇa*). Cf. Haribhadra's Abhisamayālaṁkārālokā, MS. Minaev, 41 b. 14. — 42 a. 1. — *kalpitaṁ rūpaṁ grāhya-grāhaka-ākāreṇa kalpitatvāt / vikalpitaṁ rūpam abhūta-parikalpanena jñānam eva tathā-pratibhāsa iti vikalpitatvāt / dharmatā-rūpaṁ tattvato rūpam eva çūnyatā-rūpeṇa pariniṣpannatvāt //* This subject is discussed in detail in Tsoṅ-kha-pa's Legs-bçad-sñiṅ-po, where it is directly said, that this part of the Pañcaviṁçatisāhasrikā is considered by some to contain the teaching of Yogācāra-vijñānavāda.

mediate and acute, one is made to understand (the Doctrine) in 3 ways — viz. as detailed, intermediate and abridged. So have the compilers written it down. They could not have rehearsed it in such a manner themselves (without any divine assistence). There is however no defect here, for this is a miracle produced by the blessing of the Buddha himself. [79 a.]

This is affirmed by the teacher Trilakṣa (Sthirapāla), as say the translators Ṭho-phu[336]) and Chag. As concerns the ***Saṁcaya***, we read in the commentary thereon[337]), that it had been subsequently delivered in the dialect of Magadha, in order to give satisfaction to the 4 varieties of hearers.

The aim of the Teaching was to cause all those who had adhered to false views to abstain from these and, subsequently, to direct them to the unique passage (to Salvation)[338]) — the Doctrine of Non-substantiality (and Relativity) and of Monism[339]). It is said in the ***Lalita-vistara***[340]):

> (The Buddha) has turned the Wheel of the Doctrine, —
> That of Monism and Relativity, (the Teaching)
> That there is no substance and no plurality,
> That nothing (really) appears and disappears anew,
> And that nothing (really) increases or becomes diminished.

The fact that these precepts represent the Scripture of the intermediate period is indicated in the ***Prajñā-pāramitā*** itself as follows: — And there arose the sound of the murmur of the gods in the skies: O! in Jambudvîpa the second swinging of the Wheel of the Doctrine can be witnessed. The 3ᵈ Wheel of the Doctrine is that which ascertains the essence of the Absolute Reality[341]). The

[336]) Khro-phu. His name is Jam-pai-pal (Byams-paḥi-dpal). Cf. below.

[337]) Tg. MDO VII.

[338]) *bgrod-pa-gcig-pa* = *ekāyana.*

[339]) *tshul-gcig-pa* = *eka-naya.* Cf. Abhisamayālaṁkāra, I. 62 — *samatai'ka-naya-jñatā.*

[340]) 436. 11, 12. The version of Lefmann's edition is different — *anālayaṁ niṣprapañcam anutpādam asaṁbhavam / viviktaṁ prakṛtī-çūnyaṁ dharma-cakraṁ pravartitam //*

[341]) *don-dam rnam-par-ṅes-paḥi ḥkhor-lo.* This is the name given by the Chinese commentary on the Saṁdhinirmocana-sūtra of Wen-tshig. (Tg. MDO. XXXIX, XL, and XLI. According to the Tib. tradition it is usually called *legs-par-rnam-par-phye-ba-daṅ-ldan-paḥi ḥkhor-lo (legs-phyeḥi chos-ḥkhor)* — the Teaching containing a perfect and correct discrimination (of that which does and does not exist as an Ultimate Reality.) Cf. Saṁdhinirmocana-sūtra quoted below and Tsoṅ-kha-pa's Legs-bçad-sñiṅ-po, Tsaṅ edition, 13 a. 4—5.

place where it was delivered was Malaya or Vaiçalī[342]), etc. It is said that the circle of hearers consisted of those devoted to the (3) different Vehicles, but it would be correct if we would take this to mean: "The Bodhisattvas who have entered all the different Vehicles." As concerns the time (during which it was exposed) —Ṭho-lo says that it was 12 years, —Chim-pa —10 years, Chag — 7 or 9 years and others —26 or 27 years. I myself have not seen any authoritative source for these (different varieties) of counting the time.

The Doctrine is that which definitely demonstrates the Absolute Reality. At first, the earliest Teaching completely excluded the nihilistic point of view (i. e. everything, all the elements, were considered to be real in themselves). Owing to this an (incorrect) realistic imputation could easily grow predominant. With a view to this (the Buddha) has expounded the intermediate Teaching in which a negativistic standpoint predominates. But this (Scripture of the latest period) introduces different (degrees of Reality) demonstrating (the elements in their) imputed aspect[343]) as totally non-existing[344]), (the elements in) the causally dependent aspect[345]) as having a real existence from the standpoint of the Empirical Reality[346]), and the 2 forms of the Ultimate Aspect[346a]), as representing the Absolute Reality. [79 b.] It is accordingly that which puts an end to the 2 extreme points of view, contains the direct meaning[347]) and cannot be an object of dispute. On the contrary, the other 2 (Swingings of the Wheel of the Doctrine)

---

[342]) Yaṅs-pa-can.

[343]) *kun-tu-brtags-paḥi mtshan-ñid (kun-brtags) = parikalpita-lakṣaṇa.*

[344]) Tsoṅ-kha-pa and his school object to this statement of Bu-ton that the imputed aspect is totally non-existing.

[345]) *gžan-dbaṅ-gi mtshan-ñid (gžan-dbaṅ) = paratantra-lakṣaṇa.*

[346]) *kun-rdzob = saṁvṛti.*

[346a]) *yoṅs-su-grub-paḥi-mtshan-ñid (yoṅs-grub) = pariniṣpanna-lakṣaṇa.* The 2 forms of this aspect are: 1. The Absolute as the pure and non-illusionary consciouness, as for instance the concentrated transcendental wisdom of the Mahāyānist Saint perceiving the separate unreality of the elements, and 2. the Absolute as the true and unalterable essence of existence, Cf. Khai-ḍub (Mkhas-grub), Stoṅ-thun-bskal-bzaṅ-mig-ḥbyed, Vol. I of Khai-ḍub's works, Tsaṅ edition 31 a. 1—2. — *dbye-na theg-chen-ḥphags-paḥi chos-kyi-bdag-med rtogs-paḥi mñam-bžag-ye-çes-lta-bu phyin-ci-ma-log-paḥi yoṅs-grub (= dharma-nairātmya-bodhaka-samāhita-jñāna-bhūta-aviparīta-pariniṣpanna) daṅ chos-ñid ḥgyur-med yoṅs-grub (= avikāra-dharmatā-bhūta-pariniṣpanna) gñis-te.*

[347]) *ṅes-don = nītārtha.*

are of conventional meaning and can be made an object of controversy. This is the opinion of the Vijñānavādins. It is said in the *Saṁdhinirmocana-sūtra*[348]: —Thereafter Paramārthasamudgata[349]) addressed the Buddha as follows: —The Lord has first of all, in the country of Benares, at Ṛṣipatana[350]), in the grove of the antelopes[351]), swung the Wheel of the Doctrine, demonstrating the 4 Truths of the Saint to those who had entered the Vehicle of the Çrāvakas. It was a marvellous and wonderful Teaching, similar to which none in this world, whether gods or men, had expounded before. But nevertheless, this Wheel of the Doctrine, swung by the Lord, (was not the highest form of the Teaching, expounded by him). There were (other Teachings to follow) that were more sublime than it[352]). (This earliest Teaching of the Buddha) left an opportunity for controversy, was of conventional meaning[353]) and an object of dispute[354]).

Thereupon the Lord, having begun with (the Teaching that) all the elements are devoid of a real essence of their own[355]), that they neither become originated[356]) nor disappear[357]), that they are quiescent from the outset[358]) and by their very nature merged in Nirvāṇa[359]), has swung the second Wheel of the Doctrine for the sake of those who had entered the Great Vehicle[360]), — (the Teaching) marvellous and wonderful as it demonstrates the principle of Non-substantiality (and Relativity). But, as regards this Wheel of the Doctrine swung by the Lord, there are likewise other Teachings superior (to it). It is of conventional meaning, presents an opportunity (for controversy) and can be an object of dispute.

Finally, the Lord has (again) started with the Teaching about

---

[348]) Kg. MDO. V. 24 b. 5—25 a. 4.

[349]) Don-dam-yaṅ-dag-ḥphags.

[350]) Draṅ-sroṅ-ltuṅ-ba (or lhuṅ-ba).

[351]) Ri-dvags-kyi-nags = Mṛgadāva.

[352]) *bla-na-mchis-pa.* Is explained by Wen-tshig as: "their being other teachings superior to it" and by Tsoṅ-kha-pa "as their being other teachings higher than it, viz. those of direct meaning". Legs-bçad-sñiṅ-po 12 a. 1—3.)

[353]) *draṅ-don = neyārtha.*

[354]) *rtsod-paḥi-gži = vivāda-adhikaraṇa.*

[355]) *ṅo-bo-ñid-ma-mchis-pa = niḥsvabhāvatā.*

[356]) *skye-ba-ma-mchis-pa = anutpanna.*

[357]) *ḥgag-pa-ma-mchis-pa = aniruddha.*

[358]) *gzod-ma-nas-ži-ba = ādi-çānta.*

[359]) *raṅ-bžin-gyis-yoṅs-su-mya-ṅan-las-ḥdas-pa = prakṛti-parinirvṛtta.*

[360]) *theg-pa-chen-po-la yaṅ-dag-par-žugs-pa = mahāyāna-saṁprasthita.*

the absence of a real essence with the elements and (the demonstration of the latter) as neither becoming originated, nor disappearing, as quiescent from the outset [80 a.] and as being, by their very nature, merged in Nirvāṇa. He has then swung the third Wheel of the Doctrine for the adherents of all (the 3) Vehicles, (the Teaching) miraculous and wonderful, as it gives a perfect discrimination (of that which is and is not an ultimate reality). And this swinging of the Wheel of the Doctrine by the Lord is to be regarded as unsurpassable, it gives no opportunity (for ascribing faults), is of direct meaning and cannot be an object of dispute. —

The aim of this (Teaching) was to remove the 2 extreme imputations[361]) and to cause (the converts) to adopt the middle way[362]).

According to the Mādhyamikas, the earliest and the latest Scripture are both conventional[363]), and (only) the intermediate contains the direct meaning. The passage (of the *Saṁdhinirmocana-sūtra*) just quoted, is explained (by them) as being itself of conventional meaning. Some say that (the Teaching of the latest period) is that which removes the contradiction between the first 2 divisions of Scripture. (These authorities) try to establish this on the foundation of the *Laṅkāvatāra* where it is said[364]): —

> From the Empirical Standpoint everything exists,
> But from that of the Absolute there is no (separate) reality;
> Therefore, existence and non-existence with regard to one and the some thing,
> Must not be regarded as a mutual contradiction. —

So they say, (but we answer to this): —The text quoted expresses the point of view of the Mādhyamikas, but not that of the Vijñānavādins[365]). The latter are not of the opinion that something which does exist, could at the same time be unreal as an ultimate reality[366]).

---

[361]) Realism or Eternalism (*rtag-mthaḥ = çāçvata-anta*) and Nihilism or Materialism (*chad-mthaḥ = uccheda-anta*).

[362]) *dbu-maḥi-lam = madhyama-pratipad.*

[363]) *dgoṅs-pa-can = ābhiprāyika.* [364]) Ed. Bunyiu Nanjio, p. 280.

[365]) According to the Vijñānavādins, the existence of ultimate realities (*paramārthasat*) is admitted.

[366]) According to the Vijñānavādins, there is a distinction to be made between "an ultimate separate reality" (*paramārtha-sat*) which is identical with the idea of the separate element in the causally dependent aspect (*paratantra*), and the Absolute (*paramārtha-satya*) which is the same as *pariniṣpanna-lakṣaṇa.* Khai-ḍub, Stoṅ-thun, 19 a. 2.

And the Vijñānavāda is not capable of removing the contradiction between the views of the Hīnayānists and those of the Mādhyamikas. Some call the earlier Scripture "the Wheel of the Doctrine demonstrating the 4 Truths of the Saint", that of the second period — "the Wheel of the Doctrine demonstrating the 2 Truths"[367]), and that of the third — "the Wheel of the Doctrine in which the distinction of the Truths has not been made at all". (This is incorrect,) since we have undeniable proofs that in this latest division of Scripture the 4 or the 2 Truths have been frequently mentioned.

According to some, the latest Scripture is "that of the different Vehicles", since it demonstrates different Teachings that relate to the (3) Vehicles, as it is said in the ***Lalita-vistara***[368]): —

> In different forms, (demonstrating) the resemblance
> With an illusion, a mirage, a dream,
> With the moon's reflection in the water, and the echo,
> The Lord has swung the Wheel of the Doctrine. — [80 b.]

The Paṇḍit Parahitabhadra[369]) says: — He has swung the Wheel of the Doctrine, the Teaching about the attainment of a blissful existence for those deprived of the element of (the saintly) lineage[370]). — And, according to Sajjana: — It is the Wheel of the Doctrine of the Pratyekabuddhas demonstrated to the members of that spiritual family. (As concerns this last statement), Chag says that it is contradictory to that which is said about the 3 Wheels of the Doctrine (i. e. that the first is intended for the Hīnayānists, the second for the Mahāyānists, and the third — for the adherents of all the Vehicles). This is quite clear, since no such separate Code (of the Pratyekabuddhas) exists[371]).

Now, (in reality) the Lord, having extirpated the force which calls forth speech[372]), has attained Enlightenment in perfect silence and then, up to the time of his attaining Nirvāṇa, has not uttered a single word. But, in accordance with the thoughts (and the

---

[367]) I. e. the Empirical *(saṁvṛti)* and the Absolute *(paramārtha)* reality.

[368]) 436. 15, 16. — ***māyā-marīci svapnaṁ ca dakacandra*** (sic) ***pratiçrutkā / yathai'te tathā tac cakraṁ loka-nāthena vartitam //***

[369]) Gžan-phan-bzaṅ-po.

[370]) ***rigs-med-pa = agotraka.***

[371]) Cf. Sūtrālaṁkāra, XI. 1. and commentary — ***hīnayāna-agrayāna-bhedena dvayaṁ bhavati çrāvaka-piṭakaṁ bodhisattva-piṭakaṁ ca.***

[372]) ***ṅag kun-nas-sloṅ-baḥi bag-chags = vāk-samutthāna-vāsanā.***

needs) of the living beings, he appears as if teaching (the Doctrine) in various forms[373]), as it is said[374]): —

> A cymbal on a magic circle
> Issues its sounds, being agitated by the wind,
> And although there is nothing with which it is beaten,
> Its sound is nevertheless heard.
> Similar is the voice of the Buddha which arises,
> Being called forth by the thoughts of the living beings,
> And owing to their previous virtuous deeds.
> But the Buddha (himself) has no constructive thought
> (By which his words could be conditioned).

The voice of the Buddha is therefore something inconceivable for our mind.

The Teacher has thus perceived the living beings subjected to suffering, being obscured by the pellicule[375]) of ignorance, tied by the knot of egocentristic views, suppressed by the mountain of pride, consumed by the fire of desire, wounded by the weapons of hatred, cast into the wilderness of Saṁsāra, and unable to cross the streams of birth, old age, illness, and death. And, in order to deliver them (from this suffering), from between his teeth resembling a beautiful sonant conch-shell, he stretched forth his tongue endowed with miraculous power, ejected his voice, similar to that of Brahma, and thus expounded the whole of the Doctrine.

12. [The Buddha's Attainment of Nirvāṇa[376]).]

Thereafter we have (the last) act (of the Buddha), viz. his departure into Nirvāṇa. — The Lord addressed Ānanda in order that the latter should pray him not to depart into Nirvāṇa. [81 a.] He said: — O Ānanda, he, who on the foundation of the 4 miraculous powers[377]) has repeatedly practised profound meditation, can, if

---

[373]) Cf. Conception of Buddhist Nirvāṇa, p. 210. (quotation of the Tathāgata-guhya in the XXV. Chapter of the Mādh. vṛtti).

[374]) The same idea is frequently expressed in the Uttaratantra. Cf. my translation, chapter IV. "The Acts of the Buddha."

[375]) *liṅ-tog* = *kāca*.

[376]) The narrative of the Buddha's attainment of Nirvāṇa and the following, i. e. the burial of the Buddha, the first and the second council is taken from the Vinaya-kṣudraka, Kg. ḤDUL. XI.

[377]) *rdzu-ḥphrul-gyi rkaṅ-pa bźi* = *catvāra ṛddhi-pādāḥ*.

he wishes, remain living for an aeon or even longer than that[378]. The Buddha has taken recourse to the 4 miraculous powers and has practised meditation again and again. Therefore, if the Buddha wishes, he can live during an aeon and longer than that. So he spoke to him twice and thrice, but Ānanda, being obscured by Māra, did not answer a word[379]. Then Māra the Evil One (in his turn) prayed (the Buddha) to pass away into Nirvāṇa, and the Buddha consented, saying that he would do so after 3 months[380]. Thereupon the Buddha mastered the force of life and cut away the force of life-time[381]. And, the moment he did this, the earth trembled, the stars fell down, in the 10 quarters of the sky there burst forth flames, and the gods residing in the atmospherical space, beat their drums[382]. (Ānanda) asked the cause of this and the Buddha explained to him the 8 causes owing to which the earth trembled etc.[383] And Ānanda then understood, that the Lord had cut away the force of life-time and prayed him (to continue to live), but the Buddha did not consent[384]. Thereafter, having delivered his instructions to the congregation of Capala[385], the Lord departed in the direction of Vaiçali. And, looking all the while to the right, he finally reached the grove of Çiṁçapa trees situated to the north of the villages of Vriji. There he spoke to the monks about the 3 disciplines, and after that he gradually came to another Çiṁçapa grove to the north of the village of Upabhoga. And, having demonstrated (to the monks) that the trembling of the earth was the sign, that he would soon pass away into Nirvāṇa, he said: — If (the Teaching which you intend to follow) is contained in the Sūtras, is to be found in the Vinaya and is not in conflict with the true state of things, you are to accept it as (my) Doctrine. If this is not the case, then (a teaching of some other kind) is not to be accepted[386]. [81. b.]

---

[378]) *kalpaṁ kalpāvaçeṣaṁ ca. (bskal-pa-ḥam bskal-ba-las lhag-gi bar-du).* Cf. Yaçomitra, Abhidharmakoça-vyākhyā, BB. II. 19. 15.

[379]) Vin.-kṣudr. Kg. ḤDUL. XI. 247 a. 5—6.

[380]) Ibid. 248 b. 1—249 a. 3.

[381]) Ibid. 249 a. 4—5. Cf. Yaçomitra, Abhidharmakoça-vyâkhyā BB. II. 20. 3, 4. —*jīvita-saṁskārān adhiṣṭhāya (ḥtsho-baḥi-ḥdu-byed byin-gyis brlabs-nas) āyuḥ-saṁskārān utsṛṣṭavān* /

[382]) Vin.-kṣudr. Kg. ḤDUL. XI. 249 a. 6.

[383]) Ibid. 249 b. 1—250 a. 7. [384]) Ibid. 250 a. 7—b. 6.

[385]) Xyl. *rtsa-ba-liḥi dge-ḥdun.* The Kg. has *tsa-pa-laḥi.*

[386]) Vin.-kṣudr. Kg. ḤDUL. XI. 250 b. 6—256 a. 6.

Thereafter the Buddha accepted his last alms from Cunda, the son of a blacksmith in the village of Pāpā and, having preached the Doctrine, departed to Kuçanagara[387]. (On the way) he laid himself to rest between Pāpā[388]) and the river Vasumatī[389]). Ānanda got some muddy water from the stream Kakuta and brought it (to the Buddha). The latter washed his mouth and feet and, having refreshed himself, rose up[390]). From Paṇḍaka[391]) who belonged to a great community of the Mallas and who had been converted by the Buddha, the Lord accepted 2 new pieces of cloth of the colour of gold. And, as he put them on, having cut off the fringes, his body shone brilliantly. Being asked the cause of this, he replied: — The reason is, that I am to attain Nirvāṇa this evening[392]). Then he washed himself in the river Vasumatī[393]) and, as a means of removing the grief of Cunda, said that he whose alms (the Buddha accepts) will reap merit equal to that of attaining Buddhahood and Nirvāṇa[394]). Ānanda then asked him how to pacify desire, and he said: — One must wash it away with the rain of moral purity and then arouse aversion (to this worldly life). Thereafter he gave his instructions to Kātyāyana how to deliver the precepts of the Doctrine. Then, on the way to Kuçanagara, he grew tired and lay down. Ānanda then spoke to him about the component parts of Enlightenment[395]), whereupon the Buddha rose up, went to Kuçanagara and there, in the neighbourhood of the dwellings of the Mallas, he caused a seat to be erected betwixt two Sāla-trees[396]). And, with his back to the north, he bent down on the right side, crossed his legs and lay down, having given himself up to the thoughts about the illumination[397]) (of the living beings) and to intense concentration, and having become possessed of the idea that he was now to pass away into Nirvāṇa[398]). And, as Ānanda, having grasped the seat, wept and lamented, (that he was to be separated from the Teacher), the latter appeased his grief by

[387]) Groṅ-khyer Rtsva-can. Ibid. 256 a. 6—258 a. 4.
[388]) Sdig-pa-can.
[389]) Dbyig-ldan. Ibid. 258 a. 4. sqq.
[390]) Ibid. 258 b. 1—6.
[391]) Gyuṅ-po.
[392]) Ibid. 260 b. 5—261 a. 2. [393]) Ibid. 261 a. 2—4.
[394]) Ibid. 261 a. 6—7. [395]) Ibid. 262 a. 2, 3. sqq.
[396]) Ibid. 262 b. 7—263 a. 1.
[397]) *snaṅ-baḥi ḥdu-çes = āloka-saṁjñā.*
[398]) Ibid. 263 a. 5.

speaking of the 4 miraculous attributes (with which Ānanda was to become endowed n future)[399]). [82 a.] Ānanda then asked him the reason why he was to attain Nirvāṇa here in this place[400]). The Buddha replied: — Six universal monarchs, Mahāsudarçana[401]) and the rest have passed away here, and with the Buddha, there will be altogether seven[402]). — At that moment the gods were unable to sustain the splendour of (the Buddha), the anchorite endowed with the special marks (of the super-being) and fled[403]). Ānanda then asked: — How are thy relics to be worshipped? — The Buddha replied: — Like those of a universal monarch. The body is to be wrapped in a cloth of cotton-wool and covered with 500 pieces of cloth. It is to be put into an iron coffin filled with oil. (This coffin) is to be closed with 2 iron lids, and (the whole) must be burnt on a pile of fragrant wood. The fire is to be quenched with milk, and the bones are to be put into a golden urn. Then, at the meeting-place of 4 roads, a monument is to be erected, and after that one must worship and feast[404]). Thereafter it was made known to the Mallas of Kuçanagara that the Buddha was to pass away that evening, and the Mallas accordingly came into the presence of the Lord. The latter preached the Doctrine to them, and Ānanda prescribed for them the obeisances that are to be kept by the devotees of the laity[405]).

Then there remained for the Teacher two disciples whom he had to convert personally, — Subhadra[406]) and Sunanda[407]). In order to subdue the latter, the Lord took a lute with 1000 strings and a frame of Vaiḍūrya stone. Then, having transformed himself into a Gandharva, he appeared before the doors of Sunanda and proposed a match in the skill of music. He gradually cut off all the strings with the exception of one, but the sound nevertheless remained the same. Finally, the Buddha cut off the single string that remained, likewise. But in the empty space the sound continued to ring as before. The pride of Sunanda was thus humiliated [82 b.] and he was greatly astonished. The Teacher then appeared in his true form, and Sunanda, full of faith, made his salutations and sat down in order to hear the Teaching. And, as the Lord

---

399) Ibid. 264 a. 3—b. 1. sqq. 400) Ibid. 264 b. 5—6.
401) Legs-mthoṅ-chen-po. 402) Ibid. 264 b. 7—274 a. 7.
403) Ibid. 275 b. 4, 5. 404) Ibid. 275 b. 5—276 a. 3.
405) *dge-bsñen-gyi sdom-pa = upāsaka-saṁvara.*
406) Rab-bzaṅ. 407) Rab-dgaḥ.

preached the Doctrine to him, Sunanda came to the intuition of the Truth[408]). At that time there was in Kuçanagara a Parivrājaka, named Subhadra, who, as it was said, had attained the state of an Arhat. This one heard that on the bank of the Mandakinī[409]) pond the flowers of the Udumbara garden had withered and that the cause of this was that the Buddha was about to pass away into Nirvāṇa. Thinking that it was the time to get his doubts cleared, he went to Ānanda and asked 5 times, but was not admitted (into the presence of the Buddha). The Teacher, as he knew about this, said: — This is the last time that I have to speak with a heretic. Therefore, let him come[410]). And, after he had spoken many a word to the delight of Subhadra, he said; — O Subhadra, when I attained the age of 29 years, I became a monk and then, for one-and-fifty years, have practised every possible virtue. O Subhadra, the religious discipline in which the 8-membered Path of a Saint[411]) is wanting, does not bring about the 4 results attained by an ascetic[412]). But if the eight-fold Path does exist, then these results are realized. Apart from this (eight-fold Path) there can be no real attainment of saintliness. — And as he spoke thus (Subhadra) came to perceive the Truth, became ordained by being addressed with the summons: — Come here![413]), and attained Arhatship. And then, thinking that he ought not to witness the Teacher's departure, he blessed the 5 sacred places and passed away into Nirvāṇa himself[414]).

Thereafter the Teacher delivered the following precepts: — One must not introduce into the religious order the heretics, with the exception of the Çākyas and[415]) †. The 12 classes of sacred texts are to be recited for the sake of bringing about happiness and welfare of the fourfold congregation. The teacher must be subjected to the rules of the Prātimokṣa. The old must keep together the young by providing for them necessaries of life. The young must not call the elders by name. To those who are possessed of

---

[408]) Vin.-kṣudr. Kg. ḤDUL. XI. 278 a. 5—279 b. 2. sqq.

[409]) Dal-ḥbab.

[410]) Vin.-kṣudr. Kg. ḤDUL. XI. 279 a. 6—280 a. 5.

[410]) *ḥphags-paḥi-lam-yan-lag-brgyad = ārya-aṣṭāṅga-mārga.*

[412]) *dge-sbyoṅ-gi ḥbras-bu = çramaṇa-phala.* Cf. M. Vyutp. § 46.

[413]) *tshur-çog-gis bsñen-par-rdzogs-pa = ehitvena-upasaṁpannaḥ.*

[414]) Vin.-kṣudr. Kg. ḤDUL. XI. 280 a. 5—282 b. 1.

[415]) Me-pa ral-pa-can = Agnijaṭilas (?).

faith one must speak about the following 4 subjects, viz. the apparition of the Buddha in this world, his attainment of Enlightenment, [83 a.] his teaching of the Doctrine, and his departure into Nirvāṇa[416]. — O monks, if you have doubt as regards the 3 Jewels and the 4 Truths, then ask now![417] Then he took off the garment that covered the upper part of his body and said: — O monks, it is very difficult to meet with the apparition of the Buddha. Perceive therefore now the body of the Buddha[418]. O monks, henceforth I shall speak no more: — This is the last word of the Buddha — all the elements of existence, that are caused and conditioned are liable to destruction[419]. — And, having uttered this, he became absorbed in the 4 degrees of trance (of the ethereal sphere)[420], the 4 degrees of the immaterial sphere[421], and the Cessation-Trance[422] in the direct and the reverse order[423]. After that he again entered the (first 4) degrees of trance. And then, after attaining the culminating point (of the last of these)[424], he passed away into Nirvāṇa.

The teacher Çilapālita[425], in his commentary on the Vinaya-kṣudraka, gives the following explanation which agrees with the point of view of the Kashmirian (Vaibhāṣikas): — After the (attainment of) the culminating point (in the 4th degree of trance), one comes to a neutral[426] state of the mind, which is followed by Nirvāṇa. This neutral state, being near to the culminating point before said, is called itself "the culminating point".

Immediately after (the Lord had passed away into Nirvāṇa) the earth trembled, the stars fell down, from the 10 quarters of the sky there burst forth flames and sounds of celestial music were heard[427].

---

416) Vin.-kṣudr. Kg. ḤDUL. XI. 287 b. 2—289 a. 2.

417) Ibid. 289 a. 3 sqq. 418) Ibid. 289 b. 1, 2.

419) Ibid. 289 b. 2—290 a. 5.

420) *bsam-gtan-bži = catvāri dhyānāni.*

421) *gzugs-med-bži = catvāra ārupya-samāpattayaḥ.*

422) *ḥgog-sñoms* (i. e. *ḥgog-paḥi sñoms-par ḥjug-pa) = nirodha-samāpatti.*

423) *lugs-ḥbyuṅ-lugs-zlog = anuloma-viloma.*

424) *rab-mthaḥ.* 425) Tshul-khrims bskyaṅs.

426) *luṅ-ma-bstan-pa = avyākṛta.*

427) Vin.-kṣudr. Kg. ḤDUL. XI. 290 a. 5, 6.

[The Burial of the Buddha.]

At that time Mahākāçyapa[428]) was abiding in Rājagṛha[429]). Having come to know that the Teacher had passed away, he thought: — Such is the nature of all the Phenomenal Elements. If the king Ajātaçatru hears this, he shall certainly die. Therefore one must find a means (of preventing this). — Accordingly, he said to the Brāhmaṇa Varṣaka[430]): — Go thou to the garden without delay and draw pictures (illustrating the acts of the Buddha), — how he became conceived in the womb, how he attained Enlightenment, how he swung the Wheel of the Doctrine, how he demonstrated his miraculous apparitions[431]) at Çrāvastī [83 b.], how he descended from the abode of the gods at Keçavatī and how he went to take his last rest at Kuçanagara[432]). Then place 7 wooden troughs filled with fresh butter and one — the eighth, — with finest sandal wood. And then gradually demonstrate (to the king the events in Buddha's life). Thereafter, when the king faints, thou must put him into the 7 troughs with fresh butter and the eighth with sandal wood and make him recover. — Varṣaka acted according to these instructions and gradually showed to the king (the acts of the Buddha). — This, said he, — is the arrival of the Teacher at Kuçanagara to take his last sleep. — And, as the king asked: — Has the Buddha passed away? — he did not answer a word. The king fell down in a swoon, but Varṣaka made him recover according to the instructions which he had received. And, at that moment, a certain monk who had come, uttered the following verse[433]): —

> In that grove where a pair of Sāla, —
> Those most beautiful of all the trees do grow,
> The Teacher has passed away into Nirvāṇa,
> And we have strewed flowers in that place. —

Indra said[434]): —

> Alas, the phenomenal elements are evanescent,
> They are subjected to origination and destruction.
> The pacification (of these elements) is the true bliss!

---

428) Ḥod-sruṅs-chen-po.
429) Rgyal-poḥi-khab.
430) Dbyar-byed. 431) *cho-ḥphrul = prātihārya.*
432) Vin.-kṣudr. Kg. ḤDUL. XI. 290 a. 6—b. 6.
433) Vin.-kṣudr. Kg. ḤDUL. XI. 291 b. 1.
434) Ibid. 291 b. 2.

And Brahma[435]): —

This is the culmination of all the virtue,
That can be accumulated by the living beings
And can be desired for in this world.
Here an individual, higher than whom there are none,
The Buddha who has attained the (10) powers
And is possessed of divine sight, —
This Teacher has passed away into Nirvāṇa! —

Aniruddha[436]) said[437]): —

He who, with a firm and steady mind,
Has protected (the living beings)
And has attained the motionless quiescent state,
He who was endowed with the faculty of divine vision,
Has now passed away into Nirvāṇa,
Having emitted and suspended his breath! —

And at that time some of the monks were rolling on the ground in despair, some lamented loudly, others sat (in silence) tormented by sorrow, and still others were reflecting over the essence of the Doctrine[438]).

The next day [84 a.] Ānanda summoned the Mallas of Kuçanagara, who up to the 7th day made the necessary arrangements[439]). Then, on the 7th day, the wives and daughters of the Mallas spread a canopy, and the Malla youths made a bier. The gods worshipped, offering perfumes, wreaths of flowers, incense and the like. They all entered Kuçanagara by the western gate, came into the middle of the city, then went out through the eastern gate and crossed the river Vasumatī. Thereafter the Mallas prayed to make halt at a sanctuary where they deposited the ornaments of their heads. The gods in their turn strewed flowers, so that (the feet and the legs of the body) were covered up to the knees[440]). A certain Ājīvaka, having gathered many of these flowers, went to the city of Pāpā and met with Mahākāçyapa whose grief was not appeased and who had come in order to worship (the relics of the Buddha). And, as this Ājīvaka related about the Teacher's attainment of Nirvāṇa, an old monk said: — O monks, you are now released from him who has said: — This you may do and this you may not.

---

[435]) Ibid. 291 b. 3. [436]) Ma-ḥgags-pa. [437]) Ibid. 291 b. 4.
[438]) Ibid. 291 b. 5—7. [439]) Ibid. 292 b. 1. sqq.
[440]) Ibid. 294 b. 7—295 a. 2.

I tell you: — Do what is in your power to do and do not, what you can not. — But the gods cast a veil on his words and made them unheard (to the assembly) with the exception of Mahākāçyapa[441]). Then the latter summoned the congregation: — Let us go quickly in order to see the relics of the Buddha, as long as they have not been destroyed by the flames[442]).

At that time the Mallas began to perform the funeral rites, as becoming a universal monarch. They tried to set the pile on fire, but the flame did not blaze up. Aniruddha knew that this was because Kāçyapa had not come, and said this[443]). Kāçyapa then came, opened the coffin, took off the pieces of cloth and the cotton-wool and made his salutations to the body, as it was still untouched (by the flames)[444]). Thereupon Mahākāçyapa, being the wisest and the most virtuous of the 4 great Çrāvakas, — the others being Ājñātakauṇḍinya, Cunda[445]) and Kāçyapa with the 10 powers[446]), — [84 b.] wrapped the body in new cotton-wool and in 500 new pieces of cloth, put it into the iron coffin, filled the latter with oil, covered it with 2 iron lids, and piled up the fragrant wood. And the fire then blazed forth itself[447]). Ānanda then said[448]):

The Great Leader endowed with a precious body
And possessed of miraculous powers,
Has departed into the world of Brahma.
The worldly frame of the Buddha has been covered
By 500 pieces of cloth and 1000 religious garments.
By its own lustre this body, though well-wrapped,
Has become perfectly consumed;
But two of the robes have not been burned,
The most inward and the most outward, these two. —

Thereupon the Mallas quenched the fire with milk, and from that milk there sprung forth 4 flowers: — a Javā[449]), a Pāṇḍura[450]), an Açvattha[451]), and an Udumbara[452]). The relics were then deposited into a golden urn which they placed in the middle of the town and worshipped[453]).

---

441) Ibid. 295 a. 2—295 b. 1. 442) Ibid. 295 b. 1—3.
443) Ibid. 295 b. 3—296 a. 3. 444) Ibid. 296 a. 3—7.
445) Skul-byed. 446) Stobs-bcuḥl Ḥod-sruṅs.
447) Vin.-kṣudr. Kg. ḤDUL. XI. 296 a. 7—b. 5.
448) Ibid. 296 b. 5—7. 449) *gser-can.* 450) *ser-skya.*
451) *rta-don.* 452) Vin.-kṣudr. Kg. ḤDUL. XI. 296 b. 7—297 a. 1.
453) Ibid. 297 a. 1—3.

Thereafter the Mallas of Pāpā, having heard that the Teacher had passed away 7 days before, collected a 4 membered army and declared to the Mallas of Kuçanagara: — This Teacher has a long time been dear to us. He has now passed away in the neighbourhood of your town. You must give us our portion of the relics, that we could erect a monument in our town, worship and feast. But if you do not give us (our part) we shall take it by force. — Do so, — replied the Mallas of Kuçanagara[454]). In a similar manner the members of the Kṣatriya family Puluka of Calakalpa[455]), the Krodhavas of Rāvaṇa, the Brāhmaṇas of Vaiṣṇavadvīpa[456]), the Çākyas of Kapilavastu and the Licchavis of Vaiçalī, demanded their share[457]). [85 a.] Ajātaçatru of Magadha in his turn heard that all these had gone to take their part of the relics. So he likewise set out, having mounted his elephant. But, as he thought about the merits of the (deceased) Teacher, he fell down in a swoon (from grief). Thereafter, having recovered, he sent Varṣaka, having said to him: — Ask thou in my name the Mallas, whether they are unharmed and not subjected to danger, whether they are in troubles, how they live, whether they are powerful and enjoy happiness. Then tell them as follows: — The Teacher has for a long time showed his benevolence to us and has been our preceptor. At present he has passed away in the neighbourhood of your town. Therefore give us a part of his relics. We shall erect a monument at Rājagṛha, worship and feast. — Varṣaka did as he was ordered. The Mallas said in return: — We intend to do the same. — But, — said Varṣaka, — if you shall not give us our part, we are going to fight for it. — Do so, — was the answer[458]). The wives and children of the Mallas learned the skill of archery and, in order to encounter the 4 membered armies of their antagonists, the Mallas, their forces being likewise 4 membered, marched out[459]). At that time a member of the Brahmanical family of Droṇa[460]), knowing that if there would be a struggle, there would be mutual slaughter, — said to the Mallas of Kuçanagara: — The Teacher, from the very beginning, was endowed with forbearance and has sung the praise of the latter. It is therefore ill-suited that you should kill

[454]) Ibid. 297 a. 3—b. 2.
[455]) Rtog-pa-gyo-ba. [456]) Khyab-ḥjug-gliṅ.
[457]) Vin. kṣudr. Kg. ḤDUL. XI. 297 b. 2—298 a. 1.
[458]) Ibid. 298 a. 1—b. 6. [459]) Ibid. 298 b. 6—299 a. 3.
[460]) Bram-zeḥi-rigs Bre-bo-daṅ-mñam-pa.

each other for the sake of his relics. We shall divide them into 8 parts and worship them ourselves in a golden vessel. — Do so, — said the Mallas of Kuçanagara. Then the same was told to the Mallas of Pāpā and to all the others, up to Varṣaka. [85 b.] And they all said: — Do like that[461]). — Accordingly, the relics were divided into 7 parts and each was given his part, beginning with the Mallas of Kuçanagara and ending with Varṣaka. Each of these then erected a monument in their own country, worshipped and feasted[462]). The part of the relics which was given to Rāvaṇa[463]) was carried off by the Nāgas and worshipped by them. The urn in which the relics had (first) been deposited was given to the member of the Brahmanical family of Droṇa who erected a monument in his own city. The ashes of the body fell a lot to Nyagrodhaja[464]), and that youth of Brahmanical caste built a monument in the Nyagrodha country, performed sacrificial rites and made a great feast. At that time there were thus 10 monuments and, with the 4 eye-teeth of the Buddha, altogether 14 (objects of worship)[465]).

> There were 8 parts of the relics of the Omniscient
> As they were distributed by Droṇa.
> Of these, — 7 became objects of worship in Jambudvīpa,
> And one of the parts of the Highest Being's relics,
> That of the city of Rāvaṇa, was worshipped by the king of the Nāgas.
> There remained, moreover, the 4 eye-teeth of the Highest Being.
> Of these, one tooth was worshipped in the realm of the gods,
> The second, — in the delightful city of Gāndhāra[466]),
> The third — in the realm of the Kalinga king,
> And the fourth tooth of that greatest of men
> The king of the Nāgas worshipped in the city of Rāvaṇa.
> The king Açoka, residing in Pāṭaliputra,
> Decorated richly the 7 monuments.
> And in this land subjected to his power
> These 7 monuments became adorned by objects of worship

---

461) Vin.-kṣudr. Kg. ḤDUL. XI. 299 a. 3—b. 7.

462) Ibid. 299 b. 7—300 a. 7. 463) Sgra-sgrogs.

464) Nyagrodha-skyes.

465) Vin.-kṣudr. Kg. ḤDUL. XI. 300 b. 1—6.

466) Tshig-ḥdzin.

Thus, the lords of the gods, Nāgas, and men,
The lords of men, Nāgas and Yakṣas
Payed their homage and worshipped (the relics).
(The Lord), endowed with Highest Wisdom and Commiseration,
And fully possessed of the 10 powers,
Was born in the Çākya clan and attained Enlightenment in Magadha;
In Kāçī (Benares) he has swung the Wheel of the Doctrine, [86 a.]
And, within the shelter of Kuçanagara, he has passed away into Nirvāṇa[467]).

As concerns the meaning of "Nirvāṇa", the Hīnayānistic (schools) consider it to be the complete annihilation of the stream of all the elements, the material as well as the mental, just as fire becomes extinguished after the fuel has been consumed[468]). According to some of the Mahāyānists, the Body of Bliss[469]) attains Nirvāṇa, but none of the Buddha's) adherents knows about this. (It is said that) this is a case similar to that of Indra whose death is known only to himself, whereas the gods surrounding him have no notion about it. — This is not correct, as it is said that the Body of Bliss is eternal and that the stream (of its existence) is uninterrupted[470]). Two causes of longevity have been mentioned, viz. abstaining from taking away life[471]) and giving food to others.

---

[467]) Ibid. 300 b. 6—301 a. 3.

[468]) The different points of view of the Hīnayānists regarding Nirvāṇa have been thoroughly analysed by Jam-yaṅ-žad-pa (Ḥjam-dbyaṅs-bžad-pa) in his commentary on the Abhisamayālaṁkāra (Phar-phyin-skabs-brygad-ka, Transbaikalian Chilutai Monastery edition I. 57 b. 3. sqq.). The Kashmirian Vaibhāṣikas and the Sautrāntikas following Scripture *(āgama-anusāriṇaḥ Sautrāntikāḥ = luṅ-gi-rjes-ḥbraṅs-Mdo-sde-ba)* consider Nirvāṇa to be mere annihilation. A part of the Vaibhāṣikas (acc. to Jam-yaṅ-žad-pa some of the Vaibhāṣikas following the Abhidharmakoça) and the logician Sautrāntikas *(nyāya-anusāriṇaḥ Sautrāntikāḥ = rigs-paḥi-rjes-ḥbraṅs Mdo-sde-ba)* maintain that the consciousness of the Arhat at the time of final Nirvāṇa does not become annihilated, but that it is followed by other, different states of consciousness which do not relate to the ordinary Phenomenal Existence. This idea is to be found in a more developped form with the Yogācāras who admit an eternal motionless state of the Arhat in the so-called "Unaffected Sphere" *(zag-med-kyi dbyiṅs = anāsrava-dhātu)*.

[469]) *loṅs-spyod-rdzogs-paḥi sku = saṁbhoga-kāya.* [470]) Cf. vol. I. p. 132.

[471]) *srog-gcod-pa-spaṅs-pa = prāṇātipāta-virati.*

Now, if the 2 are fully practised, if the 2 accumulations of merit are fully accomplished, and if one has taken recourse to the highest forms of meditation, on the basis of the 4 miraculous powers, it becomes possible, if one desires, to remain living for an aeon and longer. (By such factors the eternal existence of the Body of Bliss is conditioned). It is said in the Commentary to the *Anantamukha-nirhāra-dhāraṇī*[472]):

Only the Apparitional Body[473]) and not the other (forms)
Are spoken of as passing away into Nirvāṇa;
(The other 2 forms) are possessed of the factors for an
eternal existence
And it is impossible for them to pass away. —

Accordingly, it is thus said that the Apparitional Body, and not the Body of Bliss does pass away into Nirvāṇa. It has moreover been said that the Apparitional Body has attained Nirvāṇa, but this does not mean that its stream of existence is altogether annihilated. We read in the *Saddharmapuṇḍarika*[474]): — When the sons of a skilful physician do not drink the medicine, their father, having prepared a remedy, says: — Drink, as long as the remedy is there, for I am about to die. — So saying, he feigns death. The sons know that, the father being dead, there is no other who knows about a remedy. And so, in order to preserve their lives, they drink the medicine. Thereafter, [86 b.] when they have recovered from their illness, they come to know that the father did not really die. Now, (the father) did not commit the sin of lying in doing so. (Similar is the case with the Buddha's attainment of Nirvāṇa which is demonstrated by him as a means of converting the living beings). It is said in the *Suvarṇa-prabhāsa*[475]): —

The Buddha does not pass away,
And the Teaching does not cease to exist,
But, in order to bring the living beings to maturity,
The Buddha demonstrates his departure into Nirvāṇa. —

---

472) Sgo mthaḥ-yas-pa-bsgrub-paḥi-gzuṅs-kyi ḥgrel-pa. Tg. RGYUD. LXVIII. 15 b. 5. (N.)

473) *sprul-paḥi-sku* = *nirmāṇa-kāya.*

474) BB. 321. 9—323. 1. (Tathāgata-āyuṣ-pramāṇa-parivarta.)

475) This verse is quoted in Haribhadra's Abhisamayālaṁkāralokā, MS. Minaev. 103 a. 12—13. *na buddhaḥ parinirvāti na ca dharmo' ntardhīyate / sattvānām paripākāya nirvāṇaṁ tū' padarçayet //*

The *Sūtrālaṁkāra* says[476]): —

As fire blazes forth in some places,
And becomes extinct in others,
So is the Buddha for the living beings,
Seen (by some) and unseen (by others). —

It is said in the *Sūtrālaṁkāra* that the stream of existence of the Apparitional Body[477]) is uninterrupted. Now, (we have to understand this as follows): — If food is given to somebody again and again, we say: The food is given constantly and uninterruptedly. In a similar manner, (the Apparitional Body) manifests itself uninterruptedly and is therefore regarded as having a constant existence, that does not cease. Here it has passed away into Nirvāṇa, but elsewhere it abides without departing. Here it has passed away, since there are no more such beings who could be converted by beholding (the visible form of) the Buddha. (In other places) it does not pass away, since there exist such who are to be converted through the sight of the Buddha's corporeal form, like Indra and the like. It is said in the *Çūraṁgama-samādhi-sūtra*[478]): — At present, there is in the east a sphere of Buddhaic activity called "The Perfectly Adorned." There abides the Buddha Vairocana "the king of miraculous powers crowned with rays of light". The duration of his existence is equal to 700 immeasurable periods of aeons. It is said, that this Buddha represents the true form of this our Teacher. He manifests himself in 1 000 000 000 such worlds of 4 continents as ours. In some of these he becomes born, in some he manifests himself as attaining Enlightenment, in others — he swings the Wheel of the Doctrine, and in still others he demonstrates his departure into Nirvāṇa. In accordance (with all that has been said), the Buddha is not to be regarded as not having attained Nirvāṇa, inasmuch as he has removed all the Obscurations. But, on the other hand, he does not pass away, since his work is not accomplished. Is is said in the *Mahāyāna-saṁgraha*[479]): (He has attained Nirvāṇa on one side and has not attained it on the other) [87 a.], since he has removed all the Obscurations, but at the same time has not fully accomplished his

[476]) IX. 17. — *yathā' gnir jvalate' nyatra punar anyatra çāmyati / buddheṣv api tathā jñeyaṁ saṁdarçanam adarçanam //*

[477]) *sprul-sku = nirmāṇa-kāya.*

[478]) Dpaḥ-bar-ḥgro-baḥi-tiṅ-ṅe-ḥdzin-gyi-mdo. Kg. MDO. XI. 309 a. 1 — 310 a. 4. (D.)

[479]) Tg. MDO. LVI. 49 b. 4.

work. Now, it may be asked, what was his age, when he passed away? Some say, that when he was converting the Parivrājaka Subhadra and the Gandharva Sunanda, he spent a year (in converting each). Otherwise (as it is said), having been entreated by Cunda, he consented to live two years more. Thus, according to the said authorities, he passed away when he was 82 years of age. I, however, know no source (that justifies this statement). The latter disagrees with the *Aṣṭa-mahāsthāma-caitya-stotra*[480]) where it is said: — Having been entreated by Cunda, he continued to live for another 3 months. — An authority versed in the Vinaya says that, according to the *Vinaya-kṣudraka,* (Buddha) passed away 84 years of age. It is clear that this authority has not read the *Vinaya-kṣudraka,* for it is said in the latter: O Ānanda, the Buddha has attained the age of 80, and has thus met with old age and infirmity. — Therefore (it will be correct if we affirm) that he passed away when he was 80 years old. Accordingly it is said in the *Suvarṇa-prabhāsa* that the Lord has attained the age of 80, and in the *Karuṇā-puṇḍarīka* — that the Buddha's age was that of 100 years without one fifth. In many other sūtras we likewise have it stated that the Teacher lived 80 years. The *Mahāvibhāṣā* moreover says: —

In the place where he swung the Wheel of the Doctrine,
In Vaiçalī, in Paṇḍubhūmi, in the realm of the gods,
In Balaghna and in Kauçambī,
In the wilderness, in Uçirayicī,
In the Bamboo Grove, and
In the city of Kapilavastu, —
In each of these places the Lord,
The Highest of living beings abided for a year.
Twenty-three years he resided in Çrāvastī,
Four years in the place abounding with remedies[481]),
Two years he spent in Indraçailaguhā,
Five years — in the villages of Rājagṛha,
Six years he underwent the practice of asceticism and
Twenty-nine years he abided in his father's palace. —
Thus the Lord, the holiest and highest of Sages,
Attained the age of 80 and departed into Nirvāṇa. —

---

480) Tg. BSTOD. I. 95 a. 8.

481) *sman-gyi-gnas.*

As concerns the date of (the Buddha's attainment of Nirvāṇa), [87 b.] it is said in the *Mahāparinirvāṇa-sūtra* that it took place in spring, on the 15th of the month of Vaiçākha, at midnight[482]. In the commentary to the *Vinaya-kṣudraka*, the work of the teacher Çīlapālita[482a], it is said that it was at the end of autumn in the month of Kārtika on the 8th day of the ascending moon. The great Pandit Çākyaçrī says that it was on the 8th of the ascending moon of Kārtika, at midnight. —

At the time when the moon disappeared behind the mountain
The Highest of Sages passed away into Nirvāṇa. —

According to the Hīnayānists, in the evening (the Buddha) subdued the Demon of Carnal Desire[483]. At daybreak, by force of concentrated trance called the "thunderbolt-like"[484], he vanquished the Demon of Moral Defilement[485]. When the Evil One prayed the Buddha to pass away into Nirvāṇa, the Lord said that he would not depart, till he had not accomplished all his work for the welfare of the 4 kinds of adherents. In such a manner, some say, he vanquished the Demon of Death[486]. Some are of the opinion that he subdued the Demon governing the 5 groups of elements at the time when he was practising asceticism. Others affirm that he vanquished the Demon of Death and him who governs the groups of elements after having attained Nirvāṇa. Now (we know that) in the Bamboo Grove he observed the Summer Fast and at that time showed how severe and rigid observances were to be kept. Thereafter, having been entreated by the Evil One, he cut away the force of life-time[427] and mastered[488] the forces of life[489]. It is clear that by means of this he vanquished the Lord of Death and the Demon governing the groups of elements respectively[490].

---

482) Cf. Mahāvaṁsa III. 2.— *Kusinārāyaṁ yamaka-sālānāṁ antare vare Vesākha-puṇṇamāyaṁ so dīpo lokassa nibbuto* /

482a) Tg. MDO. LXXXI.

483) *lhaḥi-buḥi-bdud* = *devaputra-māra*.

484) *rdo-rje-lta-buḥi tiṅ-ṅe-ḥdzin* = *vajropama-samādhi*.

485) *ñon-moṅs-paḥi-bdud* = *kleça-māra*.

486) *ḥchi-bdag-gi-bdud* = *mṛtyu-adhipati-māra* or *maraṇa-māra*.

487) *tsheḥi ḥdu-byed* = *āyuḥ-saṁskāra*.

488) Or "blessed" (?) *byin-gyis-brlabs-pa* = *adhiṣṭhitavān*.

489) *ḥtsho-baḥi ḥdu-byed* = *jīvita-saṁskāra*.

490) Cf. Yaçomitra, Abhidharmakoça-vyākhyā, BB. II koçasthāna, 19. 12—20. 5.

Jñānagarbha[491]) says: —

By these and similar words
He demonstrated his mastery over them (the forces of life), —
This because he had vanquished the 2 Demons
And was full of Commiseration with regard to the converts. —

Accordingly, he vanquished the 2 Demons who bore respectively the character of the Lord of Death and of the 5 Groups of Elements and, being full of compassion with those who were to be converted, he pronounced the blessings (through which he made manifest his mastery over the forces of life). [88 a.] In order to show that he had the power over death, he rejected (the force of life-time). And, in order to demonstrate the power over the Groups of Elements, he mastered the vital forces. This is to be taken as a matter of fact.

According to the Mahāyanists, (the Buddha) vanquished the 4 Demons simultaneously as it is said: — Hast thou not attained Enlightenment and, at that very time, vanquished the 4 Demons? —

As concerns these 12 acts of the Buddha, we have diff rent accounts in the *Vinaya*, in the *Abhiniṣkramaṇa-sūtra* and in the *Lalitavistara*, each having its own special version. Here, in describing (the first 11 acts), we have followed the *Lalitavistara*. The act of the Buddha's departure into Nirvāṇa is rendered in accordance with the *Vinaya-kṣudraka*. The hidden meaning etc. of these accounts is to be known in detail from the *Upāyakauçalya-sūtra*[492]).

IV. $Accb_2$ c_3.[493]) Detailed Analysis of the Subjects referring to the Doctrine.

Here we distinguish 3 points: —

a_4) The way how the Teaching was rehearsed by the Compilers

b_4) The way how it abided after having been compiled.

c_4) The way how it will finally undergo destruction and cease to exist.

---

491) Satya-dvaya-vibhanga.

492) Thabs-la-mkhas-paḥi-mdo.

493) Cf. Vol. I, p. 127.

IV. $Acc_1 b_2 c_3 a_4$. **The Rehearsals of the Teaching.**
Here we have: —

a_5) (The rehearsal of) the Hīnayānistic Teaching.
b_5) (The rehearsal of) the Mahāyānistic Doctrine.

IV. $Acc_1 b_2 c_3 a_4 a_5$. **The Rehearsals of the Hīnayānistic Scripture.**

We distinguish 3 periods during which (Hīnayānistic Scripture) was rehearsed. We shall now take in consideration

The first Rehearsal.

After the monuments (harbouring the Buddha relics) etc. had thus been erected and after Çāriputra with his 80 000 followers, Maudgalyāyana with the 70 000 under his orders and the Teacher himself with his congregation of 18 000 monks had passed away[494]), the gods whose life dures many aeons began to show their contempt (toward the Doctrine), saying: — The Word of the Teacher is dispersing like smoke. The monks who possessed authority and power have likewise passed away. Therefore the 3 Codes of Scripture will never come to be expounded[495]). In order to put an end to this manifestation of contempt, Mahākāçyapa resolved to call a council of the clergy and bade Pūrṇa[496]) to assemble the monks[497]). [88 b.] Pūrṇa who was at that time abiding in the culminating state of mystic absorption looked around and beat the wooden gong, whereupon (all the monks), with the exception of Gavāṁpati[498]) assembled[499]). Pūrṇa, having received the order to summon Gavāṁpati[500]), by force of his miraculous power, flew to the palace of Çirīṣaka where Gavāṁpati was abiding, saluted him and said: — The congregation of monks with Mahākāçyapa at their head send their greetings to the reverend Gavāṁpati. There is an affair concerning the Congregation; therefore thou must speedily come. — Now Gavāṁpati was free from passion (and every kind of attachment) but, under the influence of the force of friendship (which remained with him) he asked: — O reverend Pūrṇa! Has not the Lord passed away into another world for the sake of the living

494) Vin. kṣudr. Kg. ḤDUL. XI. 301 a. 3—4.
495) Ibid. 301 a. 4—5. 496) Tib. Gaṅ-po.
497) Ibid. 301 a. 5—b. 2, 3.
498) Ba-laṅ-bdag. 499) Ibid. 301 b. 3—7.
500) Ibid. 301 b. 7—302 a. 2.

beings to be converted? Has there not been any strife, dispute and quarrel amongst the clergy, and has not any abusive language been used? Do not the heretics cause to turn back the Wheel of the Doctrine that has been swung by the Lord? Have not (these heretics) assembled and done harm to the Congregation of the Çrāvakas? Have not the (heretical) ascetics, the Brāhmaṇas, the (heretical) mystics, and the Parivrājakas who are overpowered by passion, — have they not reviled the Buddha who is akin to the sun? Have not those whose minds are covered by the darkness of ignorance caused any rupture in the unity of the Congregation? Have not the Doctrine and Discipline of the Lord, as well as the sentences and words corresponding to the Doctrine, and the philosophical teachings likewise, —have they not been rendered impure? Those who were of a virtuous behaviour, have they not got their minds diverted from reading, reciting, and taking to heart (the word of Scripture)? Are they not assembling now for telling obscene tales? With minds possessed of doubt and uncertainty [89 a], do they not consider that which is not the Doctrine to be such, and do they not speak of the real Doctrine as not being it? Do they not speak of that which is not the real Discipline as being such, and depreciate the true Discipline in saying that it is not such? The monks, obscured by the defilement of envy, do they not show contempt with those who are possessed of virtuous behaviour and who have unexpectedly come to them, instead of practising the 6 kinds of virtue that would give pleasure (to the new-comers)? The Brāhmaṇas and householders who were possessed of faith, — have they not been diverted from their belief in the Doctrine by the worthless monks and adopted heretical views? (These bad monks), — have they not taken recourse to wrong means of livelihood? Do they not live on agriculture and traffic, or maintain their life by seeking a support in worldly power? After having commenced the practice of the (12) virtues of rigid asceticism[501]), — have they not accepted shelter in the suburbs of cities, thus frustrating their obeisances of ascetics? Those who are not really ascetics, — do they not affirm to be such and by this bring confusion amongst those who are of virtuous behaviour? Now, be this as the case may be, but, O reverend Pūrṇa, (this is especially what I wish to know): — If it is right to say: "the Congregation of

---

[501]) *sbyaṅs-paḥi-yon-tan* = *dhūta-guṇa.*

monks with Buddha at their head", how is it then that thou sayest: "With Kāçyapa at heir head"? (What does this mean?) —The Teacher who abided in the practice of Highest Commiseration and brought his activity to full accomplishment, — has he passed away and become merged in the plane of the final Nirvāṇa without residue?[502]) And, as the steersman of all that lives is no more, has not the world (of living beings) become confused? He who was endowed with the 10 powers, — is he not himself overpowered by the force of Evanescence? The Teacher of the living beings, the protector who wakes us, — has he now himself fallen asleep? Has the sun of the Buddha gone down? The moon of the Lord of Sages, — has it not been devoured by Rahu and become invisible? [89 b.] The lordly enchanted tree in the region of the 33 gods, adorned by those fragrant flowers which are the component parts of Enlightenment and bearing the 4 sublime fruits of saintliness, — has it not been broken, by the elephant of impermanence? The Light of Divine Wisdom, — has it not disappeared into Nirvāṇa, — blown out by the wind of evanescence? Such were his questions[503]). Pūrṇa said in return[504]): —

> O Sage, in order to secure a long existence for the Doctrine,
> The Congregation of the Çrāvakas has come together,
> And, being assembled at that place, they pray thee
> To abide with them and join (in their work).
> The great ship, the Lord, has met with destruction,
> And the moutain of Divine Wisdom has broken down,
> But there are still numerous ascetics of 4 kinds,
> Possessed of the Highest Sublime Teaching, who are not idle.
> From them I have come here as a messenger;
> In order that the Teaching might be established,
> Thou must come with me in any case. —

Gavāṁpati said[505]): —

> Enough of this, O Pūrṇa, it is not the time to go.
> I had the intention of going to that place
> Where the Protector, the Light of World, abided.
> But, as he has now departed to that other world of perfect peace,

---

[502]) *lhag-ma-med-paḥi mya-ṅan-las-ḥdas-paḥi dbyiṅs = anupadhiçeṣa-nirvāṇa-dhātu.*

[503]) Vin. kṣudr. Kg. ḤDUL. XI. 302 a. 4—303 a. 1.

[504]) Ibid. 303 a. 2—3. [505]) Ibid. 303 a. 4—5.

Who, really wise, will go into this world?
This alms-bowl and these religious garments of 3 kinds,
Give thou to the Congregation of the monks.
I shall go there were I find peace and no further rebirth,
And pray those possessed of sublime intentions to forgive me. —

Having thus said, he manifested his miraculous power and died (on the spot). His body was consumed by fire that sprung forth from it by itself. Four streams of water then issued from it and the following four verses were heard: —

1. At present the times have become evil,
The living beings rely upon their own actions,
The Light of the World has passed away,
Therefore all must now choose their paths themselves.

2. The active elements of life, being accumulated,
Disappear at once, in a moment [90 a.];
Subjected to the suffering of birth etc. and possessed of passion,
The ordinary beings indulge in the conception of the Ego;
You must know that there is no such thing!

3. He who is wise must become attentive through constant thought,
And must be zealous in appreciating all that is virtuous.
The living beings in their multitude,
They all pass away and perish,
And the bloom of life is liable to change.

4. Having by his wisdom duly worshipped the Lord,
And brought to accomplishment all his aims,
Full of reverence and highest devotion,
Gavāṁpati has thus departed, following his Teacher[506]).

Thereupon Pūrṇa, by the force of his miraculous power, returned to the place were the Congregation was assembled, made his salutations, presented the mendicant's bowl (of Gavāṁpati) etc. and said: —

He has heard that the Body of the Lord exists no more,
And, by the force of his virtuous deeds,
He has passed away to perfect peace.

---

[506]) Ibid. 303 a. 5—b. 2.

Here are his religious garments and his mendicant's bowl;
He prays the Congregation to forgive his intentions[507]).

Thereupon Kāçyapa said[508]): — Harken ye, O monks!

This one has passed away like a Saint,
But the others must not depart to perfect peace in such a manner;
As long as there is a necessary work to do,
Those who have power must assemble and dare not depart
Like this high-minded Gavāṁpati, the receptacle
Of virtuous deeds, who resided in Çirīṣaka;
In such a way you must not think,
But assemble and exert your minds
How to act for the sake of mankind. —

Having given this order, he said: — If the precepts of the Doctrine are expounded here, many monks will come. In such a case there may arise confusion. Let us therefore go to Magadha[509]). — Well, — said (the other members of the Congregation). — Then they sent away the monks who were still under discipline[510]) and appointed Ānanda verger. Ānanda with the Congregation (in travelling to Magadha) passed through many a country district. [90 b.] But Mahākāçyapa went straightly (without roaming about), came to Rājagṛha and was seen by Ajātaçatru[511]). The latter, having been reminded of the Teacher, was about to fall from his elephant (in a swoon), but Kāçyapa held him by force, forbade him to do so any more, and said: — We desire to discuss about the precepts of the Doctrine in this godly place[512]). — Well, — said the king, — I shall provide all that is necessary. — Thus they assembled, the king having ordered to prepare seats, couches, and other requisites in the hollow of a Nyagrodha tree. The summer fast was then proclaimed.

Now, Mahākāçyapa, having perfectly examined the state of mind of Ānanda, said to Aniruddha: — Amidst this Congregation who has been praised by the Lord, there are such who are still under the rules of Discipline and are possessed of passion, hatred, infatuation, desire, and egocentristic properties. Aniruddha, having

---

507) Ibid. 303 b. 2—5.
508) Ibid. 303 b. 5—7.
509) Ibid. 303 b. 7—304 a. 4.
510) *slob-pa* = *çaikṣa*.
511) Ibid. 304 b. 5—7.
512) Ibid. 305 a. 5—6.

looked over the matter with his supernatural faculty of vision, said: — Thou must know. — The Congregation of the monks is free from all that is worthless, it is pure, possessed of that which is essential, is the field on which virtue grows, and is worthy to receive the gifts of the worldly beings. But as to Ānanda, — he is of the kind which thou hast just mentioned[513]). — By this Kācyapa saw that Ānanda was to be subdued by censure and said to him: — We here are the Highest Congregation and shall not discuss about the Doctrine with such as thee. — Therefore begone! — Ānanda trembled as if he had been struck in the most sensible part of his body. — O great Kāçyapa, be merciful! — said he. I have not committed any transgressions as regards morals, views, conduct, and means of livelihood, nor can I be accused of the slightest offence with regard to the Congregation![514]) — To this Kāçyapa said: — As thou wert all the time sitting at the Teacher's feet, what great wonder is it that thou hast not committed the 4 transgressions! But now rise up and bear evidence that thou hast not misbehaved with regard to the Congregation. — I shall show thee thy faults[515]). — [91 a.] Ānanda then rose up. The 3000 worlds trembled and the gods, full of awe, said: — Alas, Kāçyapa, whose words are true and beneficient, is thus bitterly censuring Ānanda, as we see from this elevated place[516]). — Kāçyapa said: — Thou hast summoned women to embrace religious life, heedless of the Teacher's having said to thee: — Ānanda, do not cause women to embrace religious life and do not tell them that they ought to take orders and become nuns. Why that? Because, if women take orders according to the discipline of this Doctrine, the latter will have no long duration. As, for instance, if hail descends on a field full of wild rice, the latter will be destroyed, similarly if women take orders, the Discipline of this Doctrine is not to abide for long. Has he not said that?[516]) — Ānanda replied: — I cannot be accused of want of shame and the like. But (mind thou this): — Mahāprajāpatī was the foster-mother who fed the Teacher with her breast. It would be suitable (to admit women to take orders) out of mere gratitude toward her, and in order that (the Buddha) should become possessed of the 4 kinds of adherents (including the nuns). — Thy gratitude, —

---

[513]) Ibid. 305 b. 7—306 a. 4.

[514]) Ibid. 306 a. 4—7. [515]) Ibid. 306 a. 7—b. 1.

[516]) Ibid. 306 b. 3—7.

said Kāçyapa, — has caused harm to the spiritual Body of the Buddha. The hail has fallen on the abundant field of Buddhaic activity; therefore there remains only the short period of 1000 years (for the Doctrine) to abide. In former times, when the passions of the living beings were insignificant, the Congregation of 4 kinds was suitable, but at present it was not the wish of the Teacher that this should be. It is thou who hast prayed him (to allow women to take orders), and this is thy first transgression. Bear evidence in this![517]) — Then thou hast not prayed the Teacher not to pass away into Nirvāṇa. — This was a confusion caused by the Evil One. — Just this is thy fault, — bear evidence![518]) —

Moreover, when asked, thou hast answered otherwise (than it was proper). Bear evidence in this![519]) —

Again: thou hast trampled with thy feet upon (the Buddha's) garment of fine cloth [91 b.]. — There was no companion who could have withdrawn them. — If thou hadst cast them upward into the air, the gods would have taken hold of them. — Bear evidence in this![520]) —

Furthermore: Thou hast brought muddy water (for the Teacher)[521]). — This was because 500 vehicles had passed the Kakuta river and its waters were troubled. — Thine is the fault! If thou hadst held up thy hands, the gods would have presented water of 8 different tastes. Bear evidence therefore![521]) — Further on: It has been said: — If one wishes, one may, for the sake of the Congregation, relax the strictest observances of morality and the minutiae of monastic discipline and enjoy a pleasant existence! Here thou hast not inquired about these minutiae. Now there are different indications concerning them. It is said that they consist in abstaining from (those transgressions) which are mentioned directly after: 1. the 5 forms of fall, 2. the (4) transgressions that are to be expiated through confession[522]), 3. the 90 transgressions leading to moral fall[523]), 4. the (30) transgressions requiring absolution[524]), or 5. after the indeterminate offences[525]). The consequence was that some have not observed (the minutiae)

---

[517]) Ibid. 306 b. 7—307 a. 5.

[518]) Ibid. 307 a. 5—b. 1. [519]) Ibid. 307 b. 1—2.

[520]) Ibid. 307 b. 2—4. [521]) Ibid. 307 b. 4—6.

[522]) *so-sor-bçags-pa* = *pratideçanīya*. M. Vyutp. § 162.

[523]) Ibid. § 161. [524]) Ibid. § 160.

[525]) *ma-ñes-pa* = *aniyata*. M. Vyutp. § 159.

with regard to the offences which deserve expulsion[526]), and others have not observed those indicated subsequently to the indeterminate transgressions. Owing to these circumstances the heretics have got an opportunity to revile (the Doctrine). This is another fault which thou hast committed. — I was overpowered by grief at being separated from the Teacher, — (replied Ānanda). Just this very grief of thine is not to be pardoned. Therefore bear evidence! — Again, thou hast exposed to the sight of laymen and of women the concealed private parts (of the Buddha's Body)[527]). — I know, that (the women are full of passion, replied Ānanda, but I thought that if they would see the private parts of the Buddha's Body), they would become deprived of the female organ[528]). — Just (by having such strange thoughts) thou hast committed a fault. — Bear evidence, therefore![529]) —

Furthermore, thou hast shown the Body of the Teacher to women and it has become polluted by their tears. — I thought that if such a Body would be seen, the living beings would make the Creative Effort (for Enlightenment). — Just by thinking like that thou hast committed a fault and, being thus, though slightly, possessed of desire, —depart and do not abide amongst the Highest Congregation that is completely dispassionate![530]) — Ānanda looked in the 4 directions and, full of pain and grief, spoke in a low voice: — Alas, such is my lot. The Lord has left me. On whom am I to rely, who will be my light and protection? [92 a.] At that moment the gods exclaimed: — O! victory is with the gods and the Asuras are vanquished! The Teaching has prospered! A Çrāvaka who resembles the Teacher has censured another Çrāvaka who is likewise akin to the Teacher![531]) —

Thereupon Ānanda spoke: — O Kāçyapa, have patience with me. I shall act in accordance with the Doctrine and shall not do henceforth (as I have done). Consider thou but this. — The Teacher has entrusted me to thy care. — Ānanda, said he, do not be grieved. Thou art confined to the care of Mahākāçyapa. Kāçyapa, thou

---

[526]) *pham-pa* = *pārājika*. Ibid. § 156.

[527]) *ḥdoms-kyi-sba-ba sbubs-su-nub-pa* = *koçagata-vasti-guhya*.

[528]) Sic. acc. to Vin. kṣudr. — *bdag-gis ḥdi-sñam-du bsams-so // bud-med-ni raṅ-bźin-gyis ḥdod-chags che-bas bcom-ldan-ḥdas-kyi ḥdoms-kyi-sba-ba sbubs-su-nub-pa mthoṅ-na mo-mtshan daṅ-bral-bar gyur-to //*

[529]) Vin. kṣudr. Kg. ḤDUL. XI. 308 b. 2—4.

[530]) Ibid. 308 b. 4—7. [531]) Ibid. 308 b. 7—309 a. 3.

must not be intolerant with regard to insignificant defects, but act according to my word[532]). (To this Kāçyapa said): — Thou, Ānanda, must not weep. The virtuous elements in thee are to increase and will not be diminished. I have inflicted punishment upon thee in order that thou shouldst be zealous for the sake of the Doctrine![533]) —

Thereupon Aniruddha said to Kāçyapa: If Ānanda is to be absent, how is the word of the Buddha to be compiled?[534]) —(Kāçyapa replied): — Ānanda, although he is possessed of virtuous properties, may not abide amongst us. Desires and the like are still existing with him. Therefore he must be subjected to Discipline and ought not to discuss (about the Doctrine) with us. After that he said: — Be gone thou, Ānanda! — When, by thy zeal, thou hast become an Arhat, — then we can discuss together![535]) —

Ānanda, with his eyes full of tears, and distressed at the thought that he was deprived of the Teacher, departed from that place. He went to the village of the Vriji, and there (one known as) the son of the Vriji tribe[536]) became his servant. Once, when (Ānanda) was expounding the Doctrine, this offspring of the Vriji tribe, having got a glimpse in his teacher's state of mind, said[537]): —

O Gautama, if thou doest keep off distraction
And abidest in the dark shadow of a tree,
Thou shalt attain Nirvāṇa.
Concentrate thy mind and practise profound meditation,
And thou shalt attain the state of perfect peace at an early date. —

Following this advice of the offspring of the Vrijis[538]), (Ānanda), dur ng the day [92 b] and the first part of the night, walking and sitting, became purified from mental obscuration. At midnight he washed his feet outside the monastery. Thereafter, he sunk down on his right side and, without lowering his head on the

---

[532]) Ibid. 309 a. 3—5. [533]) Ibid. 309 a. 5—6.

[534]) Cf. Mahāvaṁsa, III. 10. — *puna Ānanda-thero pi bhikkhūhi abhiyācito / sammanni kātuṁ saṁgītiṁ sā na sakkā hi taṁ vinā //*

[535]) Vin. kṣudr. Kg. ḤDUL. XI, 309. a. 6—b. 2.

[536]) Acc. to Vin. kṣudr. *tshe-daṅ-ldan-pa Bri-dziḥi-bu = āyuṣmān Vrijiputra*

[537]) Ibid. 309 b. 6.

[538]) Bu-ton has here the Tibetan equivalent Spoṅ-byed-kyi-bu.

pillow, attained the state of an Arhat[539]. Thereafter he returned (to the place of the council) in the hollow of the Nyagrodha tree[540].

Mahākāçyapa, for the sake of the monks of future times who could forget (the precepts), discussed in the morning briefly in verse, and later on in the afternoon in detail[541]. And first of all there was a discussion about the rehearsal of the Sūtras. Kāçyapa asked Ānanda whether he had energy enough and bade him to compile the Sūtras on the foundation of the resolution (of the Congregation), delivered after the vote repeated twice[542]. Thereafter the 500 Arhats spread their religious garments on the seat supported by lions on which Ānanda seated himself[543]. — I must expound all the Sūtras I have heard, thought he. — And the gods, knowing his intention, listened with reverence. Then Kāçyapa uttered the following entreaty[544]: —

O reverend Ānanda, expound thou the Sūtras,
The aphorisms which represent the highest form
Of the Doctrine that was delivered by the Lord,
The Teacher whose intention it was to help the world! —

Thereupon Ānanda, recalling into memory the virtues of the Teacher, turned his face toward Bodhimaṇḍa, folded his hands, recollected all the teachings he was to compile and began: — This is what I have once heard. The Lord was abiding in Benares, in Ṛṣipatana and in the Grove of the Antelopes. — And, as he uttered these words, the gods became full of grief and said[545]: —

Alas, everything in this world
Is, without exception, evanescent.
Even that ocean has dried up
Which was the repository of the jewels of virtue.
He, from whom the Doctrine has been heard directly
Is now enjoying the bliss of Salvation.

---

539) The expulsion of Ānanda and his attainment of Arhatship is related briefly in the Mahāvaṁsa, III. 23—25.

540) Vin. kṣudr. Kg. ḤDUL. XI. 309 b. 2—310 a. 5.

541) Ibid. 310 a. 5—b 1.

542) *gsol-ba-gñis-kyi-las* = *jñapti-dvitīya-karma-vacana*. Cf. M. Vyutp. § 266. 2, 3. Cf. also Childers, Pāli Dictionary, s. v. *ñatti (jñapti)* and *kamma-vacana.*

543) Vin. kṣudr. Kg. ḤDUL. XI. 310 b. 1—7.

544) Ibid. 311 a. 6—7.

So have I heard, — thus it is (now) summarized
And is to be heard at present. —

Thereupon (Ānanda communicated the Sūtra): — Then [93 a.] the Lord addressed the 5 monks as follows: — O brethren, this is the Doctrine that has not been heard of before, viz. that of the uneasiness (of Phenomenal Life), — the (first) principle of the Saint, — and so on.

Then Kauṇḍinya said to Kāçyapa: — I have heard this part of the Doctrine directly. It has caused the ocean of my blood and tears to be dried up, has closed the doors to the evil births, has caused the mountain of bones to be crossed, and has opened the doors to blissful existence. Through the exposition of it, I and 80 000 gods have obtained the vision of the Truth[546]). Now, to-day it is communicated as "having been thus heard" in the past. Alas, everything is evanescent without exception! — Thus saying,he descended from his elevated seat and sat down (on the ground). The others likewise descended from their seats (and said): — We have witnessed the exposition of this Doctrine directly, but now owing to the force of evanescence, the Lord can at present only be heard of (and not directly seen)![547]) —

Thereafter the Arhats, perceiving with their supernatural vision, asked Ānanda: — Is this the Word of Buddha that is acknowledged by thee? — It is the Word acknowledged by all of us, — (replied Ānanda). And, (in his turn he asked): — Is the Word acknowledged by all of you such (as I have communicated)? — It is just that, — (replied the other Arhats). — Then Kāçyapa thought: — The rehearsal of the first aphorism has not met with any objection and must therefore be the true Doctrine. — And to Ānanda he said: — How has the second aphorism been communicated? — (Ānanda continued): — So have I heard . . . etc. What is this uneasiness (of Phenomenal Existence), — the first principle of the Saint? — It is the uneasiness accompanying birth, — and so on.

How has the 3d aphorism been communicated? — O brethren, the material group of elements[548]) does not represent the Ego. —

This and the following Ānanda repeated, and the 499 Arhats [93 b.] established (that which he had said) as the kanonical

[545]) Ibid. 311 b. 2—3. [546]) *chos-kyi-mig* = *dharma-cakṣuḥ*.
[547]) Ibid. 311 b. 4—312 a. 1.
[548]) *gzugs* = *rūpa* in the sense of *rūpa-skandha*.

text[549]). The aphorisms containing the teaching about the 5 groups of elements were compiled together, forming the part concerning the 5 groups. The passages about the (12) bases of cognition were united so as to form the division dealing with the bases of cognition, the aphorisms concerning the members of the causal chain and the cognition of the 4 principles, — in the Nidāna[550]) sections. The numerous passages delivered by the Çrāvakas were combined in "the division of the Speeches of the Çrāvakas", and the sermons delivered by the Buddha, — in the part containing the Speeches of the Buddha. The aphorisms containing the teachings about the (37) characteristic features of Enlightenment were compiled so as to form the division concerning the component parts of the Path. The numerous sayings were united into the "Division of sayings", the numerous verses, — into the corresponding section[551]), the extensive parts of Scripture —into the Dīrgha-āgama, the intermediate —into the Madhyama-āgama, and the solitary sentences and the like, —into the separate passages, containing one and more sentences[552]). (Thus the division of the Sūtras) was compiled and established as the kanon. Thereupon Kāçyapa asked Ānanda, whether the Teaching was of such a compass (as had been compiled). — It is of such a compass, — replied Ānanda, —and there is nothing that is left (incompleted). —Having said this, Ānanda descended from the seat and sat down on the ground[553]).

Thereupon Upāli[554]) was asked whether he had sufficient energy and was then ordered to rehearse the Vinaya in accordance with the resolution delivered after the twice repeated vote. After Upāli had been seated on the seat supported by lions, (Kāçyapa said): — Where did the Lord lay the first foundation of Discipline? — At Benares. —For whose sake? — For the 5 monks. — He has ordered them to wear the skirt in a circular form. —

And the Arhats perceived with their supernatural vision and became convinced that this was the real Doctrine. —

Where was the second foundation of Discipline established? —(was the second question). —At Benares, for the 5 disciples, the order to wear religious robes in a circular form, —and so on.

---

549) Vin. kṣudr. Kg. ḤDUL. XI. 312 a. 2—314 a. 3.

550) Gleṅ-gži. 551) Yaṅ-dag-par-ldan-paḥi-miṅ (?).

552) *gcig-las-ḥphros-paḥi-luṅ = ekottara-āgama.*

553) Vin. kṣudr. Kg. ḤDUL. XI. 314 a. 3—b. 2. 554) N̄e-bar-ḥkhor.

Where was the third foundation of Discipline established? — In the village of Kalandaka in order that Bhadradatta[555]) should overcome his immorality. —

Thereafter, the (4 sins) meriting expulsion[556]), the (13) transgressions requiring rehabilitation by the whole of the clergy[557]), the indeterminate transgressions,[557a]), the 30 transgressions accompanied with forefeiture[558]), the (90) transgressions requiring absolution[559]), the (4) transgressions to be expiated by confession[560]) [94 a.], the numerous minutiae of Discipline, the pacification of quarrels, the supplementary rules, forfeiture, ordination, fast, punishment, calumny, the causes (of transgression), and the subject of faith, — all these were definitely indicated. In such a way the Vinaya was rehearsed, and after that Upāli descended from his seat[561]). Then Mahākāçyapa, in order to rehearse the Abhidharma, for the sake of the living beings of future times, — underwent the procedure of vote and resolution. He said: — Of the Abhidharma I shall speak myself. The Abhidharma is that which elucidates the essence of the things cognizable. It consists of the 4 methods of intense mindfulness, — etc. as before[562]).

Thereupon, as the 500 Arhats thus rehearsed the 3 Codes of Scripture, the gods exclaimed: — O! the gods have won and the Asuras have lost! — And the 500 monks received the name of "the Great Compilers"[563]).

Thereupon Mahākāçyapa spoke as follows[564]): —

The limitless Word of Him
Who was endowed with the 10 Powers
Is now compiled in this Book of the Law
For the sake of mankind.
It is possessed of light,
Since it removes the gloom of ignorance,
Wherever false views obscure and oppress the living beings. —

Then he thought[565]): — I have rehearsed the Word of the Buddha as well as I could and have (through this) to a certain extent been

---

[555]) Bzaṅ-sbyin. [556]) *pham-pa* = *pārājika.*

[557]) *lhag-ma* = *(sangha)-avaçeṣa.* [557a]) *ma-ṅes-pa* = *aniyata.*

[558]) *spaṅ-ltuṅ* = *naisargika.* [559]) *ltuṅ-byed* = *prāyaçcittika.*

[560]) *so-sor-bçags-pa* = *pratideçanīya.*

[561]) Vin. kṣudr. Kg. ḤDUL. XI. 314 b. 2—315 b. 6.

[562]) Ibid. 315 b. 6—316 a. 5. [563]) Ibid. 316 a. 5—b. 3.

[564]) Ibid. 316 b. 3—4. [565]) Ibid. 316 b. 7—317 a. 2.

of help (to the living beings). — Now, who is able (to do this work) completely? I for my part shall depart into Nirvāṇa. —

Having rehearsed the sermons of the Lord,
I have established the Path of Virtue;
This Word of the Teacher is to abide for long,
Being transferred from one (disciple) to another;
It will chastise those that are shameless
And support those who are modest.
I have been of help and stored up merit,
And the time for me to pass into Nirvāṇa has come. —

Know thou, Ānanda! [94 b.] The Teacher has passed away, after having entrusted the Doctrine to my care. As I am now to depart into Nirvāṇa, it is thou who art to be its defender. And thou, in thy turn, art to entrust it to Çānavāsika[566]).

Thereupon Kāçyapa, having worshipped the 8 monuments with the relics (of the Buddha) and the tooth (of the latter) which was preserved in the realm of the Nāgas, rose up to the abode of the 33 gods. There he beheld the tooth (of the Buddha that was kept there) without winking, placed it on the crown of his head, worshipped it and said to the gods: — Be full of attention and devotion! — Having delivered this word he returned to Rājagṛha. Ajātaçatru to whom he intended to announce his arrival was asleep. — Make him awaken and call him to me! — So said he, ascended the southern hill Kukkuṭapāda and strewed Kuça grass in the interspace between the 3 hills. Then he put on the patched cowl of the Buddha, uttered a blessing (that his corpse) should not decay till the time when the word of Maitreya would be expounded and, having demonstrated many miraculous apparitions, passed away into Nirvāṇa. Thereafter the gods worshipped, spread a cover over the 3 mountains, uttered many sounds of lamentation, and disappeared[567]).

At that time Ajātaçatru, who had dreamt that the lineage of his mother's brother belonging to the royal race had ceased, awoke and, having heard that Kāçyapa had passed away, fell in a swoon. Upon recovering, he ascended the hill, and the Yakṣas withdrew the cover (that was spread over the hills). The king, having worshipped, was about to order that the body should be burnt, but Ānanda said: — He has pronounced a blessing that his body should remain

---

566) Ibid. 317 a. 2—4. 567) Ibid. 317 a. 4—318 b. 2.

till the time when the Doctrine of Maitreya is to be expounded. The 930 millions of Çrāvakas of Maitreya will take the body (of Kāçyapa) and show it, saying: —This was a disciple of Çākyamuni, the foremost of those endowed with the 12 virtues of an ascetic. It was he who compiled the Teaching. — And it will be known that the men of this (age of ours) were small in size and the Teacher's body great. [95 a.] Then Maitreya will say: —These are the robes of Çākyamuni! — Then his adherents will assume the virtues of ascetics and become Arhats. — It is for this reason that one must not burn (these relics), but build here a monument[568]). —

Accordingly they erected a monument and worshipped. And after that a covering was again spread over the 3 mountains. Then Ānanda promised that he would show to Ajātaçatru how he would pass away into Nirvāṇa, and thereupon departed into the Bamboo Grove[569]).

Whilst he was abiding there, Çānavāsika arrived, after having fortunately crossed the sea, and asked: — I intend to celebrate the 5 years' feast. But where is the Teacher? — He has passed away! —And, as he heard this, Çānavāsika fell in a swoon. —And Çāriputra and the rest, — where do they abide? — They have likewise passed away, — (was the answer). Thereafter Çānavāsika made a 5 years' feast for Ānanda and the Congregation, at the end of which he took orders and became versed in the 3 Codes of Scripture[570]).

At that time a certain monk (was preaching in the following manner)[571]): —

> He whose life has a duration of 100 years
> Can certainly abide in ease like a duck in the water.
> And can be perceived as similar to such a duck.
> Such a uniform life is the best.

Ānanda, having heard this, said:[572]) —The Teacher has not preached like that, but: —

> He with whom life dures 100 years
> Invariably becomes born and perishes.
> The Teacher has declared that here on earth

---

568) Ibid. 318 b. 2—319 a. 4. 569) Ibid. 319 a. 4—6.
570) Ibid. 319 a. 6—b. 5. Cf. Schiefner, Tāranātha, p. 9.
571) Vin. kṣudr. Kg. ḤDUL. XI. 319 b. 6.
572) Ibid. 319 b. 6—302 a. 2.

Two kinds of individuals must be distinguished:
Those with minds full of disbelief and hatred,
And those who in their faith have gone astray.
He who has wrongly apprehended the Sūtras
Is like an ox that has fallen into a mire,
And must inevitably perish.
He has no thoughts concerning his death,
His study does not lead to knowledge and is fruitless.
Incorrect knowledge, it is like poison;
But he is really wise, whose study [95 b.]
Leads to correct knowledge and has for its result
The removal of all the Obscurations. —

The monk who had recited incorrectly said to the preceptor (with whom he studied): — Ānanda has grown old and has lost his power of memory. The preceptor said[573]): —

Subjected to the suffering of old age,
This living being has lost his memory;
He does not recollect correctly,
For his mind is overpowered by decrepitude. —

Ānanda heard this and said: — If I speak to him there will be a quarrel. It is likewise unsuitable for me to go (and remonstrate) before his teacher. I shall therefore pass away into Nirvāṇa. —

The old ones, — they all have died before,
And with these new young monks one cannot be of accord.
I am now abiding quite alone
In concentrated trance, similar to a bird.
Those who were my friends and associates
Have all of them died before and are gone.
How shall I reflect over the state of mystic absorption?
There is no suitable teacher for this here[574]). —

Accordingly he said to Çānavāsika: — The Doctrine has been entrusted by the Teacher to Kāçyapa, and by the latter to myself. I am now about to depart (into Nirvāṇa). Therefore it is thou who art to guard the Doctrine. And he foretold that in the place called Mathurā[575]) on the mountain called Murunda, Nata and Pata, the sons of a merchant would build a monastery and become alms-givers (of the church). He said moreover that Upagupta[576]),

---

[573]) Ibid. 320 a. 2—3. [574]) Ibid. 320 a. 3—7.
[575]) Bcom-brlag. [576]) N̄er-sbas.

the son of Gupta[577]), the merchant of incense, should take orders. Indeed, the Teacher had prophecied: — One hundred years after I have passed away, this one will become a Buddha, though without bearing the characteristic feature of such[578]), and perform the acts peculiar to a Buddha. — Let it be so, — said Çānavāsika[579]). — Thereafter Ānanda sent a message to Ajātaçatru and then departed into the middle of the Ganges. The king, having dreamt that the staff of his umbrella hade been broken, awoke and, after he had heard the message of Ānanda, fell in a swoon. When he recovered, he set out with his army in the direction of the Ganges[580]). At the same time the gods spoke to the inhabitants of Vaiçalī as follows[581]): —

The Saint Ānanda who is like a light for the animate world,
Has manifested his Great Commiseration for the multitude
of living beings. [96 a.]
This Sage, having removed the darkness of suffering,
Has now come to Vaiçalī, in order to attain perfect peace. —

Thereupon the Licchavis likewise proceeded toward the Ganges. At that time a Brahmanical anchorite with 500 adherents expressed the wish to take orders. Ānanda produced by magic an island in the middle of the Ganges and there (the anchorite and his followers) were ordained and became Arhats. With respect to the place and the time they became known by the name of Madhyāntika — "(those who were ordained) at noon-day[582]) or in the middle of the river"[583]). (The anchorite) then prayed that he might pass away into Nirvāṇa before Ānanda, but the latter said: — Kashmir is the place suitable for mystic absorption and the best resting-place. There, 100 years after I have passed away, a monk known by the surname of Madhyāntika is to establish the Doctrine. — Such was the prophecy of the Teacher and thou must act according to it. — I shall do so, — replied the anchorite[584]).

Thereupon Ānanda, having manifested many miraculous apparitions, passed away into Nirvāṇa. Half of his body was taken by the citizens of Vaiçalī and the other half — by Ajātaçatru.

---

577) Sbas-pa. 578) Cf. Schiefner, Tārānātha, p. 17.
579) Vin. kṣudr. Kg. ḤDUL. XI. 320 a. 7—b. 4.
580) Ibid. 320 b. 4—321 a. 2.
581) Ibid. 321 a. 2—3. 582) Ñi-ma-guṅ-pa.
583) Chu-dbus-pa. Cf. Schiefner, Tārānātha, p. 9.
584) Vin. kṣudr. Kg. ḤDUL. XI. 321 b. 4—322 a. 1.

By the sharp thunderbolt of Highest Wisdom
He split in two his body resembling a mountain.
One half was given to the ruler of men,
And the other — to the Congregation of the Lord. —

And thereupon monuments were erected at Vaiçalī and Pāṭaliputra[585]).

Thereafter Madhyāntika, in order that the prophecy of the Teacher and the order of his preceptor (Ānanda) should be fulfilled, went off to Kashmir. There he seated himself in a cross-legged position ond became absorbed in concentrated trance. This brought the Nāgas (who were residing there) into a rage. They shook the ground and sent down a heavy rain. However, by this they were incapable of moving even the fringe of (Madhyāntika's) religious garment. Then a rain of arrows and other missiles descended upon him, but these were all turned into flowers. Owing to this the Nāgas were dismayed and asked Madhyāntika what would be his orders. He said: —This place belongs to me according to the prophecy of the Buddha. — And they gave him so much ground as he could cover by sitting in cross-legged posture, [96 b.] but this space was (miraculously augmented so as to fill up) all the 9 valleys (of Kashmir)[586]). Then the Nāgas asked: — How many adherents hast thou? —500 Arhats, —replied the elder. — Now, if one of these will be absent, — we shall take the ground back again, —(returned the Nāgas)[587]). —The elder said: — Be it as it may be; in any case it has been provided for alms-givers; therefore one must introduce householders here. —Thereupon he settled there a multitude of people, and, in order that they should prosper, he went to Gandhamadana and caused saffron to grow. Thereafter he subdued the troublesome Nāgas. The latter asked him how long the Teaching was to abide there, and the elder replied, that it would exist 1000 years. They then consented to give up the ground for the time during which the Doctrine of the Lord was to exist there. — Be it so, — said the elder. Then, after he had established the church in Kashmir, (the elder Madhyāntika) passed away into Nirvāṇa[588]). The church was thereafter entrusted by Çānavāsika to Upagupta, by Upagupta — to Dhītika, by the

[585]) Ibid. 322 a. 1—4. [586]) Cf. Schiefner, Tārānātha, p. 12. sqq.
[587]) Vin. kṣudr. Kg. ḤDUL. XI. 322 a. 4—323 a. 2.
[588]) Ibid. 323 a. 2—7.

latter — to Kṛṣṇa, and by Kṛṣṇa to Sudarçana. (And they all) departed into Nirvāṇa (one after the other)[589]).

The second Rehearsal.

One hundred and ten years after the Teacher had passed away, the monks abiding in Vaiçalī were indulging in prohibited actions of which there were 10 kinds: —

Exclamations of astonishment (1), rejoicing (2),
Digging ground (3), using the sacred salt (4),
Eating on the way (5), taking the food with 2 fingers (6),
Eating not at due time (7), taking intoxicating drink (8),
Making a new rug without stitching to it a patch of the old one (9),
And begging for gold and silver (10). —
These, briefly, were the transgressions which were admitted[590]).

At that time an Arhat named Sarvakāmin[590a]) who had attained the 8 degrees of liberation (from materiality)[591]) was residing at Vaiçalī. And from the city called Dhanika[592]) there came an Arhat called Yaças[592a]) with 500 adherents who had made a turn through the country. Having arrived at Vaiçalī, they found that the monks had a large income, and they themselves obtained a great share. Having asked the reason of this, [97 a.] they came to know that 10 prohibited points were admitted[593]). Accordingly, they went to Sarvakāmin and inquired: — Is it proper that (the exclamations of astonishment) like aho! should be admitted? How is this possible? — With the monks of Vaiçalī the conduct does not harmonize with the theory. They perform religious observances and at the same time they admit such exclamations as aho! O reverend master, this is not right. — At what place has (the Lord) established the rule forbidding this? — At Campā. — Whom had he in view when he established it? — The 6 disciples. — Amongst what category of transgressions has it been counted? — Amongst the nume-

---

[589]) Ibid. 323 a. 7—b. 4.

[590]) Ibid. 323 b. 4—325 a. 4. Summary in verse 332 a. 2—3. Cf. also Mahāvaṁsa, IV. 9—11 a. and Schiefner, Tāranātha, p. 41 and 289.

[590a]) Thams-cad-ḥdod.

[591]) *rnam-thar-brgyad* = *aṣṭau vimokṣāḥ.*

[592]) Nor-can. [592a]) Grags-pa.

[593]) Vin. kṣudr. Kg. ḤDUL. XI. 325 a. 4—7.

rous minute defects. — O Elder, this first point is a transgression with regard to the Sūtras and the Vinaya. It deviates from the Teaching of the Master, and (the permission of it) is not contained in the Sūtras and is not to be found in the Vinaya. It disagrees with the Essence of the Doctrine. Therefore, when it is spoken of as admissible and has become practice, how is it possible to be indifferent with regard to it? — (Sarvakāmin) sat without answering a word.

Then, O Elder, the following is to be asked. Can exclamations of rejoicing be regarded as admissible? ... and so on, as before. — They perform religious observances, and at the same time incite the monks in attendance to rejoice and consider this to be admissible. This is not right. — (The rules forbidding it have been delivered) at Campā to the 6 disciples and (it has been counted) among the numerous minute defects.

As concerns the acts of the monks, it is considered admissible to live by agriculture (digging the ground). (This has been forbidden) at Çrāvasti to the 6 disciples and counted amongst the transgressions that require absolution[594]).

Furthermore, it is considered admissible to mix the salt that is to be kept for life-time with that which is used in general, to eat it, and make it thus an object of ordinary use. (The rules forbidding this) have been delivered at Rājagṛha to Çāriputra and (this act) is counted among the trangressions requiring absolution. Moreover, eating on the way is held to be admissible. — (The monks) having gone a yojana or a half of such, assemble and eat, with the pretext that they are travelling. This has been forbidden at Rājagṛha to Devadatta and counted among the defects requiring absolution.

Then we have "the transgression of the 2 fingers". The food that has not been left (from a previous meal) they eat, taking it with 2 fingers. This has been forbidden at Çrāvastī to numerous monks and counted among the acts requiring absolution [97 b.].

Further on, there is the transgression admitted under the pretext of illness. The monks take wine in the manner of a leech that sucks blood and, having drunk, excuse it with illness. This has been forbidden at Çrāvastī to Saugata and counted among the offences requiring absolution.

---

594) *prāyaçcittika = ltuṅ-byed.*

Next there is "the admission of a mixture". The monks mix a droṇa measure of milk with as much sour milk and eat it at undue time, considering this to be admissible. (The rules forbidding this) have been delivered at Çrāvastī to numerous monks and it is counted amongst the transgressions requiring absolution.

Then there ist the transgression concerning the rug (or carpet on which the monk sits). The monks begin to use a new carpet without patching it with the so-called Sugata span taken from the old one. The rules forbidding this have been delivered at Çrāvastī to numerous monks and it is counted among the transgressions requiring absolution.

And lastly, there is the transgression regarding gold and silver. The monks anoint an alms-bowl with fragrant species, put it on the head of a Çramaṇa, on a table or a seat, place it in a narrow passage or at the crossing-place of 4 roads, and proclaim: — This is a sublime vessel. If you deposite your gifts into it and fill it, you are to reap great merit. Accordingly, the people fill (the bowl) with gold and silver which is enjoyed (by the monks). The rules forbidding this were delivered to the 6 disciples.

Thereafter Sarvakāmin spoke (to Yaças): — Go thou and find such who would be of accord with thee, and I will be thy friend according to the Doctrine[595]). Yaças accordingly departed and spoke as he had before to Çāḍha[596]) from the city of Çoṇaka, to Dhanika[597]) from Saṁkaçya, to Kubjita[598]) of Pāṭaliputra who was enjoying the highest felicity, as he was absorbed in concentrated trance, to Ajita[599]) of Çrughna[600]), to Saṁbhūta[601]) of Mahiṣmatī[602]), and to Revata[603]) of Sahajā[604]). These said: — Thou art tired. Rest now and we shall search for those that would take our part[605]).

Thereafter the monks of Vaiçalī asked the pupils of Yaças[606]): — Whither has your teacher gone? — He is seeking for those who will aid him in executing the act of your excommunication. — Tho this the monks of Vaiçalī said: — This is not a good action. [98 a.] According to the Word of the Teacher who has passed away it is proper to maintain one's life in many different ways. As

595) Ibid. 325 b. 1—328 a. 1.
596) Gyo-ldan. 597) Nor-can. 598) Zla-sgur.
599) Ma-pham-pa. 600) Sug-na. 601) Yaṅ-dag-skyes.
602) Ma-he-ldan. 603) Nam-gru. 604) Lhan-cig-skyes.
605) Vin. kṣudr. Kg. ḤDUL. XI. 329 a. 5—7. 606) Grags-pa.

this is so, wherefore are you planning to do mischief to us? — The others replied: — You are behaving in a way that is not admissible and bring corruption into the Church. Therefore we shall in any case execute the act of your excommunication. — And as they said so, (the monks of Vaiçalī) became afraid and tried to bribe the pupils of Yaças, by presenting to them mantles, religious robes, etc.[607]). Thereafter Yaças having finished the search of those who would form his party, returned, and his pupils said to him: — Master, it would be better to forbear from this our intention. According to the Word of the deceased Teacher, it is permitted to live in many different ways. If this be so, for what reason should we plan mischief against (these monks)? — By these their words (the Arhat) understood that they had been bribed and spoke to them as follows[608]): —

He who hastens where one ought to tarry
And tarries when one ought to make haste
Is a fool who does not act when it is proper
And becomes subjected to suffering.
His lot is to be without renown,
And he is deserted by his friends.
His cause, it does not prosper,
Being like the descending moon.
But he who duly applies his mind (to fulfill his aim),
Who makes haste when it is proper and does not tarry,
Is a wise man who removes
All that is insuitable and attains bliss.
His lot is fame, he is not deserted by his friends,
And his fortune will grow like the ascending moon.

Thereafter Yaças went to the courtyard where the monks were assembled and let them put his knowledge, the result of his previous vows[609]) to a test. He struck the wooden gong, and 700 Arhats, all of them pupils of Ānanda, assembled, with the exception of one. (This one was) Kubjita who did not hear, since he was absorbed in the Cessation-Trance[610]).

Then Yaças thought: — If the names (of the monks to be ex-

---

[607]) Ibid. 329 a. 7—330 a. 3. [608]) Ibid. 330 a. 7—b. 2.

[609]) *smon-nas-çes-pa* = *praṇidhi-jñāna.*

[610]) *ḥgog-paḥi-sñoms-ḥjug* = *nirodha-samāpatti.* Vin. kṣudr. Kg. ḤDUL. 330 b. 2—3.

communicated) are called out and repeated aloud, passions will be aroused. [98 b.] One must therefore speak without mentioning names. — And he sat down at the side of the Elders[611]). At that moment Kubjita rose up from the Cessation Trance, and a certain god summoned him, saying: — Seven hundred Arhats, of the same preceptor as thyself, are rehearsing the Teaching. Therefore make haste to join them. Accordingly, by the force of his miraculous power, Kubjita flew to the place and appeared before the gate of the courtyard. As he knocked, those within asked: — Who art thou? And he replied as follows: —

There are ascetics dwelling in Pāṭaliputra
Who are profoundly learned and observe the Vinaya.
One of them has now come here,
His name being "the subduer of the senses".
It is he who is standing at the gate!

There are likewise other "subduers of their senses" (said the monks). — He then said: — I am he who has cleared all doubt. — I am he who is free from regret. — And finally: — I am Kubjita. — Then the doors were opened and he entered[612]).

Then Yaças, addressing the Elders, began: — O venerable sirs, is the license of shouting aho! admissible? Thus spoke he and further on as before, without mentioning names, viz. that such and such monks (were doing the prohibited actions). — Such a conduct is to be condemned by us! — In this manner he discussed the 10 inadmissible points in detail, and (the other Elders) gave their approval[613]). Then they went out and beat the wooden gong, causing the monks of Vaiçali to assemble. The Elders now called out the name (of those who committed the transgressions), viz. "the monks of Vaiçalī," spoke of the 10 inadmissible points at full length and said: — These are to be excommunicated by all of us. — And, for speaking thus, the 700 (Arhats) became known as "those who made the correct resolution"[614]).

Thus the second rehearsal was carried out by the 700 Arhats. The aim of it was the exclusion of the 10 inadmissible points. The time was — 110 years after the Teacher had passed away. The

---

611) Ibid. 330 b. 3—5. 612) Ibid. 330 b. 5—331 a. 5.
613) Ibid. 331 a. 5—b. 3.
614) Ibid. 331 b. 3—332 a. 2.

place was the monastery of Kusumapura[615]) at Vaiçalī, and the alms-giver of the monks was the pious king Açoka. [99 a.][616])

The third Rehearsal.

(The account of this third rehearsal) is not to be found in the Vinaya and therefore we meet here and there with disagreeing points. According to some, 137 years after the Teacher had passed away, at the time when the kings Nanda and Mahāpadma were reigning, and when the elders Mahākāçyapa, Uttara[617]) and others were residing at Pāṭaliputra, Māra the Evil One, having assumed the form of a monk named Bhadra, showed many miraculous apparitions, sowed disunion amongst the clergy and brought confusion into the Teaching[618]). At that time, when the elders Nāgasena[619]) and Manojña[620]) were living, (the clergy) became split into (various) sects. On the 63d year (after this division had taken place), the Teaching was rehearsed by the elder Vātsīputra[621]). According to others, 160 years after the Teacher had passed away, at the time when the king Açoka began to reign in the city called Kusumavistara (?)[622]), the Arhats were reading the Word of the Buddha in (4 different languages), viz. the Sanskrit[623]), Prakrit[624]), Apabhraṁça[625]), and Paiçācika[626]). Accordingly, the pupils (of the different Arhats) formed separate fractions, and this gave origin to the division into the 18 sects. In the philosophical views (of the different sects) there were many disagreeing points which brought confusion into the Church[627]). — It was for this reason that Arhats and ordinary learned monks, having assembled in the monastery of Jalandhara, rehearsed (Scripture) for a third time. This

---

615) Xyl. Ku-sma-pu-ri. Or: Puṣpapura. Cf. Mahāvaṁsa, IV. 31. — Pupphapura.

616) Mahāvaṁsa, IV. 8. — *atīte dasame vasse Kālāsokassa rājino / saṁbuddha-parinibbāṇā evaṁ vassasataṁ ahu //*

617) Bla-ma.

618) This passage is fully contained in the Tarkajvālā of Bhāvaviveka, Tg. (Pek.) MDO. XIX. 162 b. 6—163 a. 3. Cf. also Schiefner, Tāranātha, p. 52.

619) Kluḥi-sde. 620) Yid-ḥoṅ.

621) Gnas-maḥi-bu. Cf. Tarkajvālā, Tg. MDO. XIX. 163 a. 1 sqq.

622) Me-tog-gis-rgyas-pa. So also in Tarkajvālā.

623) *legs-par-sbyar-ba.* 624) *tha-mal-pa.* 625) *zur-chag.*

626) *ça-zaḥi-skad.*

627) A similar passage is contained in the Tarkajvālā, Tg. MDO. XIX. 161 a. 3. sqq.

took place 360 years after the Teacher had passed away. We read however in the ***Karuṇā-puṇḍarīka***[628]) the following prophecy: — One hundred years after I have passed away, there will appear in Pāṭaliputra a king named Açoka of the Maurya dynasty[629]). This king will cause to worship the 84 000 monuments containing my relics in a single day. — And in the ***Prabhāvatī***[630]) it is said: — Thereafter the king Dharmāçoka died, and the Arhats, in order to put an end to the practice of reciting (Scripture) in Prakrit, Apabhraṁça [99 b.] and in a dialect of intermediate character, gradually rehearsed (the kanonical texts) according to other methods. These new texts were like the sūtras which were compiled in Sanskrit[630a]). (Thereafter) the Teaching assumed 18 different forms. — I am of the opinion that (the statement of the authority just mentioned) disagrees with the texts I have quoted (before).

Others (speak about the 3d council) as follows: — The aim of it was to clear the doubts of the 18 sects as regards the spurious texts of Scripture. The time was 300 years after the Teacher had passed away. The place was the country of Kashmir and the monastery of Kuvana, and the alms-giver was Kaniṣka[631]), the king of Jalandhara. The members of the council were 500 Arhats with Pūrṇika at their head, 500 Bodhisattvas, Vasumitra and others, and 250 or 10 000 ordinary Paṇḍits. After a recitation (of the texts) had been made, it was settled, that the texts acknowledged by the 18 sects were all of them the Word of Buddha.

As concerns the division into the 18 sects, Bhavya[632]) considers that there were 2 principal fractions viz. the Mahāsanghikas[633]) and the Sthaviras[634]). Others say that there were 3, — (the 2 just mentioned) and the Vibhajyavādins[635]). The Mūlasarvāstivādins[636]) say that till the time of the 2d rehearsal there was only

---

[628]) Kg. MDO. VI. 140 a. 1—3. (N.)

[629]) Mu-raḥi rigs-kyi. [630]) Tg. MDO. LXXXIX. 182 a. 2, 3 (N).

[630a]) Sic. acc. to Tg. — *rgyal-poḥi-skad-du sbyar-baḥi mdo-sde.* The Xyl. has — *rgya-chen-poḥi skad-du.*

[631]) Xyl. Ka-ni-ka. [632]) Tarkajvālā, Tg. MDO. XIX. 163 a. 2. (Pek.)

[633]) Dge-ḥdun-phal-chen-pa. [634]) Gnas-brtan-pa.

[635]) Rnam-par-phye-ste-smra-ba. Cf. Tarkajvālā, Tg. MDO. XIX. 162 b. 1. *gžan-ñid-kyis smra-ba-ni sṅa-ma-bžin-du brjod-par-byaḥo //rtsa-baḥi dbye-ba-ni gsum-ste / ḥdi-ltar Gnas-brtan-pa daṅ / Dge-ḥdun-phal-chen-pa daṅ / Rnam par-phye-ste-smra-baḥo //*

[636]) Gži-yod-smra-ba. This and the following is an extract from Çākyaprabha's Prabhāvatī (Tg. MDO. LXXXIX. 182 a. 4—b. 7. Nar.) in abridged form.

one school viz. the Mūlasarvāstivāda. Thereafter, owing to the fact that Scripture was recited in different dialects, there arose the 17 other sects. (The texts of these fractions), they say, do not represent the Teaching of Buddha. They are not to be found in the Vinaya, since they are not included in the precepts containing the monastic obeisances. Neither are they contained in the Sūtras, since they contradict each other. They are likewise in conflict with the true Essence of the Doctrine, since they explain the Word of Scripture in another sense. — Therefore they are not the Word of the Buddha. —

We refute this statement of the Sarvāstivādins as follows: — The texts of the 17 sects are the Word of Buddha. They are to be found in the Vinaya, since they teach the Moral Discipline[636a]). They are contained in the Sūtras, as they speak of the Mental Discipline[637]). And they are not in conflict with the true Essence of the Doctrine, since they are in conformity with the Teaching of Nirvāṇa and contain the precepts relating to the Discipline of Highest Wisdom[638]). Moreover they are endowed with the 3 seals, the negation of a real Ego with regard to all the elements, etc. [100 a.] They have as their principal subject-matter exclusively the Word of the Buddha, they have been analysed by the Arhats, and have appeared as a result of the Buddha's blessings. — We read moreover in the Sūtra containing the explanation of the dream of king Kṛkin[639]), as follows: O great monarch, in thy dream thou hast seen how 18 men were pulling at a piece of cloth. This means that the Teaching of the Buddha Çākyamuni will be split into 18 sects. But the cloth, that is (the Doctrine of) Salvation, will not be torn asunder. — This passage likewise proves that (the kanonical texts acknowledged by the 18 sects) represent all of them the Word of Buddha. Vinītadeva[640]) and the author of the ***Bhikṣu-varṣāgra-pṛcchā***[641]) are of the opinion that there were 4 principal sections. Vinītadeva says: —

[636a]) *tshul-khrims* = *çila* in the sense of *adhiçila-çikṣā.*

[637]) *sems* = *citta* in the sense of *adhicitta-çikṣā.*

[638]) *çes-rab* = *prajñā* in the sense of *adhiprajñā-çikṣā.*

[639]) Cf. Schiefner, Tārānātha, p. 59.

[640]) Dul-lha. The following passage in verse is a quotation from the Nikāya-bheda-upadarçana-saṁgraha. Tg. MDO. LXXXIX. 172b. 1—3. (N.)

[641]) Cf. Schiefner, Tārānātha, p. 272.

The Eastern[642]), the Western[643]), the Himālayan[644]),
The Lokottaravādins[645]), and the Prajñaptivādins[646]), —
These five belong to the Mahāsaṁghikas.
The Mūlasarvāstivādins, the Kāçyapīya[647]),
The Mahīçāsaka[648]) and the Dharmagupta[649]),
The Bahuçrutīya[650]), the Tāmraçatīya[651]),
And the division of the Vibhajyavāda, —
These are the Sarvāstivādins.
The Jetavanīya[652]), the Abhayagirivāsins[653])
And the Mahāvihāravāsins[654]), —
These form the section of the Sthaviras.
The Kaurukullaka[655]), Āvantaka[656]), Vātsīputrīya[657]),
Are the 3 varieties of the Saṁmitīya[658]).
These are the 18 different sects,
Differing as regards their country, Doctrine and teacher.

According to the author of the *Varṣāgra-pṛcchā*[659]), 6 sects form the division of the Mahāsaṁghika, 4 sects — that of the Sarvāstivādins, 5 — that of the Saṁmitīya, and 3 — that of the Sthaviras. The Sarvāstivādins, "those who admit the reality of all (the elements)" are called so, since they maintain that (the elements as classified into) groups, component elements of an individual, and bases of cognition, or otherwise, that all the objects in the present, past, and future exist in reality. Just as the high classes establish the mundane laws and customs of a country or race, in a similar manner (these Sarvāstivādins), as they spoke in Sanskrit [100 b.] (the

---

[642]) Çar (-kyi-ri-bo-pa) = Pūrvaçaila. (Mahāvaṁsa V. 12 b—Pubbaselīyā).

[643]) Nub (-kyi-ri-bo-pa) = Aparaçaila. (Mahāvaṁsa V. 12 b—Aparaselīyā).

[644]) Gaṅs-kyi-ri-pa = Haimavata (Ibid. V. 12 a).

[645]) Ḥjig-rten-ḥdas-par-smra-ba.

[646]) Btags-par-smra-ba (The Xyl. has: Brtag-par-smra-ba. — Mahāvaṁsa V. 5 a. Paññattivādā).

[647]) Ḥod-sruṅs-sde. (Mahāvaṁsa V. 9 a. — Kassapīyā; acc. to Tarkajvālā Tg. MDO. XIX. 162 b. 1. *Char-bzaṅ-ḥbebs-pa žes-bya-ba-la kha-cig-ni Ḥod-sruṅs-pa žes zer-ba* —

[648]) Sa-sruṅ-sde (Ibid. V. 6 a, 8 a — Mahiṁsāsaka).

[649]) Chos-sruṅ-sde. (Ibid. V. 8 b. Dhammaguttika).

[650]) Maṅ-thos (Ibid. V. 5 a — Bahulikā. Cf. note).

[651]) Dmar-slob-ma. [652]) Rgyal-byed-tshal-gnas.

[653]) Ḥjigs-byed-gnas. [654]) Gtsug-lag-khaṅ-chen.

[655]) Sa-sgrags. [656]) Sruṅ-pa-pa. [657]) Gnas-maḥi-bu.

[658]) Kun-gyis-bkur-ba.

[659]) Tg. MDO. LXXXIX. 74 b. 6—75 a. 2. (N.)

language of the higher classes), represent the foundation *(mūla)* for the tradition of the other sects. For this reason they are called the Mūla-Sarvāstivādins. Their teacher was Rāhulabhadra[660]) of the Kṣatriya caste, renowned for his devotion to the (3) Disciplines. Their language was the Sanskrit, they wore a mantle which had from 25 to 29 fringes, and their badges were an Utpala flower, a lotus, a jewel, and the leaf of a tree.

The Mahāsaṁghikas were called so, since they were the clergy (Saṁgha), the greater part of which (mahā) was constituted by them. Their teacher was Mahākāçyapa, a Brāhmaṇa great in his practice of the 12 virtues of an ascetic[661]). Their language was the Prakrit, they wore from 23 to 27 fringes, and their badge was a conch-shell.

The Saṁmitīya received this name, as they taught the theories expounded by a teacher who was revered by a great number of people. Their teacher was Upāli of Çūdra caste, great in his observance of the Vinaya. Their language was the Apabhraṁça, the number of fringes (on their mantles) was from 21 to 25, and their badge was the Sorcika flower.

The Sthaviras bore this name, since they maintained to belong to the spiritual descent of the Sthavira Saints. Their chief preceptor was Kātyāyana of the Vaiçya caste, renowned for his converting the borderland. They spoke an intermediate dialect and their fringes and badge were known to be similar to those of the Saṁmitīya. According to some the language of the Mahāsaṁghikas was the intermediate dialect, that of the Saṁmitīya was the Prakrit, and that of the Sthaviras — the Apabhraṁça.

We have thus a great difference in the views of these 18 sects, but nevertheless all belong to the Church of Buddha. It is accordingly said: — It is only owing to the difference in the views that this division (into the 18 sects) has been caused. But as to different teachers, there are none[662]).

And: — The Teaching of the Lion of the Çākyas has become split into the 18 sects. This has been conditioned by the previous acts of this Teacher of the World[662a]). [101 a.]

---

[660]) Sgra-can-zin-bzaṅ-po.

[661]) *sbyaṅs-paḥi-yon-tan = dhūta-guṇa.*

[662]) In the sense that there are no different founders of the Teaching. This passage is a quotation from the Varṣāgra-pṛcchā. Tg. MDO. LXXXIX. 74 b.7. (N.)

[662a]) Ibid. 75 a. 2—3.

In such a way the Teaching was rehearsed for a 3d time. Thereafter, as the ordinary people who were not possessed of a good memory, recited Scripture incorrectly, making omissions and interpolations, — the Word of Buddha was written down in books, in order to prevent its corruption. Till that time it was recited by heart, and no written texts of it existed. According to some this is not correct, since in the *Mañjuçrī-mūla-tantra*[663]) it is said: — The son of Ajātaçatru called Upa shall cause the Word of Buddha to be written down. It is said moreover in the *Vimalaprabhā*[664]): — After the Lord had passed away into Nirvāṇa, the compilers wrote down the Teachings of the 3 Vehicles in books.

IV. Acc$_1$ b$_2$ c$_3$ a$_4$ b$_5$. The Rehearsal of the Mahāyānistic Scripture.

Tradition says that on the mountain called Vimalasvabhāva, to the south of Rājagṛha, in the assembly of a million of Bodhisattvas, — Mañjuçrī rehearsed the Abhidharma, Maitreya — the Vinaya, and Vajrapāṇi — the Sūtras. It is said moreover in the *Tarkajvālā*[665]): — The Mahāyānistic Scripture is the Word of Buddha. The chief Compilers of it were Samantabhadra, Mañjuçrī, the Lord of the secret charms[666]), Maitreya, and others. The Çrāvakas were not the chief compilers of our (Mahāyānistic) kanon, since the latter is not accessible to them. — In the *Commentary on the* 3 *Prajñāpāramitā-sūtras*[667]) it is said that according to the *Tathāgata-acintya-guhya-nirdeça*[668]) Vajrapāṇi is to be the compiler of the Teachings of the 1000 Buddhas (that are to arise in the fortunate aeon). In the *Vajrapāṇy-abhiṣeka-tantra* likewise Vajrapāṇi is spoken of as the compiler (of Mahāyānistic Scripture) [101 b.]. Accordingly, it is admitted that it was he who rehearsed

---

[663]) Kg. RGYUD XI. 442 a. 1—2. (N.) [664]) Tg. RGYUD I.

[665]) Tg. MDO. XIX. 180 a. 2—4.

[666]) Gsaṅ-baḥi-bdag-po = Guhyaka-adhipati i. e. Vajrapāṇi.

[667]) Tg. MDO. XIV. This passage is to be found in Haribhadra's Abhisamayālaṁkārālokā, MS. Minaev, 5 b. 14—6 a. 5. — *Tathāgata-guhya-nirdeça-adhikāreṇa sarvathā bhādrakalpika-sarva-tathāgatānāṁ rūpa-kāya-saddharma-kāya-rakṣāyāṁ kṛta-adhikāratvād Vajrapāṇy-abhiṣekādau pratyarpita-çāsanatvāc ca anyeṣāṁ viçeṣa-vacana abhāvād Aṭakavatī-nivāsī daçabhūmīçvaro Mahāvajradhāraḥ sarva-loka-anugrahāya Prajñāpāramitā-sūtra-ratna-saṁgītiṁ pratyadhiṣṭavantam Ārya-Maitreyādi-mahābodhisattva-gaṇam evam ityādy āha iti pūrvācāryāḥ.*

[668]) Cf. Vol. I. p. 97, note 845.

(this Scripture), reciting it to Maitreya and the rest in the form: - This have I heard, — and so on.

IV. Acc$_1$ b$_2$ c$_3$ b$_4$. The Existence of the Doctrine.

Here we distinguish:

a$_5$) The period of time during which the Teaching is to exist.

b$_5$) The prophecies concerning the persons who appeared during that time and preserved the Doctrine.

c$_5$) The acts performed by these persons who were foretold (by the Buddha).

IV. Acc$_1$ b$_2$ c$_3$ b$_4$ a$_5$. The Time of Existence of the Doctrine.

Some authorities versed in the Vinaya say that, according to the *Vinaya-kṣudraka*, the Doctrine was to have an existence of 7000 years. Owing to the admission of Prajāpatī into the religious order, this time was diminished for 2000 years, so that the whole time of the duration of the Doctrine is to be 5000 years. This statement disagrees (with the text referred to), for in the *Vinaya-kṣudraka* it is said that the Doctrine is to exist for 1000 years. In the *Bhadrakalpika-sūtra*[669]) we read that the (real) Doctrine is to have a duration of 500 years and the next 500 there will be only a resemblance of it, — so that altogether it is to exist 1000 years. In the Commentary on the *Abhidharma-sūtra*, in the story of *Suvarṇākṣamāla* we read: — O king, in thy dream thou hast seen that a multitude of people assembled, spoke, used abominable words, quarrelled and did harm to each other. — This is an omen that the Teaching of the Buddha Çākyamuni which is to exist 1000 years will finally disappear, owing to the evil teachings and disunion. In the *Abhidharmakoçabhāṣya* it is said: — They say that (the precepts of the Doctrine) are to exist for 1000 years. According to others this refers to the Doctrine viewed as the practice[670]), but the theoretical part[671]) is to have an existence longer than that. — Thus (the *Abhidharmakoçabhāṣya*) likewise speaks of 1000 years. The Sūtra on the gratitude of the Buddha[672]) says: — If the Lord permits that women enter his Congregation, the Highest Doctrine will cease to exist 500 years earlier (than it would otherwise). There-

---

669) Ibid. p. 98, note 909. 670) *rtogs-paḥi-chos = adhigama-dharma.*

671) *luṅ-gi-chos = āgama-dharma.*

672) Drin-lan-bsab-pa. Kg. MDO. XXXII. 161 a. 4—5.

fore the Lord must not allow women to enter the Congregation of the Buddha. — It is thus said that, owing to the admission of women into the religious order, the time of duration of the Doctrine has been diminished for 500 years. [102 a.] It is said in the Commentary on the *Akṣayamatinirdeça*[673]) in the passage explaining the sentence "in the subsequent period, that of the last 500 years", — as follows: — If we take the life-time of man which lasts 100 years, — the first 50 years will be the period of development. During that time the body, mind, and energy will be in a state of growth and progress. After these 50 years have passed away, the following 50 years will represent the period during which body, mind, and energy are subjected to decrease and become diminished. In a similar manner the Teaching of the Buddha Çākyamuni is to abide in Jambudvīpa for 1000 years during which it will bring fruit and become propagated. If we divide (this period) into 2 equal parts, the first 500 years will represent "the period of development", and the latter 500 we shall have to call "the period of regress".

Otherwise, it is said in the *Candragarbha-sūtra*[674]): — After I have passed away into Nirvāṇa, a resemblance of the Highest Doctrine will exist for 2000 years. And in the *Karuṇā-puṇḍarīka*[675]): —May, after I have passed away into Nirvāṇa, the Highest Doctrine exist for 1000 years. And (after that), may a resemblance of the Highest Doctrine exist for 500 years more. Thus, (according to these sūtras), the period of existence of the Doctrine is indicated as being equal to 500 years. In the Commentary on the *Vajracchedikā*[675a]) it is said: The meaning of "the last 500 years" is as follows: —5 periods of 500 years are meant here. It is said that the Teaching of the Lord is to exist during these 5 periods. The last of these is accordingly indicated here. In the *Munimatālaṁkāra*[676]) it is said: — Some are of the opinion that the Highest Doctrine of the Buddha Çākyamuni is to exist for 5 times 500 years. According to these texts the period of duration (of the Doctrine) is to be 2500 years. In the Commentary to the 3 *Prajñāpāramitā-sūtras*[677]) it is said: — The Teaching is to exist for 5000 years. If we divide

---

673) Tg. MDO. XXXV. 307 b. 3—6. (N.)
674) Kg. MDO. XXXII.. Cf. below.
675) Kg. MDO. VI. 352 b. 2—3. (N.) 675a) Tg. MDO. XVI. 234 a. 1—2. (N.)
676) Tg. MDO. XXIX. 366 a. 1—3. (N.)
677) Tg. MDO. XIV 232 b. 1—7. (N.)

each thousand of years into 2 equal parts [102b.], we shall have altogether 10 periods which are called "the 10 Chapters". In the 1st, the 2d, and 3d of these periods of 500 years respectively many Arhats, Saints who have attained the 3d Result[678]), and such who have entered the Stream[679]) are to appear. In accordance with this, the said periods are called "the Chapter of the Arhats"[680]), "the Chapter of those who do not return into the World"[681]), and "the Chapter of those who have entered the stream"[682]). These 3 are called the "Chapters of Cognition"[683]).

Thereafter, during the 4th, the 5th, and the 6th period of 500 years many Saints endowed, respectively, with Highest Transcendental Perception[684]), with Concentration of Mind and with Highest Morality are to appear. Accordingly, we have "the Chapter of Transcendental Perception"[685]), "the Chapter of Mind-concentration"[686]), and "the Chapter of Highest Morality"[687]), or "the 3 Chapters of Saintly Activity"[688]).

Then, in the 7th, the 8th and the 9th period, many teachers versed, respectively, in the Abhidharma, the Sūtras and the Vinaya are to arise. These periods are accordingly to be called "the Chapter of the Abhidharma"[689]), "the Chapter of the Sūtras"[690]), and "the Chapter of the Vinaya"[691]). These three are "the Chapters of the Theoretical Doctrine"[692]). The 10th period of 500 years is called "the Chapter of the mere outward marks"[693]), since (the monks) will bear only the external signs of the religious order, but will not be characterized by the corresponding views, conduct, and internal constitution. It is this period which is spoken of as "the last 500 years". The teacher Mañjuçrīkīrti[694]) mentions the 3 periods of Cognition, the 3 periods of Activity, the 3 periods of the Theoretical Doctrine and the period of the mere outward marks. The first of these are likewise called "the periods of the Results of Saintliness"[695]). It is said moreover in

---

678) *phyir-mi-ḥoṅ-bahi ḥbras-bu = anāgāmi-phala.*
679) *rgyun-du-žugs-pa = srota-āpanna.*
680) *dgra-bcom-paḥi leḥu.*
681) *phyir-mi-ḥoṅ-baḥi leḥu.* 682) *rgyun-du-žugs-paḥi leḥu.*
683) *khoṅ-du-chud-paḥi leḥu gsum.* 684) *lhag-mthoṅ = vipaçyanā.*
685) *lhag-mthoṅ-gi leḥu.* 686) *tiṅ-ṅe-ḥdzin-gyi leḥu.*
687) *tshul-khrims-kyi leḥu.* 688) *sgrub-paḥi leḥu gsum.*
689) *mṅon-paḥi leḥu.* 690) *mdo-sdeḥi leḥu.* 691) *ḥdul-baḥi leḥu.*
692) *luṅ-gi leḥu gsum.* 693) *rtags-tsam-ḥdzin-paḥi leḥu.*
694) Ḥjam-dpal-grags-pa. 695) *ḥbras-buḥi dus.*

the story of the venerable Nandimitra[696]): — Up to the time when the age of the human beings in Jambudvīpa will increase from 10 to 600 years, the Teaching of the Lord Çākyamuni is to exist. Now, it is clear that the indications of 1000, 1500, 2000, and 2500 years are of a conventional meaning[697]). [103 a.] In the case of these a special point has been taken into consideration, viz. the deterioration of activity and the like. It is said accordingly in the *Munimatālaṁkāra*[698]): — The "cessation" of the Highest Doctrine" means the deterioration of the saintly activity. In the Commentary on the *Vajracchedikā*[698a]) we have it explained as follows: — The destruction of the Highest Doctrine means the deterioration of it as regards devotion, reading, recitation, instruction, explanation, study, investigation, etc. The aim (of such indirect indications) was to arouse in the converts aversion (toward this wordly existence). They are in conflict with the true state of things. Indeed, they disagree with the prophecies concerning the brothers Asanga (and Vasubandhu) and with the prophecy delivered to the goddess Vimalaprabhā[699]), where it is said: — 2500 years after I have passed away into Nirvāṇa, the Highest Doctrine will become spread in the country of the red-faced (people). In the Sub-commentary on the *Abhidharmakoça*[700]) we read: — That the theoretical Doctrine[701]) is to have a long existence means that its duration will be even longer than 1000 years. This is to be regarded as correct. — (The statement) that (the Doctrine) is to exist for 5000 years we esteem to be of direct meaning[702]). Now there arises the question, as to how many years (of these 5000) have elapsed till now. The Master[703]) (Atiça) is of the opinion that the Teacher became conceived in the womb in the male-wooden-mouse-year and was born in the year of the wooden cow. In the male-earth-pig-year he became a Buddha, and in the last month of the male-wooden-monkey-year, at the time of the ascending moon, he passed away into Nirvāṇa.

[696]) Ḥphags-pa Dgaḥ-baḥi-bçes-gñen-gyi rtogs-brjod.

[697]) *draṅ-don* = *neyārtha.*

[698]) Tg. MDO. XXIX. 336 a. 3. (N.).

[698a]) Tg. MDO. XVI. 234 a. 2—3. (N.)

[699]) Lha-mo Dri-ma-med-paḥi luṅ-bstan.

[700]) Mdzod-kyi ḥgrel-bçad. [701]) *luṅ-gi-chos* = *āgama-dharma.*

[702]) *ṅes-don* = *nitārtha.* The tradition that the Teaching of Buddha is to exist for 5000 years is to be found in the Mahāvaṁsa, III. 38. — *Mahākassapa-thereṇa idaṁ sugata-sāsanaṁ / pañca-vassa-sahassāni samatthaṁ vattane kataṁ //*

[703]) Jo-bo-rje.

According to the Sa-kya hierarch[704]) the Buddha was conceived in the womb in the female-fire-hare-year, was born in that of the male-earth-dragon, became a Buddha in that of the male-water-tiger, and passed away in the female-fire-pig-year, on the 8th of the ascending moon in the last month of spring or the last month of autumn. Now, 137 years after the teacher had passed away, there appeared the king Nandin[705]), 108[706]) years after, — the king Candragupta[707]). [103 b.] Then, 231 years after there appeared the king Bhūritejas (?)[708]) and, from 724 to 814 years after him — the king Aṁçuvarman[709]) in Nepal. Then, 242 years after there appeared the Tibetan king Ṭhi-tsug-de-tan Ral-pa-can[710]). Thus, up to this time, 2955 years have passed away (since the death of the Buddha), as we have it correctly counted by the Indian and Nepalese calculators and by the Tibetan kings likewise. Nam-kha of the Chimpa tribe[711]), in accordance with the point of view of the Master (Atīça), considers that in the year of the female fire-serpent 3393 years have passed away since the death of the Buddha. Accordingly, he is of the opinion that 3458 years have passed away up to the year of the male-water-dog.

According to the school which maintains (that the Buddha was born) in the year of the dragon, i. e. the calculation of Sa-kya-paṇḍita, made at the time when, in the year of the male-fire-mouse, the departure of the venerable Kīrtidhvaja into Nirvāṇa was celebrated, —3349 years had passed away (after the Buddha's departure into Nirvāṇa). Thereafter in the year of the fire-cow, at the time of the installation of the prayer-wheel moved by water, the Lama Chö-gyal[712]) has counted 3410 years. Accordingly up to the male-water-dog-year, when the Lama Matiçrī Kun-gā-lo-ḍö-gyal-tshan-pal-zaṅ-po[713]) came to Tibet in order to become ordained, — 3455 years had passed away and the 3456th year (of the Doctrine) was lasting. Thus, (at that time) 6 periods of 500 years, representing the Chapters of the Result of the Saintly Activity and, in the "Chapters of the Theoretical Doctrine", —

---

704) Chos-rje Sa-skya. 705) Dgaḥ-byed.
706) One must evidently correct *brgya-brgyad* for *brgyad-brgya.*
707) Zla-sruṅ. Usually Zla-ba-sbas-pa.
708) Brjid-maṅs. 709) Ḥod-zer-go-cha.
710) Khri-gtsug-lde-btsan ral-pa-can.
711) Mchims Nam-mkhaḥ. 712) Chos-rgyal.
713) Kun-dgaḥ-blo-gros-rgyal-mtshan-dpal-bzaṅ-po.

455 years of "the Chapter of the Abhidharma". Accordingly, there remain 45 years of this latter Chapter and 3 periods, representing, respectively, the Chapters of the Sūtras, the Vinaya, and the mere outward marks, thus altogether 1545 years.

According to the calculations made by the Kashmirian Çākyaçri in the male-wooden-mouse-year at Ṭho-pu [104 a.] and in the year of the female-fire-hare at Sol-nag-thaṅ-chen —

At midnight on the 8th of the bright half of Kārtika[714]),
When the moon set behind the mountain,
The Lord of Sages passed away into Nirvāṇa.
And after that, one thousand
Seven hundred and fifty years,
Two months and half-a-month,
And 10 days more have passed away.
There are thus three thousand
Two hundred and forty-nine years,
Nine months, and ten days
That remain for the Doctrine to exist in future. —

According to the point of view of those who count (the time of the Buddha's attainment of Nirvāṇa) to have been the 5th of the middle-month of spring in the year of the fire-hare, and according to the tradition of the Sa-kya which counts from the male-iron-horse-year, — 1865 years have passed away up to the year of the male-water-dog. The Sa-kya hierarch says: — This point of view has its origin in India. The Saindhava Çrāvakas used every evening, during their religious service, to count: — So many years have passed away since the death of the Teacher. In such a way did they count. But, (subsequently) different errors were made in counting the seasons. This dates from the time when the teachers Udbhaṭasiddhisvāmin[715]) and Çaṁkarasvāmin[716]) became possessed of the intention of making an image of the Mahābodhi at Magadha, and when the latter itself arose from a pile of sandal-wood instead. It was thus the custom to count: —"So many years have passed away since the death of the Teacher". — The Paṇḍits of India, Kashmir, and Nepal in general follow this method, but owing to the errors that have crept in, it is not to be regarded as authoritative. Indeed, it proves to be incorrect, if we compare it with the

---

[714]) *smin-drug.* [715]) Mtho-btsun-grub-rje. Cf. Schiefner, Tāranātha, p. 64.
[716]) Bde-byed-bdag-po. Schiefner has Çaṁkarapati.

prophecy delivered to the goddess Vimalaprabhā, where "the country of the red-faced" that has been mentioned is no other than Tibet, with the number of years indicated in the prophecy concerning Nāgārjuna and others, and with the chronology of the Tibetan kings etc. According to the opinion of Rba "the country of the red-faced" means China.

Some authorities say [104 b.] that, according to the Kālacakra, up to the male-water-dog-year 1613 years have passed away, and that 187 years remain (for the Doctrine to exist). Such a statement shows a total ignorance of the true meaning of the Kālacakra.

Others say that, according to the point of view of Kamalaçīla, 2040 years have elapsed and that 460 remain. I myself have not seen any authoritative source confirming this. Therefore (in order to refute these incorrect statements) it is necessary to know that, according to the teaching contained in the chief Tantra of the Kālacakra system, up to the male-water-dog-year, 2198 years have passed away. I am of the opinion that the statement according to which (the Doctrine) is to exist up to the time when human age will be 600 years, refers to (the existence of) the monuments containing the relics (of the Buddha), etc.

IV. $Acc_1 b_2 c_3 b_4 b_5$. The Prophecies concerning the Persons who worked for the Sake of the Doctrine.

Kāçyapa, Ānanda, Çānavāsika,
Upagupta, Dhītika, Kṛṣṇa,
And Mahāsudarçana, — these are the 7 hierarchs[717])
Who are mentioned in the *Vinayakṣudraka*.

In the *Lankāvatāra* we read[718]): — Who is to be the guardian of the Doctrine, after the Lord has passed away into Nirvāṇa? — This and the following is explained in the Commentary[719]) as follows: — The succession of the hierarchs from the Buddha himself up to Dhītika is the same as in the Vinaya. (Dhītika) confined the Doctrine to the care of Bibhaka; then it was successively transferred to the venerable Buddhananda[720]), Buddhamitra, to the monk Pārçva[721]), the pupil of the latter, and then to Sunaçata,

[717]) *gtad-rabs bdun.* [718]) Ed. Bunyiu Nanjio. p. 28. — *nirvṛtte sugate ko 'sau çāsanaṁ dhārayiṣyati.*

[719]) Not to be found in the 2 Commentaries contained in Tg. MDO XLII and XLIII. [720]) Xyl. Buddhananti. [721]) Rtsibs.

Açvaghoṣa[722]), Amṛta[723]), Nāgārjuna, Āryadeva, Bāhula, Saṁghananda, the monk Arhat, Ghalaça, Kumārada, Çāyanta, Vasubandhu Manoda, Haklenayaçàs[724]) and to the monk Siṁha. It is said in the *Mahākaruṇāpuṇḍarīka*[725]) in answer to the question: Who is to be the guardian of the Doctrine after the Teacher has passed away? — O Ānanda, the monk Kāçyapa [105 a.] and thyself, ye two are to guard the Highest Doctrine for 40 years and more[726]). — Then, in the city of Mathurā[727]) on the mountains Gandhamadana[728]) and Mahāpārçva[729]), in the grove called Pankavatī[730]) there is to appear the monk called Çlanavāsa[731]), and, in the same place, the monk Nandin[732]). — On the mountain Uçīra there are to appear 44 000 monks[733]). — In the city of Pāṭaliputra, in the Mārgārāma, there will be a monk called Açvagupta[734]) and in the same city, in the grove of the ducks, — the monk called Uttara[735]). — In the country of Anga[736]), during the 5 years' feast 13 000 Arhats are to arise[737]). — In the city called Survarṇadroṇa[738]), 2 monks called Vijña[739]) and Saṁjaya[740]), in the city of Sāketana[741]), — the monk Mahāvīrya[742]) and on the northern border-land of Gandhāra[743]), — the monk Kāçyapa, — are to appear[744]). All these monks are to be greatly renowned for their miraculous achievements, their great power and faculties. They are to be praised as being possessed of intrepidity and greatly learned, mastering the Sūtras, the Vinaya, and the Abhidharma, teaching correctly and being like ships that conduce others to the apprehension (of the Doctrine). These are to be the propagators of my Teaching.

On the northern border-land, in the city of Takṣaçilā[745]), a

---

722) Rta-skad. 723) Ma-çi-ba.

724) Xyl. Ha-ka-la-ka-na-ya-na-ça (?)

725) Kg. MDO. VI. The passage quoted is rendered in an abridged form.

726) Kg. MDO. VI. 109 b. 4. sqq. 727) Bcom-brlag.

728) Ri-sbo. 729) Ṅos-che. 730) Ḥdam-bu-can.

731) Yul-slan-pa. Kg. MDO. VI. 113 a. 2—6. Cf. Schiefner, Tāranātha, p. 4 and 51.

732) Dgaḥ-ba-can. Kg. MDO. VI. 113 a. 6—b. 1.

733) Ibid. 113 b. 1—5. 734) Rta-sbas. Ibid. 114 a. 3—5.

735) Bla-ma. Ibid. 114 a. 5—7. 736) Yul Yan-lag-tu.

737) Ibid. 114 b. 1—5. 738) Gser-gyi-bre. 739) Mkhas-pa.

740) Yaṅ-dag-par-rgyal-ba-can. Ibid. 114 b. 5—7. 741) Gnas-bcas.

742) Brtson-ḥgrus-che. Ibid. 114 b. 7—115 a. 1.

743) Sbos-ḥdzin. 744) Ibid. 11. a. 3—6. 745) Rdo-ḥjog.

householder named Jāṭanika[746]) will appear. He will pay homage to my body and my disciples and, after 1000 aeons, in the age of good luck, in the world called Mahāvyūhasvalaṁkṛta[747]), he is to become the Buddha Samantaprabha[748]).

In the north, in the palace called Vistaravatī[749]), many Brāhmaṇas and householders devoted to the Doctrine are to appear. These, after their death, are to be reborn in Tuṣita. The monks at that time, for the greater part, will not act according to the Doctrine and fall into error[750]). [105 b.] And in that place a devotee of the laity called Dharmavardhana[751]) possessed of miraculous powers will likewise appear[752]). In the north, moreover, a Mahāyānist monk called Jīvaka[753]) will arise. He will restore the monuments of the Buddha that will have undergone destruction, and richly decorate them with gold and the like. After his death he is to be reborn in Sukhavatī[754]). —

In the border-woodland, in the royal palace called "the Peaceful" the king named Agnidatta[755]) is to worship the relics and the disciples of the Buddha. In that country more than 3000 Arhats are to arise[756]). In the northern border-land, in the village Hiṅgala[757]) the teeth of the Buddha will be greatly worshipped and many monks endowed with the highest morality will appear and attain all of them Nirvāṇa by the paths of the 3 Vehicles. These all will cause my Teaching to become widely spread. Do not therefore be grieved![758]) —

In the *Laṅkāvatāra* it is said[759]): —

In the southern country of Vedalya,
A monk glorious and greatly renowned,
Whose name is sounded Nāga,
Will put an end to the extremities of Ens and Non-ens,
And after he has expounded in this world
My Teaching as that of the Great Vehicle,
Higher than which there is none,

---

746) Ral-pa-can. 747) Bkod-pa-chen-pos-legs-par-brgyan-pa.
748) Kun-tu-snaṅ-ba Kg. MDO. VI. 115 a. 6—b. 4. 749) Rgyas-ldan.
750) Ibid. 115 b. 5—116 a. 3. sqq. 751) Chos-ḥphel.
752) Ibid. 117 b. 2. sqq. 753) Ḥtsho-byed. 754) Ibid. 117 b. 6—118 a. 5.
755) Mes-byin. 756) Ibid. 118 a. 7—b. 3. 757) Çiṅ-kun-skye-ba.
758) Kg. MDO. VI. 118 b. 5—119 a. 7.
759) Ed. Bunyiu Nanjio, p. 286. — *dakṣiṇā-patha-Vedalyāṁ bhikṣuḥ çrīmān mahāyaçāḥ Nāgāhvayaḥ sa nāmnā tu sad-asat-pakṣa-dārakaḥ*, etc.

He will secure the Stage of Perfect Bliss[760]),
And pass away into the region of Sukhavatī.

And in the *Manjuçrīmūlatantra*[761]) we read: —

After I, the Buddha, have passed away,
Four hundred years are to elapse,
And then a monk called Nāga will appear.
He will be devoted to the Doctrine,
And administer great help to it.
He will attain the Stage of Perfect Bliss,
Live for six hundred years,
And the mystic knowledge of the Mahāmayūrī[762])
Will be secured by that great being.
He will know the subjects of the different sciences,
And expound the Teaching of Non-substantiality.
And, after he has cast away this bodily frame,
He will be reborn in the region of Sukhavatī.
And, finally the state of Buddhahood
Is to be certainly attained by him.

Such is the prophecy concerning Nāgārjuna. —
We read moreover[763]): —

A monk bearing the name of Asanga, [106 a.]
Well versed in the meaning of the scientific treatises,
Will, in different forms, explain
The conventional and the direct meaning of the Sūtras.
By his nature he is to be one
Who teaches the Sublime Science to the living beings,
And reveals the meaning of the Sacred Texts.
He is to secure that mystic knowledge
Which is called the Female Messenger of Sala[764]) (?)
And, by the force of his magic charms,
The most sublime wisdom is to arise in him.
In order that the Doctrine should abide for long,
He will rehearse the essential meaning of the Sūtras.

---

[760]) *rab-tu-dgaḥ-baḥi-sa* = *pramuditā-bhūmi* — the first Stage of the Bodhisattva.

[761]) Ḥjam-dpal-rtsa-rgyud, Kg. RGYUD. XI. 450 a. 5—6.

[762]) Rma-rgya-chen-mo.

[763]) Mañjuçrīmūlatantra, Kg. RGYUD. XI. 450 a. 6—b. 2.

[764]) Sa-laḥi-pho-ña-mo.

He is to live one hundred and fifty years,
And, after his body will have withered away,
He is to depart into the region of the gods.
Abiding in the world of the living beings,
In the various stages of Phenomenal Life,
He will for a long time experience the Highest Felicity.
And finally, this elevated being
Is to attain Supreme Enlightenment.

This is the prophecy regarding Asanga. — (The text quoted is sometimes proceeded by the verse): —

When nine hundred years have passed away
After I have attained Nirvāṇa. —

This is not to be found in the Tantra, but has been added by the Chinese Teacher Dzog-sal[765]) in his Commentary to the *Saṁdhinirmocana*.

At the time which is to come
A monk called Arhat is to appear,
He is to know the meaning of the secret charms,
Become versed in the Tantras and greatly learned.
By uttering the charm of the Yakṣas,
He will secure a precious vessel.

In such a manner (the coming of) the monk called Arhat has been foretold[766]).

A monk possessed of great learning,
Is likewise to appear at that time.
And will be known by the surname
Of "the mother's servant"[767]).
He will compose hymns in my honour,
And, owing to his sublime virtues,
He will teach in accordance with the Truth.
His mind is to be perfectly serene,
He will be devoted to the Doctrine of the Buddhas,
Secure the secret charms that are hard to be obtained,
And which resemble those of Mañjughoṣa.
Endowed with virtuous properties and with morality,
And being greatly learned, he is to expound the Doctrine.

---

[765]) Rdzogs-gsal. [766]) Kg. RGYUD. XI. 450 b. 3 sqq. [767]) Ma-khol.

These verses and following ending with:

And he is to attain the Enlightenment of the Omniscient, —

contain the prophecy concerning Mātṛceṭa[768]).

When the Word of the Teacher here on earth [106 b.]
Will become corrupted amongst the living beings at last,
Men, famed for their zeal in the religious observances, and kings
Will appear, — there is no doubt in this, —
As, for instance, those who are known by the surname
Of "the Mother's Servant" and "the Flower"[769]).
One called Kumāra[770]) and one whose name begins with Ma
Will be attached to the Doctrine from the beginning to the end.
There will be likewise one, known by the name of Nāgāhvaya[771]),
One whose name is Ratnasambhava[772]),
One whose name begins with Ga, one called Kumāra[773]),
And one whose name begins with Ba
Are to investigate the Doctrine.
A high being with a name beginning with A
Will zealously maintain the precepts of the Teacher[774]).
(There will likewise appear one who wil be)
Adorned with all the different virtues,
The initia letter of his name being La.
A king, belonging to the adherents of the Buddha,
Will elucidate the Doctrine of the Teacher[775]).
A monk, zealous in religious practice,
Whose name begins with the letter A is to appear
From amongst the Brāhmaṇas and enter the Doctrine.
He is to reside in the city of Sāketana[776])
And is to live for eighty years[777]).
A monk whose name begins with A,
Is to appear in the southern country,
Endowed with wisdom, he will live 60 years,
And have his residence in the city of Kāçi[778]).

---

768) Xyl. Maticitra. Kg. RGYUD. XI. 449 b. 2—450 a. 4.
769) Me-tog = Puṣpa. Ibid. 472 a. 2—3. 770) Gžon-nu.
771) Klus-bos. 772) Rin-chen-ḥbyuṅ. 773) Ibid. 470 a. 3—4.
774) Ibid. 472 a. 4—5. 775) Ibid. 472 a. 5—6. 776) Gnas-bcas.
777) Ibid. 472 a. 6. 778) Ibid. 472 a. 6—7.

A devotee whose name begins with Dha[779])
Will be greatly renowned in the southern district.
He will refute all his opponents and adversaries,
Be zealous in the religious observances,
And secure the secret charms[780]).
Moreover, a holy monk
Will appear in the villages of Siṁhala
And though not a Saint, he will bear the name of a Saint[781])
And have his abode in the island of Siṁhala.
He will refute all his oponents,
And put to shame the charms of the heretics,
This one is to appear at the end of a period
Which is to be characterized by great fear[782]).
The devotees who are called
By their initial letters Da and La,
And the monks who are said to take orders,
With names that begin with Ra and Ba,
Elucidating the Doctrine of the Teacher,
Are to appear, there is no doubt in this[783]).
During the reign of the king called Kṛṣṇa[784]),
A devotee with the initial letter Ma is to appear.
He is to abide in sanctuaries and hermitages, [107 a.]
And in all the ponds and the wells likewise,
The image of the Buddha will appear to him.
And, there is no doubt in this,
He will construct ships and bridges.
And, after his body will have perished by the sword,
He will depart to the celestial regions[785]).
Thereafter, (men) whose names begin
With the initial letters Sa and Ka,
And, similarly, others, whose names are sounded,
Beginning with the letters Ra and Gha,
One whose initial letter is Ba,
And those who are called Suvaktra[786]) and Sukha[787])

---

779) This seems to be Dharmakirti. 780) Ibid. 472 a. 7—b. 1.
781) This is considered to refer to Āryadeva. Cf. below.
782) Ibid. 472 b. 1—2. 783) Ibid. 472 b. 2—3. 784) Nag-po.
785) Ibid. 472 b. 3—4. 786) Legs-bžin.
787) Legs-te-bde. The text of the Mañj.-mūla-tantra has Legs-te-sde = Susena.

Well-famed for their charity and their offerings,
Refuting the teachings of adversaries,
One who has been a merchant and the other — a physician, —
These two will perform diverse acts of charity[788]).
A renowned devotee whose name begins with Ba,
Another with the initial letter Ra,
And one with a name beginning with Va, —
These are to make the images of the Teacher[789]).
A sage whose name begins with Ma,
And similar devotees, possessed of faith are to appear.
In many ways the devotees are mentioned,
And an infinite number of them is to arise at that time[790]).
And, famed as zealous in religious practice,
They will likewise elucidate the Doctrine of the Teacher.
And, at the time, when the Church, here on earth,
Will be weakened and lose its splendour,
Then they will create the images of the Buddha,
Gladdening the heart, — there is no doubt in that.
The prophecy of Enlightenment is granted to all of them:
They shall attain Enlightenment as I have done[791]).
They are to receive the gifts of the worldly beings,
Attain the end of worldly existence in the three Spheres,
And, exhibiting great zeal in the magic charms and the Tantras,
They are to be possessed of great fame[792]).
And now, I am to speak of those,
Who, being possessed of the attributes of Brāhmaṇas,
Will be zealous in the secret charms and the Tantras,
And be acquainted with the customs of kings[793]).
In those bad and disastrous times
They will appear in all the different countries.
An eminent Brāhmaṇa whose name begins with Ba
Rich and perfectly knowing the Vedas, [107 b.]
Will traverse all the countries without exception
In the search of dispute and controversy.
And, till the limits of the earth

788) Ibid. 472 b. 4—5. 789) Ibid. 472 b. 6. 790) Ibid. 472 b. 6—7.
791) Ibid. 472 b. 7—473 a. 1. 792) Ibid. 473 a. 1—2.
793) Ibid. 473 a. 2—3.

Which is bordered by the 3 oceans,
Will indulge in disputes with the heretical opponents[794]).
And that which is the first and principal word
Which, owing to the desire of helping the living beings,
Has been uttered by the princely youth,
The charm of 6 syllables, — will be repeated by him[795]).
By means of this sublime proceeding,
He will help some and teach others.
Jaya[796]), Sujaya[797]), Yaçasvin[798]), Kalyāṇa[799]),
And then, Kulika[800]) and Dharmika[801]),
Mahavırya[802]), and Suviṣṇu[803]),
Madhu[804]) and Madhubhadra[805]),
And, moreover, Siddha[806]) and Adarpa[807]),
Rāghava[808]), and Çūdra[809]),
And in a like way another who is called Kāçījāta[810]).
Owing to the spell repeated by this youth,
These all are going to appear.
They all will be of a sublime character,
Possessed of wisdom and greatly learned[811]). —

And further on[812]): —

A Brahmaṇa whose name begins with Vi
In the city of Kusumapura
Is to propitiate the wrathful deities[813]). —

Again[814]): —

Thereupon a Brāhmaṇa greatly renowned,
With a name that begins with A,

---

794) Ibid. 473 a. 3—4. 795) Ibid. 473 a. 4—5.
796) Rgyal (-ba). Cf. Schiefner, Tāranātha p. 4.
797) Legs-par-rgyal-ba. Ibid. 798) Grags-ldan.
799) Dge-ba. Ibid. 800) Rigs-ldan. Ibid. p. 5.
801) Chos-daṅ-ldan-pa. Ibid.
802) Brtson-ldan. Ibid. Cf. also Ibid. p. 68, note 6.
803) Legs-par-khyab-ḥjug. Ibid. p. 5. 804) Sbraṅ-rtsi. Ibid.
805) Sbraṅ-rtsi-bzaṅ-po. Ibid. Schiefner has Supramadhu.
806) Grub(-pa). Ibid. p. 4.
807) Dregs-bral. Ibid. The Xyl. has: Legs-bral.
808) Schiefner, Tāranātha, p. 4.
809) Dmaṅs-rigs. Ibid. p. 5, note 1.
810) Ka-çir-skyes-pa. Ibid. p. 5, note 6.
811) Mañjuçrī-mūla-tantra, Kg. RGYUD. XI. 473 a. 5—7.
812) Ibid. 473 a. 7—b 1. 813) Khro-bo. 814) Ibid 473 b. 3—4.

One who is virtuous and knows the Doctrine and its meaning,
Will speak the Truth and subdue the senses. —

Furthermore[815]):

After that, (likewise) greatly famed,
A Brāhmaṇa investigating the meaning of the Doctrine,
And after him one, whose name commences with Ça
Is to appear in the Māla country. —

And[816]): —

Thereupon there will be greatly renowned
A Brāhmaṇa who will appear in the southern district.
The initial letter of his name is Ba (or Va.)
It is he who will make the Teaching of the Lord predominant.
He is to abide in sanctuaries and hermitages,
And the delightful reflection of the form of the Lord
Will make him the ornament of all living beings
On this earth bordered by the 2 Oceans.
Thereupon, endowed with great fame,
A Brāhmaṇa possessed of great riches
Whose name begins with the letter Na,
Will have his abode in the southern district. [108 a.]
This high being will possess the knowledge of the secret charms,
And will certainly attain Supreme Enlightenment[817]). —

There are many who consider these two (last) prophecies to refer to Vasubandhu and Dignāga, but they are both alike unsuitable. Indeed, (these prophecies) are given quite apart from the religious devotees (to whom both Vasubandhu and Dignāga belong). Neither do we have (in the prophecies just quoted) the acts and the characteristic features (of both). —

I am now to speak of those
Who are to appear in Central India.
There will be a Brāhmaṇa called Pūrṇabhadra[818]),
Famed for discipline and pure morality.
Then, Pūrṇa[819]) who is to reside at Mathurā,
And one whose name begins with Bha and Vasunetra[820]),

---

815) Ibid. 473 b. 5. 816) Ibid. 473 b. 7—474 a. 1.
817) Ibid. 474 a. 1—2.
818) Gaṅ-ba-bzaṅ. Cf. Schiefner, Tāranātha p. 5.
819) Gaṅ-ba. Ibid. 820) Nor-gyi-spyan. Ibid.

Who are to be praised and revered by kings.
The Brāhmaṇas thus indicated
Will pay homage to the Teaching of the Buddha[821]). —

We have moreover[822]): —

On the border of the woodland
That is near to the eastern ocean,
A Sage, one of the Lohitas, and another
In the north, in the country of snow, — etc.

Some consider that this is an indication of the Great Translator who was born in Ya-brog[823]). But, as (this prophecy) is contained in that section which refers to kings, —this must be accurately investigated. —

In connection with this prophecy it is said[824]): —

In the west, in the delightful region of Kāçī,
And in the country called Mūrdhāna,
There is to appear a king
Whose name will be Pañcamasiṁha[825]). —

We have moreover the following[826]): — One hundred years after the Teacher will have passed away, in the city of Kusumapura there will appear the king Açoka who will live 150 years and worship the monuments of the Buddha during 87 years[827]). After him, the king named Vigataçoka[828]) will worship these monuments for 76 years[829]). Thereafter, the king Vīrasena[829a]) will rule for 70 years[830]) and will be succeeded by the king Nanda[831]). The latter's reign will dure 56 years[832]) and his friend will be the Brāhmaṇa Pāṇini[833]). Then there will appear the king Candragupta [108 b.][834]), and after him his son called Bindusāra[835]) who will

---

821) Mañjuçrī-mūla-tantra. Kg. RGYUD. XI. 474 a. 3—4.

822) Ibid. 462 b. 6—7. 823) Ya-ḥbrog. 824) Ibid. 462 b. 7.

825) Seṅ-ge-lṅa.

826) The following passages represent likewise a prophecy of the Mañjuçrī-mūla-tantra which is rendered by Bu-ton in prose.

827) Ibid. 443 a. 6 sqq.

828) Mya-ṅan-bral. The Xyl. of Bu-ton's text has Mya-ṅan-med-bral = Vigatāçoka. In such a form this name appears likewise in Tārānātha. Mañjuçrī-mūla-tantra, Kg. RGYUD. XI. 446 a. 5 sqq.

829) Ibid. 446 a. 7. 829a) Dpaḥ-boḥi-sde.

830) Ibid. 446 b. 1—4. 831) Dgaḥ-bo. Ibid. 446 b. 4.

832) Ibid. 447 a. 7. 833) Ibid. 447 a. 7—b 1.

834) Zla-ba-sbas-pa. Ibid. 447 b. 2. 835) Sñiṅ-po-thig-le. Ibid. 447 b. 4.

rule for 70 years. The minister of these kings Cāṇakya[836]), (owing to his deeds) will depart to hell.

After the monk Nanda has died, another called Candanapāla will appear and will live 300 years[837]). Thereafter, the king called Bhadanta[838]) will burn down the temples and the monuments from the eastern country and up to Kashmir and massacre the monks[839]). After him there will be a king called Buddhapakṣa[840]) who will be succeeded by the king Sarvābhirāma[841]) who is to live 300 years. The son of the latter, Gambhīrapakṣa[842]) will reign in the Pañcāla[843]) country.

In the northern Himālaya, in the country called the Godly[844]), there is to appear the king Manuṣyadeva[845]) who will attain the age of 80 years[846]). In China there will be a king named Hiraṇyagarbha[847]) who is to live 150 years[848]). In his country —

> The Bodhisattva, the great hero,
> Mañjughoṣa who is endowed with great light.
> Perceived by all in that pure region,
> Is to abide in the form of a child[849]). —

In the north, a king called Turuṣka is to live 300 years[850]), and after him he who is called Turuṣka-Mahāsammata[851]). The latter is to attain the age of 200 years[852]).

In the west, beyond Ujjayinī[853]), a king named Çīla[854]) is to rule for 300 years[855]), and after him a king called Cala[856]) who is to live for 54 years and 5 months[857]). — Of the greater part of

---

836) Tsa-na-ka. Ibid. 448 a. 5—b 1.
837) Ibid. 452 a. 3 sqq. 838) Btsun-pa. 839) Ibid. 452 a. 4—6.
840) Saṅs-rgyas-phyogs. Ibid. 452 b. 3—4.
841) Thams-cad-mṅon-dgaḥ. Ibid. 452 b. 4—6.
842) Zab-moḥi-phyogs. 843) Lṅa-len. Ibid. 452 b. 6—7 sqq.
844) Lha-ldan. 845) Miḥi-lha. 846) Ibid. 453 a. 4—5.
847) Dbyig-gi-sñiṅ-po. Cf. Schiefner, Tārānātha. p. 14, note 2.
848) Mañj.-mūla-tantra. Kg. RGYUD. XI. 453 b. 3—454 a. 1.
849) Ibid. 454 a. 2—3. 850) Ibid. 454 a. 3—5.
851) Tu-ru-ṣka maṅ-pos-bkur-ba. Schiefner, Tārānātha, p. 2 has Çākamahāsammata.
852) Mañj.-mūla-tantra, Kg. RGYUD. XI. 454 b. 1—4.
853) Ḥphags-rgyal.
854) Ṅaṅ-tshul. Also translated (in the Tantra) as Tshul-khrims (445 b. 5.)
855) Sic. acc. to Bu-ton, but Tantra (455 b. 2.) — *lo-ni sum-cu-dag-tu-yaṅ / rgyal-srid gnod-pa-med-par bya //*
856) Gyo-ba. 857) Ibid. 455 b. 5.

these kings it has been prophecied that they are to attain Enlightenment. The reigns of many other kings have moreover been foretold, but I do not write about them, since I fear that it will take too much place.

Furthermore, we read in the *Nātha-abhyudaya-tantra*[858]): — A certain fisherman, having been swallowed by a fish, will die and be reborn as the Yogin called Dārika[859]). This one will cast wine into the river Ganges and in an hour an island called Badaha will appear. [109 a.] The result of the charms (of this magician) is that the Ḍākas and Ḍākinīs will be rendered powerless. —

And[860]): — In the country of Oḍiviça[861]) there will appear a man possessed of the faculty of mystic meditation which he will excercise with great energy. He will be a follower of the precepts of Rāmaṇi. His name (is spelt as follows): — The letter Ka of the first phonetic class is adorned with the first vowel (i. e. A). Then comes the 4th letter of the 7th class (Ha), being as if slightly mounted on the latter Na. This unique and powerful Yogin will secure the 8 great principal magical properties[862]). The person spoken of here is Kahnapa or Kṛṣṇacārin[863]). The 6 pupils of the latter are to secure the Great Seal[864]) by means of which everything which has a separate and physical reality will be rejected. —

Again[865]): — The foremost of the Paṇḍits, known by the name of Dharmakīrti, — he and 6 other persons, acting for the sake of the Doctrine and abiding in virtuous conduct are to secure the magical properties. After that, the guardians of the Doctrine named Mahila, Çaṁkara[866]), Bhavyaghoṣa, and Sahasrakarṇa[866a]). will in 13 years attain the magical properties. —

Furthermore[867]): — In the south, a city called Ajārayoginī is to appear, and there a magician named Nāgārjuna will bestow royal power upon Gopāla who will sit mounted on a Çiṁçapa tree.

---

[858]) Sic. acc. to Xyl. Mgon-po-mṅon-par-ḥbyuṅ-baḥi-rgyud. In the Kangyur (Derge ed.) this work is called Mahākāla-tantra-rāja. Kg. RGYUD. V. 66 b. 4—5. (D.)

[859]) Cf. Schiefner, Tārānātha, p. 127, 177, 249, 278.

[860]) Kg. RGYUD. V. 67 b. 3—4. [861]) Xyl. O-ru-bi-sa.

[862]) *grub-pa* = *siddhi*. Or: *dṅos-grub-chen-po*.

[863]) Nag-po-spyod-pa-pa.

[864]) *phyag-rgya-chen-po* = *mahāmudrā*. Ibid. 67 b. 5.

[865]) Ibid. 68 b. 1—2.

[866]) Xyl. Saṁkara. Kg.: Pāgara (Sāgara)

[866a]) Xyl. Sahaprakarṣa, Kangyur: Sahasrikārṇa. [867]) Ibid. 68 b. 4—5.

And, after the death of (the latter's) son, the nephew of Vahana and other kings are to appear. —

In the *Kālacakra-uttara-tantra*[868]) it is said: —

The monk Nāgārjuna, the source of all the virtuous properties
Administering help to all living beings,
The teacher called Sthiramati[868a]), those who are endowed
With 10 000 magical powers over the duration of life,
Those who attain their aim on the Path of the 10 virtues, —
Āryadeva, Kambala[869]), Açvaghoṣa, Dignāga [109 b.],
Parahitāçaya[869a]), Candrapadma[869b]), and Padmānkura[870]),
Avigraha, Açeṣakṛṣṇa, the king of Bhasalakalpa, and the king Indrabhūti[871]): —

And furtheron[872]): —

He who is called Jñāna, Vajraghaṇṭa[872a]), Kuṇṭha[872b])
Those drinking wine from skulls, bearing the trident,
The ornaments of bones, the wine-cup,
And the hand-drum, — as he who is called Kṛṣṇālavāla.

In accordance with all these passages, the persons mentioned are said to be the guardians of the Doctrine. Some say that no prophecies have been delivered with regard to those who were endowed with the attributes of the Yogins (i. e. the Tantric magicians). This is however to be refuted by the passages which we have just quoted. —

In general, as regards the preservation of the Doctrines of the Buddhas, the exposition of them, and the action according to them, we know that, especially, the teachings of the 1000 Buddhas are preserved, rehearsed, and protected by Vajrapāṇi. The Doctrine of this Buddha is preserved by Mañjuçrī, Vajrapāṇi, Brahma, Indra, etc. It is said in the *Mañjuçrī-mūla-tantra*: —

---

868) Kg. RGYUD. I. 206 a. 3—6. (N.)
868a) Blo-brtan. The Kg. has Ḥod-brtan.
869) Lva-baḥi-na-bzaḥ. 869a) Gžan-la-phan-paḥi bsam-pa.
869b) Sic. Xyl. Zla-ba-padma. The Kg. has Btsun-pa Padmaḥi-myu-gu.
870) Padmaḥi-myu-gu. 871) Xyl. Indrabodhi.
872) Ibid. 199 b. 3—4. 872a) Rdo-rjeḥi-dril-bu.
872b) (?) Xyl. Lag-ltuṅ. Kg. Lag-rdub. Perhaps Lag-rdum. In Cordier's Index du Bstan-Ḥgyur I p. 171 we find the name Kuṇṭha (Varāhakuṇṭha) as the author of the Çrīvajra-bhairava-sādhana (Kuṇṭha = phyag-rdum = lag-rdum — "he with the mutilated hand.")

The Lord of Sages will pass away into Nirvāṇa,
And, in order to protect the Highest Doctrine,
There will be one who appears in the form of Mañjuçrī,
Of him who constantly preserves the Doctrine. —

In particular, the protectors of the Doctrine are the 16 Sthaviras, viz.

1. Panthaka[873]), — in the realm of the 33 gods,
2. The Sthavira Abhedya[874]) in the Himālaya,
3. Kanaka[874a]) —(Bhāradvāja), —in the western continent Godhanya,
4. Bakula[875]), — in the northern continent Kuru,
3. Bhāradvāja, — in the eastern continent Videha,
6. Mahākālika[876]), in Tāmradvīpa,
7. Vajrīputra[877]), — in Siṁhaladvīpa,
8. Rāhula[878]), in Priyangudvīpa,
9. Çrībhadra[879]), — in Yamunādvīpa,
10. Gopaka[880]), — on the mountain Bihula,
11. Nāgasena[881]), — on the Urumunda mountain,
12. Vanavāsin[882]), — on the Saptaparṇa mountain,
13. Kṣudrapanthaka[883]), — on the Gṛdhrakūṭa,
14. Kanakavatsa[884]), — in Kashmir,
15. Angiraja[885]), — on the Kailāsa mountain, — and
16. Ajita[886]), — in the Crystal Wood of the Sages.

Each of the 16 is surrounded by numerous Arhats. Without passing away into Nirvāṇa [110 a.], they will act according to the Word of the Buddha and protect the Doctrine.

IV. $Acc_1 b_2 c_3 b_4 c_5$. The Acts performed for the Sake of the Doctrine by the Persons who had been foretold by the Buddha.

The Life of Nāgārjuna[887]).

Four hundred years after the Buddha had passed away, in the south, in the country of Vidarbha, there dwelt a rich Brāhmaṇa who had no children. It had been prophecied to him in a dream that, if he would invite 100 Brāhmaṇas to a religious feast, a son would be born to him. He acted accordingly, told his prayers

---

873) Lam-pa. 874) Mi-phyed-pa. 874a) Gser-can. 875) Xyl. Bhakula. 876) Dus-ldan-chen-po. 877) Rdo-rje-moḥi-bu. 878) Sgra-gcan-ḥdzin. 879) Dpal-bzaṅ. 880) Sbed-byed. 881) Klu-sde. 882) Nags-gnas. 883) Lam-phran. 884) Gser-gyi-beḥu. 885) Yan-lag-ḥbyuṅ. 886) Ma-pham-pa. 887) Cf. Grünwedel, Edelsteinmine, B. B. p. 12 sqq.

and, 10 months after, a child was born. When (the father) showed him to the sooth-sayers, the latter said that, although the marks (of the boy) were lucky, he could not live longer than 10 days. (The father) asked how one could help in this matter. — It was said that if he would invite 100 Brāhmaṇas to a religious feast, (the life of the boy) could be made to last 7 months and, by another invitation of 100 monks likewise to a religious feast, (the boy) could be made to live 7 years. But, said they, these is no means (to make him live) longer than that. (The father) accordingly did as he was told. When the end of the 7 years drew near, the parents who were unable to bear the sight of the dead body of their son (which they would soon have to behold), sent him to travel with a servant. So he gradually went and went and, having come to behold the face of Khasarpaṇa[888]), finally came to the gates of Nālanda[889]). There he began to recite the hymns of the Sāmaveda which were heard by the Brāhmaṇa Sāraha who was residing there. (The latter) led him in, and as (the boy) related to him the circumstances owing to which he was thus travelling about, the teacher told him that if he would become a monk, it could be possible to find a means (of prolonging his life). Accordingly, he took orders, (and his teacher) consecrated him on the magic circle of Amitāyus, the Conqueror of the Lord of Death, and made him recite the magic formula (of Amitāyus). Especially, he made him recite (these charms) during the evening and the night when his 7th year was to elapse and thus he became delivered from the Lord of Death. Then he showed himself to his parents who greatly rejoiced. After that he studied with the Brāhmaṇa Sāraha the texts of the Çrī-Guhyasamāja etc. with all the necessary instructions. Then he prayed Rāhulabhadra[890]), the abbot of Nālanda [110 b.] to be his preceptor, became regularly ordained and was known as the monk Çrīmān[891]).

Some time after, when he was occupying the post of the waiter (or verger)[892]) of the Congregation of Nālanda, a great famine (happened in that country). Çrīmān got from the intermediate continent[893]) the elixir producing gold, and, having obtained gold by means of it, was able to procure for the members of the Con-

[888]) The Xyl. has Khar-sa-pā-ṇi. Cf. Schiefner, Tārānātha, p. 144.
[889]) The Xyl. has here and further on throughout: Nālendra.
[890]) Sgra-gcan-ḥdzin-bzaṅ-po. [891]) Dpal-ldan. [892]) *Žal-ta-pa.*
[893]) *gliṅ-bar.*

gregation their noon-tide meals, so that they could keep the summer-fast. But the members of the Congregation asked: — How was it possible (for thee) to procure the noon-tide meals at a time when everything is wanting, when we are awaiting death and abide (in a country) wasted by famine? — And, when he told them about the manner (in which he produced the meals) as just mentioned, they said: — Without asking the permission of the Clergy, he has procured for it unrighteous means of livelihood. He must therefore be expelled from this place and, (in order to be purified from this guilt), construct 10 000 000 monasteries and sanctuaries. —

After that he secured by propitiation the mundane and supermundane magical powers. At that time, a monk named Çaṁkara[894]) having composed a treatise called *Nyāyālaṁkāra*[895]) consisting of 1 200 000 Çlokas, refuted everyone (who chanced to dispute with him). In order to subdue (this monk, Çrīmān) expounded the Doctrine at Nālanda. Whilst he was holding his sermon, 2 boys listened to his exposition of the Doctrine and then vanished beneath the earth. (The teacher) asked who these 2 were, and it was said, that they were Nāgas. The teacher bid them to fetch the mould of the Yakṣas for the temples and monuments he had to build. They, accordingly, informed the Nāga king, and he bade them to invite the teacher. The latter, having received the invitation and, knowing that (by accepting it), he would attain a great aim, descended into the region of the Nāgas and expounded the Doctrine there. The Nāgas then prayed him to stay with them, but he said that he had come to seek the clay with which to build the sanctuaries, and, likewise, in order to carry off (the Prajñāpāramitā-sūtra) of 100 000 Çlokas. There is no time for me to stay, — said he, — but I may come afterwards. So he took with him plenty of clay, the *Çatasāhasrikā*, and the *Svlpākṣara*[896]). It is said that a small part of the *Çatasāhasrikā* was not delivered to him by the Nāgas. Thereafter he built with that clay 10 000 000 sanctuaries etc. [111 a.] and the Nāgas became his friends. He thus subdued the greater part of them with the exception of some who were not present in the Nāga-region. Henceforth he was known by the name of Nāgārjuna. Thereafter, having produced gold at Puṇḍra-

[894]) *Bde-byed.* [895]) Or: Yuktyalaṁkāra = Rigs-paḥi-rgyan.

[896]) *Yi-ge-ñuṅ-ṅu.* One of the small Prajñā-pāramitā-sūtras (Kg. RGYUD XII).

vardhana[897]), he distributed abundant alms. An old Brāhmaṇa and his wife to whom he gave at that time much gold, became devoted to him. The old man made himself his attendant, heard the Doctrine (from him) and, having died, was reborn as the teacher Nāgabodhi[898]). Thereafter (the teacher) went to the eastern country of Paṭaveça where he built many temples. In the country of Radha he did the same and intended to transform into gold a rock resembling a bell, but was hindered by the gods. After that he went to the northern continent Kuru and, on the way there, in the town called Salama, (he met with) a boy called Jetaka, to whom he prophecied, by means of palmistry, that he would be a king. Having come to the continent of the Kuru, he hung his clothes on the branch of a tree and washed. As his clothes were then carried away by the Kurus, and he protested saying: — These clothes are mine, — they returned that in their language and according to their views "mine" was the same as "ours". Having fulfilled his mission there, he departed. In the meantime, the boy mentioned before, had become king, and presented Nāgārjuna with many precious jewels. (Nāgārjuna) in exchange delivered to him "the Rosary of Jewels of the Doctrine" *(Ratnāvalī)*.

(In sum) the acts performed by this teacher for the sake of the Doctrine are as follows: — He became the attendant of the clergy, built a great number of sanctuaries and temples, made at Vajrāsana an enclosure like a diamond net, and constructed the edifice for the sanctuary of Çrīdhānya-kaṭaka[899]).

His activity in the field of science is as follows: — In metaphysics his chief works are: —

Those which have as their principal subject-matter the philosophical system of the Mādhyamika, shunning both the extremities. These are: 1. The collection of the Mādhyamika-stotras (in which the doctrine) is expounded in accordance with Scripture and 2. The (6) fundamental Mādhyamika treatises[900]) where the teaching is vindicated by logical means.

The works which are dedicated to the practical side of the Doctrine are: — The *Sūtra-samuccaya*[901]), teaching in accordance with Scripture, the *Svapna-cintāmaṇi-parikathā*[902]), demonstrating

---

[897]) Li-kha-ra-çiṅ-ḥphel. [898]) Kluḥi-byaṅ-chub.

[899]) Dpal Ḥbras-spuṅs. [900]) Cf. vol. I. p. 50, 51.

[901]) Mdo-kun-las-btus-pa, Tg. MDO. XXX. 172 b.—253 a. (Pek.)

[902]) Rmi-lam-yid-bžin-gyi-nor-bu. Tg. MDO. XXX. 219—221.

by logical means, purifying the minds of the Mahāyānists and awakening to life the element of saintliness[903]) of the Çrāvakas. [111 b.]

The work demonstrating the chief principles of the conduct of householders is the *Suhṛllekha*[904]), and that which is chiefly dedicated to the conduct of monks is the *Bodhigaṇa*[905]).

In the division of the Tantras his works are: — The *Tantrasamuccaya*[906]), — a brief exposition of the theoretical and the practical side (of the Tantras), the *Bodhicitta-vivaraṇa*[907]) where the theory is clearly exposed, the *Piṇḍīkṛta-sādhana*[908]) demonstrating the Initial Development[909]) in an abridged form, the *Sūtra-melāpaka*[910]), the *Maṇḍalavidhi* of 20 verses, the *Pañcakrama*[911]) demonstrating the Final Development[912]), etc. —

Moreover, we have by him medical works as the *Yogaçataka* etc.[913]) In the science of worldly policy[914]) we have his *Jana-poṣaṇa-bindu*[915]) containing the precepts delivered to inferiors, and the *Prajñā-çataka*[916]), consisting of instructions delivered for ministers. Then we have the *Ratnâvalī*[917]) in which the theoretical and practical part of the Mahāyānistic Doctrine are demonstrated together for the use of kings. Furthermore, he has composed the *Pratītya-samutpāda-cakra*[918]), the *Dhūpa-yoga-ratna-mālā*[919]), works on alchemistry and others. All these are independent treatises. —

---

[903]) *rigs = gotra.*

[904]) Bçes-sbriṅ. Tg. MDO. XXXIII. 74—81. (Pek.).

[905]) Byaṅ-chub-kyi-tshogs. [906]) Rgyud-kun-las-btus.

[907]) Byaṅ-chub-sems-ḥgrel. Tg. RGYUD. XXXIII. 42—50 (Pek.); also MDO. XXXIII. 221—226.

[908]) Sgrub-thabs-mdor-byas. Tg. RGYUD. XXXIII. 1—12 (Pek.).

[909]) *bskyed-rim = utpatti-krama.*

[910]) Mdo-bsre. Full title. Çrī-Guhyasamāja-mahā-yoga-tantra-utpatti-krama-sādhanam Sūtra-melāpakam nāma (Rnal-ḥbyor-chen-poḥi rgyud Dpal Gsaṅ-ba-ḥdus-paḥi bskyed-paḥi-rim-paḥi bsgom-paḥi thabs Mod-daṅ-bsres-pa). Tg. RGYUD. XXXIII. 12—17. (Pek.)

[911]) Rim-pa-lṅa-pa. Tg. RGYUD. XXXIII. 50—64 (Pek.).

[912]) *rdzogs-rim = saṁpanna-krama.*

[913]) Sbyor-ba-brgya-pa. Tg. MDO. CXVIII. 1—5 (Pek.).

[914]) *lugs-kyi-bstan-bcos = nīti-çāstra.*

[915]) Skye-bo-gso-thigs. Tg. MDO. CXXIII.

[916]) Çes-rab-brgya-pa. Ibid. and XXX. Cf. vol. I.

[917]) Or: Mādhyamika-ratnâvalī. Tg. MDO. XCIV.

[918]) Rten-ḥbrel-gyi ḥkhor-lo. Tg. MDO. CXXIII. 34—42. (Pek.).

[919]) Spos-sbyor. Ibid. fol. 29.

The Commentaries written by him on other works are the *Guhyasamāja-tantra-ṭīkā*[920]), the *Çālistambaka-kārikā*[921]) and others. —As concerns the *Caturmudrā-niçcaya*[922]) it is said in the *Āmnāya-mañjarī*[923]) that it hat not been composed by Nāgārjuna. The teacher Prajñākaramati, in his Commentary on the *Bodhicaryāvatāra* says that the teacher Nāgārjuna has likewise composed a Compendium of Discipline[923a]). In such a way did Nāgārjuna act for the sake of the Doctrine for 600 years.

At that time the king Antīvāhana[924]) or Udayanabhadra[925]) had a son, the prince Çaktimān[926]). When his mother gave him a very fine mantle, he said: —This will be of use to me at the time when I shall assume the royal power. To this the mother said: — Thou shalt not come to reign. —Thy father and the teacher Nāgārjuna have found out a means of producing an elixir securing longevity. (The duration of life of thy father) is to be the same as that of the teacher. [112 a.] (Upon hearing this, the youth) went to Çrīparvata, to the place where the teacher Nāgārjuna was abiding. The latter raised his head and began to preach the Doctrine to him. The youth tried to cut off (the teacher's) head with his sword, but failed, whereupon the teacher said: — An insect has perished (before), having been cut down by me with a halm of Kuça grass. The consequence[927]) (of this deed) is lasting upon me. Owing to it my head can be cut off with a Kuça halm. The youth, accordingly cut it off in such a way, (and after he had done that), from the foundation of the neck there was heard a verse: —

I shall now depart to the region of Sukhavatī,
But (afterwards) I am to enter this body again.

The youth then went away, having carried off the head. But (subsequently) a female yakṣa took possession of it and deposited it within the distance of a yojana (from the body). The head and

---

920) Gsaṅ-ḥdus-ḥgrel-pa. Tg. RGYUD. XXVII.

921) Sa-lu-ljaṅ-paḥi-mdo-tshigs-su-bcad-pa-bsdus-pa. Tg. MDO. XXXIII. 213—216 and XXXIV. 22—25 (Pek.).

922) Phyag-rgya-bži-pa. Tg. RGYUD. XLVI. 82—84.

923) Man-ṅag-sñe-ma. Full title: Çrī-Sampuṭa-tantra-rāja-ṭīkā Āmnāya-mañjarī-nāma. The work of Abhayākaragupta, Tg. RGYUD. XIX.

923a) Bslab-pa-kun-las-btus-pa = Çīkṣā-samuccaya.

924) Mthar-ḥgro-žon. Cf. Schiefner, Tāranātha, p. 304.

925) Bde-spyod-bzaṅ-po. 926) Nus-ldan.

927) *rnam-smin* = *vipāka*.

the body did not decay, but every year drew nearer to each other. Finally they united and again worked for the weal of the Doctrine and the living beings. (In the name) Nāgārjuna, Nāga (has the following signification): — 1. Born from (that ocean) which is the Essence, the Plane of the Absolute[928]) (just as the real Nāga is born in the sea), 2. not abiding in the 2 limits or extreme views of Eternalism[929]) and Nihilism[930]), (just as the real Nāga knows no limits as regards his abode), 3. securing the possession of the treasury of the Jewels of Scripture (just as the Nāga possesses immense wealth in gold and jewels), 4. endowed with an insight (that is like fire), burning down and illuminating (akin to the fiery eyes of the Nāga).

Arjuna has the meaning of "he who has secured power". Accordingly, the teacher is Arjuna since he is: 1. The guardian, the ruler of the kingdom of the Doctrine and 2. the subduer of the hosts of enemies, that is of all the sinful powers of this world. Being united, these two component parts form the compound name Nāgārjuna. It is said accordingly in the *Prasannapadā*[931]):

> I bow before that Nāgārjuna who has rejected
> The adherence to the two extreme points of view,
> Who has become born in the ocean of the Supreme Buddha's Wisdom,
> And has, out of mercy, exposed all the depths
> Of the treasury of the Highest Doctrine[932]), as he has cognized (it himself)[933]).
> The fires of whose Doctrine consume that fuel
> Which is (every) hostile, disagreeing view,
> And dispell, up to this very day
> The mental darkness of the world[934]).
> Whose incomparable wisdom and words are like a mass of arrows,

---

[928]) *chos-dbyiṅs = dharma-dhātu.* [929]) *rtag-mthaḥ = çāçvata-anta.*

[930]) *chad-mthaḥ = uccheda-anta.*

[931]) Tshig-gsal. B. B. p. 1. Cf. also Conception of Buddhist Nirvāṇa, p. 81.

[932]) I read acc. to the Tib. text *dam-chos-mdzod-kyi = saddharma-koṣasya.* Cf. Conception of Buddhist Nirvāṇa, Corrigenda.

[933]) *yo'nta-dvayāvāsa-vidhūta-vāsah saṁbuddha-dhī-sāgara-labdha-janmā / saddharma-kosasya gambhīra-bhāvaṁ yathānubuddhaṁ kṛpayā jagāda. / /*

[934]) *yasya darçana-tejāṁsi paravādi-matendhanam / dahanty adyāpi lokasya mānasāni tamāṁsi ca //*

Perfectly secure (for him) the victory and the sovereignty
in the 3 Spheres of Existence
Over all the world of converts including the gods,
And vanquish those hosts of enemies, — (the forces of)
Phenomenal Existence[935]. —

[112 b.] And[936]: —

Composed by Nāgārjuna, the Bodhisattva
Who has departed to Sukhavatī, after having
Let his head be cut off and delivered it to him
Who had come in request of it.

Some authorities maintain that in the *Mahāmegha-sūtra* the following is to be read: — 400 years after I have passed away, this Licchavi will become a monk called Nāga and will propagate my Doctrine. Finally, in the world called Prasannaprabhā[937]) he will become the Buddha called Jñānākaraprabha[938]). Now we read in the *Mahāmegha*: — In the south, in the country called Ṛṣila[939]) will appear a king named Vipatticikitsaka[940]). When the latter will be 80 years of age, the Highest Doctrine is to undergo destruction, and only remnants of it will be left. At that time, on the northern shore of the rivulet called Sundarabhūti[941]) near the village Mahāvāluka[942]), the dwelling-place of virtuous people, on the ground belonging to the Vaiçyas Bra-go-can (?) a Licchavi youth who by his appearance causes delight to all living beings, will be born, bear my name and expound the Doctrine of the Buddha. This youth, in the presence of the Buddha Nāgakulapradīpa[943]), will make the vow to give up his life for the sake of the Doctrine and the Teaching of the Lord. — It is he who is to propagate the Doctrine. — So is it to be read, but it is not clear, whether (this passage) really refers to Nāgārjuna. Some are of the opinion that (the words "bearing my name" refer to) the reli-

---

[935]) *yasyā'sama-jñāna-vacaḥ-çaraughā nighnanti niḥçeṣa-bhavāri-senāṁ / tridhātu-rājya-çriyam ādadhānā vineya-lokasya sadevakasya // Nāgārjunāya praṇipatya tasmai* . . .

[936]) This verse is not contained in Prof. de la Vallée Poussin's edition of the Prasannapadā.

[937]) Daṅ-baḥi-ḥod.

[938]) Ye-çes-ḥbyuṅ-gnas-ḥod. This prophecy of the Mahāmegha-sūtra is quoted in the Mādhyamika-avatāra-bhāṣya B. B. 76. 17—77. 4.

[939]) Draṅ-sroṅ-byi-boḥi-yul. [940]) Rgud-pa-gso-ba.

[941]) Mdzes-ḥbyor. [942]) Bye-ma-chen-po. [943]) Klu-rigs-sgron-ma.

gious name of Nāgārjuna which is (said to have been) Çākyamitra[944]). This however must be scrutinized. It is said, moreover, that according to *Mahābherī-sūtra*[945]), Nāgārjuna has been foretold to attain the 8th Stage, but this must likewise be examined. —

The Teacher Āryadeva.

The (spiritual) son of Nāgārjuna was the teacher Āryadeva. The latter was miraculously born[946]) *in the island of Siṁhala in* the petals of a lotus-flower and was adopted by the king of that country. When he grew up, he went to the place were the teacher Nāgārjuna was residing, entered his school [113 a.], and became proficient in all the branches of science and all the heterodox and orthodox philosophical systems. At that time there lived a heretical teacher called Mātṛceṭa[947]) who had propitiated the god Maheçvara and was exceedingly powerful, so thaṭ no living being could match him. This teacher, having caused great harm to the Doctrine of Buddha and seduced the greater part (of the people) to the heretical teachings, came to Nālanda. The Nālanda monks sent a message to Nāgārjuna who was residing on the Çrīpavrata. The teacher Āryadeva (who was abiding with him) said that he would subdue (the heretic) and went (to Nālanda). On the way there the goddess of a tree begged him to grant her an eye, and he accordingly presented her with one of his eyes. Thereafter, as he had vanquished the heretic, (the monks said): — Who is this one-eyed? — Āryadeva replied: —

> The Terrific One[948]), though he has 3 eyes,
> Cannot perceive the Absolute Truth;
> Indra, though endowed with 1000 eyes,
> Is likewise unable to see it.
> But Āryadeva, who has only one eye,
> Has the intuition of the true Essence
> Of all the 3 Spheres of Existence.

(The heretical teacher) was vanquished by (the words of) the Doctrine, was converted to Buddhism, and became a great Paṇḍit. —

Tradition says that the teacher (Āryadeva) has attained the 8th Stage. But, as the *Mañjuçrī-mūla-tantra*[949]) speaks of him: —

---

944) Çā-kya-bçes-gñen. 945) Rṅa-bo-cheḥi-mdo.

946) *rdzus-te-skyes-pa = upapāduka.*

947) Ma-khol. 948) Maheçvara. 949) Cf. above.

Though not a Saint he will bear the name of a Saint, — this must be accurately examined. —

This teacher has composed the following works: —

1. The *Mādhyamika-catuḥçatikā*[950]), demonstrating the meaning of Non-substantiality in detail.

2. The *Mādhyamika-hastavāla-prakaraṇa*[951]), — an abridged exposition (of the same subject).

3. The *Skhalita-pramathana-yukti-hetu-siddhi*[952]), refuting the challenges of opponents.

4. The *Jñāna-sāra-samuccaya*[953]), demonstrating the chief characteristic points of the philosophical[954]) and the Tantric systems.

In the Tantric literature his works are: —

Those containing the exposition of the theoretical part of Tantra, as:

1. The *Caryā-melayana-pradīpa*[955]), on the foundation of the mixed Sūtra and Tantra Scripture.

2. The *Citta-āvaraṇa-viçodhana*[956]), demonstrating the same subject by logical means. [113 b.]

3. The *Catuḥ-pīṭha-tantra-rāja-maṇḍala-upāyikā-vidhi-sāra-samuccaya*[957]), referring to the magical rights for (attaining) the power of bringing living beings to maturity.

4. The *Catuḥpīṭha-sādhana*[958]), demonstrating the Initial Development[959]).

5. The *Jñāna-ḍākinī-sādhana*[960]).

6. The *Eka-druma-pañjikā*[961]), demonstrating the magic rites, the offerings, the final Development[962]), etc.

---

[950]) Dbuma-bži-brgya-pa. Tg. MDO. XVIII.

[951]) Dbu-ma-lag-paḥi-tshad. Ibid. 24 a. 8—b. 5. (Pek.)

[952]) Ḥkhrul-pa-zlog-paḥi gtan-tshigs-grub-pa. Ibid. 20 b.—24 a.

[953]) Ye-çes-sñiṅ-po-kun-las-btus. Ibid. 29—31.

[954]) *mtshan-ñid.*

[955]) Spyod-pa-bsdus-paḥi-sgron-ma. Tg. RGYUD. XXXIII. 121 b—127.

[956]) Sems-kyi-sgrib-sbyoṅ. Tg. RGYUD. XXXIII. 121 b.—127.

[957]) Gdan-bžiḥi dkyil-chog-sñiṅ-po-mdor-bsags. Tg. RGYUD. XXIII. 142—172.

[958]) Gdan-bžiḥi-sgrub-thabs. Ibid. 91—101.

[959]) *bskyed-rim* = *utpatti-krama.*

[960]) Ye-çes-mkhaḥ-ḥgro-maḥi-sgrub-thabs. Or: Jñāneçvarī-sādhana. Tg. RGYUD. XXIII. 129—141.

[961]) Çiṅ-gcig-gi dkaḥ-ḥgrel. Ibid. 173—177.

[962]) *rdzogs-rim* = *saṁpanna-krama.*

It is said moreover that he is the author of the *Pradīpa-uddyotana-abhisaṁdhi-prakāçika-vyākhyā-ṭīkā*[963]), but we must examine whether this is chronologically correct or not. —

The Teacher Nāgabodhi.

As concerns the teacher Nāgabodhi who was likewise the pupil of the master Nāgārjuna, tradition says that he was versed in all the heterodox and orthodox philosophical systems, beheld the countenance of his tutelary deity and attained the magic power of longevity, owing to which he abides up to this day on the Çrī-parvata. He has composed the *Guhyasamāja-maṇḍala-vidhi*[964]), the *Pañca-krama-ṭīkā*[965]) and many other works. —

The Teacher Candragomin.

The teacher Candragomin was born in the east, in Bengal, and, whilst still a youth, became greatly learned. Having married Tārā, the daughter of the king of Vārendra, he lived with her (for some time). Once, as the maid-servant was calling his wife: Tārā!, he pondered and came to the insight that it was unsuitable that the wife and the tutelary deity (who was the goddess Tārā) should bear one name. He accordingly prayed (his wife) to forgive him, and made his intention to depart. He was however seized by his friends who asked him why he was going away and he told them the reason why. The king came to know this and said: — If he will not live with my daughter, throw him into the Ganges. — The hangmen, accordingly, prepared to cast him into the river, but the teacher addressed a prayer to Tārā, and the latter miraculously produced an island in the middle of the Ganges, showed her countenance quite clearly, and blessed him. And up to this day, tradition calls that spot "the island of Candra"[966]). Thereafter he was rescued by fishermen and, the king of Vārendra having become devoted to him, he grew to be an object of reverence and finally came to Nālanda. There he was asked what sciences he knew. He replied that he knew the grammar of Pāṇini [114 a.],

---

[963]) Sgron-gsal-gyi ḥgrel-bçad. Tg. RGYUD. XXX and XXXI.
[964]) Gsaṅ-ḥdus-kyi dkyil-chog. Tg. RGYUD. XXXIII. 149—165.
[965]) Tg. RGYUD .XXXIV. 174—212.
[966]) Cf. Schiefner, Tārānātha, p. 150, 151.

the *Mañjuçrī-nāma-saṁgīti*[967]), and the hymn of 150 verses[968]). (The monks) accordingly understood that he was greatly learned, bade him welcome and bestowed great honour upon him. At that time he composed many short tracts on medicine and the like. But the most revered Lord of the World[969]) himself bade him to commence the composition of numerous Mahāyānistic treatises, and after that he wrote the Commentary on the *Candrapradīpa*[970]), the *Kāya-traya-avatāra* and many other works.

At that time there was (in Nālanda) a pupil, a monk of the Kṣatriya race who had trespassed, and had committed many sinful deeds. In order to subdue (this monk, Candragomin) wrote the *Çiṣya-lekha*[971]). He has moreover composed a grammatical treatise consisting of 32 chapters and 700 çlokas[972]), in accordance with the rules of Pāṇini. The supplementary parts of this work are: —

The *Dhātu-sūtra*[973]),
The *Upasarga-vṛtti*[974]),
The *Varṇa-sūtra*[975]),
The *Uṇādi-sūtra*[976]),
Rules concerning the case- and the tense-terminations etc.

In such a manner he subdued the trespassing pupil. Once he chanted a hymn in praise of Mañjughoṣa, and the head of the latter's statue bent down and listened. (The hymn of Candragomin) accordingly became known as the "Praise of Mañjughoṣa with the bent neck"[977]).

At that time the teacher Candrakīrti had composed a fine grammatical treatise in verse called *Samantabhadra*[978]). Candragomin thought that, as his work was not so good, it should be destroyed, and threw it into a well. But the Lord of the World said to him: — Thou hast composed (this treatise), being possessed

---

[967]) (Ḥjam-dpal)-mtshan-brjod. Tg. RGYUD. LIX. Cf. Schiefner, Tāranātha, p. 152. [968]) Ibid.

[969]) Rje-btsun-ḥjig-rten-dbaṅ-phyug = Bhaṭṭāraka Lokeçvara, i. e. Avalokita. [970]) Zla-ba-sgron-maḥi ḥgrel-pa.

[971]) Slob-ma-la-spriṅ-ba. Tg. MDO. XXXIII.

[972]) The fundamental Vyākaraṇa-sūtra of Candragomin (Tg. MDO. CXVI. 1—36) has 6 chapters.

[973]) Dbyiṅs-kyi-mdo. Tg. MDO. CXXXII. 312—323.

[974]) Tg. MDO. CXVI. 36—41.

[975]) Yi-geḥi-mdo. Ibid. 41—42.

[976]) Ibid. 365—369. [977]) Cf. Schiefner, Tāranātha, p. 153.

[978]) Kun-tu-bzaṅ-po. Cf. Cordier, Index du Bstan-ḥgyur, II. p. 488.

of high altruistic thoughts[979]), (owing to which) it will be of great help (to the living beings). Therefore draw it out again. This Candragomin did. The well (into which he had thrown the book) became known as the well of Candra, and it was said that he who drank from it became possessed of acute intellectual faculty[980]). Thereafter (Candragomin) entered upon a controversy with Candrakīrti. After having asked the Lord of the World what answer he was to give that day, [114 b.] he accordingly replied in such a manner. Candrakīrti became possessed of doubt, hastened out and saw the Lord of the World as he was teaching (Candragomin) how to answer. — O great Saint, — prayed Candrakīrti, — do not do so this day. — And (the form of Avalokiteçvara turned to stone, remaining with the forefinger erected. Up to this day (that statue of Avalokiteçvara) is known as "the most merciful with the raised fore-finger"[981]). In such a manner Candragomin, possessed of great merit, exercised his activity as a guardian of the Doctrine. —

The Teacher Candrakīrti.

Candrakīrti (in his turn) was born in the south in Samana. Having got thoroughly trained in the subjects of the Sūtras and Tantras, and relying upon the word of Nāgārjuna and Āryadeva[982]), he became a great Paṇḍit, was blessed during 500 successive births and had the power of milking a cow that was drawn on a picture[983]) as well as that of hurling a column of stone without touching it with his hand.

He has composed the Commentaries on the Mādhyamika treatises (of Nāgārjuna) and on the *Catuḥçatikā*[984]), — the main text of the *Mādhyamika-avatāra* and its Commentary. The most celebrated of his works are the (2) Commentaries which are spoken of as "those which resemble the sun and the moon". These are: The Commentary on the *Mūla-mādhyamika*[985]) called the *Prasanna-padā*[986]) and the Commentary on the *Guhya-samāja-tantra*, bearing the title of *Pradīpa-uddyotana*[986a]). These are known as "the

---

[979]) *lhag-paḥi-bsam-pa* = *adhyāçaya*.

[980]) Cf. Schiefner, Tāranātha, p. 155. [981]) Ibid. p. 154.

[982]) Klu-sgrub yab-sras. [983]) Cf. Schiefner, Tāranātha, p. 148.

[984]) Tg. MDO. XXIV. 33 b.—273 b.

[985]) The Mūla-mādhyamika is called here by the abridged title Rtsa-çe i. e. Rtsa-baḥi-çes-rab = Prajñā-mūla. [986]) Tshig-gsal.

[986a]) Gsaṅ-ḥdus-ḥgrel-pa Sgron-gsal. Tg. RGYUD. XXVIII. 1—233.

2 most clear works". Now, Buddhapālita and Candrakīrti are the chief representatives of the Mādhyamika-prāsangika school[987]) or of the Loka-prasiddhi-varga-cāri-mādhyamikas[988]). The teacher Bhavya and the rest are the Mādhyamika-sautrāntikas[989]). Jñānagarbha[990]), Çrīgupta[990a]), Çāntirakṣita[991]), Kamalaçīla[992]), Haribhadra[993]) and others belong to the school of the Yogācāra-Mādhyamikas[994]). The theory of Nāgārjuna and Āryadeva has been explained (from the standpoint of these different branches of the Mādhyamika school). It is said in the ***Prasannapadā***[995]):

Nāgārjuna was endowed with the instructions of Rāhulabhadra, and Āryadeva has followed the word (of Nāgārjuna). They have clearly expounded the precepts of the Doctrine during a ong period of time. The pupils of these have analysed (this Mādhyamika) teaching and have become fully possessed of a discrim native mind. These have likewise vanquished all the heretics [115 a.] and have for a long time expounded the Doctrine[996]).

---

[987]) Dbu-ma-thal-ḥgyur-ba.

[988]) Ḥjig-rten-grags-sde-spyod-paḥi dbu-ma-pa.

[989]) Mdo-sde-spyod-paḥi-dbu-ma-pa.

[990]) Ye-çes-sñiṅ-po. [990a]) Dpal-sbas. [991]) Ži-ba-ḥtsho.

[992]) Padmaḥi-ṅaṅ-tshul. [993]) Seṅ-ge-bzaṅ-po.

[994]) Rnal-ḥbyor-spyod-paḥi-dbu-ma-pa. [995]) Cf. above note 936.

[996]) In the work of Tsoṅ-kha-pa's pupil Khai-ḍub (Mkhas-grub) called Stoṅ-thun-bskal-bzaṅ-mig-ḥbyed (Tsaṅ edition vol. I. 37 a. 1 sqq.) we have a short account concerning the Mādhyamika-ācāryas and their different points of view. It is said as follows: — The standpoint of Nāgārjuna and Āryadeva was that of the Prāsangikas. However (in their works) no direct discrimination between the Svātantrika and Prāsangika point of view and no refutation of the former has been made. Subsequently, the teacher Buddhapālita composed his Commentary on the Mūla-mādhyamika and explained the theory of Nāgārjuna and Āryadeva from the Prāsangika standpoint. After that the teacher Bhāvaviveka likewise composed a Commentary on the Mūla-mādhyamika (the Prajñāpradīpa) and made many refutations concerning the points commented by Buddhapālita. It is he who has first founded the Svātantrika system. The followers of each of these 2 (schools i. e. of Buddhapālita and Bhāvaviveka) are accordingly called by the earlier Tibetan authors "the Mādhyamikas adhering to the different fractions" (Phyogs-ḥdzin-paḥi Dbu-ma-pa = Pakṣa-grāhiṇo Mādhyamikāḥ). Bhāvaviveka has moreover composed independent works of his own, viz. the main aphorisms of the Mādhyamika-hṛdaya (Dbu-ma-sñiṅ-po) with the auto-commentary Tarkajvālā (Rtog-ge-ḥbar-ba). In these he has expounded the Svātantrika theories and the activity of the Bodhisattvas in detail. Thereupon the teacher Jñānagarbha composed the Svātantrika work Mādhyamika-satya-dvaya (or: Satya-dvaya-vibhanga). This teacher, as well as Bhāvaviveka are

Āryadeva's pupil Mātṛceṭa has likewise composed a great number of treatises and has acted for the sake of the Doctrine. We do not however give his biography, for fear that it would take too much place.

The Biography of the Brothers Āryāsanga and Vasubandhu[997]).

(It is known) that the Highest Doctrine had 3 times suffered from foes. For the first time (this happened as follows): — An old woman belonging to the heretics once said: — When the wooden gong of the Buddhists is beaten, from its sound the words "confound! destroy!" [998]) can be distinctly heard. One must see whether such sounds are harmful for us or not. An investigation was accordingly made and the following meaning apprehended: —

Let the brains of the false heretics be confounded
By the beating of this drum of the 3 Jewels,
Who are worshipped by the gods, the Nāgas and the Yakṣas!

(The enraged heretics) then made war (upon the Buddhists) and destroyed the church[999]).

Thereafter, (when it had been restored again) and was to a certain extent thriving, it happened that the king of Central India sent to the Persian king[1000]) a garment of very fine cloth as a present. But, as on the part (of that garment) which was to cover the heart, there was something resembling a foot-print,

---

the representatives of the system which maintains the reality of external objects from the Empirical Standpoint and does not admit the existence of introspective perception (*raṅ-rig* = *sva-saṁvedana*). Thereafter the teacher Çāntirakṣita composed the Mādhyamika-alaṁkāra and laid the foundation to another school of the Mādhyamikas which denies the Empirical Reality of the External World, acknowledges the introspective perception, but on the other hand does not consider consciousness to have an Ultimate Reality (differing in this from the Yogācāra-vijñānavādins). The Mādhyamika-ālokā and the 3 Bhāvanā-krama of Kamalaçīla, as well as the texts of Vimuktasena, Haribhadra, Buddhajñāna-pāda, Abhayākaragupta, etc. agree with Çāntirakṣita in the main standpoint (which is that of the Yogācāra-mādhyamika-svātantrika, whereas Bhāvaviveka and Jñānagarbha express the point of view of the Sautrāntika-mādhyamika-svātantrikas). — As we have seen, Bu-ton counts Jñānagarbha among the Yogācāra-mādhyamikas.

997) Thogs-med-sku-mched. 998) *ḥgems.*

999) Cf. Schiefner, Tārānātha, p. 81. 1000) Stag-gzig-gi-rgyal-po.

(the Persian king) said that this was an evil charm to harm him, invaded (Central India) and destroyed (the Buddhist temples)[1001].

Thereupon, after the Doctrine had again enjoyed a period of some prosperity, it happened that 2 heretical beggars came to a Buddhist monastery in search of alms. As (the novices) poured a shower of wash-water upon them, they became enraged and, having propitiated the sun, burned down many Buddhist temples with the sacred texts contained in them[1002]. At that time a woman of the Brāhmaṇa caste called Prasannaçīlā[1003] had the following thought: —Three times have foes brought harm to the Abhidharma which is the foundation of the Teaching, and no one who would be able to expound it can be found. I, being a woman, am likewise incapable of doing it. But, if I give birth to sons, I will make of them propagators (of the Doctrine). Accordingly, from her union with a Kṣatriya, (a son named) Asanga, and, (later on) from another union with a Brāhmaṇa, (a second son named) Vasubandhu were born. [115 b.][1004]. The mother drew on their tongues the letter A and performed all the other rites in order to secure for them an acute intellectual faculty.

When they grew older, they asked about the business of their fathers. But the mother said: — I have not born you for that. You must purify your minds and expound the Doctrine. — Accordingly, the younger brother departed to Kashmir to the teacher Sanghabhadra. The elder in his turn became possessed of the intention of propagating the Doctrine, after having secured the help of Maitreya. In order to propitiate (the latter) he took up his abode in the cave of the mountain Kukkuṭapādaparvata. For 3 years he made his propitiation, but as he did not see the slightest sign of success, he was greatly disappointed. Having gone out, he saw an old man who was making needles out of a pole of iron by rubbing it with a piece of cotton. How have the needles been produced? — asked he. The old man replied: —

> If a man possessed of moral strength
> Wishes to accomplish something,
> He never meets with failure,
> However difficult the work may be.

[1001]) Cf. Schiefner, Tāranātha, p. 94. [1002]) Ibid. p. 95 sqq.

[1003]) Gsal-baḥi-tshul-khrims. Schiefner has: Prakāçaçīlā.

[1004]) Cf. Schiefner, Tāranātha, p. 107 sqq.

If he does not lose his patience,
He can break mountains with the palm of his hand.

Accordingly, (Asanga) continued his propitiation for another 6 years, and thus spent altogether 9 years (in his meditation). Then he went out and saw how a rock was gradually destroyed by drops of water and by the wings of birds (that constantly touched it in their flight). But, after he had propitiated for 12 years and saw no sign (of success) he became full of grief and went out again. As he was about to go away, he saw a dog; the lower part of its body was eaten by worms, but the upper part (was still free) and it was barking and biting. (Asanga) became full of Commiseration and, seeing that if he were to remove the worms, the latter would perish and if not, — the dog would die, he became resolved to cut flesh from his body and remove (the worms) by attracting them with it. Accordingly, he went to the town called Acinta and, having pledged his mendicant's staff, obtained a golden knife. (With this) he cut off flesh from his body. Then, thinking that if he would take (the worms) with his hand, they would nervertheless perish, he shut his eyes and was about to take them off with his tongue. (At that moment) the dog disappeared, and he beheld Maitreya, full of light. (And thus did he adress him): —

O my father, my unique refuge,
I have exerted myself in a hundred different ways,
But nevertheless no result was to be seen.
Wherefore have the rain-clouds and the might of the ocean,
Come only now when, tormented by violent pain,
I am no longer thirsting? [116 a.] —

With such efforts have I tried to propitiate (thee), but not even a sign did appear. Scant is therefore thy Commiseration. — In such a way did he reproach (Maitreya). The Venerable One said: —

Though the king of the gods sends down rain,
A bad seed is unable to grow.
Though the Buddhas may appear (in this world)
He who is unworthy cannot partake of the bliss[1005]).

I was here from the very beginning, but thou couldst not see me, owing to thy own obscurations. Now, as great Commiseration

---

[1005]) Abhisamayālaṁkāra VIII. 10. — ***varṣaty api hi parjanye naivā' bījaṁ prarohati / samutpāde' pi buddhānāṁ nā' bhavyo bhadram açnute //***

has become originated in thee, thou hast got purified and canst now behold me. (In order to see) that this is really so, raise me up on thy shoulder and show me (to the people). — Asanga did so, and as Maitreya could not be perceived (by anyone else, Asanga) believed (that his words were true).

Now, what is thy desire? — (asked Maitreya). Asanga replied: — I am searching for instructions, how to expound the Mahāyānistic Doctrine. — Then take hold of my robes, — said (Maitreya) and they rose up to the Tuṣita heavens. (There Asanga) is said to have resided for 1 moment according to the time-calculation of the gods, which moment is equal to 50 or 53 human years. The scholiast of the *Yogacaryā-bhūmi* in his turn says that he resided there 6 months and heard (the Doctrine of Maitreya). Accordingly he listened to (the exposition of) the Prajñāpāramitā-sūtras, the great *Yogacaryā-bhūmi*, and numerous Mahāyānistic Sūtras. Then he prayed (Maitreya) to compose a treatise elucidating the meaning of these texts and, as a consequence, the 5 works of Maitreya were delivered to him. Such was the state of things according to the teacher Haribhadra and others. In the *Marmakaumudī*[1006]) we read: — After the (Mahāyānistic) Scripture had been rehearsed, (there were topics) contained in it, which were of exclusively profound meaning and exceedingly hard to apprehend. As there was no possibility of understanding (these subjects), the Saint Maitreya, guided by mercy, in order to make them intelligible, has elucidated them by means of the *Abhisamayālaṁkāra-kārikā-çāstra.* There are some who say that Maitreya has composed (this treatise) later at the request of Āryāsanga. Others say that Haribhadra and the rest commit an error in affirming this, and that it was communicated (to Asanga) after having been composed before. This opinion of the others (we do not share).

Moreover, some consider that [116 b.] according to the point of view of the teacher Ratnākaraçānti, the *Abhidharmasamuccaya*

[1006]) The work of Abhayākaragupta, one of the 21 Commentaries on the Abhisamayālaṁkāra. Tg. MDO. XI. 3 b. 5—4 a. 1. Cf. also Haribhadra's Abhisamyālaṁkārālokā, MS. Minaev, 57 a. 16—b. 1. sqq. — *vidita-samasta-pravacana-artha-labdha-adhigamo' py Āryāsangaḥ punarukta-bāhulyena apunarukta-pradeçe' pi pratyeka-pada-vyavaccheda-adarçanena gāmbhīryāc ca Prajñāpāramitārtham unnetum açaktau daurmanasyam anuprāptaḥ / tatas tam uddiçya Maitreyeṇa bhagavatā Prajñāpāramitā-sūtraṁ vyākhyātam Abhisamayālaṁkāra-kārikā-çāstraṁ ca kṛtam / tac chrutvā punar Āryāsangena Ācārya-Vasubandhu-prabhṛtibhiç ca vyākhyātam //*

was likewise composed by Maitreya. However we follow the usual tradition, viz. that Maitreya is the author only of the 5 treatises bearing his name.

Having heard (the exposition of these treatises, Asanga) returned into the human world. Thereafter he composed his great treatise in 5 divisions[1007]) in which the Mahāyānistic Code, i. e. the chief subjects of the Yogācāra Doctrine, or, (otherwise) all the 3 Codes of Scripture have been thoroughly dealt with. The contents of this work is summarized in the 2 short treatises likewise composed by him[1008]), the ***Abhidharmasamuccaya*** being a summary (of the teaching that is) common to all the 3 Vehicles. Some say that, since the teacher Abhayākaragupta calls the ***Abhidharmasamuccaya*** a Mahāyānistic treatise, it is not proper to consider it to be a compendium relating to all the 3 Vehicles. There is no mistake in this. It is a Mahāyānistic treatise, but this does not contradict the fact that it demonstrates the subjects that refer to all the 3 Vehicles. Moreover, Āryāsanga, having written down the 5 treatises of Maitreya, composed ***the Tattva-viniçcaya***[1009]) in which the subjects of the ***Abhisamayālaṁkāra*** and the ***Prajñā-pāramitā*** are demonstrated *(en regard)*, the Commentary on the ***Uttaratantra***[1010]), the Commentary on the ***Saṁdhinirmocana-sūtra***[1011]) and other works. He has attained the 3d Stage of Bodhisattva perfection and has through this worked for the weal of the Doctrine. It is said in the ***Prasphuṭapadā***[1012]), the work explaining the Small Commentary[1013]): — The teacher Asanga has attained the 3d Stage called Prabhākarī. — Nevertheless, in order to convert Vasubandhu, he

[1007]) Cf. vol. I. p. 54, 55, 56.

[1008]) The Mahāyāna-saṁgraha and Abhidharma-samuccaya. Ibid. p. 56.

[1009]) De-ñid-rnam-ṅes. Cf. the introductory verses to Haribhadra's Abhisamayālaṁkārāloka — *bhāṣyaṁ tattva-viniçcaye racitavān prajñāvatām agraṇī / Āryāsanga iti prabhāsvara-yaçāḥ* . . . Tsoṅ-kha-pa in his Legs-bçad sñiṅ-po, Tsaṅ Ed. 20 b. 2—4. is of the opinion that this Tattva-viniçcaya could not have been composed by Asanga.

[1010]) Known in the Tibetan tradition by the abridged title Thogs-ḥgrel = Asanga-vṛtti, its full title being Mahāyāna-uttaratantra-çāstra-vyākhyā. (Tg. MDO. XLIV.) Translated by me with the main work and published in the Acta Orientalia, vol. IX. Cf. my introduction to it, p. 90 and 93.

[1011]) Tg. MDO. XXXIV.

[1012]) Tg. MDO. VIII. 9 b. 5—6. (N.)

[1013]) Ḥgrel-chuṅ. This is the Commentary of Haribhadra on the Abhisamayālaṁkāra (without direct reference to the Prajñā-pāramitā-sūtras), called Sphuṭārthā (Ḥgrel-pa Don-gsal), Tg. MDO. VII.

has taught from the standpoint of the Vijñānavāda[1014]). (In the *Mādhyamika-alaṁkāra*) it is said: —

The subject-matter here are the 2 Aspects of Reality,
Which are vindicated by Logic and Scripture,
Which have been expounded by Maitreya and Asanga,
And are likewise acknowledged by Nāgārjuna.

In the *Cittamātrālaṁkāra*[1015]) we have, in the place were this verse is explained, as follows: — Maitreya is a Bodhisattva abiding on the 10th Stage, Asanga is a Bodhisattva on the 3d Stage, and Nāgārjuna is a Bodhisattva who has attained the first Stage[1015a]).

Now, in the Commentary on the first part of the *Yogacaryābhūmi*[1016]) it is said: — [117 a.]

I make my salutations to him who is called Asanga,
Who for the sake of helping the living beings,
Has secured, by the force of the Dharmasrotaḥ-samādhi,
The nectar of the Highest Doctrine that poured forth
From that precious vessel, — the mouth of the Saint
Maitreya,
And has drunk it by means of his ears.

And at the end of the *Vivaraṇa-saṁgraha*[1017]): —The Saint Asanga has crossed the sea of his own philosophical Doctrine and that of others, has attained the special form of meditative trance called the Dharmasrotaḥ-samādhi[1018]), and has touched with his head the feet of the Holy Unconquerable (Maitreya) resembling immaculate lotus flowers. — Some say that according to these passages, Asanga was abiding in the state of meditation called Dharmasrotaḥ. As this state exists on the Path of Accumulating Merit[1019]), (Asanga) is not really a Saint, but is conventionally called so, just as a

---

1014) According to the standpoint of the Mādhyamikas which is acknowledged by the Tibetan tradition, a Saint (Ārya) who has attained the Stages of Bodhisattva perfection, must in any case be an adherent of the Mādhyamika point of view.

1015) Sems-tsam-rgyan, the work of Ratnākaraçānti. Full title: Mādhyamika-alaṁkāra-vṛtti Mādhyamika-pratipadā-siddhi. Tg. MDO. LXI. The verse quoted is: fol. 120 a. 1—2. (N.)

1015a) Ibid. fol. 120 a. 5.

1016) Saḥi-stod-ḥgrel. Tg. MDO. LIV. 77 b. 4. (N.)

1017) Tg. MDO. LIV. 77 a. 7—b. 1.

1018) *chos-rgyun-tiṅ-ṅe-ḥdzin.*

1019) *tshogs-lam* = *saṁbhāra-mārga.*

cause is sometimes metaphorically designated by the name of the effect (which it produces)[1020].

This is not correct. It is true that the Teacher Haribhadra speaks of the Dharmasrotaḥ-samādhi as attained on the Path of Accumulating Merit. He does not however say that it ceases to exist after that. Therefore (Haribhadra's statement) does not prove the fact of (Asanga's being) a worldling. In the Great Sub-commentary on the *Sūtrālaṁkāra*[1021]) it is said that the Dharmasrotaḥ-samādhi ends simultaneously with the Stage of Action in Faith[1022]). And in the Sub-Commentary of Bhadanta Asvabhāva[1023]) we read that the Dharmasrotaḥ-samādhi represents the Degree of Highest Mundane Virtues[1024]). Now the latter and the Path of Illumination become originated directly one after the other. It is thus perfectly clear that Asanga is a Saint in the direct sense of the word. It is said that the duration of his life was 500 years, but (in reality) he lived 150 years. And the Mahāyānistic Doctrine became greatly spread owing to him.

[The Teacher Vasubandhu.]

Vasubandhu received his education in the school of Sanghabhadra in Kashmir. A great number of Pratyekabuddhas had before expressed in their entreaties the desire that that country should be the place were the Abhidharma was to be greatly spread. Moreover, in the point concerning the medical instructions[1025]) (of the *Vinayavastu*) it was foretold to be the most sublime spot, suitable for the highest transcendental contemplation[1026]). [117 b.] (Accordingly) some time before, the Arhats Çāntimān, Kubjita[1027]) and many others had composed a treatise called the *Mahāvibhaṣa* containing 100 000 Çlokas in which the 7 Abhidharma treatises and the Vinaya were summarized. In the *Prabhāvatī*[1028]) it is said that this work was composed by Upagupta. In the Commentary of Yaçomitra[1029]) the work is called "the Commentary resembling

---

[1020]) *kāraṇe kāryopacārāt.* [1021]) Tg. MDO. XLVI.

[1022]) *mos-pas-spyod-paḥi-sa* = *adhimukti-caryā-bhūmi.*

[1023]) Btsun-pa No-bo-ñid-med-paḥi ḥgrel-bçad. Tg. MDO. XLV. 110b. 2. (N.)

[1024]) *ḥjig-rten-paḥi chos-kyi-mchog* = *laukika-agra-dharma.*

[1025]) Luṅ-sman-gyi-gži. [1026]) *lhag-mthoṅ* = *vipaçyanā.*

[1027]) Sgur-po. [1028]) Tg. MDO. LXXXIX. 91 b. b, 92 a. 6.

[1029]) Rgyal-sras-ma. This is the name by which Yaçomitra's Abhidharmakoça-vyākhyā is known in the Tibetan tradition, Rgyal-sras = Rājaputra, being an epithet of Yaçomitra.

the ocean"[1030]). This is a poetical comparison of the Vibhāṣā with an ocean. *It does not mean that "the Ocean" (Sāgara) is* another name for the Vibhāṣā, just as "the Vibhāṣā-Treasury" (Vibhāṣākoça)[1031]) by which name the work is sometimes designated. *(Vasubandhu) studied the* ***Vibhāṣā*** *and the* 7 Abhidharma-treatises and apprehended without difficulty. After that he resolved to go back to India. At that time the customs were surveyed by a Yakṣa who robbed Vasubandhu of the image of his tutelary deity and thrice sent him back. But, as Vasubandhu had no riches except the Doctrine that was in his mind and could not be taken from him, he was at length permitted to pass and came to Nālanda where his elder brother had composed numerous treatises. Having heard the contents of these, (Vasubandhu) said: —

Alas, Asanga, residing in the forest,
Has practised meditation for 12 years.
Without having attained anything by this meditation,
He has founded a system, so difficult and burdensome,
That it can be carried only by an elephant![1032]) —

In such a way he expressed his contempt with the Mahāyānistic Doctrine and with the person who expounded it. The elder brother heard about this and, knowing that the incorrect activity (of Vasubandhu) would be of no use (to the latter), resolved to convert him. So he ordered two of his pupils to take the ***Daçabhūmaka*** and the ***Akṣayamati-nirdeça***, went to the younger brother and said to him: — Recite these in the morning and in the evening. — Vasubandhu, having done as he was ordered, said in the evening: — The Great Vehicle possesses good factors, but the result seems to deviate (from the correct path). — But at daybreak (he spoke otherwise): — The factors and the result are both of them sublime. Cut out this my tongue which has depreciated (such a Doctrine)! [118 a.] Accordingly he sought for a razor to do this, but the 2 pupils said: — Do not seek to cut out thy tongue. Thy elder brother possesses a means for removing thy obscurations. Go therefore to him. —(Vasubandhu) accordingly went and repeatedly listened to the exposition of the Doctrine. When the religious questions were being settled by means of controversy, the younger brother had quick and sudden flashes of idea[1033]), whereas the elder re-

---

[1030]) B. B. I. 8 — Abhidharma-bhāṣya-sāgara. [1031]) Bye-brag-bçad-mdzod.
[1032]) Cf. Schiefner, Tāranātha, p. 119. [1033]) ***spobs-pa*** = ***pratibhāna.***

quired some time in order to give a good answer. What is the cause of this? — asked Vasubandhu. — (Asanga replied): — Thou hast been a Paṇḍit during 500 repeated births, and therefore the Analytic Wisdom acquired by thee in thy previous existence is exceedingly great. With myself this is not the case. Therefore, I give reply after having questioned my tutelary deity. — (Vasubandhu) then prayed to show him (this deity). Asanga said that it was necessary to pray the Most Venerable One (Maitreya) and, having done this, said: —Thou art an ordinary worldly being. As thou hast formerly depreciated the Great Vehicle, thou art not worthy of seeing (Maitreya) in this life. In order to remove thy obscurations, thou must compose numerous Commentaries on the Mahāyānistic sūtras and read the *Uṣṇīṣa-vijaya*[1034]). In the next birth thou shalt then meet (with Maitreya). Thereupon (Vasubandhu) became full of faith in his elder brother and said: —

My brother resembles a Nāga,
And I am like the Cātaka bird.
The king of the Nāgas sends down rain,
But it does not enter the beak of the bird. —

He then secured that mystic power which is peculiar to the word of Maitreya, composed the aphorisms of the *Abhidharmakoça* and sent them with presents to Sanghabhadra. The pupils of the latter said: —The words "so they say", "this is affirmed"[1035]) (which Vasubandhu uses when quoting the opinion of the Vaibhāṣikas with which he does not agree) show a depreciation of our philosophical system. But (the teacher said) that Vasubandhu, being skilful in composing treatises, had only used poetical forms of expression. He greatly rejoiced and composed a Commentary (on the *Abhidharmakoça*) in accordance with the Sūtras. Later on (Vasubandhu) wrote his own Commentary (on the *Koça*) and sent it (to Sanghabhadra). The latter said: — This Commentary refutes the main text, is itself in conflict with Scripture and Logic, and can be defeated by means of both. One must make (Vasubandhu) destroy it with his own hands. [118 b.] Accordingly, he composed a treatise containing his objections (with the work of Vasubandhu) and then resolved to go to India. Vasubandhu heard about this and thought: —The teacher Sanghabhadra is profoundly versed in the

1034) Gtsug-tor-mam-rgyal. Cf. Schiefner, Tāranātha, p. 121.
1035) *lo* or *grag* = *kila*. Cf. Abh. koça, I. kār. 3.

Doctrine of the Vaibhāṣikas. It is therefore difficult to refute him and, moreover it is unsuitable that I should vanquish him. I would better go to Nepal, having declared that I go to see the self-originated sanctuary. He accordingly departed to Nepal. Thereafter the teacher Sanghabhadra set forth with the numerous monks who were his adherents, so that the horizon was red from the colour of their religious robes, and arrived at Nālanda where he attained Nirvāṇa. —

The teacher Vasubandhu, whilst he was residing in Nepal, once came to see a monk called Handu who, though bearing the outward attributes of a monk, did not act according to the religious rules and obeisances and carried (on his shoulder) a pot of wine. Alas! the Doctrine will undergo ruin, —said Vasubandhu, became full of grief, recited the *Uṣṇīṣa-vijaya-dhāraṇī* in the reverse order and died. A monument was erected at that place, which is said to exist till the present day. —

In short (Vasubandhu) entered the religious order after having been a high-born representative of the Brāhmaṇa caste, he had been a Paṇḍit during 500 previous births, had apprehended the meaning of 99 or 80 divisions of the *Çatasāhasrikā* and appreciated them in his mind, had recited aloud for 12 days, having confined himself in a tub of oil, was possessed of the wealth *[vasu]* of the Highest Wisdom and, having propagated the Doctrine out of mercy, had become the friend *[bandhu]* of the living beings. It is accordingly said[1036]): —

> It (the *Abhidharmakoça*) is composed by him who is called
> Vasubandhu,
> Who, being the highest of Sages, was spoken of by the
> living world
> As the Second Buddha, and was the true friend of the living
> beings. —

We read moreover in the Commentary on the first part of the *Yogacaryā-bhūmi*[1037]): —

> The Saint Asanga [119 a.] has adorned that enchanted tree
> which is the Buddha.
> With the rain of the flowers of words that spring forth
> from its branches which are the sermons (of the Lord).

1036) Abhidharmakoça-vyākhyā, B. B. 1. 4—6.
1037) Tg. MDO. LIV. 77 b. 4—5. (N.)

His younger brother represents the treasury of Wisdom and is full of glory.

It is he, the most venerable, to whom I make my salutations. —

The teacher thus greatly praised, has composed the following works: —

1. The main aphorisms of the *Abhidharmakoça* and the Commentary thereon which explain the Scripture of the first period and investigate it by the sharp weapon of Logic,

2. The Commentary on the text of the (3) *Prajñā-pāramitā Sūtras* in which the subjects of the Scripture of the intermediate period are demonstrated from the idealistic standpoint[1038]),

3. The 8 *Prakaraṇas* in which the Latest Scripture is spoken of as being of direct meaning[1039]).

Moreover, he has composed numerous Commentaries on Sūtras, viz. the *Daçabhūmaka*,[1040]),

the *Akṣayamati-nirdeça*[1041]),

the *Gayāçirṣa*[1042]).

the *Ṣaṇmukha-dhāraṇī*[1043]),

the *Caturdharmaka*[1044]), etc.

Furthermore, his is the Commentary on the *Dharma-dharmatā-vibhanga*, as well as numerous other works. In the Commentary on the *Aṣṭasāhasrikā* it is said:[1045])

[1038]) Cf. vol. I. p. 53. According to Tsoṅ-kha-pa's Gser-phreṅ, (Labraṅ Edition I. 5 a. 4. sqq.) and the Skabs-brgyad-ka of Jam-yaṅ-żad-pa (Chilutai Edition I. 5 b. 6) the standpoint of Bu-ton regarding the authorship of this work is considered to be incorrect. The said authorities maintain that the author of this Commentary on the Prajñā-pāramitā was not Vasubandhu, but the Kashmirian Daṁṣṭrāsena, as is acknowledged by the older tradition.

[1039]) *ṅes-don* = *nītartha*. Cf. vol. I. p. 56, 57.

[1040]) Tg. MDO. XXXIV. 130—335. (Pek.)

[1041]) Tg. MDO. XXXV.

[1042]) Tg. MDO. XXXIV. 90—96. (Pek.)

[1043]) Ibid. 81—83. (Pek.)

[1044]) Ibid. 83—84. (Pek.)

[1045]) Cf. above, note 1009.— *bhāṣyaṁ tattva-viniçcaye racitavān prajñāvatām agraṇī Āryāsanga iti prabhāsvara-yaçās tat-kartṛ-sāmarthyataḥ / bhāvābhāva-vibhāga-pakṣa-nipuṇa-jñānābhimānonnata ācāryo Vasubandhur arthakathane prāptādaraḥ paddhatau //* The *paddhati (gžuṅ-ḥgrel)* mentioned by Haribhadra in this verse is considered by Bu-ton as being the Commentary on the 3 Prajñā-pāramitā-sūtras (Tg. MDO. XIV) just mentioned. — Tsoṅ-kha-pa is of the opinion that this *paddhati* is a separate Commentary on the Pañcaviṁçati-sāhasrikā. He says that Bu-ton has confounded this text with the Commentary on the 3 Prajñā-pāramitā-sūtras, owing to the fact of its being sometimes designated by the title Gnod-ḥjoms which is likewise applied to the latter Commentary.

The Saint Asanga endowed with the most magnificent glory,
And being the foremost of those possessed of Highest Wisdom,
Has composed the Commentary establishing the true state of things[1046]);
Inspired by this work, the teacher Vasubandhu, exeedingly proud
Of his knowledge, skilful in the field of discrimination
Of that which is a reality by itself and not, (has composed)
His Commentary and obtained fame by his exposition of the meaning.

According to the tradition, this teacher had 4 pupils who were even more learned than himself[1047]). These are: —

1. The Teacher Sthiramati[1047a]).

This was a Paṇḍit more learned (than Vasubandhu) in the Abhidharma. At the time when the teacher Vasubandhu resided in Bhāgavihāra, sitting in a brazen tub filled with oil and reading aloud the 80 divisions of the *Çatasāhasrikā*, a dove was constantly listening to him. [119 b.] Finally, this dove died and was reborn in Daṇḍakāraṇya[1048]) as the son of a Çūdra. Immediately after he was born, he asked: —Where is my teacher? — Who is thy teacher?,— was the question.—Vasubandhu,—said he. Thereupon the father, having inquired from the merchants who were going to Central India, came to know that (Vasubandhu) was residing there. Accordingly, when the boy grew a little older, he went to the teacher Vasubandhu. The latter began by teaching to him the alphabet, and the boy studied, till he became proficient in the 5 sciences. Whilst he was still a child, he made an offering to the statue of Tārā that was at Nālanda, by putting into the hand (of the statue) a handful of beans, thinking (that the goddess) would eat them. He accordingly presented his beans, but they rolled down. Again he offered them and again they rolled down. Thinking that it was unsuitable for him to eat himself, if the goddess did not accept his offering, he presented again and again. And, as the beans again rolled down, the child began to weep. Then the goddess appeared directly before him and said: — Weep not; I have blessed thee. Therefore go home in peace! —

1046) Tattva-viniçcaya, Cf. above.
1047) *raṅ-las-mkhas-pa.*
1047a) Cf. Schiefner, Tāranātha, p. 129.
1048) Mthaḥ-ḥkhob-ḥdra-ma.

After that he became possessed of unimpeded Highest Wisdom. That statue, in its turn, became known as "Tārā with the beans".

This teacher has studied the *Ratnakūṭa* up to the 49th chapter and it is said that he has composed a Commentary to it[1049]). At that time the fame of his learning became widely spread. The king Çrīharṣa, the alms-giver of the teacher Guṇaprabha, once asked who was at that time famous in the field of the Doctrine? — The answer was: —

> The venerable Guṇaprabha has been made a Paṇḍit through royal grace,
> But only the teacher Sthiramati is the one who has mastered all the sciences.

This teacher has composed the Commentary on the *Abhidharmakoça* called the *Karakāçani*[1050]) [120 a.], the Commentary on the *Abhidharma-samuccaya,* the Commentaries on the 8 treatises (of Vasubandhu) and numerous other works.

A certain Tibetan mentions the following tradition: — After the (heretical) beggar had, by propitiating the sun, caused the sacred texts to be burnt, the teacher Sthiramati, having recited the *Ratnakūṭa* by heart, became full of pride and said: —

> If you put my wisdom on one side,
> And the knowledge of others on the opposite,
> And weigh both on a balance,
> My wisdom will turn to be the heavier. —

As the consequence of this pride he became reborn as a pig. Having examined the sound of his grunting, he thought: —

> Before, I have been the teacher Sthiramati,
> But now, owing to my pride,
> Have been reborn in the belly of a sow.
> However, afterwards, when I have died,
> I will depart to the region of Tuṣita. —

According to my opinion, this (legend) is contradictory as regards time. Moreover, the persons of whom the Buddha had foretold that they were to be the guardians of the Doctrine, cannot fall into Evil Births.

The pupil of Sthiramati was Pūrṇavardhana[1051]), and it is said

---

[1049]) Tg. MDO. XXXVII. 244—350. (Pek.)

[1050]) Tg. MDO. CXXIX. and CXXX.

[1051]) Gaṅ-ba-spel.

that the pupils of the latter were Jinamitra and Çīlendrabodhi[1051a]). This however must be examined.

The pupil of Vasubandhu who proved greater than his teacher in the field of Logic, was —

2. The Venerable Dignāga.

He was of Brāhmaṇic caste and was ordained by a teacher of the Vātsiputrīya sect. Having received a perfect education in the school of worldly sciences, he received from his preceptor the instructions about the concentrated meditation for the removal (of the Obscurations). Then he was told to meditate over the principle of the Ego which was said to be inexpressible as being neither identical with the groups of elements, nor differing from them[1052]). Having accordingly practised meditation, he could nowhere find such an Ego. Thinking that he was possessed of internal and external Obscurations, he kindled four great fires at the four directions and stripped his body of its clothing. (Having done this), he opened his eyes as wide as he could, but in spite of all his searches throughout the 10 quarters of the sky, he did not find the Ego. Whilst he was thus acting, he came to be seen by his friends who inquired [120 b.] the preceptor about this. The preceptor asked Dignāga wherefore he was doing so, and the answer was: — I am searching for the Ego. — The preceptor said: — Thou art overthrowing our own philosophical system. Therefore, be gone! — I have the power of refuting the preceptor by means of Logic, — thought Dignāga, — but it is not suitable for me to do so. Accordingly, he departed and finally came to the teacher Vasubandhu. With the latter he studied the texts of the 3 Vehicles, and became especially versed in the *Vijñānavāda* and in Logic. Thereafter the teacher, (knowing that) the cause of the Phenomenal Life of the living beings was the ignorance of the Truth, made it his intention to remove this (ignorance) and bring about the origination of its antidote, i. e. Highest Wisdom. For this sake he composed the Commentary on

---

[1051a]) Cf. Cordier, Index du Bstan-ḥgyur II. p. 396 (on vol. LXVIII.) — Pūrṇa-vardhana alias élève de Sthiramati, et maître de Jinamitra et Çīlendrabodhi. The editors of the Peking Tangyur acknowledge the tradition in regard of which Bu-ton expresses doubt.

[1052]) This is the standpoint of the Vātsiputrīyas. Cf. Conception of Buddhist Nirvāṇa, p. 31, note 1.

the *Abhidharmakoça*[1053]), the Commentary on the *Guṇāparyanta-stotra*[1053a]), the *Ālambana-parīkṣā*[1054]) and other fragmentary works, 100 in number. But, as these treatises were mere fragments (without any system) he resolved to compose the *Pramāṇasamuccaya* in which (all the small treatises) would be united in one. Accordingly, in the cavern known by his name, he wrote on the side of a rock: —

> I salute him who is the personified Logic,
> Who pursues the weal of the living beings,
> The Teacher, the Blessed One, the Protector[1055]).
> And, in order to demonstrate the means of Logical Proof,
> I shall unite here under one head
> The different fragments from all my other treatises[1056]). —

As he thus wrote down just this salutation and that which he intended to expound, the earth trembled, a light blazed forth, a tremendous sound of thunder was heard, the legs of the heretical teachers became stiff like wood, and many other ominous signs appeared. At that time a heretical teacher named Kṛṣṇamunirāja[1057]) was residing in the neighbourhood. This (teacher), perceiving with his most subtle supernatural faculty of vision, understood that (all the ominous signs) were produced by the force of Dignāga's words. Full of envy, he came by the track of the teacher when the latter had gone out for alms, and twice rubbed out the inscription. [121 a.] The teacher therefore wrote down the verse for a third time, and at the end: — Who has rubbed out this verse which has been written down by me? If this has been done out of mere mockery and jesting, one ought not to do so, for my verse pursues a great aim. If it is out of envy, (then it is likewise useless), since the verse is in my mind and cannot be rubbed out (from it). But

---

[1053]) Abhidharma-koça-marma-pradipa, Tg. MDO. LXX. 144—286. The text in the Tangyur represents nothing, but an abridged rendering of Vasubandhu's auto-commentary.

[1053a]) Tg. BSTOD. I. 234—237. The Stotra itself is the work of Ratnadāsa

[1054]) Tg. MDO. XCV. 177—179.

[1055]) The Sanskrit text of the first half of this verse is preserved in Yaçomitra's Abhidharmakoça-vyākhyā, B. B. p. 3. — *pramāṇa-bhūtāya jagad-dhitaiṣiṇe praṇamya çāstre sugatāya tāyine* /

[1056]) Iyengar restores this as follows: — *pramāṇa-siddhyai sva-kṛti-prakīr-ṇanāt nibadhyate viprasṛtam samuccitam* // Cf. Schiefner, Tāranātha, p. 132, 133, etc.

[1057]) Nag-po-thub-rgyal. Tāranātha has simply Kṛṣṇa.

if he (who has done this) is able to enter upon controversy in order to upset (my theses), let him show himself and we shall discuss. — So did he write. Again the ominous signs appeared and again (the heretic) came. Seeing the words "we shall discuss" he remained there. When the teacher, having made his turn for alms, came back, they met, and the Doctrine (of each of them) was made the pledge of conquest. So they began to dispute, and the heretic was vanquished twice and thrice. (Then the teacher said): — Thou must now adopt my Doctrine. The heretic was enraged, caused flames to burst out from his mouth, and burned down all the requisites of the teacher; the latter himself underwent the danger of being consumed. (Dignāga), full of grief, thought: — Surely, it was my intention to act for the sake of all living beings. But now I see that I cannot further the weal even of one single heretic. Therefore I shall do better if I realize the bliss of Quiescence for the benefit of my own self[1058]). He threw upward the peace of chalk (with which he had written), thinking: — As soon (as the chalk) touches the ground, I will give up my Creative Effort (of a Bodhisattva). But (the chalk) did not fall on the ground, and (suddenly) Mañjuçrī himself appeared before him saying: — My son, do not, do not do so. Thou hast met with Hīnayānistic teachings, and unworthy thoughts have become originated in thee. Know thou that this host of heretics can do no harm to this thy work. I will be thy protector till the time when thou shalt attain the Stages (of a Bodhisattva). And in future times thy work will be the unique authority[1059]) for all scientific treatises. In such a manner, as some say, did (Mañjuçrī) grant his assistance (to Dignāga). In Dharmottara's Commentary on the *Pramāṇa-viniçcaya*[1060]) it is said: — [121 b.] At the time when the teacher Dignāga was practising meditation in a solitary cavern, in one of the Stages (of this meditation) he became averse to the Saṁsāra and possessed of the desire of turning away from the cause of the living beings and of attaining deliverance exclusively for himself. At that moment the Saint Mañjuçrī appeared before him and said: — My son, thou hast become possessed of a state of mind fearing every contact with sinful beings. Accordingly, though thy mind has the power of helping all that lives, thou nevertheless showest indiffe-

---

1058) I. e. seek the salvation of the Hīnayānist Saint.
1059) Lit. "the eye". 1060) Tg. MDO. CIX and CX.

rence (to their cause). Wherefore is this so? — The answer was: — O Lord, this Phenomenal Life is endowed with much suffering and is hard to bear. I am unable to sustain it, and my mind that is attached to the sinful living beings, becomes unsteady. I see thee now, but of what use will this be (to me) if thou dost not bless me? — Mañjuçrī replied: — My son, as long as thou hast not attained the Stages of a Bodhisattva, I myself will be thy guide. — Having spoken thus, he became invisible. — In the Commentary of the Kashmirian Jñānaçrī[1061]) we read: — As long as thou hast not attained the state of a Buddha. —

The teacher (Dignāga), accordingly, composed the ***Pramāṇa-samuccaya*** with its autocommentary, refuted all the heretics, and greatly furthered the spread of the Doctrine. One of his pupils was Īçvarasena[1062]) who was versed in the 5 branches of science and composed a Subcommentary on the ***Pramāṇa-samuccaya.*** —

[The Teacher Dharmakīrti.]

The pupil of Īçvarasena was Dharmakīrti. The latter was born in the southern kingdom of Cūḍāmaṇi[1063]) in a heretical Brāhmaṇic family and, while still a child, became well trained in grammar. Once, as he took from his uncle, the heretical teacher Kumārila[1064]) the garments of a Brāhmaṇic heretical ascetic [122 a.], the uncle spoke abusively to him and drove him away. The teacher then made his resolve to vanquish all the heretics. Accordingly, he took orders in the Buddhist church, received the necessary training, and then expressed his special wish of studying the ***Pramāṇa-samuccaya*** with the teacher Īçvarasena 3 times. Having heard to its exposition, he first understood it in the conception of Īçvarasena. The second time he understood it so, as Dignāga himself (intended its meaning to be), and seing that there were errors in the views of Īçvarasena, he prayed to expound it a third time. (Īçvarasena) said: — Dignāga had no other pupil who were like me. I myself have no other pupil akin to thee. It is not the custom to give an explanation on every separate point. I have commented twice. There is no use of explaining now (the dubious points) exclusively. There are other affairs of a Paṇḍit that are to be attended

---

1061) Ibid. CX. 1062) Dbaṅ-phyug-sde.
1063) Gtsug-gi-nor-bu.
1064) Gžon-nu-ma-len. Cf. Schiefner, Tārānātha, p. 177. note 5.

to. Prepare stuff for a wick and oil (for a lamp), and in the evening I shall explain again. (Dharmakīrti) did so. After having perfectly cognized that the effect makes it possible to cognize the character of the cause[1065]) (that has produced it) he told this to the teacher in the form of a *pūrvapakṣa*. Içvarasena was delighted and said: — Now take the part of an opponent (*pūrvapakṣa*) against the erroneous points of my system and compose a Commentary on the *Pramāṇa-samuccaya*. — In such a way he expressed his consent. —

Thereafter, the teacher, in order to apprehend the secret terms of the Sāṁkhya system, assumed the form of a slave, became the servant of his uncle's wife and, as the latter was very pleased with him, he told her that it was necessary for him to inquire about the weak points of the system. She said: — Ask thou at the time of merriment and thou shalt apprehend. Accordingly, he fastened a cord to the leg of the woman. At every difficult point he pulled the cord, and (the woman having told him), he apprehended all that he wanted, [122 b.] came to know the secret points of the system[1066]), and became known as superior (to all his adversaries). At that time he issued the following proclamation: — If there is somewhere a learned man, may he enter upon dispute (with me). — After this had been made known, the greater part (of the heretical teachers) fled to other countries. Those who tried to dispute were vanquished by (the words of) the Doctrine, entered the Path of it and made the following solemn utterance; —

If the sun of sublime speech
That is called Dharmakīrti goes down,
The elements of virtue that were awakened will die
And all that is sinful will again rise up. —

And those who sung his praise, said: —

We salute the teacher,
Him who is called Dharmakīrti,
Who is preeminent by vanquishing his adversaries
Amongst the heretics, skilful in Logic and Speech.

Thereafter the teacher travelled through many countries and cities and finally came to the gates (of the residence) of the king Ut-

---

[1065]) I. e. the *kārya-anumāna*.
[1066]) Cf. Schlefner, Tāranātha, p. 177.

phullapuṣpa[1067]). The king asked: — Who is at present famed as a Paṇḍit? — (The teacher) replied: —

> O Utphullapuṣpa, thou who art endowed with great merit, say
> Who is victorious in all the countries except me,
> Who am possessed of perfect Wisdom (like) Dignāga,
> Of purest speech like Candragomin,
> And am skilful in the prosody that comes from the poet Çūra?![1067a]) —

Art thou Dharmakīrti? — asked the king. — By this name I am known, — was the answer. The king then invited him to reside (with him) and became his alms-giver. After that (Dharmakīrti) composed his 7 treatises[1068]) and, finally, an auto-commentary on the first chapter of the *Pramāṇavārtika*. These treatises became current in the various schools, but (the scholars) for the greater part did not understand them. There were however a few who did apprehend their meaning, but these, moved by envy, declared them to be incorrect and fastened them to the tail of a dog. But the teacher said: — The dog will make its way through villages and hamlets, and the treatises will in such a manner become spread about. And, as they say, he wrote at the head of the *Pramāṇavārtika* as follows: — [123 a.] The living beings for the greater part are attached to that which is base and are not possessed of wisdom and energy. Therefore they not only care not for sublime words, but, polluted by envy, show hatred (in regard of them). For this reason, the thought that this (treatise) will be of help to others does not exist with me. But the mind which, during a long period of time, has become accustomed to fine words, will find delight in it, since it arouses its zeal. —

After that he ordered the Paṇḍit Devendrabuddhi[1069]) to compose a Commentary (on the *Pramāṇa-vārtika*. Devendrabuddhi did this once and gave it (to the teacher) for review, but (Dharmakīrti) washed it away with water. Devendrabuddhi wrote it another time, but (the teacher) burnt it with fire. After having composed it again, Devendrabuddhi presented it to the teacher saying: — The greater part (of the hearers) are unworthy and time does not

---

[1067]) Me-tog-rgyas-pa. Tāranātha (Schiefner p. 181, note 3) has Me-tog-kun-tu-rgyas-pa.

[1067a]) Ibid.   [1068]) Cf. vol. I. p. 44, 45.   [1069]) Lha-dbaṅ-blo.

wait. Therefore, as I have been instructed, I have made a summary and have composed here a commentary on the difficult points. — Dharmakīrti said: — The meaning which is expressed by suggestions and indirectly does not appear as it should be, but that which is expressed directly has a correct form. — However, thought he, — my Logic will never be rightly understood. —And, as runs the tradition, he added at the end of the *Pramāṇa-vārtika*: — Just as a river disappears in the ocean, so (this my science) will disappear and perish. —

The pupil of Devendrabuddhi was Çākyabuddhi who composed a Subcommentary. It is said that the pupil of this latter teacher was Prabhābuddhi[1070]). Some say that Yamāri[1071]) was the pupil of Dharmakīrti himself, that (the author of) the *Pramāṇa-vārtika-alaṁkāra*[1071a]) obtained instructions from the dead body (of Dharmakīrti), that the pupil (of this author) was Vinītadeva and the pupil of the latter Dharmottara. But in the Commentary it is said that Dharmottara was the pupil of Dharmākaradatta[1072]) and Kalyāṇarakṣita[1073]). Yamāri has composed a Subcommentary on the *Pramāṇa-vartika-alaṁkāra*[1073a]). Vinītadeva and Çaṁkarānanda[1074]) have written Commentaries on the 7 Treatises. [123 b.] So runs the tradition. —

The pupil of Vasubandhu who excelled him in the knowledge of the Prajñā-pāramitā was —

3. The Saint Vimuktasena.

He was the principal of many great monasteries, belonged (at first) to the sect of the Kaurukullakas and was the nephew of the teacher Buddhadāsa[1075]). He attained the Stage of Joy[1076]), and heard the Word of the Buddha himself. He composed the *Pañca-viṁçati-sāhasrikā-ālokā*[1077]), a Commentary on the *Abhisamayālaṁkāra* in correspondence with the *Pañca-viṁçati-sāhasrikā*,

---

1070) Ḥod-kyi-blo. 1071) Xyl. Dza-ma-ri.

1071a) The work of Prajñākaragupta, Tg. MDO. XCIX. and C.

1072) Chos-ḥbyuṅ-byin. 1073) Dge-sruṅ.

1073a) Full title: Pramāṇavārtika-alaṁkāra-ṭīkā Supariçuddhā nāma, Tg. MDO. CIV. 208—345, CV., CVI. and CVII.

1074) Bde-byed-dgaḥ-bo. Cf. Schiefner, Tāranātha, p. 188.

1075) Saṅs-rgyas-ḥbaṅs. Cf. Cordier, Index du Bstan-ḥgyur II, p. 273.

1076) *rab-tu-dgaḥ-ba = pramuditā.*

1077) Ñi-khri-snaṅ-ba, Kg. MDO. I. For the full title of this work, cf. vol. I, note 270.

elucidating the subjects of the *Prajñā-pāramitā*. The Bhadanta Vimuktasena has composed the *Abhisamayālaṁkāra-vārtika*[1078]), and is considered by some to be the pupil of Ārya Vimuktasena. —

[The Teacher Haribhadra.]

(Now comes) in particular the biography of the teacher Haribhadra. In the eastern Khadira forest, in the trunk of a high tree there dwelt a tree-sprite. Now it happened that a shepherd of that country had died, and his beautiful wife was tending the sheep (in his stead). The tree-sprite mentioned had sexual intercourse with her, and (from their union) a remarkable son was born who was named Gopāla[1079]). His father put him in possession of precious jewels, and, by the force of his virtues, he obtained the royal power over the whole of the country. It is by this king that the monastery of Nālanda was buillt. Gopāla's queen who had no power over the king, resolved to bring him under her influence and asked a Brāhmaṇa to give her magical power in order to accomplish this. The Brāhmaṇa brought from the Himālaya an enchanted drug, sealed it and handed it over to (the queen's) slave-girl. The latter, whilst crossing a bridge, fell down, and (the drug) was carried away by the stream, gradually reached the ocean, and was seized by the Nāga king who swallowed it up. Thus, by the force of the drug, the Nāga king, the sovereign of the ocean, became subjected to the power of the queen, united with her, [124 a.] and from this union a son named Çrīmad Dharmapāla[1080]) was born. — At the time when, at an auspicious hour, the religious ceremonies were performed (over the child), the head of a serpent haughtily rose up. The king, enraged, resolved to cut it off, but a ring was shown to him, on which he beheld the characters of the Nāgas. He then continued to worship and after that devoted himself to the education (of the child)[1081]). When the latter grew up, he became possessed of the desire of building a temple more magnificent than all the others, and inquired the sooth-sayers (on this subject). The sooth-sayers said that it was necessary to make a wick out

---

[1078]) Tg. MDO. II.Tsoṅ-kha-pa in his Gser-phreṅ (Labraṅ Ed. I. 7 a. 6 and further on) expresses doubt as regards the authorship of this work.

[1079]) Cf. Schiefner, Tārānātha, p. 202.

[1080]) Dpal-ldan Chos-skyoṅ. Cf. Schiefner, Tārānātha, p. 208 and 209. According to Tār. this is not Dharmapāla, but Devapāla.

[1081]) Cf. Schiefner, Tārānātha, p. 209.

of the cotton belonging to ascetics and Brāhmaṇas, to get oil from the houses of kings and merchants, to fetch an oil-burner from a place of penance, and to place the burning lamp before the tutelary deity. — If thou shalt address an entreaty, the serpent of Dharmapāla will throw the lamp away, and at the place (where it falls) the temple must be built. This was done, but there suddenly appeared a raven, that threw the lamp into a lake. (The youth) was distressed, but in the night the king of the Nāgas with 5 serpent-heads came to him and said: — I am thy father, and I will cause this lake to dry up. Thou shalt build thy temple in the place of it. (In order to bring this about) thou must perform sacrifices for 7 weeks. This was accordingly done. On the 21st day the lake was dried up and (in its place) the monastery of Odantapuri was built.

This king had 4 sons, — a king, a Paṇḍit, a magician, and (another) king who was of sinful conduct. The latter feared that he would be deprived of riches, but his father put him in possession of a precious jewel. This (4th son) had himself a son called Devapāla who was possessed of the power of solemn entreaty[1082]) and was full of faith in the Prajñā-pāramitā. This (son) stole the jewel of his father and gave it to a monk who was explaining the Pāramitā. The father, having come to know about this, said: — Jewels are necessary for kings, but monks are known to be of scant desires and modest. Thou (O monk) art not like that! — [124 b.] He then ordered the monk to be strangled and took away the jewel. The monk, in his turn, had made the entreaty to become immediately, after his death, reborn as the son of his pupil, the prince (Devapāla). This accordingly took place, and he became the king Mahīpāla[1083]), one who was full of faith in the Prajñā-pāramitā and searched for the means of expounding it (in the different countries). At that time the teacher Haribhadra who belonged to the Kṣatriya caste took orders, became versed in all the hetorodox and orthodox philosophical systems and especially studied during a long period of time the subjects of the Prajñā-pāramitā. Having learned from his preceptor Vairocanabhadra the means of propitiating Maitreya, he made this propitiation and beheld in a dream a monk of the colour of saffran and of sublime appearance who said to him: — Go thou to east, to Khasarpaṇa. — Having awakened, Haribhadra went there and remained for 3 days fasting and reflecting over his

---

1082) *smon-lam-gyi-stobs* = *praṇidhāna-bala*. 1083) Sa-skyoṅ.

dream. At day-break he dreamt again and beheld above the fragrant temple[1084]) of the Odantapuri-vihāra, in the skies, amidst dense masses of clouds, the upper part of the body of a god who, issuing from the clouds, was worshipping with various articles of worship. —What art thou doing? —asked Haribhadra. — I am worshipping Maitreya in order that he should expound the *Aṣṭasāhasrikā*, — was the answer. Then (Haribhadra) looked during a long time and beheld the countenance of Maitreya who was of the colour of gold, the crown of whose head was adorned with a Caitya and whose right hand was making the gesture[1085]) peculiar to (the Buddha) who expounds the Doctrine. Having saluted and worshipped him, (Haribhadra) addressed to him the following question: — At present, there are many Commentaries elucidating thy treatise[1086]). Which of these am I to follow? — Thou must perfectly apprehend the texts of all (the different authors), select all that is correct and compose thyself a separate treatise (of thy own). — Such was the instruction Haribhadra received. Having awakened [125 a.] and worshipped, Haribhadra set forth from the east to the west in order to find an almsgiver (to aid him) in the composition of his works. The king Mahīpāla, having heard that the teacher Haribhadra was greatly learned, sent a messenger to invite him. Haribhadra accepted the invitation and composed, in accordance with the Commentary of the Saint (Vimuktasena), the summary of the *Pañcaviṁçati-sāhasrikā* in 8 chapters[1087]), the Great Commentary on the *Aṣṭasāhasrikā*[1088]), the Commentary called *Sphuṭârthā*[1089]) the Commentary on the *Saṁcaya*[1090]) called *Subodhinī*[1091]), the *Prajñā-pāramitā-bhāvanā*, etc. So runs the tradition. In the Great Commentary on the *Aṣṭasāhasrikā*[1092]) it is said that this work was composed at the monastery of Trikaṭuka[1093]) under the patronship of Çrīmad Dharmapāla. The teacher Prajñākaramati says: — The master Haribhadra, pursuing the weal of

---

[1084]) *gandhola* i. e. *gandhālaya*. [1085]) *phyag-rgya* = *mudrā*.

[1086]) I. e. the Abhisamayālaṁkāra.

[1087]) Le-brgyad-ma, Tg. MDO. III, IV, and V.

[1088]) The Abhisamayālaṁkārālokā. Tg. MDO. VI.

[1089]) Don-gsal-ḥgrel-pa, Tg. MDO. VII.

[1090]) Tg. MDO. VII. [1091]) Rtogs-par-sla-ba.

[1092]) MS. Minaev, 409b. 1—6. — *tasmin sarvaguṇākare Trikaṭuka-çrīmad-vihāre cubhe / dānālabdha-mahodayasya karaṇād devasya dharmātmanaḥ ... Çrī-Dharmapālasya vai / /*

[1093]) Tsha-ba-gsum. Cf. Schiefner, Tārānātha, p. 219.

the living beings, saw that, in the elucidation of the Prajñā-pāramitā, there were many different opinions expressed in the different works, and that the Commentaries in their explanations were contradicting each other. He accordingly became deeply grieved by this. But, whilst he was abiding in solitude, the most merciful Lord Maitreya, in order to appease his grief, exposed to him the Prajñā-pāramitā in connection with the teaching of the process of Illumination.[1094]) Such is the tradition I have heard. — The teacher Dharmamitra says that (Haribhadra), having caused pleasure to his teacher for 17 years, was favoured by Maitreya in a dream (who expounded the Doctrine to him). However, the teacher (Haribhadra) himself says that he borrowed (the material for his works) from the 4 great Commentaries and, especially, has based upon the treatises of the 2 Saints (i. e. Asanga and Vimuktasena). [125 b.] It is said in the Great Commentary[1094a]): — Here the explanations of the Saint Asanga etc. have been written down. Therefore it (the Commentary) is to be regarded as authoritative. And: — As I have perceived the meaning, owing to the aid of the Saint Vimuktasena. —

[The Teacher Buddhajñānapāda.]

The pupil (of Haribhadra) was known by the name of Buddhajñānapāda[1095]) and received the consecration from Mañjuçrī. Once he concealed himself from his teacher in a crowd and lost his eyes (as a punishment), but having begged to forgive him he was given eyes that could see by day and by night. This teacher, at the request of his pupil Guṇamitra, composed the Commentary on the *Saṁcaya*[1096]). He has written moreover 14 works on the Scripture of the *Guhyasamāja*, — the *Mukhāgama*[1097]), the *Samantabhadra-sādhana*[1098]), the *Samantabhadrā*[1099]), the *Ātmasādhana-avatāra*[1100]), the *Viçva-cakra*[1101]), the *Ratnajvālā*[1102]), the *Mahā-*

[1094]) *mṅon-rtogs* = *abhisamaya.*

[1094a]) MS. 57 a. 14—16. — *Āryāsanga-prabhṛtīnām eva idaṁ vyākhyānaṁ likhyata iti pramāṇī-kartavyam.*

[1095]) Saṅs-rgyas-ye-çes-žabs. [1096]) Tg. MDO. VIII.

[1097]) Žal-gyi-luṅ. Tg. RGYUD. XXXIX. 20—23. In the Xyl. this work is called Ḥjam-dpal-žal-gyi-luṅ = Mañjuçrī-mukha-āgama.

[1098]) Sgrub-thabs Kun-tu-bzaṅ-po. Ibid. 33—42.

[1099]) Kun-tu-bzaṅ-mo. Full title: Yan-lag-bži-paḥi sgrub-thabs Kun-tu-bzaṅ-mo = Caturanga-sādhana-upāyikā Samantabhadrā. Tg. RGYUD. XXXIX 42—51. [1100]) Bdag-sgrub-pa-la-ḥjug-pa. Ibid. 63—75. The Xyl. has: Bdag-grub-par-ḥbyuṅ-ba. [1101]) Sna-tshogs-ḥkhor-lo. [1102]) Rin-chen-ḥbar-ba.

mūla-jñāna[1103]), the *Gāthā-koça*[1104]), the *Mukti-tilaka*[1105]), the *Bodhi-citta-tilaka*[1106]), the *Mangala-vyākhyā*[1107]), the *Caturtha-avatāra*[1108]), works on offerings, burning sacrifices, worship, magic circles, the Propitiation of the Lord of the Waters[1109]) etc., as runs the tradition. —

The pupil of Vasubandhu who excelled him in the knowledge of the Vinaya was —

4. The Teacher Guṇaprabha.

It is said in the Commentary (?): — The venerable teacher Guṇaprabha of Brāhmaṇic descent was a great authority in the Vinaya of the Ārya-mūla-sarvāstivādins. He has crossed the ocean of the orthodox and heterodox philosophical systems, has got his faculty of high wisdom increased by the nectar of the Discipline of Buddha's Doctrine, and has zealously and essentially realized the sublime precepts of the Lord. —[126 a.]

This teacher, endowed with such merits, has composed the *Vinaya-sūtra*[1110]), the *Ekottara-karma-çataka*[1111]), the Commentary on the Chapter on Morality of the *Bodhisattva-bhūmi*[1112]), and the autocommentary on the *Vinaya-sūtra*[1113]). Some consider the *Ekottara-karma-çataka* to be the work of Vinītadeva.

Now, according to some authorities, the teacher (Guṇaprabha) was the pupil of Upagupta, and according to others, the pupil of Sudarçana. — This is an anachronism and is therefore to be rejected as a mistake.

The adherents of the old Vinaya say that Sudarçana delivered the teaching (of the Vinaya) to Anāgāmin, and the latter — to Anivartitabuddhi (?)[1114]) who in his turn exposed it to Guṇaprabha.

[1103]) Rtsa-baḥi-ye-çes-chen-po.

[1104]) Tshigs-su-bçad-paḥi-mdzod.

[1105]) Grol-baḥi-thig-le. Tg. RGYUD. XXXIX. 56—63.

[1106]) Byaṅ-chub-sems-kyi-thig-le.

[1107]) Bkra-çis-rnam-bçad. [1108]) Bži-pa-la-ḥjug-pa.

[1109]) Rje-btsun-ḥphags-pa Gnod-ḥdzin chu-dbaṅ-gi sgrub-paḥi-thabs = Bhaṭṭāraka-ārya-Jambhala-jalendra-sādhana, Tg. RGYUD. XXXIX. 75—77.

[1110]) Ḥdul-baḥi-mdo. Tg. MDO. LXXXVII. 1—109.

[1111]) Las-brgya-rtsa-gcig. Ibid. 109—298.

[1112]) Byaṅ-saḥi tshul-khrims-leḥuḥi ḥgrel-pa = Bodhisattva-bhūmi-çīla-parivarta-bhāṣya. Tg. MDO. LIV. 229—240.

[1113]) Tg. MDO. LXXXIII. and LXXXIV.

[1114]) Blos-mi-ḥbebs.

This however needs an investigation. It is said that Guṇaprabha attained the age of 400 years. This statement, as well as that according to which his pupil was Çākyaprabha — is false. Indeed we read in the *Prabhāvatī*[1115]): My preceptor was Puṇyakīrti[1116]) who resided in Magadha, was the ornament (of that country) and greatly famed. From him I have heard (the Teaching) and now expound this my Commentary on the rules of the Vinaya that is to be the foundation of the teaching of the Arhats. — And further on:[1117]): — I have composed a Commentary elucidating the meaning, thinking: — May my teacher, the master Çāntiprabha[1118]) who abides far away and whose fame is all-pervading, grant me his point of view which I try to secure by recollection. — Thus (Çākyaprabha) himself says that he is the pupil of Puṇyakīrti and Çāntiprabha. In the *Triçata-kārikā*[1119]) it is said that (Çākyaprabha's) pupil was Çākyamitra.

Çākyaprabha has composed the *Triçata-kārikā* and the Commentary thereon called *Prabhāvatī*. On the *Vinaya-sūtra* a Commentary has been composed by Dharmamitra[1120]) who is considered by some to have been the pupil of Guṇaprabha. [126 b.] It is said moreover that the pupil of Çākyaprabha was Siṁhamukha, and the pupil of the latter — Jinamitra, but this must be scrutinized.

The Biography of the Bodhisattva Çāntideva.

Seven wonderful stories are known (about this teacher): —

The way how he secured his tutelary deity (1),
The splendour of his acts in Nālanda (2),
The refutation of his opponents (3),
The stories of the Pāṣaṇḍakas (4), of the beggars (5),
Of the king (6), and of the victory over the heretical teacher (7).

[The Story how Çāntideva met with his Tutelary Deity.]

In the southern country of Saurāṣṭra[1121]), the king Kalyāṇavarman[1122]) had a son born to him who was called Çāntivarman[1123]). The latter, whilst still a youth, studied many different sciences.

1115) Tg. MDO. LXXXIX. 183 b. 3—4. (N.)
1116) Bsod-nams-grags-pa. 1117) Ibid. 183 b. 6—7.
1118) Ži-ba-ḥod. 1119) Tg. MDO. LXXXIX. 83 a. 4.
1120) Vinayasūtra-ṭīkā, Tg. MDO. LXXXV and LXXXVI.
1121) Yul-ḥkhor-bzaṅ-po. 1122) Dge-baḥi-go-cha.
1123) Ži-baḥi-go-cha.

In particular, he learned from a certain exorcist[1124]) the methods of propitiating Mañjuçrī[1125]), made this propitiation and came to behold the countenance (of the deity).

Now, it happened that his father died and he was to be crowned king the next morning. But in the evening (before this was to happen), he beheld in a dream Mañjuçrī who was sitting on the throne which he was to occupy the morrow himself and who said to him: — My son, this seat belongs to me. I am thy protector. That I and thou shouldst sit on one seat can by no means be suitable[1126]). — Having awakened, Çāntideva understood that it was impossible for him to reign. So he fled and took orders in Nālanda with Jayadeva[1127]), the foremost of 500 Paṇḍits. Henceforth he was known by the name of Çāntideva.

[The Activity of Çāntideva in Nālanda.]

As concerns his internal conduct, — (it is known that) he heard the Doctrine from the Saint (Mañjuçrī), meditated over it and composed treatises of profound meaning. But, in his external life, he was known to the others as doing nothing else but eating, sleeping and walking about. Owing to this fact he was designated by the 3 nicknames of "Bhu" "Su" "Ku"[1128]), and the other monks, looking at his outward behaviour, thought: — The business of monks is the study of the 3 Wheels of the Doctrine [127 a]. This one is not possessed of the knowledge of either of them. He is thus unworthy to enjoy the alms granted by the faithful and must therefore be cast out. We shall read the Sūtras by turn, and then he will go away himself (as he knows nothing). Accordingly they summoned him to recite the Sūtras, but he replied that he was unable to do so, and prayed his preceptor: — Thou must bid me (to recite). The teacher commanded him (to read), and after that he consented. And, as some were of the opinion, that he knew nothing and all doubted of his knowledge, the monks, in order to try him, erected a lofty seat amidst a crowd of people. It was not clear how he could ascend this seat. But he pressed it down with his hands and mounted it. At this the greater part (of the hearers) were amazed. Thereafter he asked: — What am I to

1124) Ku-su-lu. Cf. Sarat-Chandra-Das, dictionary, p. 19, 20.
1125) Ḥjam-dpal-rnon-poḥi sgrub-thabs = Tīkṣṇa-Mañjuçrī-sādhana.
1126) Cf. Schiefner, Tāranātha, p. 163.
1127) Rgyal-baḥi-lha. 1128) *bhuj*, *sup* (*i. e.* *svap*) and?

read, — that which has or that which has not been known before? And they prayed him to read that which was new and unknown. Now, as the *Çikṣāsamuccaya* was too large a work and the *Sūtra-samuccaya* too abridged, he recited the *Bodhicaryāvatāra*[1129]) which in few words communicated an extensive subject-matter. And, after he had recited the verse of the Chapter on Highest Wisdom[1130]): —

When neither Ens nor Non-ens (appear before the mind), etc. he rose up into the air, higher and higher. Finally, his body became invisible, but the voice continued to resound. And, after the recitation was completed, he appeared again[1131]).

Thereafter, those who were possessed of a good memory, rehearsed the work as they had heard it. But, as (after the rehearsal) there appeared (different versions), viz. of 700, of 1000, and of more than 1000 verses, there arose doubt (as to which was the correct one). (Çāntideva) had said: — The Compendium of Discipline (the *Çikṣā-samuccaya*) must be looked over again and again. — And: — the short Summary, the Compendium of the Sūtras *(Sūtra-samuccaya)* must be looked over now. As these works were unknown, and as one had heard that he was residing in south, near the sanctuary of Çrīdakṣiṇa[1132]), 2 monks were sent to invite him. [127 b.] Having met with him, they asked (about the works). He told them that the *Çikṣā-samuccaya* and the *Sūtra-samuccaya* were to be found in the store-room of his school-house, written in the small characters of the Paṇḍits. As to the Bodhicaryāvatāra, he said that the version of 1000 verses was the right one. Thereafter he gave his instructions how to explain these works and act according to them. —

[Çāntideva's Victory over the Heretics.]

After that he departed to the east, where he took part in a great dispute. By the force of his miraculous powers, he reconciled (those who were quarrelling) and gave pleasure to all.

1129) Or: Bodhisattvacaryāvatāra (Byaṅ-chub-sems-dpaḥi spyod-pa-la ḥjug-pa).

1130) Çer-le, i. e. Çes-rab-kyi-leḥu = Prajñā-pariccheda or Prajñā-pāramitā-pariccheda. Bodhicaryāvatāra IX. 35. — ***yadā na bhāvo nā' bhāvo mateḥ saṁtiṣṭhate puraḥ / tadā' nya-gaty-abhāvena nirālambā praçāmyati //***

1131) Cf. Schiefner, Tārānātha, p. 165.

1132) Dpal-gyi-yon-can. Cf. Schiefner, Tārānātha, p. 166.

[The Conversion of the Pāṣaṇḍakas.]

Then, in a district lying not far to the west of Magadha, he took up his abode in the place where 500 adherents of the Pāṣaṇḍaka teaching were residing. Once, as a great disaster occurred in that country, and all food and beverage became exhausted, (the Pāṣaṇḍakas), greatly suffering, were searching one who could obtain for them means of livelihood. Finally, they selected (Çāntideva) as their chief and put themselves under his commands. The teacher got a bowl full of rice, blessed it, and made it suffice for all. After that he caused them to abstain from the Pāṣaṇḍaka teaching and to adopt Buddhism[1133]). —

[The Feeding of the Beggars.]

Thereupon a great famine happened in that country. Thousands of beggars, tormented by hunger and thirst, were near to their end. The teacher obtained means of livelihood, expounded the Doctrine and gave delight to all[1134]). —

[Çāntideva's Help to the King.]

Thereafter it happened that in the east, the king of Ariviçana was troubled by a riot. Some who were dissatisfied with the means of livelihood (they obtained) surrounded the king, intending to do him harm. As in such a manner the king would have been killed, there was a necessity of granting gifts (to those who were dissatisfied). (Çāntideva) came to the king's rescue and protected him. Now, the teacher had nothing but a wooden sword stamped with the seal of Mañjuçrī. The courtiers saw this and said to the king: —This man is a cheat; look at the instrument in his hand! [128 a.] The king, enraged, said (to Çāntideva): — Draw out thy sword! O Lord, —entreated the teacher, —this may bring harm to thyself. — May I be harmed, — replied the king, — nevertheless draw it out in any case! —Then, O Lord, thou must shut one eye and look with the other, — prayed Çāntideva. The king did so, but when the sword was drawn out, the one eye that saw could not sustain the shining (of the sword) and was blinded. The king then begged for forgiveness, entrusted himself to the protection of Çāntideva and was converted to Buddhism[1135]).

1133) Ibid. p. 167. 1134) Ibid. 1135) Ibid. p. 164.

[Çāntideva's Victory over Çankaradeva.]

Thereafter the teacher went to the south, to Çrīparvata where he lived as one who had devoted himself to the propitiation of Ucchūṣman[1136]), with the attributes of a beggar, naked and substituting on wash-water. Whilst he was thus abiding, Kacalahā, the female slave of the king of Khatavihāra, saw that the wash-water she had poured out reached the body of the teacher and began to boil. At that time a heretical teacher called Çankaradeva made it known to the king: — The day after to-morrow I shall draw in the skies the magic circle of Maheçvara. If you are unable to destroy it, I shall burn down all the Buddhist images and books, and make you adopt the Brāhmaṇic Doctrines. The king assembled the clergy and related the matter to them. And, as none of them could express his readiness to destroy the magic circle, the king became deeply grieved. But then the slave-girl related what she had seen before, and the king gave the order to seek (for Çāntideva). After they had searched for him everywhere, they found him sitting under a tree and told him the matter. He said: — I have the power (of destroying the magic circle). You must prepare for me an urn full of water, a pair of garments, and fire. This was done. Then, as in the evening the teacher went off murmuring, they all became possessed of doubt. Two days after, the magic circle was drawn. When the eastern quarter was just finished, the teacher, [128 b.] by the force of concentrated trance, called forth a mightly wind by which the magic circle was blown away, the herbs, trees and cities likewise were all of them either swept down or shaken so that they nearly fell. The people who lived (in those towns) were swept away. The heretical teachers were scattered and, like small birds by the wind, were carried away into the different regions. (Everything) was covered with great darkness. But then the teacher ejected a light from his forehead by which he showed the way to the king and queen. As they were without clothes and covered with dust, he gave them the water (that had been prepared before) to wash, covered them with the new clothes, and warmed them by the fires, thus causing delight to them. Thereafter the temples of the heretics were destroyed, and (the people) were converted to Buddhism. And up to this day that place is known as "the spot where the heretics were vanquished"[1137]). —

1136) Xyl. U-tshu-smaḥi spyod-pa. Cf. Ibid. p. 166. 1137) Ibid. p. 167.

Now, this master himself speaks of his own person as of an ordinary being, but the teacher Prajñākaramati calls him a Saint. Kṛṣṇa[1138]) says of him that he touched with his head the lotus-like feet of Mañjughoṣa. The teacher thus spoken of has composed 3 works: The ***Çikṣāsamuccaya***, an exposition in detail, the ***Sūtrasamuccaya***, an abridged Compendium of the Teaching, and the ***Bodhicaryāvatāra*** which exposes an extensive subject-matter in few words. According to the tradition, 100 Commentaries on the Bodhicaryāvatāra were extant in India, but only 8 have been translated into Tibetan. —

The History of the Grammatical Literature.

In the ***Lankāvatāra-sūtra***[1139]) we have the prophecy: — The author of (the treatises on) Grammar will be Pāṇini. — And in the ***Manjuçrī-mūla-tantra*** it is prophesied that (this Pāṇini) is to attain Enlightenment[1140]). Now the history of the grammatical treatises composed by the Brāhmaṇa Pāṇini and others is as follows: — At first, in the region of the 33 gods, a god named Sarvajñāna composed a great grammatical treatise. [129 a.] This was used by the gods, (subsequently) ceased to exist, and did not, therefore, appear in Jambudvīpa. Thereafter Çakra, the king of the gods, likewise composed a grammatical work called ***Indravyākaraṇa***. This work was perfectly apprehended by the sage Bṛhaspati who demonstrated it to the children of the gods and became known as the preceptor of the gods or the teacher of grammar. And thinking: —None except myself is skilful in grammar, —he became possessed of great pride. But the king of gods got an urn full of water from the ocean, took a drop of it by means of a halm of Kuça grass and said to Bṛhaspati: — The science of grammar as a whole is like the ocean. That part of it which I know is like the water of this urn, and that which thou knowest is only like this drop. Bṛhaspati was greatly disappointed, and thought that he would never be able to teach grammar again. But Indra said to him: — Though this be so, still thou must teach as far as thou knowest. — Such was his commandment, and (Bṛhaspati), not daring to disobey it, declared that he would not teach on the 4 auspicious days, but

---

1138) Nag-po-pa.

1139) Ed. Bunyiu Nanjio, p. 366. — ***Pāṇiniṁ çabda-nrtāıam . . .***

1140) Kg. RGYUD. XI. 447 a. 7—b. 1. (Nar.) — ***bram-zeḥi khyeḥu Pā-ṇi-ni / ṅes-par ñan-thos-byaṅ-chub-tu / ṅa-yis luṅ-bstan-byas-pa-yin //***

that all the other time he would expound. Accordingly, up to this day, the Brāhmaṇas observe the 4 auspicious days, saying: —

On the 8th day the teacher will be oppressed,
On the 14th — the pupils will be oppressed,
On the day of the new-moon the science will be oppressed,
On the first day everything will be oppressed. —

This treatise (the *Indravyākaraṇa*) came likewise to Jambudvīpa and was expounded there.

Thereupon, when it had ceased to exist, the Brāhmaṇa Pāṇini appeared. At first, being desirous to study grammar, he showed the lines of his hand to a fortune-teller who told him that he would not be possessed of the knowledge of grammar. Then he drew (the corresponding) line with a sharp knife, and set out in search of a teacher, but did not find any. Thereafter he propitiated Mahādeva who showed his countenance to him and asked: — What doest thou desire? — I wish to study grammar, — replied (Pāṇini). Then the god blessed him (129 b.] and simultaneously uttered the sounds "A", "I", "U". By this Pāṇini came to apprehend the whole of the grammatical science. So runs the legend. The Buddhists say, that (Pāṇini) came to the knowledge of Grammar through having propitiated Avalokita, and this agrees with Scripture. It is said in the *Mañjuçrī-mūla-tantra*[1141]):

Pāṇini, the Brāhmaṇa's son,
Has been prophesied by me
To attain the Enlightenment of the Çrāvakas;
And he shall likewise secure the charm
For propitiating the High Lord of the Universe. —

This teacher (Pāṇini) has composed a grammatical treatise containing 2000 rules which is known as the *Pāṇinīya-vyākaraṇa*. On this treatise a king of the Nāgas[1142]) composed a Commentary called the *Mahābhāṣya* consisting of 100000 Çlokas which became widely spread.

In later times, the king Udayana[1143]) had a wife who knew some parts of grammar. Once, when she and the king were washing, the king sprinkled water (upon her). The queen said: — "*Mamodakāsiñca*"[1144]) which in the Sanskrit language means: Do not sprinkle

---

1141) Cf. the preceding note and Schiefner, Tāranātha, p. 53 and 54.
1142) Çeṣa = Patañjali. 1143) Bde-spyod.
1144) Similarly in Tāranātha, Schiefner, p. 74.

water upon me. — The king, having applied the words to his barbaric language, understood them as: — Get me a broth of sesamum, — and ordered a slave to prepare such. The queen was distressed and, thinking it better to die than to be the companion of such an ox-like husband, intended to commit suicide. The king then asked her what was the matter, and she related the story (of Pāṇini) which we have given above. Thereafter Sarvavarman[1145]) the maternal uncle of the king said to him: — I shall propitiate Kumāra Kārttikeya[1146]) and obtain the magical power of the word; therefore thou must say to the queen: — Thou must not do so (i. e. must not commit suicide). — The king did so and the queen was consoled.

Sarvavarman made his propitiation, and Kumāra Kārttikeya showed his countenance to him and asked what he wanted. — I wish to study Grammar, — replied Sarvavarman. Then Kārttikeya began with "*Siddho varṇa-sama-āmnāyaḥ*"[1147]) [130 a.] and explained up to the 15th Chapter. Then (Sarvavarman) became full of pride and exclaimed: — I have found it out! Kārttikeya then turned his vehicle and, as the tail of the peacock (on which he was mounted) appeared behind, Sarvavarman exlaimed: — O Kalāpa! I pray, forgive me! Now, *Kalāpa* means a mass, any aggregate of component parts. Sarvavarman applied it to the peacock's feathers. In connection with this (Sarvavarman's work) became known under the name of *Kalāpa*. Thereafter (Sarvavarman) taught it to the king, the latter came to understand it, and the queen was pleased. —

Now, as the work did not contain all the parts of grammar, Sarvavarman and the Brāhmaṇa Vararuci[1148]) made additions to it, and it was issued as consisting of 400 Çlokas and 24 chapters. The Paṇḍit Durgasiṁha[1149]) has composed a Commentary to it[1150]). (Another) Commentary called the *Çiṣyahitā*[1151]) was written by the Paṇḍit Yaçobhūti[1152]). Then there appeared the *Candra-vyā-*

[1145]) Sic. acc. to Xyl. Cf. Schiefner, Tārānātha p. 76. Perhaps: Çarvavarman. In Cordier's Index to the Tangyur we have s. v. Kalāpa-sūtra the designation of its author as: — Saptavarman, Sarvavarman, Çarvavarman, Īçvaravarman or Dbaṅ-phyug-go-cha. Cf. vol. I. p. 47, note 456.

[1146]) Gžon-nu Smin-drug.

[1147]) Xyl. Siddho varṇa-samaṁ naye. Cf. Schiefner, Tārānātha, p. 75.

[1148]) Mchog-sred. [1149]) Bgrod-dkaḥ-seṅ-ge.

[1150]) Tg. MDO. CXVI. 110—125. (Pek.) [1151]) Slob-ma-la-phan-pa.

[1152]) Grags-ḥbyor. Tg. MDO. CXVI. 125—163 or CXXXII. 1—295 (Pek).

karaṇa on which the maternal uncle of Candragomin, Dharmadāsa[1153]) has composed a Commentary consisting of 6000 Çlokas, and the teacher Ratnamati[1154]) a Sub-commentary of 12 000 Çlokas. This Sub-commentary in its turn has been elucidated by the Paṇḍit Pūrṇacandra[1155]) in a work of 36 000 Çlokas. Thereafter the Paṇḍit Rājaçrī has made a Compendium of the *Kalāpa* and the *Candra-vyākaraṇa*; his work is known as the *Rājaçrī-vyākaraṇa.* Finally in later times, the Paṇḍit Smṛti has composed a work on Grammar for the use of Tibetans, called the *Āyudhopama-vacanamukha*[1156]). A detailed history of these grammatical treatises, as well as of the works on Poetics, Dramatical Composition, Medicine, etc. is to be found elsewhere. —

On the Lost Parts of the Kanon.

In such a way the persons who were foretold by the Buddha have preserved the Doctrine by preaching and acting according to it. But at present only a part (of the Kanon) exists, its complete form having been lost. In the *Vyākhyāyukti*[1157]) it is said:—[130 b.]

As the basis for the correct rehearsal is lost,
We know that (the Kanon) is not complete. —

Now, the *Duḥkha-skandha-sūtra*[1158]), the *Udayana-paripṛcchā*[1159]), the *Guru-sūtra*[1160]), the Sūtra of Ānanda[1161]), the Sūtra of Kāçyapa[1162]) and many others had disappeared and were not to be found at the time when Vasubandhu lived. In the *Ratnakūṭa* which consisted of 100 000 chapters, there remain only 49, of the *Mahāsamaya*[1163]) which likewise contained 100 000 chapters — only 60, and of the *Avataṁsaka*, similarly of 100 000 chapters — only 40 chapters. Of the *Lankāvatāra* which consisted of 36 000 (Çlokas) we have only 3600, of the *Ghana-vyūha*[1164]) of 12 000 verses only 1300, of the *Mahāmegha* which contained 100 000 verses, — only a few chapters, of the *Samādhirāja*, — only 15 divisions, of the

---

[1153]) Chos-kyi-ḥbaṅs. [1154]) Rin-chen-blo-gros.
[1155]) Zla-ba-gaṅ-ba.
[1156]) Smra-sgo Mtshon-cha. Tg. MDO. CXVI. 273—278. (Pek.)
[1157]) Aga monastery edition 97 b. 6.
[1158]) Sdug-bsṅal-gyi-phuṅ-poḥi-mdo.
[1159]) Ḥchar-byed-kyis-žus-pá. [1160]) Bla-maḥi-mdo.
[1161]) Kun-dgaḥ-boḥi-mdo. [1162]) Ḥod-sruṅs-kyi-mdo.
[1163]) Ḥdus-pa-chen-po.
[1164]) Rgyan-stug-po-bkod-pa.

Ekottarika-āgama[1165]) in which there were from 1 to 100 subjects, — only from 1 to 10. As concerns the *Nirvāṇa* — and the *Smṛtyupasthāna-sūtra*[1166]), their translation has not been finished. Of the *Çūraṁgama-sūtra*[1167]) that had 10 000 Çlokas, only 1 chapter (has been translated). In the *Mahā-tathāgata-uṣṇiṣa*[1168]), the *Mahā-adhigama*[1169]), and the *Candragarbha-paripṛcchā*[1170]) there was a great number of chapters. Of each of these chapters many passages have not been translated at all. Of the translations made previously, the greater part has likewise disappeared. Moreover, many Sūtras quoted in the great Chinese Commentaries are not to be found. Other Sūtras, as the *Mahā-vyavadāna-bhūmi*[1171]) have their abode in the realm of the gods. The detailed *Prajñā-pāramitā-sūtra* containing 1 000 000 000 Çlokas is preserved in the abode of the king of the Gandharvas, [131 a.] the intermediate (of the detailed), of 10 000 000 Çlokas, in the realm of the king of the gods, and the abridged (of the detailed), that is the *Çatasāhasrikā*, exists in it complete form in the region of the Nāgas.

As concerns the Tantric Scripture, it is said in the *Jñāna-vajra-samuccaya*[1172]) that the *Kriyā-tantra*[1173]) numbered 4000 texts, the *Ācāra-tantra*[1174]) 8000, the *Kalpa-tantra*[1175]) 4000, the Tantras containing (the teaching of) both (the *Kriyā* and *Ācāra*) — 6000, the *Mahā-yoga-tantra*[1176]) — 12 000, and the *Mahā-anuttara-yoga-tantra*[1177]) — 14 000. Each Tantra consists of a great number of Fundamental and Explanatory Tantras, etc. Of these the *He-vajra*[1178]) of 100 000 verses, the *Guhya-samāja* of 25 000 verses, *Mahā-Çaṁvara-abhidhāna*[1179]) of 500 000 verses, the *[Çaṁvara]-Uttaratantra*[1180]) of 100 000 verses, the *Kālacakra* of 12 000 verses, the *Yoga-anuvidyā*[1181]) of 36 000 verses, the *Māyājālā*[1182]) of 16 000 verses, the *Mahāmāyā* of 18 000 verses, the great *Raktayamāri-*

1165) Gcig-las-ḥphros-pa. 1166) Dran-pa-ñer-gžag.
1167) Dpaḥ-bar-ḥgro-baḥi-mdo.
1168) De-bžin-gçegs-paḥi-gtsug-gtor-chen-po.
1169) Rtogs-pa-chen-po. 1170) Zla-ba-sñiṅ-pos-žus-pa.
1171) Rnam-par-sbyoṅ-baḥi-sa-chen-po. 1172) Ye-çes-rdo-rje-kun-las-btus.
1173) Bya-baḥi-rgyud. 1174) Spyod-paḥi-rgyud.
1175) Rtog-paḥi-rgyud. 1176) Rnal-ḥbyor-chen-poḥi-rgyud.
1177) Rnal-ḥbyor-chen-po-bla-na-med-paḥi-rgyud.
1178) Ḥdar-byed-kyi-gliṅ-na (?) Kye-rdo-rje.
1179) Bde-mchog-mṅon-pa-brjod-par-chen-po.
1180) (Bde-mchog-gi) (?) rgyud-phyi-ma. 1181) Rnal-ḥbyor-rjes-su-rig-pa.
1182) Sgyu-ḥphrul-dra-ba.

tantra[1183]) of 300 000 verses, the *Tārā-abhyudaya-tantra*[1184]) of 700 Chapters, the *Hayagrīva-kalpa*[1185]) of 700 Chapters, the *Amogha-pāça-tantra*[1186]) etc. are said to exist in the region of the gods, in Çambhala, Uḍḍiyāna, etc.

Moreover, in India, Kashmir, Nepal, Kaṁsadeça[1187]), China, the Great China[1188]), Persia, Campaka, in the monkey-realm, in the country of the Golden-eyed, in Rugma, Ramya[1189]), Tāmradvīpa[1190]), Siṁhaladvīpa, [131 b.] Priyangudvīpa, Yamunādvīpa, Suvarṇadvīpa[1191]), Makha, Khaçya, Gyiljoṅ, Shaṅ-shuṅ, Bru-sha, A-sha, Sum-pa, Sahor, Mi-ñag, the country of Jaṅ, of the Yogurs, the Thogar, Uḍḍiyāna, Dramila[1192]), Andhra[1193]), Cola, Kalinga, and other great kingdoms as well as in the districts of Tibet, as the Teaching was expounded, disappeared, and again began its existence in them, the Scriptures of the 3 Vehicles, either complete or incomplete, in parts, have been preserved. It is said, likewise, that a great number of sacred texts exist in the region of the Nāgas. In the *Çiṣya-lekha* we read[1193a]). —

The Teaching which is like a precious jewel,
Being sublime and indestructible,
And which shows the Path of Purity,
Has been contemplated with reverence by the hooded Nāgas,
Like the diamonds in their diadems, and disperses
The darkness for those who dwell in the depths of the earth.

IV. Acc$_1$b$_2$c$_3$c$_4$. The Way how the Doctrine will cease to exist.

It is said in the *Candragarbha-paripṛcchā*[1194]): — O Lord, how will the Highest Doctrine finally cease to exist? Owing to what

---

1183) Gçin-rjeḥi-gçed-dmar-poḥi-rgyud.

1184) Sgrol-ma-mṅon-par-ḥbyuṅ-baḥi-rgyud.

1185) Rta-mgrin-gyi-rtog-pa. 1186) Don-yod-žags-paḥi-rgyud. 1187) Li.

1188) Bu-ton makes the difference between Rgya-nag = Cina and Rgya-nag-chen-po = Mahācīna.

1189) Ram-ma. 1190) Zaṅs-gliṅ. 1191) Gser-gliṅ.

1192) Ḥgro-ldiṅ-baḥi-yul.

1193) Loṅ-baḥi-yul. Bu-ton evidently read Andhadeça, "the country of the blind" instead of Andhradeça. 1193a) Tg. MDO. XXXIII. 71 a. 4—5. (N.)

1194) Kg. MDO. XXXII. 216 b. 6—220 b. 4. The prophecy concerning the cessation of the Doctrine is treated in the Kangyur like a separate text: Ḥphags-pa Zla-baḥi-sñiṅ-pos žus-paḥi mdo-las saṅs-rgyas-kyi bstan-pa gnas-pa daṅ ḥjig-paḥi tshul luṅ-bstan-pa.

factors is it to disappear, and who will be the cause of its destruction? — (The Buddha replied): — After I have passed away, during 500 years, a great number of living beings is to appear, who will act according to my Doctrine and obtain deliverance. Thereafter, during 500 years there will appear many who practise meditation. But the kings, the ministers, and the ordinary living beings[1194a]) who were devoted to the Doctrine will subsequently become less in number. Thereupon, during another 500 years, a great number of teachers who expound the Highest Doctrine, and who lead the living beings to salvation will appear. The number of the Çrāvaka Arhats will however become diminished. The kings [132 a.] and the greater part of the living beings will become mere hearers, but will not apply energy to realize (the precepts) and to live according to them. In such a way faith will become weakened. The protectors of the Highest Doctrine will grow distressed, and those who are not devoted to the Highest Doctrine will become more powerful than before. The kings of Jambudvīpa will invade each other with war and disturbances will arise[1194b]) . When 300 years of these 500 will have passed away, the gods and Nāgas[1194c]) who live according to the Doctrine will no more exist, and the living beings will cease to believe in the Highest Doctrine. Even those who are virtuous will not act according to the precepts. And, as they will have no energy, their achievements will be likewise feeble. The 4 chief colours and those derived from these 4, as well as the smells, tastes, etc. will become weak. There will be likewise famine and plagues befalling men and cattle. When 200 years will have remained, the monks will no more act according to the Doctrine and search for worldly gain and renown. They will lack Commiseration, will not live morally, and will depreciate those who act righteously according to the Doctrine. They will appropriate riches and objects of enjoyment, rely upon the orders of temporal power, rule kingdoms, be the messengers of kings, and seek to please them. They will sow disunion between the kings

---

[1194a]) Sic. acc. to the Kg. — ***rgyal-po daṅ blon-po daṅ sems-can-phal-rnams kyaṅ*** . . . The Xyl. has: ***rgyal-po daṅ sems-can phal-cher.***

[1194b]) The Kg. has after this (fol. 217 a. 3): ***bdud-kyi ris kyaṅ ḥphel-bar-ḥgyur-ro*** — the family of the Evil One will likewise increase. This passage is left out in the Xyl.

[1194c]) The Kg. has = ***lha klu-la-sogs-pa sems-can-sruṅs-ma-rnams.*** — The gods and the Nāgas who protect the living beings.

and their subjects, and will seek means of livelihood by traffic and gain. Those acting according to the Highest Doctrine, will not do so by realizing it in harmony with their internal constitution, but will only act for outward show, and turn hypocrites. At that time all the gods and Nāgas, devoted to the Doctrine will abandon the lands where the monks live in such a way, and will not abide there anymore. The hosts of Māra and other foes of the Doctrine will appear there and become powerful. [132 b.] The kings, ministers, etc. will lose faith and will no more draw a distinction between virtue and sin. They will inflict wounds upon the Highest Doctrine, and will rob and carry away the property of the 3 Jewels and that of the Congregation. They will have no shame in committing sinful deeds and will destroy the images and sanctuaries, so that the objects of worship will grow scant. But then, by the force of the virtue the monks and householders acting according to the Doctrine who are to appear and will abide in some places, rain and snow will descend in different countries at due time, prosperous years will come, human and animal diseases will grow less, and (a time of) happiness for the lands will appear.

But this is not to have a long duration. For the greater part there will be manifold suffering and uneasiness. At that time, 3 kings, neither of Indian, nor of Chinese descent, Yavana, Palhika and Çakuna[1194d]) will appear. These will not act according to the Highest Doctrine, will conduct wars, fight and quarrel and will lay waste many districts in the west and in the north. The sanctuaries and temples in these countries they will destroy, and burn down with fire, and rob the objects of worship, the property of the 3 Jewels etc. These 3 kings will be in mutual strife and the reign of each of them will not be happy. But then, at a certain time, they will become allies, unite in one kingdom, collect a great army, and take possession of Gāndhāra, Mahādeça, and other countries lying on this side of the Ganges.

At that time, on the other side of the Ganges, to the south, in the country of Kauçambi, there will be a king named Mahendrasena. This king will have a son called Duḥprasahahasta[1195]) with an iron mark on his forehead and with the lower part of his body,

---

[1194d]) Sic. acc. to Kg. (fol. 217 b. 4) The Xyl. has: Balabū and Çikuna. We could perhaps translate: "The Grecian, the Persian and the Scythian kings".

[1195]) The Xyl. here and further on: Duprasaha. Kg.: Dusprasahasta.

up to the elbows stained with blood [133 a.]. At that time to 500 ministers 500 sons will be born who will be stained with blood up to their waists. At the same time the king will become possessed of a colt that will speak. And, the evening on which that (colt is to be born) a rain of blood is to descend from the skies. The king will ask the meaning of these omens from an anchorite possessed of the 5 forms of supernatural perception and the latter will utter the following prophecy: — O sovereign, thy son will moisten the soil of Jambudvīpa with blood, and thereafter he will make himself the Lord of Jambudvīpa. Thereupon, after 12 years will have passed away since the birth of the prince, the allied forces of the 3 kings mentioned before, Yavana and the rest, 300 000 in number with the kings at their head, will invade the realm of the king Mahendrasena. Thus war will break out, and the king will be distressed and lament. As he will thus abide in sorrow, his son Duḥprasahahasta will ask: Father, wherefore art thou grieved? — And the father will say: — I am grieved, because the armies of the 3 kings have appeared in our country. — To this the son will reply: — Father, do not be distressed, I shall vanquish these armies. — Well, — will say the father. Thereafter, the prince will put 500 Pāṣaṇḍakas, sons of ministers and others at the head of an army of 200 000 men. At the time of battle, the iron mark on the prince's forehead will appear distinctly, the whole of his body will become of iron, with terrible fury he will charge and conquer. After the victory, the army of Duḥprasahahasta will return and the father will say: — My son, thou hast fought with such an army of 3 kings and hast conquered. [133 b.] Well hast thou done. Henceforth thou art to rule the kingdom, and I in my turn will embrace religious life. — And, obeying to his orders, the son will assume the reign. Thereafter, during 12 years he will fight with the armies of the 3 kings and will gradually vanquish a great number of these forces. He will capture the 3 kings themselves and cause them to be put to death. Thereupon he will make himself emperor of Jambudvīpa. Then the king will say to his ministers: — The fact that I have become the Lord of Jambudvīpa should make me rejoice. But great is the sin (I have committed) by causing so many living beings to be killed. Therefore I am grieved. What am I to do in order to be purified from this sin? — The ministers will say: — In the country of Pāṭaliputra there is a teacher of the Doctrine versed in the 3 Codes, the son of the Brāhmaṇa Agnidatta called Çiṣyaka[1196]) who abides in a monastery. If he is invited he will be able to purify thee from thy sin. The king will be delighted, and, having invited the monk Çiṣyaka, will ask him: — By what means can I become purified from my sins? — The monk will reply: — Thou must worship the 3 Jewels for 12 years and seek their protection. If thou doest this, thou canst be purified from thy guilt. — Then the king will send messengers to whatever monks will be living in Jambudvīpa in order to assemble them all at Kauçambi and will not allow them to practise their religious obeisances in other countries. But the monks on the way, will for the greater part perish from wild beasts, savages, floods etc., — and only 100 000 will come into the king's presence. These will come, and the king will make a feast, offer presents to them and worship. Thereafter [134 a.] the members of the Congregation will ask each other. — Where is thy teacher? Where are thy pupils? Where are thy friends, thy associates in the observances? And they will relate how such and such were killed by wild beasts and savages, were carried away by the flood, had died, being overcome by illness, and so on. Each of them will become full of grief, they will shed tears and beat their breasts. Then the king will bid them not to be grieved, but the members of the Congregation will not listen to him. The king will be distressed, will turn his face down and fall asleep. And whilst sleeping he will utter the following entreaty: — From the Congregation of monks who are mere worldly beings I will have no protection. O may I behold the countenance of an Arhat! And the gods of this world will say to him whilst he is dreaming: — On the mountain Gandhamadana[1197]) there abides an Arhat called Surata[1198]), the son of the merchant Sudhana[1198a]). If he be invited he will purify thee from thy guilt and clear all thy doubts. —And the king, in accordance with the dream will, immediately after awakening, send messengers, invite the Saint, worship him and make his salutations. Then, on the 14th day of that month, the Congregation will assemble, and of those

---

[1196]) Slob-ma-can. Corrected acc. to Kg. (fol. 218 b. 3—4) — bram-ze Agnidattaputra . . . miṅ ni Çiṣyaka ste Slob-ma-can. The Xyl. has: bram-ze Akan-dra-dhaḥi-bu. (Sic!)

[1197]) The Xyl. has Gandhamahāna.

[1198]) Des-pa.

[1198a]) Corr. acc. to Kg. (fol. 219 a. 5) Su-dha-na-pu-tra ra-rna-ça (?) ste tshoṅ-dpon Nor-bzaṅs-kyi bu żes-bya-ba rab-tu-byuṅ-ba Su-ra-ta ste Des-pa . . .

who have newly taken orders some will pray the teacher Çiṣyaka to expound the Vinaya. But Çiṣyaka will say: — If a man has lost his eyes and has no ears and nose, of what use is a mirror to him? I can teach the Vinaya, but ye will not act according to it and will not preserve your morals. What use is it therefore of teaching the Vinaya to you? Then the Arhat Surata, with a voice resembling the roar of a lion, will say: — I have observed the precepts of the Doctrine of Buddha the Lord, and, up to this day, I have not lost the slightest part of it. [134 b.] Thou must not speak like that, but expound the Vinaya. — Thus will he speak, and the teacher Çiṣyaka, having recognized in him an Arhat, will be full of shame and sit without uttering a word. Then the pupil of Çiṣyaka, the monk called Angada[1199]) will rise up from his seat and say to the Arhat: — How canst thou, thyself immoral and ignorant of the Vinaya, show contempt with our teacher who is versed in the 3 Codes of Scripture? — And, coming into a rage, he will strike the Arhat and kill him. Thereafter the Yakṣa Dadhimukha[1200]), devoted to the Highest Doctrine, will seize a thunderbolt, appear visibly and say to the monk Angada: — Wherefore hast thou killed the Arhat? — Then he will strike him with his thunderbolt and kill him. After that the monk Kerāda will kill Çiṣyaka, and then all the monks will kill each other, so that not one of them will be left. Thereafter the gods, Nāgas and the other guardians of the Doctrine who abide in the skies, will for the greater part become distressed. They will weep, and their tears will fall down on earth as a rain of blood and fire. The skies will turn yellow, black and red and there will be lightning and great thunder. From the body of the star called Dhūmaketu black smoke will come forth, owing to which the sun, the moon, etc. will lose their shine. At that time the gods of the region of the Thirty-three, the Mother Mahāmāyā and others will come. They will lament, collect all the coloured garments of the monks and carry them to the region of the 33 gods. Then the king will ask: — From where comes this great noise?— And they will say to him: — There arose a quarrel amongst the members of the clergy and they have killed each other. — The king, distressed, will rise up [135 a.] and at

---

[1199]) The Xyl. has Dpuṅ-rgyan. Kg. (fol. 219 b. 3): Çi-ṣya-kaḥi slob-ma dge-sloṅ Aṁ-ga-da ste Dpuṅ-gi-tshogs-ḥjigs-su-ruṅ.

[1200]) Žo-gdoṅ.

daybreak will go to the outward temple to see. There he will behold some of the monks with their heads cut off, some with their arms and legs severed from the body, and others with their eyes cast out, having thus in different ways met with their death. Full of grief, he will search for the bodies of the Arhat and of Çiṣyaka, the teacher versed in the 3 Codes. He will take them under his right and his left arm-pit and say: — The Arhat was to me like a father [1200a]). The teacher of the 3 Codes was the treasury of the Doctrine. Now, as they both have died, I shall henceforth have no pleasure in life. My kingdom — I will give it to anyone who wishes to have it. — Thus saying, he will shut his eyes and cease to look about. Then the ministers in order to appease the grief of the king, will give to 500 men the appearance of monks. They will not, however, shave their heads and beards with a razor, but will burn them with fire. They will dress them in the hide of black and red cattle [1200b]), will come into the king's presence and say: — 500 monks have arrived. — The king, delighted, will open his eyes, and behold (the so-called monks) dressed in the hide of cattle and with their hair and beards singed. Then he will order to bring the sacrificial tools for worshipping the 3 Jewels and will perform the sacrificial rites. Thereafter he will question (the new-comers) concerning the Doctrine. But, as they will not know even a single word of it, the king will again become full of grief. And after that he will collect the corpses of the monks, cause them to be burned, and perform the funeral rites. —

At that time all the supports of the Highest Doctrine in Jambu-dvīpa will meet with an end. Thereafter gold will be transformed into bad silver and stone, silver will be changed, into bad brass and stone, brass — into copper, and pearls — into horn. Of the 6 tastes [135 b.] only 2, viz. the bitter and the sour will remain. —

And in the prophecy of Sanghavardhana [1201]) etc. it is said: — The cast images etc. will be taken into the realm of the Nāgas.

[1200a]) Corrected arr. to Kg. (fol. 220 a. 3): *dgra-bcom-pa ṅaḥi pha yin.* The Xyl. has *ṅaḥi ma yin* "mother".

[1200b]) The Xyl. leaves out (Kg. fol. 220 a. 4—5) — *tshon sna-brgya yaṅ dehi-tshe nub-pas ban-de lṅa-brgya yaṅ chos-gos mi-bdog-nas phyugs nag-po* etc. — At that time the hundred different colours will have ceased to exist. Therefore, as it will be impossible (to obtain for) the 500 monks religious robes, they will dress them, etc.

[1201]) Dge-ḥdun-ḥphel-gyi lun-bstan-pa.

All the writings will become corrupt, all the clothes will be coarse, all the tastes except the bitter and the stringent and all the jewels will disappear. The kings themselves will die from grief that the Doctrine is to exist no more. —

All this is said in accordance with (the prophecy that) the Doctrine is to exist 2000 years. In the Sub-commentary to the ***Abhisamayālaṁkāra***, composed by Dharmamitra[1202]), it is clearly said that such facts have likewise taken place before. —

In general the causes owing to which the Doctrine ceases to exist, are the cessation of the force of a Buddha's previous vows and entreaties and the fact that the converts to the Teaching are no more to be found. As concerns the conditions, it is said that a Doctrine ceases to exist owing to 3 such conditions, viz. 1. The deterioration of the religious ascetics from their philosophical views and observances, 2. the loss of devotion to the church from the part of the alms-givers, and 3. impediments caused by Māra, by the gods of the latter's realm and by malignant ghosts *(preta)*. With regard to the Doctrine of this our Teacher it is clearly said that the conditions for its cessation are the first two. As concerns the time of cessation it is said that, according to the ***Prajñaptiçāstra***, (the Doctrine) will disappear when human age will be 40 years. Chag says that it will happen at the period when it will be 30 years. I, however, have not seen any authoritative source affirming this. —

We read moreover in the ***Karuṇāpuṇḍarīka***[1203]): — After the cessation of Buddha Çākyamuni's Highest Doctrine, the relics (of the Buddha) will sink down to the golden foundation of the earth. Then, when the Sahālokadhātu[1204]) will become deprived of precious jewels, these relics will become a Vaiḍūrya stone called Ketumati[1205]) which will remove all poverty. Thereafter these relics [136 a.] will rise up till Akaniṣṭha. A rain of flowers will then descend and, from that rain, the names of the 3 Jewels and other different words of the Doctrine will be heard. The gods abiding in the World of Desire and in the Ethereal Sphere will hear these words of the Doctrine and remember their previous virtuous deeds. They will descend into Jambudvīpa and convert men to the 10

[1202]) Tg. MDO. VIII. 121 a. 8. (Pek.) Cf. vol. I. note 1246.

[1203]) Kg. MDO. VI. 354 a. 3—355 b. 1. (N.) The passage in the Xyl. is condensed.

[1204]) Mi-mjed-kyi-ḥjig-rten-gyi khams. [1205]) Tog-gi-blo-gros.

virtues. Moreover, the flowers in the skies will be transformed into diverse precious jewels and will descend into the Sahālokadhātu. And all strife and the like of the living beings in the Sahālokadhātu will be pacified and there will be prosperity and abscence of illness. The living beings who will perceive these jewels, touch, and enjoy them, will be rendered irretrievable from (the Doctrine of) the 3 Vehicles. Then the relics will again take up their abode in the depths of the golden foundation of the earth. In a similar manner, at the times of war and famine, and when the 3 intervening ages will come, those relics will be transformed into precious sapphires, will rise up to Akaniṣṭha and abide there. As before, the rain of flowers will descend, the Words of the Doctrine will be heard, a rain of jewels will come down, and all hostile elements will be pacified. Then the relics will again come to abide in the depths of the golden foundation of the earth. —

In the *Nandamitra-avadāna*[1206]) it is said: — When the age of men will have the duration of 700 years, the 16 great Elders (Sthaviras) will assemble together all the collections of sacred books belonging to the Doctrine of Çākyamuni wherever they might be. [136 b.] Then they will make a sanctuary of the 7 kinds of jewels and circumambulate (the sacred books) deposited there. Then, having seated themselves down cross-legged, they will say: — Praise be to the Lord, the Tathāgata, the Arhat, the Perfect Supreme Buddha Çākyamuni! — Having made this salutation, the Elders will pass away into the final Nirvāṇa. The sanctuary of the 7 kinds of Jewels will disappear and abide below, in the golden foundation of the earth. After that, the Teaching of the Buddha Çākyamuni, the Highest Doctrine will cease to exist, and thereupon 70 millions of Pratyekabuddhas will appear in this world. Thereafter, when the age of the living beings will have a duration of 80 000 years, the Tathāgata Maitreya will make his apparition on earth. — In the ***Bodhisattva-piṭaka*** it is said that in the intervening age, from the time when human age will be reduced to 10 years and till the coming of Maitreya, in the period of growth, 80 000 Pratyekabuddhas will appear. According to some sources, the Buddha Maitreya will appear 570 000 000 years after the attainment of Nirvāṇa by the Buddha Çākyamuni. —

1206) Dgaḥ-baḥi-bçes-gñen-gyi-rtogs-brjod. Tg. MDO. XC.

Conclusion.

1. The Teaching of the Lord which is a lamp made of precious jewels,
   And is the treasury of all the virtues that lead to the super-bliss (of Salvation)[1207],
   By the force of time comes to its end
   And fades away like a flower deprived of moisture.

2. Now the Doctrine will not abide for long,
   Human life is unsteady like a torch exposed to the wind,
   The consequences of former deeds, the passions, and the Lord of Death are full of power,
   Therefore be devoted to the Doctrine and secure its treasures![1208]

3. This history the monk of Çākya's (spiritual) descent
   Who is in the power of this age and deprived of true concentration,
   Bu-ton with the large mouth and resembling a parrot, has written down.
   May he by the virtue of this soon come to see the countenance of the Invincible (Maitreya)! [137 a.]

Of the History of Buddhism entitled "the Jewellery of Scripture" finished the 2d Chapter "On the rise of the Doctrine in this world in general".

1207) *ṅes-legs* = *niḥçreyasa*.

1208) *rin-chen grub* — an illusion to Bu-ton's personal name.

IV B. The History of Buddhism in Tibet

The second general topic is the way how the Doctrine took its origin in Tibet. We have here 3 sub-divisions: —

a) The early period of the propagation of the Doctrine.

b) The subsequent period of propagation.

c) The index of the doctrinal works translated during these 2 periods.

IV B a. The Earlier Period of Propagation.

As concerns the way how the human generation first appeared in Tibet, we read in the Commentary on the *Devātiçayastotra*[1209]) that at the time when the 5 Pāṇḍavas[1210]) were fighting with the 12 armies of the Kauravas[1211]), the king Rūpati with 1000 warriors, in the disguise of women, fled into the rocky district of the Himālaya. Of these (the Tibetans) are considered to be the offspring. In the Tibetan legends it is said that (the Tibetans) are the descendants of a monkey and the fiendess of a rock. A detailed account of this is to be found elsewhere.

As regards the genealogy of the Tibetan kings, some say that (their ancestor) was the 5th descendant of Prasenajit the king of Kosala, according to some it was the 5th descendant of the youngest, feeble son of Bimbisāra. Still others say that at the time when the Tibetans were oppressed by 12 petty chiefs of the demons and Yakṣas, the king of Vatsa, Udayana[1212]), had a son born to him, whose eyelids were overhanging and whose fingers were connected with a web. As the child with such distinctive marks appeared, (the king) was frightened and ordered him to be put into a leaden box and thrown into the Ganges. (The boy) was however found

[1209]) Lha-las-phul-du-byuṅ-baḥi bstod-paḥi ḥgrel-pa. The work of Prajñāvarman, Tg. BSTOD. I.

[1210]) Skya-bseṅ-bu lṅa.

[1211]) Sgra-ṅan. The Xyl. has erroneously Dgra-ṅan.

[1212]) Ḥchar-byed.

by a peasant who brought him up. When he grew older, and the story (how he was found) was related to him, he became full of grief and fled to the Himālayas.

Gradually he passed by the Hla-ri Yöl-wa[1213]) and came out into the plain of "Tsan with the 4 gates"[1214]). The Bön priests who came from the Mu-thag[1215]) and Mu-kā[1216]) declared that he was a god. [137 b.] After they had asked him who he was and he replied: — I am a mighty one[1217]), — they inquired from where he came and he pointed with his finger to the sky. After their efforts to comprehend the language of each other turned to be unsuccessful, (the Böns) placed him on a wooden throne which they loaded on the necks of four men and said: — We shall make him our lord. — Therefrom he derived his name of Ña-ṭhi-tsen-po[1218]) "the neck-chaired Mighty One". It was he who became the first king of Tibet.

His son was Mu-ṭhi-tsen-po[1219]), the son of the latter Tiṅ-ṭhi[1219a]), the son of this one So-ṭhi, the latter's son Ye-ṭhi, the son of this one — *Dag-ṭhi*[1220]), and the son of the latter — Si-ṭhi-tsen-po[1221]). These are accordingly called the 7 Ṭhi. Up to the time of the latter the worship called the Döl-bön[1222]) was spread. Of the 3 sons of this king, one who was called Ja-ṭhi[1223]) received the surname of Pu-de-k'uṅ-gye[1224]). His son was A-ço-leg[1225]), and the son of the latter — I-ço-leg who built the Chin-bar-tag-tse[1226]), — the first fortified castle. The son of this king was T'o-ço-leg who had a son called K'u-rub-leg. The latter's son was Ḍoṅ-je-leg[1227]), and the son of this one — Tho-ço-leg. These six are known as the "6 Good-Ones of the Earth"[1228]). The son of the last of these kings was Gye-śa-nam-śin-de[1229]) and the son of this one — De-nöl-nam[1230]). From the time of the latter and up to Ṭhi-thog-je-thog-tsen[1231]) there was a long succession of kings. As the 26th of this line, there appeared the king Tho-tho-ri-ñan-tsen[1232]). When the latter attained the age of 16 years and was

---

1213) Lha-ri-yol-ba. 1214) Btsan-thaṅ-sgo-bži. 1215) Dmu-thag.
1216) Dmu-skas. 1217) Btsan-po. 1218) Gñaḥ-khri-btsan-po.
1219) Mu-khri-btsan-po. 1219a) Diṅ-khri. 1220) Gdags-khri.
1221) Sri-khri-btsan-po. 1222) Rdol-bon. 1223) Bya-khri.
1224) Spu-lde-guṅ-rgyal. 1225) A-ço-legs.
1226) Ḥchiṅ-bar-stag-rtse. 1227) Ḥbroṅ-rje-legs.
1228) Saḥi legs drug. 1229) Rgyal-za-rnam-zin-lde.
1230) Lde-snol-gnam. 1231) Khri-thog-rje-thog-btsan.
1232) Tho-tho-ri-gñan-btsan.

abiding on the summit of the palace Yam-bu-la-gaṅ, a casket fell from the skies, and when its lid was opened, the ***Karaṇḍavyūha-sūtra***[1233]), the 100 ***Precepts***[1234]) ***concerning Worship*** and a golden Caitya were found within. The casket received the name of the "Mysterious Helper" and was worshipped (by the king). The latter came to live 120 years and came to witness the dawn of the Highest Doctrine[1235]); up to that time the kingdom had been ruled by the Bön. In a dream (which this king had) it was prophesied to him that on the 5th generation one would come to know the meaning of these (sacred texts which he had miraculously obtained). His son [138 a.] was Ṭhi-ñan-śuṅ-tsen[1236]) who in his turn had a son named Ḍo-ñan-de-ru[1237]). The latter's son was Tag-ri-ñan-śig[1238]) who was born blind. After this son had ascended the throne, he worshipped "the Mysterious Helper" and through this his eyes became opened. He received his surname owing to the fact that he beheld on the Tag-ri a wild sheep (ñan)[1239]) that was going about. The son of this king was Nam-ri-sroṅ-tsen[1240]). The latter (in his turn) had from his wife Thse-poṅ-s'a-ḍi-s'a-thö-kar[1241]) a son endowed with special marks of beauty and with the form of Amitābha abiding on his head. He was born in the year of the fire-cow and received the name of Ṭhi-de-sroṅ-tsen[1241a]). The form of Amitābha on his head was encircled by a wreath of poppies. Thirteen years of age he ascended the throne and brought under his power all the petty chieftains of the borderland who offered him presents and sent their messages (of submission). —

As at that time no writing existed in Tibet, the son of Anu of the Thon-mi tribe was sent with 16 companions (to India) in order to study the art of writing. After having studied with the Paṇḍit Devavidyāsiṁha[1242]), they shaped, in conformity with the Tibetan language, (the alphabet) consisting of 30 consonants[1243]) and 4 vowels[1244]). The form (of these letters) was given a resemblance

---

[1233]) Za-ma-tog-bkod-pa. Kg. MDO. VII.

[1234]) Pan-goṅ-phyag-rgya-pa. Kg. MDO. XXIV.

[1235]) Lit.: "Found the head of the Highest Doctrine" (***dam-paḥi-chos-kyi dbu brñes***).

[1236]) Khri-gñan-zuṅ-btsan. [1237]) Ḥgro-gñan-lde-ru.

[1238]) Stag-ri-gñan-gzigs. [1239]) *gñan*. [1240]) Gnam-ri-sroṅ-btsan.

[1241]) Tshe-spoṅs-za-ḥbri-za-thod-dkar.

[1241a]) Khri-lde-sroṅ-btsan. [1242]) Lhaḥi-rig-pa-seṅ-ge.

[1243]) *gsal-byed.* [1244]) *āli.*

with the Kashmirian characters. After (this alphabet) had been definitely formed at the Maru temple of Lhasa, (Thon-mi) composed 8 works on writing and grammar, and the king studied them 4 years abiding in seclusion. The *Karaṇḍavyūha-sūtra*, the 100 *Precepts*, the *Ratnamegha-sūtra* and others were then translated (into Tibetan).

As at that time the Tibetan subjects were disregarding the royal power, (the king) introduced laws harmonizing with the 10 virtues and converted the Tibetans to Buddhism. Owing to this he is known by the name of Sroṅ-tsen-gam-po[1245]) — "Sroṅ-tsen the most accomplished".

Thereafter, from southern India, (the statue of) the 11 faced Avalokita of finest sandal wood which had become originated by itself was brought. [138 b.] The king then took in marriage Ṭhi-btsun, the daughter of the Nepalese king Aṁçuvarman[1246]). This princess brought with her the images of Akṣobhya-vajra[1247]), Maitreya, and Tārā, the latter being of sandal wood. After that the king married the Chinese princess Oṅ-co, — the daughter of the Chinese Emperor Seṅ-ge-tsen-po[1248]), who brought with her the statue of the Buddha which was afterwards placed in the Ṭhul-naṅ[1249]) temple. Thereupon Ṭhi-btsun had the desire of building a monastery, but had not the power of doing this. (The king) saw that the ground of Tibet was like (the body of) a she-devil that had fallen on her back, and that it was necessary to press (this she-devil) down. Accordingly, on the right shoulder (he caused to build) the monastery of Ka-tshe[1250]), on the left one-Ṭha-nḍug[1251]), on the right leg — Tsaṅ-ḍam[1252]), and on the left — Ḍom-pa-gyaṅ[1253]), these being "the 4 monasteries of the 4 flanks"[1254]). Then, on the right elbow, (the monastery of)Koṅ-po-p'u-chu[1255]), on the left — Hlo-ṭ'ag-khom-thiṅ[1256]), on the right knee — Ka-ṭ'ag[1257]), and on the left Ṭ'a-t'um-tse[1257a]), "the 4 subduers of the borders"[1258]) were constructed. Thereafter on the palm of the right hand Luṅ-nö[1259]) of Jaṅ-tshe[1260]) and on that

---

[1245]) Sroṅ-btsan-sgam-po. [1246]) Ḥod-zer-go-cha. [1247]) Mi-bskyod-rdo-rje.
[1248]) Seṅ-ge-btsan-po. [1249]) Ḥphrul-snaṅ. [1250]) Ska-tshal.
[1251]) Khra-ḥbrug. [1252]) Gtsaṅ-ḥgram. [1253]) Grom-pa-rgyaṅ.
[1254]) Ru-bžiḥi gtsug-lag-khaṅ bži. [1255]) Koṅ-po-bu-chu.
[1256]) Lho-brag-khom-mthiṅ. [1257]) Ska-brag.
[1257a]) Bra-dum-rtse. [1258]) Mthaḥ-ḥdul bži. [1259]) Rluṅ-gnod.
[1260]) Byaṅ-tshal.

of the left one — the Dan-loṅ-thaṅ-ḍön-ma of Kham[1260a]), on the right foot — Jam-ṭin[1261]) of Maṅ-yul, and on the left — the P'um-thaṅ-pa-ṭ'o-kyer-chu[1262]) of Mon-yul were built and many other monasteries besides. Thereafter, in the middle of the lake O-thaṅ, (the king) made a foundation of stone covered with wood. Cement having been made out of the mould of the Nāgas and earth having been brought with the help of a goat, the ground was levelled and the monastery of Lhasa, the Rä Ṭhul-naṅ[1263]) was built. From the working-tools heaped up in the northern projection of the temple there appeared by itself the form of Avalokita with 11 faces and was prayed to stay. —

Thereafter the king departed to the 5 peaked mountains of China, and built there 108 temples. The Chinese queen Oṅ-co (in her turn) built the temple of Ra-mo-che. At that time the Indian teacher Kusara, [139 a.] the Brāhmana Çaṁkara, the Nepalese teacher Çīlamañju, the Chinese teacher Hva-çaṅ Mahādeva-tshe, the translator Thon-mi Saṁbhoṭa, his pupil Dharmakoça, and Dorje-pal of Hla-luṅ translated and edited a certain number of the kanonical texts. —

The King (Sroṅ-tsen-gam-po) is regarded as the incarnation of Avalokita and there exists a biography of him by 2 monks of Li. This king ruled 69 years and died 82 years of age. At that very time the queen Oṅ-co said: — Let the statue of Çākyamuni[1264]) be brought from Ra-mo-che and placed in the projection of Ṭhul-naṅ. Let the door be covered with plaster, and may Mañjuçrī write upon it. — And, with Ṭhi-btsun (and the king), they all 3 coalesced with (the statue of) Avalokita and passed away. The ministers then made (the statues of) the 2 tutelary deities change their places, thus acting according to the testament.

The son of this king was Maṅ-roṅ-maṅ-tsen[1264a]), his son — K'uṅ-sroṅ-k'uṅ-tsen[1265]), the son of the latter Du-sroṅ-maṅ-po-je-lo-nam-ṭhul-gyi-gyal-po[1266]), and the son of this one — Ṭhi-de-tsug-ten[1267]). The latter built the fortress of Lhasa, the Phu-

---

[1260a]) Ḥdan-kloṅ-thaṅ-sgron-ma. [1261]) Byams-sprin.
[1262]) Bum-thaṅ-spa-gro-skyer-chu. [1263]) Ras ḥphrul-snaṅ.
[1264]) The Tib. has here and further on Lha Çākya-mu-ne (sic).
[1264a]) Maṅ-roṅ-maṅ-btsan. [265]) Guṅ-sroṅ-guṅ-btsan.
[1266]) Ḥdu-sroṅ-maṅ-po-rje-blo-nam-ḥphrul-gyi-rgyal-po.
[1267]) Ṭhi-de-gtsug-brtan.

nam-sä[1268]) of Chim, the T'ar-phur-khar-hlag[1269]), the Do-mad-liṅ-chu-ṭhi-tse[1270]), the Ga-chu-çar-go of the Red Cliff[1271]), the Phaṅ-thaṅ-ka-med[1272]), the Ka-chu-pan-chuṅ, the Ḍin-zaṅ of the Red Cliff[1273]), etc.

Mūlakoça of Lan-ka[1274]) and Jñānakumāra of Ñag[1275]) translated the Sūtras *Karmaçataka*[1276]) and *Suvarṇaprabhāsottama*, as well as works on Mathematics and Medicine and furthered the spread of the Doctrine.

(The king Ṭhi-de-tsug-ten) had a son called Je-tsha-hla-pön[1277]) who married the daughter of the Chinese Emperor Gyim-çaṅ-[139 b.] oṅ-co. The son of these died. (The princess) united with the grandfather and worshipped the statue of Çākyamuni. Thereafter, a boy endowed with special marks of beauty was born in the year of the male-earth-horse. At the time when the king departed in order to visit Phaṅ-thaṅ, the boy was carried off by Na-nam-s'a[1278]), was brought up as the son of the latter and became known by the name of Ṭhi-sroṅ-de-tsen[1279]). When he was still a child, Saṅ-çi and others, altogether 4 in number, were sent to China in search of kanonical works. At that time a Chinese Hva-çaṅ who was endowed with the supernatural faculties spread the rumour that the Tibetan messengers were incarnations of Bodhisattva Saints and recommended to treat them as such. (The messengers) came, were honoured by the Chinese Emperor and sent back in the company of a Hva-çaṅ. When they returned to Tibet, the king had died and, as the prince was still a child, the ministers violated the laws and customs, banished those who were acting according to the Doctrine, and made arrangements to send the statue of Çākyamuni back to China. But as 300 men were incapable of moving it, they buried it in sand and made of the temple a slaughter-house. At that time the Na-nam Ṭhi-thog-je-thaṅ-la-bar[1280]) died, having broken his back. Cog-ṭ'u-kye-pa-ṅe-gyal-goṅ[1281]) likewise died, having withered away. (After that the ministers) said: — This is a punishment for our having buried

---

1268) Phu-gnam-sral. 1269) Dar-ḥphur-mkhar-lhag.
1270) Mdo-smad-liṅ-chu-khri-rtse. 1271) Brag-dmar du Sga-chu-çar-sgo.
1272) Ḥphaṅ-thaṅ-ka-med. 1273) Brag-dmar-ḥbrin-bzaṅs.
1274) Blan-ka. 1275) Gñags. 1276) Las-brgya-pa.
1277) Ḥjad-tsha-lha-dpon. 1278) Sna-nam-za.
1279) Khri-sroṅ-lde-btsan. 1280) Khri-thog-rje-thaṅ-la-ḥbar.
1281) Cog-gru-skyes-pa-ṅes-rgyal-dgoṅ.

the deity under sand. — Accordingly, they hoisted the statue on a pair of mules and brought it to Kyi-roṅ[1282] in Maṅ-yul. Nevertheless, after that Khar-ṭ'ag[1283] and Ḍiṅ-s'aṅ[1284] were both destroyed. At that time the nephew and niece of Ba-laṅ-lag-gi-pä-sal-naṅ[1285], — a brother and a sister had both died. The Hva-çaṅ made magical implements owing to which the maiden a year after was reborn as his own son, in whom the remembrance (of previous existence) appeared. This one, (when he grew up) was selected by the prince as the governor of Maṅ-yul and was sent there. At that time Saṅ-çi, having arrived, took up his abode in solitude at Chö-ṭag[1286]. Thereafter, Thi-sroṅ-de-tsen, having attained the age of thirteen, ascended the throne. [140 a.] When the biography of this father and grandfather was related to him, the Doctrine was likewise mentioned (in the narrative). (The king) got the sacred texts that were concealed, expressed the wish to study them, and became full of faith. The Chinese Me and Go, and the Pandit Ananta, these 3 were appointed to translate (the texts). The translation was accordingly begun, but the minister Ma-sh'aṅ-ṭ'om-pa-kye[1287] and others caused impediments to this. The ministers who were devoted to the Doctrine, sent Saṅ-çi to Maṅ-yul. Sal-naṅ[1288] did not remain at Maṅ-yul, but went to India and presented his sacrificial offerings at Mahābodhi and Çrī-Nālanda. In Nepal he met with the preceptor Bodhisattva[1289] and invited him to Maṅ-yul. Thereafter he built a monastery, made the Creative Effort for Enlightenment, and was henceforth known by the name of Ye-çei-vaṅpo[1290] (Jñānendra). The teacher (Bodhisattva) whom he prayed to come (afterwards) to Tibet, gave his instructions and his consent and departed to Nepal.

Then, having studied the kanonical works that had been concealed, (Jñānendra) had an interview with the king at the palace of Luṅ-tshug[1291], held a discussion with him concerning the Doctrine, and related to him the biography of Bodhisattva. — Hide thyself, — said the king. — By the by I will make Sh'aṅ-ñams'aṅ[1292] discuss over the matter. — Thereafter Sh'aṅ-ñam-s'aṅ, Gö-ṭhi-s'aṅ[1293] and the other ministers, devoted to the Doctrine,

[1282]) Skyid-groṅ. [1283]) Mkhar-brag. [1284]) Ḥbrin-bzaṅ.
[1285]) Ba-laṅ-glag-gi-sbas-gsal-snaṅ. [1286]) Chos-brag.
[1287]) Ma-žaṅ-grom-pa-skyes. [1288]) Gsal-snaṅ.
[1289]) I. e. the teacher Çāntirakṣita. [1290]) Ye-çes-dbaṅ-po.
[1291]) Rluṅ-tshugs. [1292]) Žaṅ-ñam-bzaṅ. [1293]) Ḥgos-khri-bzaṅ.

received the orders to act for the sake of the latter. Ñam-s'aṅ said:—Ma-sh'aṅ[1294]) is very powerful and is hostile to the Doctrine. Therefore it will be impossible to attain any result. — Gö said: — I know a means of action, but you must assist me in the affair. — The king and the ministers gave their approval, and, after Gö had reflected (over the means of action), they cast Ma-sh'aṅ-ṭ'om-pa-kye alive into a grave and covered the aperture with a block of stone. Thereupon [140 b.] Jñānendra was sent to invite the Ācārya Bodhisattva. Laṅ-ṭ'oṅ-na-ra[1295]), Ñer-tag-tsen-toṅ-s'i[1296]), and Ḍaṅ-gya-ra-le-s'i[1297]), — these 3 were afterwards despatched to meet them. After they had met at Maṅ-yul, and Laṅ-ṭ'oṅ-na-ra with the Ācārya had been left there, (the Ācārya) payed his respects to the governor in his palace. On this occasion the officials of Sh'aṅ said: — One must investigate whether he mutters the bad spells of the south or of Nepal or not. Accordingly, Saṅ-çi, Seṅ-k'oṅ-hla-luṅ-s'i[1298]) and Me-lan of the Chim-pa tribe were sent (to get information on the subject), but they did not understand the language (of the Ācārya). They then prayed the Kashmirian Ananta to be interprete, and inquired of what kind the Ācārya was. And, as it was said that he was virtuous and had no obscene thoughts, he was invited to the palace and, with the Kashmirian Ananta as translator,—he expounded in the palace Luṅ-tshug for 4 months the teaching of the 10 virtues, of the 18 component elements of the individual, and of the 12-membered causal chain. This brought the malignant deities of Tibet into a fury. Phaṅ-thaṅ was carried away by a flood, lightning struck in Mar-po-ri, and diseases befalling men and cattle broke out. The Tibetan subjects declared that this was a consequence of the propagation of a false doctrine, and the Ācārya was sent back to Nepal.

Then, after a long time, Sal-naṅ of Ba[1299]) was sent to China in search of kanonical texts. Saṅ-çi and others, 30 in number, were in their turn despatched in order to invite the Ācārya again. At that time a Hva-çaṅ of China said: — In 6 months and 6 days an incarnation of the Saint Açvaghoṣa will come. — (The Tibetan envoy came), was favoured by the Chinese Emperor, got from the Hva-çaṅ the instructions concerning the concentration of mind, and communicated them to his companions. (When Sal-naṅ had

---

[1294]) Cf. above. Note 1287. [1295]) Laṅ-groṅ-sna-ra.
[1296]) Gñer-stag-btsan-stoṅ-gzigs. [1297]) Sgraṅ-rgya-ra-legs-gzigs.
[1298]) Seṅ-goṅ-lha-luṅ-gzigs. [1299]) Sba.

returned from China, the king said to him): — The Ācārya has not up to this time been invited; go therefore (and fetch him). — Sal-naṅ accordingly went to Nepal and invited the Ācārya. Thereafter, when he had come back, he met the king in Ḍin-s'aṅ of the Red Cliff and said to him: —As the demons of Tibet are not subdued, they do not admit that one acts for the sake of the Doctrine. [141 a.] They are powerful and endowed with huge bodies. It is therefore necessary to subdue them. Now there exists a teacher called Padmasambhava who is endowed with great power and dexterity. You must invite him (in order to pacify the devils). — The king having declared that this was told to him in a dream, sent Maṅ-je-sal-naṅ of Ba[1300]), and Seṅ-k'oṅ-hla-luṅ, with 5 attendants, viz. Dorje-dud-jom[1301]) of Na-nam, Jñānasiddhi of Ce[1302]), Çākyaprabha of Chim, Jayarakṣita of Ṭ'aṅ-ti and Çrīsiṁha[1303]) of Çü-pu[1304]). The teacher came to know about this and went to K'uṅ-thaṅ in Maṅ-yul, where they met. Thereafter he gradually proceeded forward, subduing the malignant deities. Having come to Ha-sa-po-ri, he met with the king and then went to Mal-ṭoi-phu[1305]), and subdued all the Tibetan demons. Thereafter the teacher was invited to Sam-yä and established his residence there.

The Ācārya Bodhisattva in his turn, examined the ground, took the monastery of Odantapuri as a model and made a plan containing the forms of the mount Sumeru, the 12 continents, both the sun and the moon, all these surrounded by a circumference of iron. In the female-fire-hare-year the foundation was laid, and first of all the temple of Avalokita was built, and images for which the men of Tibet served as patterns, were sculptured. The queen Che-va-tshe-peṅ S'a-mar-gyal Me-tog Dolma[1306]) built the Khamsum-s'aṅ-khaṅ-liṅ[1307]), (the queen) Pho-yoṅ-s'a-gyal-mo-tsün[1308]) built the U-tshal-ser-khaṅ-liṅ, and (the queen) Ḍo-s'a-jaṅ-chubman[1309]) — the temple of Ge-gyä-je-ma-liṅ[1310]). In the female-earth-hare-year the work was accomplished. The Ācārya Bodhi-

---

1300) Sba Maṅ-rje-gsal-snaṅ.
1301) Rdo-rje-bdud-ḥjoms. 1302) Lce. 1303) Dpal-gyi-seṅ-ge.
1304) Çud-pu. 1305) Mal-groḥi-phu.
1306) Che-ba-tshe-speṅs Za-dmar-rgyal Me-tog Sgrol-ma.
1307) Khams-gsum-zaṅ-khaṅ-gliṅ.
1308) Pho-yoṅs-za-rgyal-mo-btsun. 1309) Ḥbro-za-byaṅ-chub-sman.
1310) Dge-rgyas-bye-ma-gliṅ.

sattva and Padmasambhava performed the rites of consecration and a feast was celebrated during 13 years. In the sheep-year 12 monks of the sect of the Sarvāstivādins were invited [141 b.], and it was put to the test, whether the Tibetans could become monks or not. For this purpose 7 men were selected and ordained as monks. According to some, the 3 elder ones of these were Mañjuçrī of Ba[1311]), Devendra of Tsaṅ[1312]) and Kumudika of Ṭ'aṅ. The 3 younger ones were Nāgendra of Khön[1313]), Vairocana of Pa-k'or[1314]) and Ācārya Rin-chen-chog of Ma[1315]). The intermediate one was Katana of Laṅ[1316]). The preceptor of these was said to be Dānaçīla, and their religious names were Jñānendra, etc. (According to others), the Ācārya Bodhisattva, having been made preceptor, first of all Ja-ṭhi-s'i[1317]) took orders and became possessed of the 5 supernatural faculties. Thereafter, Sol-naṅ of Ba, Ṭhi-sh'er of Bā, Çīta of Saṅ, Vairocana Rakṣita of Pa-k'or, Jinottamaghoṣa[1317a]) of Ran-la, Nāgendrarakṣita[1318]) of Khön, Ācārya Rin-chen-chog of Ma, and Leg-ḍub[1319]) of Tsaṅ, — 7 in number, who received the religious names of Jñānendra, Çrīghoṣa, etc. (were ordained). These are spoken of as "the 7 selected ones"[1320]). If we examine the ends of their names and take in consideration that the name of Bodhisattva was Çāntirakṣita, it will be clear that they were the pupils of the latter. The spiritual ancestral line of preceptors[1321]) was: — Çāriputra, Rāhula[1322]), Nāgārjuna, Bhāvaviveka, Çrīgupta, Jñānagarbha and the preceptor Bodhisattva. The portraits of these were painted on the northern wall of Sam-yä.

Thereafter the teacher Padma transformed the sands of Ṅan-çoṅ into fertile ground, forced the Tsaṅ-po river to flow downward, and performed other miraculous acts. Then he took the silver urn in which the king used to keep fresh water for washing, cast it into the air and, having obtained the water of the gods of the colour of milk, prayed the king to refresh his body. The ministers however were displeased with this and sent him away.

Furthermore, the Indian teachers Vimalamitra, Buddhaguhya[1323]), Çāntigarbha, Viçuddhasiṁha [142 a.] with the Tibetan

---

[1311]) Dbaḥ. [1312]) Rtsaṅs.
[1313]) Ḥkhon. [1314]) Pa-gor. [1315]) Rma. [1316]) Glaṅ.
[1317]) Bya-khri-gzigs. [1317a]) Rgyal-ba-mchog-dbyaṅs.
[1318]) Kluḥi-dbaṅ-po-bsruṅ-ba. [1319]) Legs-grub.
[1320]) Sad-mi mi bdun. [1321]) mkhan-brgyud. [1322]) Sgra-can-zin.
[1323]) Saṅs-rgyas-gsaṅ-ba.

translators, viz. the 7 selected ones, Dharmāloka[1324]), the Bande Nam-khā, Ratnasena of Ḍo[1325]), Nam-par-mi-tog-pa[1326]), Çākyaprabha[1327]) and others interpreted and translated numerous kanonical works. The Tantric exorcist[1328]) Dharmakīrti having been invited, the rites of consecration of the Yogavajradhātu[1329]) and other magic circles in the Düd-dül-ṅag-pa-liṅ[1330]) were performed. The Kashmirian Paṇḍits Jinamitra, Dānaçīla and others established the rules of monastic discipline in the Nam-dag-ṭhim-khaṅ-liṅ[1331]). The Chinese Hva-çaṅ and others underwent the practice of meditation in the Mi-yo-sam-ten-liṅ[1332]), works on Grammar and Dictionaries were composed in the Da-jor-tshaṅ-pai-liṅ[1333]), treasures were stored up in the Ḳor-dzö-p'e har-liṅ[1334]), and the kanonical works were discussed in the monastery of Vairocana. By these and other similar works the Doctrine was fully and thoroughly introduced.

In the year of the dragon the teachers residing in the palace of Den-kar[1335]), the translators Ban-de Pal-tseg[1336]), the Ban-de Nāgendra[1337]) and others made a list of the titles of the sacred texts that were translated in Tibet, as well as the number of divisions[1338]) and Çlokas contained in them, and wrote all this down in the form of a catalogue.

Thereafter the Ācārya Bodhisattva declared that no heretics would appear in Tibet, but that the church of the Buddha would itself be split into 2 sects, and that dispute and controversy would take place. Therefore, — said he, — when that time will come, you must invite my pupil Kamalaçīla and, after a controversy will have been held, all strife will be pacified and the true form of the Teaching established. — Thus did he prophesy and soon, having been kicked by a horse, he went to his rest.

Thereafter Çrīghoṣa[1339]) was appointed teacher and expounded the Doctrine. Jñānendra fled and gave himself up to meditation in Hlo-ṭ'ag[1340]). The number of pupils of the Chinese Hva-çaṅ [142 b.] Mahāyāna increased. These favoured nihilistic views and

---

1324) Chos-kyi-snaṅ-ba. 1325) Sgro Rin-chen-sde.
1326) Rnam-par-mi-rtog-pa. 1327) Çākya-ḥod. 1328) Sṅags-ḥchaṅ.
1329) Yo-ga-rdo-rje-dbyiṅs. 1330) Bdud-ḥdul-sṅags-pa-gliṅ.
1331) Rnam-dag-khrims-khaṅ-gliṅ. 1332) Mi-gyo-bsam-gtan-gliṅ.
1333) Brda-sbyor-tshaṅs-paḥi-gliṅ. 1334) Dkor-mdzod-pe-har-gliṅ.
1335) Ldan-dkar. 1336) Dpal-brtsegs. 1337) Kluḥi-dbaṅ-po.
1338) Bam-po. 1339) Dpal-dbyaṅs. 1340) Lho-brag.

did not exert themselves in the practice of virtue, saying: — By acting according to the Doctrine, by virtuous acts of body and speech, one cannot become a Buddha. One attains the state of the latter by abiding in perfect inactivity. — The Tibetans, for the greater part, found pleasure (in such a conception of the Doctrine) and studied the system (of the Hva-çaṅ). Çrīghoṣa, Ratna of Ba and a few others who adhered to the system of the Ācārya Bodhisattva did not agree (with the Hva-çaṅ) neither in the theory nor in the practice, and there was strife (between the 2 parties). When the king gave the order that one should follow theoretically and practically the system of the Ācārya Bodhisattva, the Tön-mün-pa[1341]) (the Chinese party) were enraged, armed themselves with sharp knives and threatened to kill all the Tsen-min-pa (the adherents of Bodhisattva)[1342]). The king, distressed, sent for Jñānendra in order to summon him. Twice (the envoys) sought and did not find him. They were then sent for a third time with the directions to kill (Jñānendra) if he did not come. Accordingly, they came into a cavern, 12 fathoms deep, and having descended (and found Jñānendra there), they prayed him to come. Thinking that if he would not go, he would be killed or would have to commit suicide, he went and told the king that it was not proper to summon him, since the commandments of the teacher (Bodhisattva) were of another kind. By this the king was reminded (of the Ācārya's instructions) which he had forgotten, and sent a messenger to invite the teacher Kamalaçīla. This the Hva-çaṅ came to know and, having obtained the *Çatasāhasrikā* and other Sūtras of profound meaning, taught and explained them, and composed the *Dhyāna-svapna-cakra*[1343]), "the Attainment of the state of Absorbtion", refuting the challenges directed against the preceeding work, "the Repeated Attainment", "the Reverse Side of the System", vindicating the theory by Logic, "the Sources in the form of 80 Sūtras"[1344]), proving it by means of Scripture, etc. In all these works it was demonstrated that the action according to the Doctrine was unnecessary, and that it was sufficient to abide in a state of sleep. And, seing that the *Saṁdhinirmocana-sūtra* disagreed with his views and conduct, (the Hva-çaṅ) cast it away with a kick. At that time Jñānendra [143 a] prayed the king to

1341) Ston-mun-pa. Cf. below.
1342) Cf. below.
1343) Bsam-gtan-ñal-baḥi-ḥkhor-lo.
1344) Mdo-sde-brgyad-cu-khuṅs.

listen himself to the exposition of the precepts of the Ācārya. The king was delighted and said: — You are my Ācārya! — Thereafter the teacher Kamalaçīla arrived. The king seated himself in the middle, the Hva-çaṅ was given a place to his right and the teacher (Kamalaçīla) to his left side. The Tsen-min were placed so as to form the retinue (of Kamalaçīla). The king, having handed to both wreaths of flowers, declared: — Ye two are to hold a controversy. To him who conquers, the vanquished must present his wreath and dare no longer abide here! —

Then the Hva-çaṅ spoke: — If one commits virtuous or sinful deeds, one comes to blissful or to evil births (respectively). In such a way the deliverance from the Saṁsāra is impossible, and there will be always impediments to the attainment of Buddhahood. (The virtuous and the sinful deeds) are just like white and black clouds which alike obscure the sky. But he who has no thoughts and inclinations at all, can be fully delivered from Phenomenal Life. The absence of any thought, search, or investigation brings about the non-perception[1346]) of the reality of separate entities. In such a manner one can attain (Buddhahood) ot once, like (a Bodhisattva) who has attained the 10th Stage. —

To this Kamalaçīla himself answered as follows: — Thou sayest thus that one ought not to think about anything whatever. But this means the negation (or rejection) of the Highest Analytic Wisdom likewise. Now as the latter represents the foundation of the Divine Wisdom of a Saint, the rejection of it necessarily leads to the negation of this sublime Transcendental Wisdom. If Analytic Wisdom is absent, what meditator can come to abide in a state where there is no constructive thought? — If one has no thought concerning any of the elements of existence and does not direct the mind upon them, this does not mean that one can cease to remember all that one has experienced and to think of it. If I think: — [143 b.] I must not recall in my mind any element of existence, — such a thought will itself be an intense recollection and activity of the mind. If the mere absence of (consciousness and) recollection is regarded as sufficient, it follows that in a swoon or at the time of intoxication one comes to the state where there is no constructive thought. Now, (in reality) without correct analysis there is no means of attaining the liberation from constructive

1346) *mi-dmigs-pa* = *anupalambha*.

thought. If we merely cease to reflect and have no discrimination, how can we come to the cognition of the Non-substantiality of all the elements? —And, without the cognition of Non-substantiality, it is impossible to remove the Obscurations. Therefore, the incorrect representation can be cast away only by means of the correct Analytic Wisdom. For this reason it is not proper to say, that one does not reflect, when in reality it is the reverse. Without recollection and correct activity of the mind, how can one come to remember the place of former residence[1346]) and attain Omniscience? And how will it be possible to extirpate the passions? — But the Yogin who reflects over an object by means of correct Analytic Wisdom, cognizes all the external and internal elements in the present, past, and future as non-substantial, has all thought-construction pacified within him, and rejects all the evil doctrines. On this foundation he becomes skilful in expedients and in the manifestation of Highest Wisdom. And, having through this cleared all the Obscurations, he can attain the state of a Buddha. —

Thereafter the king said: — All the adherents (of Kamalaçīla) must likewise make their objections. —Accordingly Çrīghoṣa spoke as follows: — The Chinese are of the opinion that one has to enter (the Stage of a Buddha) at once, but not by gradual practice. According to them, the 6 Transcendental Virtues are to be taken as the mere negation of their reverse. Highest Charity[1347]) is thus viewed only as the absence of greadiness. The fact of abstaining from every kind of appropriation thus represents the Highest Transcendental Charity. So they have it in connection (with each of the 6 virtues) up to that of Highest Wisdom. [144 a.] For a long time after the Teacher had passed away, there were no disagreeing points in (the main points of) the Teaching. At present, contrary to the 3 varieties of the Mādhyamikas, the Tön-mün-pa wish to attain Buddhahood at once, and (pretend to) do so without searching and cognition. Of course, there are many methods of acting, but the very process of attaining Enlightenment, as well as the result of it is only one; (therefore it is impossible to attain it by means of a way that is quite unsuitable for this). —

Then spoke Jñānendra: — The attainment (of Buddhahood) at once and the action by degrees must both be investigated. If

---

[1346]) *ṅon-gyi gnas rjes-su-dran-pa = pūrva-nivāsa-anusmṛti.*

[1347]) *sbyin-paḥi pha-rol-tu-phyin-pa = dāna-pāramitā.*

the action by degrees is right, then (in doing nothing) you cannot be possessed of the factors of attainment and will be very unlike us. And, if you attain (Buddhahood) at once, what are you doing at present? You must be Buddhas from the very beginning and, (according to your point of view), there will be no fault in admitting this. Now, when you ascend a mountain, you must do it step by step, but you are not capable of doing it at once. In a similar manner, if it be difficult to attain the first Stage (even by degrees), what is there to say of the attainment of Omniscience? According to the point of view of us, the Tsen-min-pa, it is necessary to become trained in the 3 kinds of Analytic Wisdom, then, on the basis of all the different subjects of Scripture, to apprehend correctly the meaning of the latter, to receive training in the practice of the 10 virtues, to attain steadfastness by the means of profound meditation, to enter the first Stage and come to the guiltless state (of a Bodhisattva)[1348]), and then, passing through gradual training on the 10 Stages, to attain Buddhahood by means of the 10 virtues. — If we admit your point of view, it follows that the Accumulations of Merit need not to be brought to accomplishment, mental training is not required, and the knowledge of the worldly matters is unneccessary. But, in such a case, how can the knowledge of everything cognizable be attained? If you do nothing and only sleep, you will not even take food and thus die of hunger! And, in such a way, where and when are you to attain Buddhahood? If you walk without searching and investigating, you will needs fall; where and when can you thus cognize the Truth? —

Thus and more spoke he in detail and the Tön-mün-pa were incapable of giving an answer. They gave the wreath of flowers to the teacher, and declared themselves vanquished. [144 b.] Co-ma-ma[1349]) and other (adherents of the Hva-çaṅ) were distressed and, having smitten their bodies with stones, died, as runs the tradition.

Thereafter the king gave the following order: — Henceforth, as concerns the theory, one must adopt the system of Nāgārjuna. With regard to the practice, — one must become trained in the 10 kinds of virtuous conduct and in the 10 Transcendental Virtues.

1348) *(byaṅ-chub-sems-dpaḥi) skyon-med-pa* = *(bodhisattvasya) nyāma.*

1349) Co-rma-rma.

As to the Tön-mün views, the propagation of these is not to be permitted! — Accordingly the Hva-çaṅ was sent back to China, and his books were collected and kept concealed in a store-house. Now, Tön-mün and Tsen-min are Chinese words signifying "simultaneists" and "gradualists". —

Later on, four Chinese butchers, sent by the Hva-çaṅ, killed the teacherKamalaçīla by squeezing his kidneys. Jñānendra passed away, having refused to take food. The king in his turn died 69 years of age, and was held to have been an incarnation of Mañjuçrī. His son, Mu-ne-tsen-po assumed the reign in the male-water-tiger-year, caused 4 great religious services to be celebrated at Sam-yä, and thrice established equality between the rich and the poor of his Tibetan subjects. Having reigned for a year and 7 months, he died 17 years of age, having been poisoned by his mother. After that, his younger brother, Ṭhi-de-tsen-po[1350]), then 4 years of age, was made king, and was (later on) known by the surname of Se-na-le[1351]). (This king built the Kar-chuṅ-gya-de[1352]) and greatly furthered the spread of the Doctrine. Five sons were born to him: Ṭhi-de-sroṅ-tsen[1353]), Ral-pa-cen-tsaṅ-ma[1354]), Ṭhi-dar-ma-u-t'um-tsen[1355]), Hla-rje-hlün-ḍub[1356]), and Ṭhi-chen-po[1357]). Ral-pa-cen who was considered to be the incarnation of Vajrapāṇi began to reign 18 years of age and built the palace of Ön-caṅ-do[1358]) with 9 storeys. Before, in the time of his forefathers, the teacher Bodhisattva, [145 a.] Jñānendra, Sh'aṅ-gyal-ñen-ña-s'aṅ[1359]), Lön-ṭhi-sh'ir-saṅ-çi[1360]), the translators Jñānadeva-koṣa, Khyi-ḍug[1361] of Ce[1362]), the Brāhmaṇa Ananta and others created a literary language that contained many words unintelligible to the Tibetans. Besides, different translations were made from the Chinese, from the language of Li and Sahor, etc. Owing to this there were many different renderings of words and the study of the Doctrine became very difficult. Seeing this, the king issued the following order: — The Aparāntaka teachers[1363]) Jinamitra, Surendrabodhi, Çīlendrabodhi, and Bodhimitra, the Tibetan

---

[1350]) Khri-lde-btsan-po. [1351]) Sad-na-legs.
[1352]) Skar-chuṅ-rgya-sde. [1353]) Khri-lde-sroṅ-btsan.
[1354]) Ral-pa-can-gtsaṅ-ma.
[1355]) Khri-dar-ma-u-dum-btsan. [1356]) Lha-rje-lhun-grub.
[1357]) Khri-chen-po. [1358]) Ḥon-caṅ-rdo.
[1359]) Žaṅ-rgyal-ñen-ña-bzaṅ. [1360]) Blon-khri-bžlr-saṅ-çi.
[1361]) Khyi-ḥbrug. [1362]) Lce. [1363]) Ñi-ḥog-gi-mkhan-po.

teachers Ratnarakṣita and Dharmatāçīla, the skilful translators Jñānasena[1364]), Jayarakṣita, Mañjuçrīvarman, Ratnendraçīla and others are to translate the Hīnayānistic and Mahāyānistic Scriptures into Tibetan directly from the Sanskrit[1364a]). The titles are to be registered and written down so as to form an index. In no case are the rules of translation to be violated, and one must make the translations so that it could be possible for everyone to study. — Moreover, the texts translated before were re-edited in the new language, 3 different forms of instructions were made, and it was prescribed that the Hīnayānistic Scripture other than that acknowledged by the Sarvāstivādins, and the secret charms were not to be translated. Finally, measures as the *Droṇa*[1365]), *Srań, Sho*, and others were introduced, in accordance with those of India. To every ecclesiastic 7 families were appointed, from which he was to receive his alms. (The king himself honoured the members of the clergy) by making of his head a seat for them and by touching their feet with his head. He made war with China, was victorious, and the numerous reports of his generals were written down on the Long Stone[1366]) in Lhasa.

Now, as the government of the city was entrusted to a monk, the ministers who rejoiced in sinful deeds were enraged [145 b.] and made secret machinations in order to violate the precepts of the Doctrine. The king's son Tsań-ma who had taken orders was expelled to Ṭ'omo. Scandalous talk was spread about that the queen Ṅań-tshul-ma and the great Bande Yon-ten-pal[1367]) had secrete intercourse with each other. Finally, the great Bande was murdered and the queen committed suicide. The king himself, 36 years of age, in the female-iron-bird-year was assassinated by Pä-gyal-to-re[1368]) and Co-re-leg-ma[1369]) who turned round his neck. Thereafter, the Tsen-po Lań-dar-ma-u-dum-tsen took possession of the kingdom. The devil-like Pä-gyal-to-re who was appointed minister for inward affairs, the minister Na-nam-gyal-tsha-ṭhi-sum[1370]) and others did much that was contrary to the

---

1364) Usually known by his Tibetan equivalent — Ye-çes-sde.

1364a) Cf. Cordier, Index du Bstan-ḥgyur, II. p. 487. All the translators and Paṇḍits just mentioned are indicated as those who have compiled the Mahāvyutpatti.

1365) Bre-bo. 1366) Rdo-riṅs. 1367) Yon-tan-dpal.

1368) Dpas-rgyal-to-re. 1369) Co-re-legs-smra.

1370) Sna-nam-rgyal-tsha-khri-gsum.

precepts of the Doctrine. The school-house where the Lotsavas and Paṇḍits had translated the kanonical works was destroyed, the translations remained inachieved, and the consecration of the Ōn-caṅ-do was not performed. Thereafter, when the king grew older, a devil took possession of his mind, and he ordered that all the monks were to renounce to religious life. To all those who did not wish to give up the distinctive marks of monkhood, he ordered to give bows, arrows, drums and tambourins, and sent them to transact the business of hunters. Those who disobeyed were put to death. As the king was not able to remove the statue of Çākyamuni, he ordered to hide it, having buried it in sand, barred the doors of the temple, covered them with plaster and ordered to draw upon them the picture of a monk drinking wine. The doors of Sam-yä and Ra-mo-che were likewise plastered with mould, an.. the books for the greater part hidden amidst the rocks of Lhasa.

Then, some time after, Pal-gyi-dorje of Hla-lun who was practising meditation at Yer-pai-lhai-ñiṅ-po[1371]) heard about all this, and the Highest Commiseration with the king[1372]) became originated

---

[1371]) Yer-paḥi-lhaḥi sñiṅ-po.

[1372]) It seeme strange that Laṅ-dar-ma's assassin, setting out to murder the king, should have "thoughts of Commiseration" with respect to him. But, in accordance with the Tantric standpoint, the murder itself is committed out of Commiseration. This is clearly expressed in Tripiṭakamāla's Naya-traya-pradīpa, Tg. RGYUD. LXXII. 26 a. 5—7. — *gaṅ yaṅ chos bstan-pa-la-sogs-pas sdig-pa-las ldog-par- mi-nus-la / ma-bzlog-na-ni ñes-par-spyod-pa ma-bzad-pa byas-paḥi phyir dmyal-ba-la-sogs-paḥi sdug-bsṅal-las gdon-par mi-nus-so // deḥi-phyir ni sṅags-pas Gçin-rje-gçed-la-sogs-paḥi tiṅ-ṅe-ḥdzin daṅ sṅags daṅ rygud-kyi sbyor-bas bsad-pa yaṅ rjes-su-snaṅ-ba yin-no // de-lta-bus ḥchi-ba-ni gñis-su-med-paḥi tiṅ-ṅe-ḥdzin-la so-sor-brten-pas bde-ḥgror skye źiṅ byaṅ-chub-kyi-sems-kyi sa-bon-la rjes-su- źugs-pas deḥi dgos-pa chen-po-ñid-du ḥgyur-ba-ñic yin-no //* There are some whom it is impossible to divert from sin by teaching (to them) the Doctrine and the like. But, if they are not converted, they will continue to commit sinful deeds of great violence, and it will be therefore quite impossible to rescue them from the sufferings of hell and the like (which will be the consequence of their deeds). It is for this reason that, in accordance with the Tantric proceeding, as for instance we have it in the transic meditation an spells of Yamāri and the like, the taking away of life (of a living being in order to save him) is permitted. He who is caused to die in such a manner can subsequently take recourse to the transic meditation comtemplating the unity of the Universe *(advaya-samādhi)*, can assume a blissful state of existence, and can further the origination of the mind directed toward Enlightenment *(bodhi-citta)*. Therefore (the act of killing such a being in order to transfer him to a blissful existence) is of great help (and furthers the weal of this being).

in him. He mounted a white horse, having smeared it black with coal, put on a fur-coat with the white side inward and the black one outward, took an iron bow and an iron arrow, came to Lhasa, saw the king as he was reading the inscriptions of the Long Stone, [146 a.] dismounted before him as he was sitting with his body leaning on the sanctuaries of the monastery and of that of Gānden. Having approached him, he lowered his knee and at the same time, bent his bow. The king, in his turn, thought that he was saluting him. At the first salutation he bent the bow. At the second he fitted the arrow, and at the third he loosened the bow-string. The arrow, parting, struk the breast (of the king). (Pal-dorje) said: — I am the black demon Ya-sh'er. If a sinful king is to be killed, it must be done in such a manner. With these words he fled. A great clamour arose in Lhasa: — The king has been murdered; hasten to the pursuit of the assassin! — (Pal-dorje) then washed the horse in the lake of Mi-nag, put on his coat, having turned it with the white part outward, and, saying:— Now I am the white demon of the skies[1373]), continued his flight. It was thus impossible for the pursuers to get hold of him. Some say that they lost sight of him at Draṅ-sroṅ-srin-po-naṅ[1374]) others — at Ṭ'ib-se-ḍom-gyi-phu[1375]), and still others — at Than-mo-do-riṅ after it had grown dark. Thereafter, having taken with him the *Abhidharma-samuccaya*, the Vinaya text *Prabhāvatī*, and the *Karmaçataka*, (Pal-dorje) departed to Kham. Now, of the Paṇ-ḍits, some were banished and some driven out of the country. The greater part of the Lotsavas had fled, and Tiṅ-ṅe-dzin-s'aṅ-po[1376]) of Ñaṅ, Rin-chen-chog of Ma, and others were killed by murderers who were sent to them. In such a manner the Doctrine was rooted out.

Now, the eldest wife of Laṅ-dar-ma declared that she was pregnant with a child, and then, after she had sought and found a little child, she showed it saying: — It has been born to me yesterday. — The ministers said to this: — A child born a day before cannot have teeth. Let him carefully preserve the instructions of his mother![1377]) Accordingly the boy became known by

---

[1373]) *gnam-theḥu-dkar-po.* [1374]) Draṅ-sroṅ-srin-po.

[1375]) Grib-se-sgrom-gyi-phu. [1376]) Tiṅ-ṅe-ḥdzin-bzaṅ-po.

[1377]) The context is not quite clear — ***mdaṅ skyes-paḥi bu-chuṅ-la so mi-ḥbyuṅ-ste / yum-gyi bkaḥ brtan-du-chug gsuṅs-pas / yum-brtan źes-grags-te /***

the surname of Yum-tan[1378]) (preserving his mother's word). His son was Ṭhi-de-gön-po[1379]), and the son of this one — Gön-ñen. The latter in his turn had 2 sons — Rig-pa [146 b.] -gön-po[1380]) and Ñi-ö-pal-gön[1381]). The son of Rig-pa-gön was Ṭhi-de-po[1382]), and the latter's son — Ṭhi-ö-po[1383]). This one had 3 sons: A-tsa-ra, Gön-po-tsen[1384]), and Gön-po-tseg[1385]). The son of Ñi-ö-pal was Gön-cö[1386]) and the son of the latter was Tsha-nal Ye-çei-gyal-tshen[1387]). — This is the elder line.

The younger queen (of Laṅ-dar-ma) had a son born in the year of the wooden cow. As she feared that the elder queen would kill the boy or carry him away, she held watch over him, keeping him constantly in the light, — of the sun at day-time and of that of a lamp by night. Owing to this he was called Ö-sruṅ[1388]) — "guarded by light". This son ascended the throne and died 63 years of age. His son was Pal-khor-tsen-po[1389]) who began to reign with 13 years and died, aged 31. He had 2 sons, — Ṭa-çi-tseg-pa-pal[1390]) and Ṭhi-kyi-de-ñi-ma-gön[1391]). The first of these became king and had in his turn 3 sons, — Pal-de[1392]) the eldest, Ö-de[1393]) the intermediate, and Kyi-de[1394]) the youngest. Ñi-ma-gön having been banished to Ña-ri, built in Pu-raṅ a castle called Ñi-s'uṅ and lived there. He had 3 sons: The eldest, Pal-gyi-de-rig-pa-gön[1395]) ruled the country of Mar, the intermediate — Ṭa-çi-de-gön[1396]) was in possession of Pu-raṅ and the youngest — De-tsug-gön[1397]) governed Sh'aṅ-sh'uṅ. The latter prince had 2 sons, — Khor-de[1398]) and Sroṅ-de. At that time in Ü and Tsaṅ religious discipline, the exposition of the Doctrine, and the study and preaching of it had altogether ceased. The stewards of the monasteries wore skirts with collars, called themselves Sthaviras and Arhats, and said that they were observing the monastic rules. In reality, they kept them only during the short time of the 3 summer months. Then, having declared that the time of fast had passed away,

---

1378) Yum-brtan. 1379) Khri-lde-mgon-po.
1380) Rig-pa-mgon-po. 1381) Ñi-ḥod-dpal-mgon.
1382) Khri-lde-po. 1383) Khri-ḥod-po. 1384) Mgon-po-btsan.
1385) Mgon-po-brtsegs. 1386) Mgon-spyod.
1387) Tsha-nal Ye-çes-rgyal-mtshan. 1388) Hod-sruṅs.
1389) Dpal-ḥkhor-btsan-po. 1390) Bkra-çis-brtsegs-pa-dpal.
1391) Khri-skyid-lde-ñi-ma-gön. 1392) Dpal-lde.
1393) Ḥod-lde. 1394) Skyid-lde.
1395) Dpal-gyi-lde-rig-pa-mgon. 1396) Bkra-çis-lde-mgon.
1397) Lde-gtsug-mgon. 1398) Ḥkhor-lde.

they did no more observe (the rules prescribed for the clergy). The exorcists [147 a.] did not understand the meaning of the Tantras and indulged in adultery and the like.

IV. Bb. The Subsequent Propagation of the Doctrine in Tibet.

At the time of the persecution of the Doctrine by Dar-ma, 3 men[1399]) viz. Rab-sal of Tsaṅ[1400]), Yo Ge-juṅ[1401]) of P'o-t'oṅ-pa and Mar Çākyamuni of Tö-luṅ[1402]) were abiding in meditation on the Pal-chu-vo-ri[1403]). They chanced to see the monk Khyi-ra-je-pa[1404]), asked what the news were, and came to know that the king had rooted out the Doctrine. They then loaded the Vinaya texts on a young mule, fled to the upper Ña-ri and, having made their way through Gar-log, they reached the land of Hor. They had the intention of introducing the Doctrine into this land of a different race and language, but were unable of doing this. So they went to the P'e-ro-tsha-tshon in the southern Amdo and again gave themselves up to meditation in the *Ma-luṅ-dorje-ṭ'ag-ra-an-chuṅ-nä-dzoṅ-ṭ'ar-rig-çel-gyi-yaṅ-gön*[1405]). Thus they were seen by the shepherds of Ma-chu who told about them to the people of Goṅ-ka[1406]). Now, Mu-s'ug-la-bar who was virtuous and worthy and who had attained the stage of Action in Faith[1406a]) went to see them and, having become full of devotion, prayed to be admitted into the religious order. Accordingly, the text of the Vinaya was handed over to him (by the meditators) who said: — Read this! If thou wilt believe we shall ordain thee. — He read, became full of faith, and shed tears. And, at that very place he was made a novice, Tsaṅ having become his principal[1407]), and Yo — his teacher[1408]). He received his religious name from both principal and teacher and was called Ge-va-rab-sal[1409]). Later on, owing to his sublime mind, he became known as Goṅ-pa-rab-sal[1410]) "he with

---

[1399]) Ḥjad-kyi gyel-mi. (?) [1400]) Gtsaṅ Rab-gsal.

[1401]) Gyo Dge-ḥbyuṅ.

[1402]) Stod-luṅs-pa Smar Çākya-mu-ne. (sic.)

[1403]) Dpal-chu-bo-ri. [1404]) Khyi-ra-byed-pa.

[1405]) Rma-luṅ-rdo-rje-brag-ra-an-chuṅ-gnas-rdzoṅ-dar-rig-çel-gyl-yaṅ-dgon.

[1406]) Dgoṅs-ka.

[1406a]) *mos-pas-spyod-paḥi sa* = *adhimukti-caryā-bhūmi.*

[1407]) *mkhan-po.* Here and further on Tsaṅ for Rab-sal of Tsaṅ. Cf. above.

[1408]) *slob-dpon.* Yo is an abbreviation of Yo Ge-juṅ. (Gyo Dge-ḥbyuṅ). Cf. above. [1409]) Dge-ba-rab-gsal. [1410]) Dgoṅs-pa-rab-gsal.

sublime thoughts". Thereafter he requested to become fully ordained as a monk, but they told him that not less than 5̄ monks had the right to do this. Now, before [147 b.] he had seen 3 monks who had been ordained by Pal-dorje of Lha-luṅ and who were abiding in Loṅ-thaṅ[1411]). He searched for them, and, having met with Pal-gyi-dorje, repeated his request. But (Pal-gyi-dorje) said: — I have killed the king and cannot therefore fill up the number required. I shall therefore seek (for others). Accordingly, he found the Chinese Hva-çaṅs Ke-vaṅ and Gyi-vaṅ and sent them. Thereafter, when the year of his noviciate had passed, (Goṅ-pa-rab-sal) was ordained by the conclave of 5 (monks). His former principal and teacher became such anew. Mar was appointed as his esoteric teacher[1412]), and the 2 Chinese monks were the assistants.

Thereupon, 5 years passed away, and then 5 men of Ü, viz. Lag-pa-lam-pa Lu-mē tshul-ṭhim[1413]), Çei-rab-ḍiṅ Ye-çei-yon-tan[1414]), Rag-çi Tshul-ṭhim-juṅ-nä[1415]), Tshul-ṭhim-lo-dö[1416]) of Ba, and Ye-çei-lo[1417]) of Sum-pa, and 5 men of Tsaṅ, viz. from Gurmo Rab-kha-pa Lo-tön[1418]) and Dorje-vaṅ-chug[1419]), Çei-rab-seṅ-ge of Çab-go-ṅai-tshoṅ-tsün[1420]), the 2 brothers Ö-gye of Ṅa-ri[1421]), and U-pa-t'e-kar-pa[1422]) of P'o-t'oṅ, — altogether 10 men came and prayed Tsaṅ[1423]) to ordain them. But he said: — I am old and cannot take pupils under my care. Address yourself therefore to the Great Lama[1424]). — Accordingly, they repeated their request to the latter, but this one said: — Five years have not yet passed away, since I have been ordained myself. I cannot therefore be a principal. But Tsaṅ said in his turn: — Be such, as an exception! — Thus the Great Lama was made principal, Tsaṅ and Yo became respectively the moral preceptor and the esoteric teacher, and Mar with the Hva-çaṅs were the assistants. Thereafter the Great Lama said: — Lo-tön, as he is powerful, must protect the church, Lu-mē, being highly revered, is to be principal, Tsoṅ-ge[1425]), as

---

1411) Kloṅ-thaṅ. 1412) *gsaṅ-ston.*

1413) Klag-pa-lam-pa Klu-mes tshul-khrims.

1414) Çes-rab-ḥbriṅ Ye-çes-yon-tan.

1415) Rag-çi tshul-khrims-ḥbyuṅ-gnas.

1416) Rba Tshul-khrims-blo-gros. 1417) Ye-çes-blo.

1418) Lo-ston. 1419) Rdo-rje-dbaṅ-phyug.

1420) Çab-sgo-lṅaḥi tshoṅ-btsun Çes-rab-seṅ-ge.

1421) Mṅaḥ-ris-pa Ḥod-brgyad sbung ñis.

1422) U-pa-de-dkar-pa. 1423) I. e. Rab-sal.

1424) I. e. Goṅ-pa-rab-sal. 1425) I. e. Tshoṅ-tsün Çei-rab-seṅ-ge.

he has an acute mind, is to become preceptor, Ḍiṅ, as he is skilful in transacting business, is to be the custodian of the place [148 a.]. Thereafter the greater part of them went upward (that is to Tibet proper), but Lu-mē remained studying the Vinaya with Ye-çei-gyal-tshen of Ḍum[1426]). At that time the younger brother of Rag-çi and the younger brother of Ba[1427]) came to meet them. They encountered at Loṅ-thaṅ and the 2 juniors, having come to faith, took orders, Lo having become their preceptor and the 2 seniors — their teachers. This is the reason why the 2 Ba and the 2 Rag are always mentioned together. Then Lo-tön said: — You are to remain here. I in my turn shall make friends with these merchants that go to Ü and Tsaṅ, depart with them and see if I can propagate the Doctrine there. If I am able to do this, I shall remain, and you must likewise come. If not, I shall come back. Accordingly, he made company with the merchants of Dan-ma. Now, as these merchants, thinking that in Sum-ṭhaṅ[1428]) some commercial affairs could be transacted, were about to return, he said to them: — Do not carry on your trade here, but go to Tsaṅ. In Gur-mo there is a man called Lo-nä-tsug-na[1429]). To him you must say: — Thy son has taken orders, and thou must now reside in Ü. Having thus spoken, he encouraged them to go. Accordingly, they had good luck in their trade, and up to this day, Gur-mo is a commercial centre, having become such by the grace of Lo-tön. The next year Lu-me said to his principal: — I am going to Ü and Tsaṅ and pray thee to give me an object of worship. (The principal) gave him a Bon-pa cap which he had ceased to wear and which was covered with yellow ground, as it had been thrown into a pit. — Wear this and remember me, — such were the teacher's words. Thereupon Lu-mē went upward to Central Tibet, and soon they all came to Ü. Now, in former times the place of residence of the learned and the monks was Lhasa. But recently it had become the place of slaughter and massacre and it was therefore not proper for them to go there. So they went instead to Sam-yä. After that Lu-me took possession of Ku-chu, [148 b.] and his spiritual descent maintained the U-chal[1430]) and U-tse.[1431]) The

---

1426) Grum Ye-çes-rgyal-mtshan.
1427) Rba, i. e. Rba Tshul-khrims-blo-gros. 1428) Sum-ḥphraṅ.
1429) Lo-nad-gtsug-na. This is evidently the father of Lo-tön.
1430) Dbu-chal. 1431) Dbu-rtse.

spiritual descent of Rag-çi occupied the Ge-gyä[1432]), and Ḍiṅ[1433]) the S'aṅ-khaṅ[1434]). Thereafter the 5 monks of Ü declared that it was necessary to build places of residence for themselves. Accordingly Lu-mē built the La-mo-chag-t'eu[1435]). He had 4 pupils: —

1. T'u-mar Tshul-ṭhim-juṅ-nä[1436]), built the Sol-nag-thaṅ-chen; the fraternity residing there was called the Thaṅ-kor[1437]);

2. Sh'aṅ Na-nam Dorje-vaṅ-chug[1438]) built the Ra-tshag-t'ar-gyal. The fraternity of it was called the Sh'aṅ-kor[1439]);

3. Dog Jaṅ-chub-juṅ-nä[1440]) built the Yer-pa-pa-raṅ. The filial fraternities belonging to his spiritual descent built the S'ad-kyi-ḍiṅ-va[1441]), Chu-çul-gyin-po, Pu-de-hlo-k'oṅ[1442]), Yol-thaṅ, Lab-so, Ḍal-ma-thaṅ[1443]) and Kha-rag-so-cig. Thereafter, in Tsaṅ they built the Sh'ui-kun-ga-ra-va[1444]) and Tshal-mig[1445]). In Kyi-çö, *Dog[1446]) and Sum-pa Ye-çei-lo-ḍö[1447]) built the Yu-go-khaṅ* mar[1448]). The spiritual descent of them is called the Dog-tsho-kor[1449]).

4. Laṅ Ye-çei-çei-rab[1450]) became the principal of Gyal-sar-gaṅ[1451]), of Lag-da-hla-khaṅ[1452]) and of the 2 Tshal-chuṅ. The filial branches of these are called the Laṅ-kor.

Sum-pa Ye-çei-lo-ḍö built Me-ru[1453]) in Ḍö-thaṅ. This monastery was destroyed and there was no fraternity belonging to it.

Rag-çi built the temple of Rag-çi-ṭhä-og[1454]).

Ba built the Yuṅ-gur[1455]), and subsequently became the principal of Lan-pa-cil-bu[1456]). His pupil Mal Sem-pa-çei-rab[1457]) built the Tö-lug-tsha-thog[1458]) and thereafter assumed the principality

---

[1432]) Dge-rgyas. [1433]) Ḥbriṅ i. e. Ḥbriṅ Ye-çes-yon-tan.
[1434]) Zaṅs-khaṅ. [1435]) La-mo-chag-deḥu.
[1436]) Gru-mar Tshul-khrims-ḥbyuṅ-gnas. [1437]) Thaṅ-skor.
[1438]) Sna-nam Rdo-rje-dbaṅ-phyug. [1439]) Žaṅ-skor.
[1440]) Rdog Byaṅ-chub-ḥbyuṅ-gnas. [1441]) Gzad-kyi-ldiṅ-ba.
[1442]) Spu-sde-lho-goṅ. [1443]) Gral-ma-thaṅ.
[1444]) Gžuḥi-kun-dgaḥ-ra-ba. [1445]) Ḥtshal-mig.
[1446]) I. e. Rdog Byaṅ-chub-ḥbyuṅ-gnas.
[1447]) Sum-pa Ye-çes-blo-gros.
[1448]) Gyu-sgo-khaṅ-dmar. [1449]) Rdog-tsho-skor.
[1450]) Glan Ye-çes-çes-rab. [1451]) Rgyal-gsar-sgaṅ.
[1452]) Glag-mdaḥ-lha-khaṅ. [1453]) Rme-ru.
[1454]) Rag-çi-ḥphrad-ḥog. [1455]) Yuṅs-ḥgur.
[1456]) Lan-pa-spyil-bu. [1457]) *Mal Sems-pa-çes-rab.*
[1458]) Stod-lugs-tsha-thog.

in the temple of Thag-ma and Mön-ḍa[1459]. His spiritual descent is called Ba-tsho.

The younger Ba built the temple of Gye-re-tshar-nai-da-ḍoṅ[1460] and subsequently became the principal of Sh'oi-che-khaṅ[1461] [149 a.].

Rag-çi then became the principal of Ka-tshal-t'ar-sh'a and the fraternity founded there and descending from him is called the Rag-tsho.

The younger Rag-çi assumed the principality of Ge-gyä[1462]. His pupil Tha-sh'i-gyal-phag[1463] likewise maintained the rule there. His pupil Sh'aṅ-tsun-çei-rab-phag[1464] built the Ta-ḍē of Lan-pa. *The fraternity thus founded is called "the spiritual line of Rag-çi the junior".*

Ḍiṅ built the Ṅan-lam-ci-mo[1465] and after that maintained the principality of Kar-chuṅ and, subsequently, of Ñe-thaṅ-ḍag-na[1466]. In the interspace between these two he built the Ḍaṅ Ra-mo-che. The fraternity founded in the latter monastery was called the "Lower Community of Ḍiṅ"[1467]. That residing at Ṅan-lam-pa is known as the higher (or upper) fraternity of Ḍiṅ[1468], and that of Lu-goṅ is "the intermediate fraternity of Ḍiṅ".

Lo-tön Dorje-vaṅ-chug of Tsaṅ built the Gyan-k'oṅ[1469]. He had 24 pupils.

Gya Çākya-sh'on-nu[1470] built the La-tö-mar-la-thaṅ[1471]; it was divided into the middle section of K'ul-tog-hla-khaṅ[1472] in the centre, and the others which are known by the name Gya-tsho.

Kyo Çei-rab-dorje[1473] built the T'on-mo-ri. The "upper section" (of the fraternity there) is founded by him.

Tag-lo-sh'ön-tsön[1474] *built the temple of* Tag-lo, and the fraternities that represent his spiritual descent are known as the Tag-tsho.

A-me Sh'u-cig-ma maintained the principality of Ṭhaṅ[1475] and Ḍag-mar[1476]. The fraternities founded by him are the Sh'u-tsho.

1459) Mon-gra. 1460) Gye-re-mtshar-snaḥi-mdaḥ-groṅ-lha-khaṅ.
1461) Gžoḥi-ḥchad-khaṅ. 1462) Dge-rgyas.
1463) Mthaḥ-bži-rgyal-ḥphags. 1464) Žaṅ-btsun-çes-rab-ḥphags.
1465) Ṅan-lam-spyi-mo. 1466) Sñe-thaṅ-brag-sna.
1467) Ḥbriṅ-tsho-smad-pa. 1468) Ḥbriṅ-tsho- stod-pa.
1469) Rgyan-goṅ. 1470) Rgya Çākya-gžon-nu.
1471) La-stod-mar-la-thaṅ. 1472) Gul-rtog-lha-khaṅ.
1473) Skyo Çes-rab-rdo-rje. 1474) Stag-lo Gžon-brtson.
1475) Ḥphraṅ. 1476) Brag-dmar.

Dar[1477]) Çākya-yon-tan maintained the principality of S'ü-po[1478]). His spiritual descent is the Dar-tsho.

Li Lo-ḍö-sh'on-nu[1479]) built the Jo-mo and his spiritual descent is called the Li-tsho.

In the 5 divisions of Mä[1480]) and the Gyan-k'oṅ-mai-kor[1481]), Lag Jaṅ-chub-gyal-tshen[1481a]) built the Chu-mig and the fraternity founded there is the Lag-tsho.

Chag Mi-ga Çei-rab la-ma built the Ñem[1482]), and Ṅog Ye-çei-juṅ-nä[1483]) built the Paṅ-kar-hla-luṅ[1484]). These two have no spiritual descent. [149 b.]

Laṅ-tsün-jam-pa[1485]) built the Khom-phug and subsequently maintained the principality of Tsaṅ-ḍam[1486]). After that, in Phum-thaṅ, Chag-sa, Dri-gog, Ma-gö, Tön-ṭhöl-ma[1487]) etc. the Upper[1488]) and the Lower[1489]) Laṅ-tsho were located.

Go-va Ye-çei-yuṅ-druṅ[1490]) maintained the principality of Bre-lha-khaṅ[1491]). His pupil Ce-tsün Çei-rab-juṅ-nä[1492]) built the Sh'a-lu-ma and then went to India where he took the vows again. Whilst he was travelling, Go-va-yuṅ-druṅ maintained the principality of Sh'a-lu. Here there were 4 primary and 6 secondary sections. The spiritual descent is called "the division of the 100 of Sh'a-lu"[1493]).

Gyi Ye-çei-vaṅ-po[1494]) built the Khar-luṅ[1495]) of Çaṅ, subsequently — Gya-re-laṅ-ra[1496]) and on the way between them — Ro-kam of Mu-çaṅ[1497]). The fraternity of Laṅ-la is called Laṅ-ra-kor. The sections belonging to the Tsug-gi U-luṅ bear the name of the U-tsho. Both are spoken of as the "lower Gyi-tsho. From Laṅ-ra the principality was maintained over the Ṭhii-chad-gön-pa[1498]).

Thereafter the pupil of A-me, Sh'aṅ-tön-tshul-phag[1499]) go-

---

1477) Ḥdar. 1478) Gzus-po. 1479) Li Blo-gros-gžon-nu.
1480) Smad-kyi Iṅa-la. 1481) Rgyan-goṅ-mahi skor.
1481a) Glag Byaṅ-chub-rgyal-mtshan. 1482) Sñems.
1483) Rṅog Ye-çes-ḥbyuṅ-gnas.
1484) Spaṅ-dkar-lha-luṅ. 1485) Glaṅ-btsun-byams-pa.
1486) Gtsaṅ-ḥgram. 1487) Ston-khrol-ma. 1488) Stod.
1489) Smad. 1490) Mgo-ba Ye-çes-gyuṅ-druṅ.
1491) Sbre-lha-khaṅ. 1492) Lce-btsun Çes-rab-ḥbyuṅ-gnas.
1493) Ža-lu-brgya-skor. 1494) Gyi Ye-çes-dbaṅ-po.
1495) Mkhar-lun. 1496) Gya-re-glaṅ-ra.
1497) Mu-çaṅs-kyi Ro-skams.
1498) Ḥkhris-kyi-ḥchad-dgon-pa. 1499) Žaṅ-ston-tshul-ḥphags.

verned the C'a-gyā[1500]. Another pupil of A-me, Coṅ-po Thar-pa-rin-chen had 4 pupils. — S'u-tön-phan-ṭ'ag occupied the principality of Ḍei-ce-tsham[1501]) and Gyan-khar-tag-luṅ[1502]). The communities belonging to these are called the S'u-tsho. Ce-tsün-kar-po[1503]) governed the Aṅ-yig and Yuṅ-tön-dza-ka-ris-pa ruled over Or. The fraternities founded by him became united with the A-mei-kor. Therefore there is no separate spiritual descent (from this teacher).

Çab-tse[1504]) founded the Çab-tse-lha-khaṅ; the community thereof is called the Koṅ-tsho and another section is styled the Kyi-tsho.

A-me, from the Kha-che-gön-pa[1505]) ruled over the Se-kyil-ter. Of the higher section of it there were 3 filial branches called the Ōn-pa-sh'aṅ.

Ṭhi-tön-tsön-bar[1506]) maintained the principality of Çoṅ-na-ra. The section belonging to it is the Ṭhi-tsho [150 a.] Sa -be-tsün-chuṅ maintained the rule of Ḍan-chuṅ, and his spiritual descent is styled the Ḍan-chuṅ-kor.

Gya-tön Āryadeva maintained the Go-ru-du-na[1507]), and his descent is called the Gya-tsho.

The abbot Sh'on-nu Çākya maintained the Sa-phug, and his descent bears the name of Sa-tsho. The upper section of it had 4 divisions which were known as "the upper Kyi-tsho".

The spiritual son of A-me, Paṅ[1508]) maintained the Thii-kyaṅ, and Sh'aṅ-tsün-sö-nam-ḍag held the rule of the C'a-gyā. These 2 are spoken of as the intermediate Kyi-tsho.

The disciple descending from the higher Kyi-tsho, Sh'on-nu-juṅ-nā maintained the Gyan-khar-thur-la[1509]). The monastic division belonging to it is known as the Thur-tsho.

Kyi-ṭsun Pal-gyi-ye-çei[1510]) occupied the principality of the Ḍuṅ-kün-ga-ra-ba[1511]). The fraternity of it is a filial branch of the higher Kyi-tsho.

The Tshoṅ-tsho had 9 secondary divisions[1512]). In the higher Tshoṅ-tsho there were the 2 sections of Kal-kor[1513]) and Gyan-kor.

1500) Bya-rgyas. 1501) Sgreḥi lce ḥtshams.
1502) Rgyan-mkhar-stag-luṅ. 1503) Lce-btsun-dkar-po.
1504) Çab-rtse. 1505) Kha-chad-dgon-pa.
1506) Khri-ston-brtson-ḥbar. 1507) Sgo-ru-du-sna. 1508) Spaṅ.
1509) Rgyan-mkhar-thur-la. 1510) Kyi-btsun Dpal-gyi-ye-çes.
1511) Ḥbruṅ-kun-dgaḥ-ra-ba. 1512) Khral-tsho. 1513) Skal-skor.

In the intermediate Tshoṅ-tsho there were likewise 2, viz. the Nä-sar[1514]) and Nä-ñiṅ[1515]). The lower section had 5 sub-divisions.

At the time when Tshoṅ-tsün was maintaining the Tsii-kyi-yaṅ-ben[1516]), A-me entrusted to him the Tsii-hla-khaṅ which was subsequently conferred to Ba-tsün Lo-ṭ'ö yon-tan. After the latter had become principal, the section ruled by him was called the Ba-tsho. His pupil Yol-chö-vaṅ maintained the Kye-nä-ñiṅ[1517]). The section belonging to it was called the upper Ba-tsho.

Yol-thog-beb[1518]) maintained the Caṅ-ra. Tag-pa-jo-btsun held the principality of the Ce-pe[1519]). These 2 represent the intermediate Ba-tsho.

The section located in Tsii is known as the lower section of Ba. Thereafter the Ñan-tsho was entrusted to A-me and, subsequently, to his pupils Rva Lo-ḍö-s'aṅ-po and to Kham-pa. Rva occupied the Ṅur-mig[1520]), and Kham-pa — the Cag-khar[1521]). The sections founded by them are called the Rva-tsho and the Kham-tsho, [150 b.] and both were known as the Ñan-tsho-kor.

The Tag-tshal-gyi-c'a-chö-khar-po-che[1522]) was likewise given to A-me and subsequently entrusted by the latter to his pupil Gya-gyal-bu-tshul-seṅ[1523]). Gya was entrusted to Koṅ-po-ye-juṅ[1524]) of Gyä. Koṅ- po maintained both the Mui nä-mo-che[1525]) and the Ja-chö[1526]) and founded the Gyä-t'a-thaṅ. These divisions are called the Ja-chö-kor.

Thereafter the Yön-dag-mo-ñö-mö-mön-ḍo in Mar-çul was given over to A-me and entrusted by him to his pupil Mar-pa Dorje-ye-çei and by the latter to his own pupil Ne-po Ḍag-pa-gyal-tshen[1527]) who maintained the principality of Roṅ-khar-phug. Subsequently, A-me founded the Kyag-tsham-tag-tshal-kyü-thaṅ and gave it to Mar-pa who in his turn built the Ṭhan-ma-gaṅ-po. With the Lag-ḍoi as a fourth they became known as the "4 children of Mön-ḍo" which bore a similarity with a mother. They were all called the Mön-ḍo-kor[1528]).

Moreover, subsequently, A-me, having maintained the prin-

1514) Gnas-gsar. 1515) Gnas-rñiṅ. 1516) Rtsis-kyi-yaṅ-dben.
1517) Skyegs-gnas-rñiṅ. 1518) Yol-thog-ḥbebs. 1519) Lce-spe.
1520) Ṅur-smrig. 1521) Lcags-mkhar.
1522) Stag-tshal-gyi-bya-chos-mkhar-po-che.
1523) Rgya Rgyal-bu-tshul-seṅ. 1524) Rgyas Kon-po-ye-ḥbyuṅ.
1525) Dmuḥi gnas-mo-che. 1526) Bya-chos.
1527) Sne-po Grags-pa-rgyal-mtshan. 1528) Smon-gro-skor.

cipality in Ser-gyi-goṅ-ṭhog[1529]), entrusted it to his pupil Sh'aṅ-pa-tshor-thö[1530]). The latter built the Ser-gyi-ḍag-çö[1531]) and then maintained the Tsen-po-diṅ[1532]), the Tsii-kyi-yaṅ-ben, the Ra-sog-tshar-la, and the Tag-tshal-kar-po-che[1533]). (All) these were entrusted to his pupil, Ba-ge-thoṅ[1533a]). The latter maintained the P'a-t'o of Roṅ and entrusted it to his pupil Ḍe-tsün-ṅön-mo[1534]). These sections are called the T'o-tsho.

Now, at the time when the secondary sections had assembled to hold council together, there appeared 3 inferior monks. When they were asked: — Whither has your preceptor gone? — they replied that he had died. If this be so, —(said the others), —you are living like orphans. And thencefrom they were known as T'o-tsho, — "the section of the orphans". All these divisions (taken together) are called "the 5 lower Tsoṅ-tsho". The principal monastery of all the 9 Tshoṅ-tsho was the Ṅo-liṅ[1535]).

Furthermore, A-sh'a Ye-çei-yuṅ-druṅ, the son of A-sh'a Go-vo-che[1536]), [151 a.] who had the wish of going to Kham in order to become a monk, arrived at Lhasa. And, on the lower part of a staircase leading to the upper storey of one of the buildings of Lhasa (he saw) the form of Çrī-Mahākāla that was painted there. When (A-sh'a) ascended, it was only a picture (that was before him), but when he descended, Mahākāla appeared directly (before him), holding a skull containing a human head mixed with blood which he was eating with a spoon made of a human rib. To him (A-sh'a) addressed his entreaty, and (Mahākāla) said: — I will be the protector of thy Doctrine. —Therefore, during a month, thou must circumambulate me. — This is the reason why the A-tsho (the section founded by A-sh'a) is so powerful.

Thereafter A-sh'a went to the school of Kham and prayed Ṭe-vo-chog-la[1537]), the pupil of the Great Lama (Goṅ-pa-rab-sal) to grant him the favour (of ordaining him). The teacher said: — I shall make the offering of water and then come! But, as the teacher died suddenly without having granted his favour, A-sh'a was considered to have received the consecration by the mere

---

1529) Ser-gyi-sgoṅ-khrog.
1530) Žaṅ-pa-tshor-khrod. 1531) Ser-gyi-brag-çod.
1532) Btsan-po-sdiṅs. 1533) Stag-tshal-mkhar-po-che.
1533a) Rba Dge-mthoṅ. 1534) Bra-btsun-sṅon-mo.
1535) Sṅo-gliṅ. 1536) Ḥa-ža-mgo-bo-che.
1537) Kre-bo-mchog-bla.

words "I will make the offering of water and then come". He is accordingly known as "the novice of the water-offering". After he had been made principal, he maintained the Na-nam-dre-dă[1538]), and subsequently, the U-yug-dai-ra-ça[1539]), as well as the Tag-gi-nă-mo-che[1540]) situated between the former two. His pupil, Çeu-te-nam-pa maintained the Lhan-gyi-so-thaṅ, and subsequently the Khor-re-kya-gaṅ[1541]), the Ñaṅ-ro-p'ŭ-do[1542]), the Khor-re-p'a-khor, and the Lhan-gyi-dro-çoṅ in gradual succession. His pupil, Sog Tshul-ṭhim maintained the Bo-tsho-thaṅ and had himself a pupil Paṅ Dul-dzin[1543]) who maintained the Tag-gi-pen-can[1544]). The pupil of this one Nub Rin-chen-ḍag[1545]) occupied the principality of Khu-luṅ-lha-t'al and, from Ra-ça, ruled over U-yug-sal-gaṅ. All these (monastic divisions) were called the A-tsho.

Moreover, Ḍe-sh'on-tshul went to Kham in the purpose of taking orders. [151 b.] Having met with Ya-s'i-p'ön-tön[1546]), the pupil of the Great Lama, in the Ṭhi-kha-khar-ma of Kham, he prayed him to grant his favour. (P'ön-tön) said: — Be it so, — but died before the vows were made and accepted. Ḍe in his turn declared: — I have been ordained, since the disciple (of the Great Lama) has said: — Be it so. — Accordingly, he was known as the one who was ordained by (the words) "Be it so". He maintained the Ja-tshaṅ of Ta-nag-phu[1547]), and, subsequently the Ja-phug of Çaṅ[1548]). We have 8 monasteries representing the filials of Ja Tshaṅ. This division is called the Ḍe-tsho.

In such a manner the 10 men started their propagation (of the Doctrine). However, as Sum-pa of Ŭ and the 2 brothers Ŏ-gye left no descent, (the new founders) are known as "the Six Men". A-sh'a and Ḍe are not included in their number.

Some say that the disciple of the teacher Bodhisattva was Ratna of Ba, that the latter ordained Hla-luṅ Rab-jor-yaṅ[1549]), that this one in his turn ordained the Great Lama Goṅ-pa-rab-sal, whose disciple was Ye-k'oṅ Ye-çei-yuṅ-druṅ[1550]). The latter is said to have ordained Ḍum Ye-çei-gyal-tshen, and this one — Lu-mē and the rest.

1538) Sna-nam-ḥdre-brdas. 1539) Ḥu-yug-mdaḥl-ra-ça.
1540) Stag-gi-gnas-mo-che. 1541) Ḥkhor-re-skya-sgaṅ.
1542) Ñaṅ-ro-bud-mdo. 1543) Spaṅ-Ḥdul-ḥdzin.
1544) Stag-gi-span-can. 1545) Snubs Rin-chen-grags. 1546) Ya-ži-bon-ston.
1547) Rta-nag-phuḥi Bya-tshaṅ. 1548) Çaṅs-kyi bya-phug.
1549) Lha-luṅ Rab-ḥbyor-dbyaṅs. 1550) Ye-goṅ Ye-çes-gyuṅ-druṅ.

In a certain testament it is to be read that Ratna of Ba (was ordained), the Ācārya Bodhisattva having become his principal, and Dānaçīla and Jinamitra — his teachers. Ba ordained Yo-ge, the latter — Goṅ-pa-sal, this one — Mañjuçrī of Ḍo[1551]), this one — Ḍum Ye-çei-gyal-tshen, and the latter — Lu-mē.

Rig-ral says that the 10 men of Ü and Tsaṅ were ordained by Ḍum, the disciple of the Great Lama. This requires proof. Moreover, some are of the opinion that Yo and the rest belong to the spiritual descent of Jinamitra. Others in their turn affirm that this genealogy is to be counted from Çāntirakṣita. This must likewise be scrutinized.

Thus, 70 years after the Church had ceased to exist in Ü and Tsaṅ, it was again introduced there by the 10 men of these provinces. [152 a.] At the time when the 10 arrived at Ü, an old woman said: — When I was 6 years of age, I last saw a monk. — And how old art thou now? — asked they. — Seventy-six, was the answer. So runs the tradition. Some say that (from the time of the persecution up to that of the restoration) 108 years had elapsed.

Rig-ral affirms the following: — From the time of the 6 men and up to the coming of Ratnabhadra[1552]) there was no study and preaching of the Doctrine, and there existed only a resemblance of the latter. Then, after the king had become alms-giver, the Lotsavas and Paṇḍits translated the kanonical works. This is the intermediate period of the spread of the Doctrine. Thereupon, without the assistance of the king, Ṅog and others have made their translations. This time is to be regarded as that of the latest propagation of the teaching.

This is not correct. (Rig-ral) himself admits that (from the time of the ten) the vows of monkhood were perfectly pure. The statement that there was only a resemblance of the Doctrine is therefore contradictory. (Rig-ral) affirms this saying: "Since there was no study and preaching". This is likewise incorrect. Indeed, the Vinaya with the necessary instructions had been exposed by the Paṇḍit Jinamitra to the translator Lui-gyal-tshen, to Yo-ge-juṅ etc., by the latter to the Great Lama, by him to Ḍum, by this one — to Lu-me, and by the latter — to S'ü Dorje-gyal-tshen. This one had 4 pupils: — Lan tshul-jaṅ[1553]), Ka-chu-pa Tshul-juṅ[1554]), Ne-po Ḍag-gyal[1555]), Jim-pa-çar-ö[1556]). The pupil of Ne-

[1551]) Sgro. [1552]) Rin-bzaṅ i. e. Rin-chen-bzaṅ-po.
[1553]) Klan-tshul-byaṅ. [1554]) Tshul-ḥbyuṅ.
[1555]) Sne-po Grags-rgyal. [1556]) Ḥjims-pa-çar-ḥod.

po was Sog Tshul-ṭhim-la-ma, the pupil of Ka-chu-pa was Ñaṅ-tsham[1557]) Rin-chen-la-ma, and pupil of Jim-pa — Ko-Khyim-pa Ye-çei-la-ma. The exposition of the Vinaya with the necessary instructions was conducted by these 3 and delivered to Gya Dul-dzin Vaṅ-chug-tshul-ṭhim, to his pupil Ma-tsho Jaṅ-dor, to Ja Dul-dzin[1558]), to Kyi-po Tshul-phag, and up to Ça-mi and the rest. Moreover the teaching of the Abhidharma had been uninterruptedly conducted by Jinamitra, by Ka[1559]), Cog[1560]), and Sh'aṅ, by Nam-naṅ-da-vai-dorje[1561]), Pal-gyi-dorje, by Gyal-ba-ye-çei of Ba, by Chog-gi-ye-çei of Cog-ḍu[1562]), [152 b.], Se-tsün Sh'ön-nu[1563]), Gar-mi Yon-tan-yuṅ-druṅ, Khu-tön Çei-rab-tsön-ḍü[1564]), Rva-ṭhi S'aṅ-bar[1565]), Gya Gyal-bu-tshul-le[1566]), Ḍaṅ-ti[1566a]) Dar-ma-ñiṅ-po, to his pupils, Ban and Rog etc.

The discrimination (made by Rig-ral) between an intermediate and a later propagation of the Doctrine is likewise false. There was no "intermediate" propagation at all, since there occurred no interruption. The earlier and the later propagation are regarded as 2 different periods, with the view that the Doctrine, having been rooted out by Laṅ-dar-ma, had, for a certain number of years, ceased to exist in Ü and Tsaṅ. The Pandit Tsan-nag-pa likewise says that there was "the later period of propagation" (without counting an intermediate one). In such a way, the fire of the Doctrine, having begun in lower Tibet, spread and expounded through Ṅa-ri. The king Khor-de entrusted the kingdom to his younger brother Sroṅ-de and himself took orders, having adopted the religious name of Ye-çei-ö[1567]). He acknowledged the Vehicle of Philosophy[1568]) to be the Word of the Buddha, but as concerns the Tantras, he was in doubt as to their being the true teaching, since the tantric exorcists indulged in perverse acts, as that of deliverance through sexual extasy, etc. Accordingly, he selected 21 young men, Rin-chen-s'aṅ-po and others and sent them to India in order to study the Doctrine. But, with the exception of

---

1557) Ñaṅ-mtshams. 1558) Bya Ḥdul-ḥdzin.
1559) Ska i. e. Ska-pa Dpal-brtsegs.
1560) I. e. Cog-ro Kluḥi-rgyal-mtshan.
1561) Nam-naṅ Zla-baḥi-rdo-rje.
1562) Cog-gru Mchog-gi-ye-çes. 1563) Se-btsun-gżon-nu.
1564) Khu-ston Çes-rab-brtson-ḥgrus.
1565) Rva-khri Bzaṅ-ḥbar. 1566) Rgya Rgyal-bu-tshul-le.
1566a) Braṅ-ti. 1567) Ye-çes-ḥod. 1568) *mtshan-ñid-theg-pa.*

Rin-chen-s'aṅ-po and Leg-pai-çei-rab, they died without having achieved their study. Rin-chen-s'aṅ-po became profoundly versed in all the branches of Tantra and philosophy and, having invited the Paṇḍits Çraddhākaravarman, Padmākaragupta, Buddhaçrīçānta, Buddhapāla, Kamalagupta, and others, achieved the translation of the philosophical part of the Kanon and of the 4 divisions of Tantra. In particular, many texts of the Yogatantra, the Guhyasamāja etc. were translated and the Tantric parts of Scripture revised. [153 a.]

Gyal-vai-çei-rab of Sh'aṅ-sh'uṅ, having invited the Paṇḍits Dharmapāla and Prajñāpāla, took orders and then, having gone to Nepal, studied the practical Vinaya with Pretaka. His pupils Pal-jor, Jaṅ-chub-seṅ-ge of Sh'iṅ-mo-che, and others, in gradual succession, propagated the teaching of the Higher Vinaya. The Princely Teacher (Ye-çei-ö) built the monastery of Sh'aṅ-sh'uṅ-tho-liṅ and became the householder of numerous Lotsavas and Paṇḍits. The son of his younger brother Sroṅ-de called La-de invited the Paṇḍit Subhāṣita. This king had 3 sons, — Ō-de[1569]), the lay prince Sh'i-va-ö and the ecclesiastic Jaṅ-chub-ö. Of these three, the latter gave gold to 5 men, Nag-tsho Tshul-gyal etc. and ordered them to select the translator Gya Tson-ḍü-seṅ-ge[1570]) as their chief, and to invite a good Paṇḍit. Accordingly, they invited Dīpaṁkaraçrījñāna[1571]) who was the son of Kalyāṇaçrī the king of Bengal, and who had received a brilliant education at the monastery of Vikramaçīla[1572]). (Dīpaṁkaraçrījñāna) accordingly accepted their invitation and came, since he had obtained a corresponding prophecy from Tārā. On the way Gya Tson-ḍü-seṅ-ge died and they arrived, *having appointed* Nag-*tsho to be interprete*. When they came to the sleeping chamber of the great translator Rin-chen-s'aṅ-po, the latter first made his salutation, and then the Paṇḍit addressed a hymn of praise to each of the images of the Tantric deities that were in the translator's room. The great translator was delighted, and they held together many discussions on religious questions. (The translator) again made his salutations and prayed to expound the Doctrine. After that they made numerous translations, and especially put in order the

---

1569) Ḥod-lde. 1570) Rgya Brtson-ḥgrus-seṅ-ge.

1571) Usually known as Jo-vo-rje "the Great Master" or Atīça.

1572) The Xyl. has Bri-ka-ma-la-çi-la (sic!)

texts of the Yoga-tantra in accordance with the explanations of Ānandagarbha and added numerous instructions to them.

By the by the Great Master (Dīpaṁkaraçrījñāna) [153 b.] went to Ü and delivered numerous instructions to his pupils Khu, Ṅog, and Ḍom[1573]. In particular, he delivered to Ḍom the precepts of the Ka-dam-pa[1574] which thenceforth became expounded. The Great Translator Rin-chen-s'aṅ-po subdued the Nāga Kar-gyal and refuted the false exorcists by means of the Doctrine. Tradition says that he secured the proximate factors of Deliverance and passed away to heaven in his bodily form[1575]. His assistant Ḍag-jor-çei-rab translated the works of the cycles of Çaṁvara and Varāhī, logical treatises, etc. and likewise passed away to heaven in his bodily form. The inferior translator Bar-chö-s'aṅ, after having translated the so-called "Six texts of the Lotsavas" (?)[1576], departed to the 5 mountains.

The translators who had first been with the Great Master and, moreover, Çākyaprabha, Yöl-cog Dorje-vaṅ-chug, Ge-vai-lo-ḍö translated and revised a great number of works. The prince Sh'i-va-ö in his turn translated the *Çrīparamādiṭīkā*[1577], the logical work of Çāntirakṣita[1578] etc.

At the time of the princely teacher Ye-çei-ö 2 Paṇḍits, Smṛti and Sūkṣmadīrgha[1579] came, having been invited by the Nepalese Padmaruci. But as the translator had died in Nepal of cholera, the 2 Paṇḍits who did not know the Tibetan language, roamed about in Ü and Tsaṅ, and Smṛti was forced to become a shepherd in Ta-nag. Subsequently Cal-se-tsab Sö-nam-gyal-tshen[1580] invited him to Man-luṅ[1581] and studied the Doctrine with him. Thereafter, having gone to Kham, (Smṛti) established the school of the Abhidharmakoça at Dan-loṅ-thaṅ[1582]. Subsequently, having become proficient in Tibetan, he made numerous translations of his own works, as the *Catuḥpīṭha-ṭīkā*[1583], the cycle of *Mañjuçrī-*

[1573]) I. e. Khu-ton (Khu-ston) Çei-rab-tson-ḍü (Çes-rab-brtson-ḥgrus). Ṅog (Rṅog) Lo-dan-çei-rab (Blo-ldan-çes-rab) and Ḍom (Ḥbrom)-tön.

[1574]) Bkaḥ-gdams-pa. [1575]) *mkhaḥ-spyod-du-gçegs.*

[1576]) Lo-tsaḥi-chos-drug.

[1577]) Dpal-mchog. Tg. RGYUD. LIV. 57—297, LV and LVI. 1—227.

[1578]) Ži-ba-ḥtshoḥi tshad-ma. This is Çāntirakṣita's Tattvasaṁgraha, Tg. MDO. CXIII. 1—159. [1579]) Phra-la-riṅ-ba.

[1580]) Dpyal-se-rtsab Bsod-nams-rgyal-mtshan.

[1581]) Sman-luṅs. [1582]) Ḥdan-kloṅ-thaṅ.

[1583]) Tg. RGYUD. XXIII. 1—89.

guhyāpanna[1584]), the *Mantra-artha-vipaçyinī*[1585]), and many others. [154 a.] Subsequently, he went to Li-chu-ser-khab and composed there the *Vacanamukha*[1586]). The Paṇḍit Sūkṣmadīrgha became the curator of Roṅ-pa Chö-s'aṅ and Roṅ-pa came to the knowledge of numerous kanonical texts.

The king Ö-de invited Sunayaçrī[1587]).

His son Tse -de invited the Kashmirian Jñānaçrī and, Khyaṅ-po Chö-tsön[1588]) having been appointed as interprete, the *Vajra-çikhara-tantra*[1589]), the Ācāra-tantras, the *Pramāṇa-viniçcaya*[1589a]) and the Commentary thereon, composed by Jñānaçrī himself[1590]), were translated.

Moreover Candrarāhula having been invited, the Lotsava Tiṅ-ṅe-dzin-s'aṅ-po[1591]) carried out the translation of the *Pramāṇa-samuccaya*[1592]) and other works.

Ṅog Lo-dan (çei-rab) was sent by Tse-de to Kashmir, studied Logic with Parahitabhadra[1593]) and Bhavyarāja[1594]), and the treatises of Maitreya with the Brāhmaṇa Sajjana[1595]), Amaragomin[1596]), and others. After Vaṅ-de[1597]) had become alms-giver, he (Ṅog Lo-dan-çei-rab) translated the *Pramāṇavārtika-alaṁkāra*[1598]) etc.

1584) Tg. RGYUD. LX. 127—178. — Ārya-Mañjuçrī-nāma-saṁgīti-guhya-āpanna-upāyika-vṛtti Jñāna-dīpa (Ḥphags-pa Ḥjam-dpal-gyi mtshan yaṅ-dag-par-brjod-paḥi gsaṅ-ba-daṅ-ldan-paḥi sgrub-paḥi thabs-kyi ḥgrel-pa Ye-çes-gsal-ba), and Tg. RGYUD. LXI. 38—41. — Guhya-āpanna-upāyika-sūtra-vidhi (Sgrub-thabs gsaṅ-ba-daṅ-ldan-paḥi thig-gi-cho-ga).

1585) Sṅags-don-rnam-gzigs. 1586) Smra-sgo. Tg. MDO. CXVI.

1587) The Xyl. has here and furtheron Sunyaçrī. 1588) Chos-brtson.

1589) Rdo-rje-rtse-mo. In the Kg. RGYUD. VIII we have the Vajra-çikhara-mahā-guhya-yoga-tantra, Karmavajra and Sh'on-nu-tshul-ṭhim (Gžon-nu-tshul-khrims) being indicated as translators.

1589a) Tg. MDO. XCV. 250—329. (Pek.) The Tangyur text is a translation made by Ṅog Lo-dan-çei-rab with the assistance of the Paṇḍit Parahitabhadra.

1590) Tg. MDO. CX. 209—355. (Pek.) Translators the same as indicated by Bu-ton.

1591) Tiṅ-ṅe-ḥdzin-bzaṅ-po.

1592) The Tangyur text of the Pramāṇasamuccaya is a translation made by the Paṇḍit Kanakavarman and the Lotsava Dad-paḥi-çes-rab.

1593) Gžan-phan-bzaṅ-po. 1594) Skal-ldan-rgyal-po.

1595) He is the Paṇḍit who assisted in the translation of the Uttaratantra and Uttaratantra-vyākhyā.

1596) Go-mi-ḥchi-med. With the assistance of this Paṇḍit Lo-dan-çei-rab translated the Abhisamayālaṁkāra. 1597) Dbaṅ-lde.

1598) Tshad-ma-rgyan. Tg. MDO. XCIX and C. Translators acc. to Tg. Lo-dan-çei-rab and Bhavyarāja.

Ṭhi Ṭa-çi Vaṅ-chug Nam-kha-tsen[1599]) likewise became an alms-giver of translators and lived 17 years in Kashmir and 34 years in Tibet. The Paṇḍits Sthirapāla[1600]), Atulyadāsa[1601]), Sumatikīrti, Amaracandra, and Kumārakalaça[1600a]) translated a great number of texts, taught at Saṅ-duṅ-neu-thog and other places, and furthered the spread of the *Sūtrālaṁkāra*, the works of Dharmottara, the *Bodhicaryāvatāra* etc. The service rendered by them is of exclusive importance.

P'a-tshab Ñi-ma-ḍag[1602]) studied 23 years in Kashmir, invited the Paṇḍit Kanakavarman, and explained the works of the Mādhyamika cycle. [154 b.] His pupils were the "Four Sons of P'a-tshab" and others.

Ḍog-mi Çākya-ye-çei invited the Paṇḍit Gāyadhara, gave him 500 pounds of gold, and translated the *He-vajra-pañjara*[1603]), the *Saṁpuṭa*[1604]) the *Rali*[1605]), the *Arali*[1606]), these four and other

---

1599) Khri Bkra-çis-dbaṅ-phyug Nam-mkhaḥ-btsan.

1600) Ḥbum-phrag-gsum-pa. Cf. Schiefner, Tāranātha, p. 249.

1600a) Gžon-nu-bum-pa. (The Xyl. has . . . ḥbum-pa.)

1601) The Xyl. has Atulyadāça. 1602) Pa-tshab Ñi-ma-grags.

1603) Kyeḥi rdo-rjeḥi-gur. Kg. RGYUD. I. No. 10. In the Kg. the full title of this work is Ārya-ḍākinī-vajra-pañjara-mahā-tantra-rāja-kalpa. Translators acc. to Kg. — the same as with Bu-ton.

1604) Saṁpuṭa-nāma-mahā-tantra, Kg. RGYUD. III. No. 8. Acc. to Kg. translators — the same.

1605) This is a division of Tantric works called by Bu-ton the Bde-mchog Ra-liḥi-rgyud (Rali-Çaṁvara-tantras). These are: — 1. Guhya-vajra-tantra-rāja (Tg. RGYUD. IV. No. 1), 2. Guhya-sarva-cchinda-tantra-rāja (Ibid. No. 2), 3. Cakra-saṁvara-guhya-acintya-tantra-rāja (Ibid. No. 3), 4. Khasama-tantra-rāja (Ibid. No. 4), 5. Mahā-khasama-tantra-rāja (Ibid. No. 5), 6. Ṛatna-mālā-tantra-rāja (Ibid. No. 7), 7. Mahā-samaya-tantra-rāja (Ibid. No. 8), 8. Mahā-bala-tantra-rāja (Ibid. No. 9), 9. Jñāna-guhya-tantra-rāja (Ibid. No. 10), 10. Jñāna-mālā-tantra-rāja (Ibid. No. 11), 11. Candra-mālā-tantra-rāja (Ibid. No. 13), 12. Ratna-jvāla-tantra-rāja (Ibid. No. 14), 13. Sūrya-cakra-tantra-rāja (Ibid. No. 15), 14. Jñāna-rāja-tantra-rāja (Ibid. No. 16), 15. Vajra-ḍāka-guhya-tantra-rāja (Ibid. No. 17), 16. Jvalāgni-guhya-tantra-rāja (Ibid. No. 18), 16. Amṛta-guhya-tantra-rāja (Ibid. No. 19), 17. Çmaçāna-alaṁkāra-tantra-rāja (Ibid. No. 20), 18. Vajra-rāja-mahā-tantra (Ibid. No. 21), 19. Jñāna-āçaya-tantra-rāja (Ibid. No. 22), 20. Rāga-rāja-tantra-rāja (Ibid. No. 23), 21. Ḍākinī-saṁvara-tantra-rāja (Ibid. No. 24), 22. Ḍākinī-guhya-jvāla-tantra-rāja (Ibid. No. 25), 23. Vajra-bhairava-vidāraṇa-tantra-rāja (Ibid. No. 26), 24. Agni-mālā-tantra-rāja (Ibid. No. 27), 25. Vajra-siddha-jāla-saṁvara-tantra-rāja (Ibid. No. 28), 26. Mahābala-jñāna-rāja-tantra-rāja (Ibid. No. 29), and 27. Cakra-saṁvara-tantra-rāja Adbhuta-çmaçāna-alaṁkāra (Ibid. No. 30).

1606) In the Kg. RGYUD. IV we have: Vajra-arali-mahā-tantra-rāja (No 37), and Rigy-arali-tantra-rāja (Nr. 38). Translators acc. to Kg. — the same.

Cycles of Propitiation[1607]) belonging to the Mother-Tantras[1608]) with the supplementary instructions to them.

Hlā-tsā[1609]) of Gö-khug[1610]) went to India 3 times and studied the Doctrine with 72 Paṇḍits who had attained the mystical powers. In particular he took recourse to the aid of Çāntibhadra, Rāhulabhadra etc., and translated the works on the Guhyasamāja belonging to the school of Nāgārjuna[1611]), works belonging to the cycle of Çaṁvara[1612]), Vajraḍāka[1613]), Catuḥpīṭha[1614]), Mahāmāyā[1615]), Hevajra[1615a]) etc.

Gyi-co Da-vai-ö-s'er[1616]) translated the *Kāla-cakra [-garbha]*[1617]),

---

1607) Sgrub-skor.

1608) Ma-rgyud. 1609) Lhas-btsas.

1610) Ḥgos-khug. Cf. Cordier, Index I. p. 99. — du monastère de Ḥgos et de la tribu Khug (originaire du district de Rta-nag, province du Gtsaṅ inférieur).

1611) Gsaṅ-ḥdus-ḥphags-skor. Tg. RGYUD. XVII—XXXII.

1612) Kg. RGYUD. IV, No. 32.

1613) Çrī-vajra-ḍāka-nāma-mahā-tantra-rāja, Kg. RGYUD. II, No. 6. In the Tangyur we have, belonging to this Cycle and translated by this Lotsava, the Çrī-vajra-ḍāka-nāma-mahā-tantra-rājasya vivṛttiḥ, Tg. RGYUD. IX. 1—238, the work of Bhavabhaṭṭa. Translators acc. to Kg. the same.

1614) Çrī-Catuḥpītha-mahā-yoginī-tantra-rāja, Kg. RGYUD. IV, No. 39, Translator acc. to Kg. the same. In the Tg. we have, translated by this Lotsava, 1. Çrī-Catuḥpīṭha-tantra-rājasya ṭīkā Smṛti-nibandha. Tg. RGYUD. XXII. 260—407, the work of Bhavabhaṭṭa; 2. Çrī-Catuḥpīṭha-tantra-rāja nāma-maṇḍala-upāyikā-vidhi Sāra-samuccaya, Tg. RGYUD. XXIII. 142—172, the work of Āryadeva; 3. Çrī-Catuḥpīṭha-sādhana-upāyikā, Ibid, XXIII. 179—185; 4. Çrī-Catuḥpīṭha-tattva-catuṣka, Ibid, 202—207, the work of Jetāri.

1615) Kg. RGYUD. IV, No. 36. Translator acc. to Kg. the same. In the Tg. we have, translated by this Lotsava and belonging to the Cycle of Mahāmāyā: 1. Guṇavatī Çrī-Mahāmāyā-ṭīkā, Tg. RGYUD. XXIII. 223—249, the work of Ratnākaraçānti; 2. Mahāmāyā-tantrasya vṛttiḥ Smṛti-nāmā, Ibid. 249—271, the work of Kṛṣṇavajra; 3. Mahāmāyā-sādhana-maṇḍala-vidhi. Ibid. 288—305, the work of Kukkuripāda.

1615a) The works of this Cycle translated by Hlā-tsā are: — 1. Hevajra-nāma-mahātantra-rāja-dvikalpa-māyasya *pañjikā Smṛti-nibandha*, Tg. RGYUD XVII. 169—228, the work of Kṛṣṇa; 2. Çrī-Hevajra-pañjikā Muktikāvalī. Ibid. 262—349, the work of Ratnākaraçānti.

1616) Gyi-co Zla-baḥi ḥod-zer.

1617) Kg. RGYUD. I. No. 5. In the Tg. we have, translated by this Lotsava and belonging to the Cycle of Kālacakra: 1. Çrī-Kālacakra-garbha-alaṁkāra-sādhana, Tg. RGYUD. 206-218, the work of Bhadrabodhi; 2. Kāla-cakra-upadeça Ibid. 218—220.

the *Buddhakapāla*[1618]), *Vajra-amṛta*[1618a]), (works of the cycle of) Çaṁvara[1618b]) etc.

Mar-pa Chö-kyi-lo-ḍö[1619]) of Hlo-ḍag[1620]) went jo India 3 times, became the pupil of the Guru Nāḍapāda[1621]), Maitrīpāda, Çāntibhadra[1622]), Pha-mthiṅ[1623])(?) and others studied the instructions to the Guhyasamāja, Çaṁvara, Mahamāyā, Catuḥpīṭha, etc. and augmented the number of the students of the Tantras of Propitiation.

Phag-pai-çei-rab of S'aṅ-kar studied with the Paṇḍits Araṇyaka[1624]) (?) of Kashmir, Tejodeva, Parahitabhadra and others, and made translations of (works belonging to the cycles of) Yogatantra, Uṣṇīṣa[1624a]), Vajrapāṇi of Sugatigarbha[1625]), and Vaiçravaṇa[1625a]),

---

1618) Saṅs-rgyas-thod-pa. Full title: Buddha-kapāla-nāma-yoginī-tantra-rāja. Kg. RGYUD. IV, No. 35. Translator acc. to Kg. the same. In the Tg. we have, translated by him and belonging to the Cycle of Buddhakapāla: 1. Çrī-Buddhakapāla-tantrasya pañjikā Jñānavatī nāma, Tg. RGYUD. XXIV. 119 — 168, the work of Saraha; 2. Çrī-Buddhakapāla-sadhana. Ibid. 251—256, author ditto; 3. Çrī-Buddhakapāla-nāma-maṇḍala-vidhi-krama-pradyotana, Ibid. 257—271. Author ditto.

1618a) Rdo-rje-bdud-rtsi, Kg. RGYUD. V, No. 4. Translator not mentioned.

1618b) In the Tg. we have: Çrī-varja-ḍāka-tantrasya Tattva-susthirā-nāma pañjikā, Tg. RGYUD. VIII. 238—254.

1619) *Mar-pa-* Chos-kyi-blo-gros. 1620) Lho-brag.

1621) Bla-ma Nā-ro. 1622) Ži-ba-bzaṅ-po.

1623) Cf. Schiefner, Tārānātha, p. 249 and 330. 1624) Dgon-pa-pa.

1624a) Gtsug-tor-gyi-skor. The works translated by Phag-pa-çei-rab, belonging to this Cycle are: — 1. Ārya-sitātapatrā-aparājitā-nāma-upāyikā. The work of Candragomin, Tg. RGYUD. LXIX. 196, 197. (Pek.); 2. Ārya-tathāgata-uṣṇisa-sitātapatrā-aparājitā-pratyangirā-nāma-dhāraṇī-sādhana. The work of Candragomin, Ibid. 204—206; 3. Author and title ditto. Ibid. 210—211; 4. Ārya-tathāgata-uṣṇiṣa-sitātapatrā-nāma-dhāraṇī-vidhi. Author ditto. Ibid. 211, 212.; 5. Uṣṇīṣa-sitātapatrā-vidhi. The work of Çūraṁgavajra, Ibid. 217, 218; 6. Ārya-tathāgata-uṣṇīṣa-sitātapatrā-aparājitā-nāma-maṇḍala-vidhi. The work of Padmāṁkuça, Ibid. 227—234; 7. Ārya-sitātapatrā-nāma-sañcaka-vidhi. Author ditto, Ibid. 234—238.

1625) Phyag-na-rdo-rje Ḥgro-bzaṅs-kyi-skor. These are: 1. Bhagavan-nīlāmbara-dhara-Vajrapāṇi-sādhana. Tg. RGYUD. LXVIII. 291, 292; 2. Nīlāmbaradhara-Vajrapāṇi-bali-vidhi, Ibid. 292, 293; 3. Nīlāmbaradhara-Vajrapāṇi-nāga-bali-vidhi, Ibid. 293, 294; 4. Gaṇacakra, Ibid. 294, 295; 5. Vajrapāṇi-maṇḍala-vidhi, Ibid. 295—298.

1625a) Rnam-thos-sras-kyi-skor. These are: — 1. Mahārāja-Vaiçravaṇa-sādhana. Tg. RGYUD. LXXII. 276—278; 2. Vaiçravaṇa-sādhana, Ibid. 284 — 285, the work of Çūraṁgavarman; 3. Vaiçravaṇa-kalpa. Ibid. 285, 286; 4.

the Great Commentary on the *Bodhicaryāvatāra*, (works of the cycle of) Çaṁvara[1625b]) etc. Dar-ma-ḍag of Ñan[1626]) lived in India 12 years, studied with the Paṇḍit Mati, invited the Paṇḍit Sunayaçrī, and translated the Great Commentary on the *Bodhicaryāvatāra*, (works of the cycles of) Tārā[1627]), of the Custodians of the Faith[1627a]) etc. [155 a.]

The youths Dab Khor-lo-ḍag[1628]), Sal-pa-ḍag of Poṅ-sh'o[1629]) and Mi-ñag-tsa-mi Saṅ-gyä-ḍag of Tsoṅ-kha, having taken recourse to the help of the Paṇḍit Abhayākaragupta, translated (works on) the *Kālacakra*, the *Niṣpannayogāvalī*[1630]), the *Munimatālaṁkāra*[1631]), the *Āmnāyamañjarī*[1632]) and other works.

The translator of Ṭ'e-vo[1633]), — Çei-rab-pal, with the assistance of that very Paṇḍit, translated the *Marmakaumudī*[1634]) etc. Rin-chen-ḍag of Pha-ri invited the Paṇḍit Amoghavajra and translated the *Amoghapāça*[1634a]), the *Pañcarakṣā*[1635]), the works on the Cycle

---

Mahārāja-Vaiçravaṇa-kalpa Çaṁkara-vidhi (? kalpa)-viçva-koça. Ibid. 286—287.

1625b) These are: — 1. Padārtha-prakāçikā nāma Çrī-Çaṁvara-mūla-tantra-ṭikā. Tg. RGYUD. VII. 400—503. (Pek.) The work of Vīravajra; 2. Çrī-cakra-saṁvara-tantra-rāja-Çaṁvara-samuccaya-nāma-vṛtti, Tg. RGYUD. VIII. 1—151, the work of Indrabhūti; 3. Mūla-tantra-saṁgraha-hṛdaya-abhidhāna-uttaratantra-mūla-mūla-vṛtti. Ibid. 151—286, the work of Çūraṁgavajra.

1626) Gñan Dar-ma-grags.

1627) Sgrol-maḥi-skor. In Bu-ton's Index we have the Sgrol-ma spyiḥi sgrub-thabs ascribed to Nāgārjuna and translated by Darma-ḍag. It is indicated by Bu-ton (fol. 207 a. 2—b. 1) as not contained in the Tangyur *(Bstan-ḥgyur-du ma-chud)*.

1627a) Of this Cycle we have, translated by Dar-ma-ḍag, the Ucchūṣma-Jambhala-sādhana. Tg. RGYUD. LXXII. 295—296. The work of Mati or Āryamati.

1628) Gdab Ḥkhor-lo-grags.

1629) Spoṅ-žo Gsal-pa-grags.

1630) The Xyl. has Phreṅ-ba-skor-gsum. This evidently refers to a work the title of which ends with "Phreṅ-ba" (= mālā or āvalī). In the Tg. RGYUD. LXXXIV we have the work of Abhayākaragupta: Çrī-Mañju-vajra-ādi-krama-abhisamaya-samuccaya-niṣpanna-yoga-āvalī. (fol. 114—188).

1631) Thub-pa-dgoṅs-rgyan. Tg. MDO. XXIX. 71—398.

1632) Man-ṅag-sñe-ma. Tg. RGYUD. XIX.

1633) Bre-bo- Lo-tsa-ba.

1634) Gnad-kyi-zla-zer. Tg. MDO. XI. 1—256. (Pek.)

1634a) Don (i. e. Don-yod)-žags-pa. This is the Ārya-Amoghapaça-panca-deva-stotra, the work of Erapati. Tg. RGYUD. LXVIII, No. 30.

1635) Bsruṅ-ba-lṅa.

of *Vijaya-vidāraṇī*[1636]), of Çaṁvara[1636a]), the *Sādhana-çataka*[1637]), etc.

Log-kya[1638]) Çei-rab-tseg translated the (works of the) Cycles of *Mañjuçrī-nāma-saṁgīti*[1639]), and of Tārā, the *Mādhyamika-avatāra*[1640]), etc. His pupil Mal-gyo Lo-ḍö-ḍag-pa translated the (works of the Cycles of) Çaṁvara and Tārā belonging to the system or Sūryagupta[1641]).

Çei-rab-ḍag-of Ḍo[1642]) went to Kashmir and, having invited the Paṇḍit Somanātha[1643]), translated the detailed instructions to the *Kālacakra*[1643a]), the Commentary on the *Hevajra-tantra* by Vajragarbha[1644]), the Commentary on the first part of the *Tantra of Vajrapāṇi*[1645]) etc. The translators Thö-pa-gā[1646]) of Pa-reg, Chö-bar of Ma-pan[1647]), and Tshur[1647a]) studied with the Indian Paṇḍit Vajrapāṇi and translated the works belonging to the Cycle of the *Mahāmudrāsiddhi*[1648]), the *Hṛdayasiddhi*[1649]), the 3 Cycles

---

1636) Rnam-rgyal-rnam-ḥjoms.

1636a) The works belonging to the Cycle of Çaṁvara and translated by Rin-chen-ḍag are: — 1. Çrī-cakra-saṁvara-pañjikā. Tg. RGYUD. VI. 159—280. The work of Bhavabhaṭṭa; 2. Samanta-guṇa-çālinī. Tg. RGYUD. VII, 177—233. The work of Vīravajra; 3. Yoginī-saṁcārya-nibandha. Tg. RGYUD. XII. 139—160. The work of Tathāgatarakṣita; 4. Çrī-Çaṁvara-sañcaka-vidhi-Tg. RGYUD. XIII. 86, 87. The work of Prajñārakṣita; 5. Cakra-saṁvara-sādhana. Ibid. 87—91. The work of Jayabhadra; 6. Çrī-Çaṁvara-maṇḍala-upāyikā. Ibid. 91—125. Author ditto. 1637) Sgrub-thabs brgya-rtsa. Tg. RGYUD. LXXI. No. No. 1—94. 1638) Glog-skya. 1639) Mtshan-brjod.

1640) The translators of the Mādhyamikāvatāra indicated in the Tangyur are the Paṇḍit Tilakakalaça and Ñi-ma-ḍag (Sūryakīrti) of Ba-tshab.

1641) Sgrol-ma Ñi-ma-sbas-paḥi-lugs. Tg. RGYUD. XXVI. No.No. 3—8, etc.

1642) Ḥbro Çes-rab-grags. 1643) Zla-ba-mgon-po.

1643a) In the Tg. we have, translated by Somanātha and Çei-rab-ḍag: 1. The Great Commentary on the Kālacakra called Vimalaprabhā, Tg. RGYUD. I and II, and 2. Çrī-Kālacakra-tantra-rājasya seka-prakriya-vṛtti Vajra-pada-udghāṭinī. The work of Dārika, Tg. RGYUD. IV. 48—87.

1644) Rdo-rje-sñiṅ-ḥgrel. Full title: Hevajra-piṇḍārtha-ṭīkā, Tg. RGYUD. XV. 1—139. The translators acc. to the Tg. are: Maitrīpāda and Çei-rab-ḍag.

1645) Phyag-rdor-stod-ḥgrel. In Bu-ton's index (fol. 209 a. 6—b. 1) we have the indication of Phyag-na-rdo-rje-dbaṅ-bskur-baḥi-rgyud-kyi-stod-ḥgrel — Commentary on the first part of the Vajrapāṇy-abhiṣeka as "not found".

1646) Thos-pa-dgaḥ. 1647) Rma-ban Chos-ḥbar.

1647a) The name of this Lotsava is Ye-çes-ḥbyuṅ-gnas = Jñānākara.

1648) Phyag-rgya-chen-po-grub-paḥi-skor.

1649) Sñiṅ-poḥi-skor. The works belonging to these Cycles and translated by the said 3 Lotsavas are to be found in the Tg. RGYUD. XLVI, viz. No. No. 12, 14, 16, 21, 23, 24, 25, 27, 28, 29, 32, 40, 41.

of *Doha*[1650]), the *Dohakoça*[1651]), the works on the Cycle of Çaṁvara by Maitrīpāda[1651a]) etc.

Kun-gā-dorje of Cal[1652]) studied with the Nepalese teacher Haṅ-du the White[1653]), and invited the Paṇḍit Çūnyatāsamādhi[1654]) from whom he received a great number of instructions.

Rva Dorje-ḍag studied with the Nepalese Mahākāruṇika and translated the 3 Cycles of Kṛṣṇa-Yamāri and Bhairava [155 b.][1655]), the Cycle of *Heruka-abhyudaya*[1656]) etc.

Bön-po Rva Chö-rab invited the Paṇḍit Samantaçrī and translated the *Kālacakra*, the *Varāhy-abhibhāva*[1657]), and the *Mahākāla-tantra-rāja*[1658]).

Sh'aṅ Çei-rab-la-ma invited the Paṇḍit Amoghavajra and translated the Cycle of Kṛṣṇa-Yamāri[1658a]) in detail.

Gyü Mön-lam-ḍag[1659]) studied with the Paṇḍit Parahita and translated the *Saṁvara-udaya*[1660]).

Sh'va-ma Seṅ-gyal secured the assistance of the Paṇḍit Maṇibhadrarakṣita[1661]) and others and translated the *Pramāṇa-samuccaya* with the Commentary thereon.

Mar-pa-t'o-pa Chö-kyi-vaṅ-chug of Ya-ḍog[1662]) translated the

---

1650) Tg. RGYUD. XLVII and XLVIII.

1651) Do-ha-mdzod. 1651a) Tg. RGYUD. XIII. 143—149.

1652) Dpyal Kun-dgaḥ-rdo-rje. 1653) Haṅ-du-dkar-po.

1654) Stoṅ-ñid-tiṅ-ṅe-ḥdzin.

1655) *Dgra-nag Ḥjigs-byed-kyi skor. In the Tg. we have the following works* belonging to the Cycle of Bhairava and translated by Dorje-ḍag of Rva: 1. Çrī-Bhairava-sādhana. Tg. RGYUD. XLIII. 208, 209; 2. Vajra-Bhairava-gaṇa-cakra. Ibid. 209—211. The work of Ratnākaraçānti; 3. Chucchundara-kalpa. Ibid. 211, 212; 4. Mahā-vajra-Bhairava-homa-vidhi. Ibid. 212—216. The work of Amogha-vajra.

1656) Tg. RGYUD. XII.

1657) Phag-mo-mṅon-ḥbyuṅ. Full title: Ḍākinī-sarva-citta-advaya-acintya-jñāna-vajra-varāhy-abhibhāva-tantra-rāja. Kg. RGYUD. IV. No. 33. Acc.. to Kg. the translators are: Gāyadhara and Gyi-co Da-va-ö-s'er (Zla-ba-ḥod-zer).

1658) Acc. to Bu-ton: *Mgon-po-mṅon-ḥbyuṅ* = Nātha-abhyudaya (or: —abhibhāva). Kg. RGYUD. V, No. 9. Cf. above note 858.

1658a) *In the Tg. we have, translated by this Lotsava:* — 1. Çrī-Kṛṣṇa-Yamāri-cakra-vidhi. Tg. RGYUD. XLIII. 235—237. The work of Amogha-vajra; 2. Karma-sahāya-karaṇa. Ibid. 237, 238; 3. Sad-dravya-adbhuta-vikurvita-saṁbhajana-vidhi. Ibid. 238, 239; 4. Çrī-Vajra-Bhairava-stuti. Ibid. 246. The work of Amoghavajra.

1659) Rgyus Smon-lam-grags. 1660) Sdom-ḥbyuṅ.

1661) Nor-bzaṅ-sruṅ-ba.

1662) Ya-ḥbrog-gi Mar-pa-do-pa Chos-kyi dbaṅ-phyug.

Commentaries on the Çaṁvara-tantra belonging to the Cycle of Propitiation[1663]), in detail.

Chö-kyi-s'aṅ-po of Cal, lived in India 10 years, studied with the teacher of Vajrāsana — Niṣkalaṅka and translated the Cycles of Çaṁvara and Rakta-Yamāri. It is he who ordained the Kashmirian Çākyaçīla as a Çramaṇera.

The translator of Ṭho-phu, — Jam-pai-pal[1664]) invited the Paṇḍit Çrī Jaganmitra-Ananta who is known by the surname of Mitrayogin. He translated the Cycle of Çaṁvara-Ekajaṭā[1664a]), the Svacitta-viçrama-upadeça[1665]), the Sugata-çāsana-ratna-vohittha[1666]), etc.

Thereafter, having invited the Kashmirian Paṇḍit Buddhaçrījñāna, he translated the Commentary on the *Abhisamayālaṁkāra* called *Prajñā-pradīpa*[1667]), the *Jinamārga-avatāra*[1667a]), the 100 Methods of Propitiation of Avalokiteçvara[1668]), etc.

After that the Paṇḍit Cākyaçrībhadra of Kashmir was invited, and Cal Chö S'aṅ translated the Great Commentary of Nāḍapāda[1668a]), and the Paṇḍit gave him numerous explanations and instructions. This Paṇḍit was accompanied by the inferior Paṇḍits Vibhūticandra, Dānaçīla, the Nepalese Sanghaçrī, [156 a.] Sugataçrī and others, their number being nine. Vibhūti and Dānaçīla lived in Tibet a long time and made translations of their own works.

Jam-pai-pal translated the *Vinaya-puṣpamālā*[1669]) and received the instructions to it. Moreover he translated the *Vajramālā*, works belonging to the Cycle of Çaṁvara etc.

[1663]) In the Tg. RGYUD. XII we have, translated by him: 1. Bhagavacchrī-cakra-Çaṁvarasya sādhanam Ratna-cūḍāmaṇi (fol. 284—294); 2. Çrī-cakra-Çaṁvara-maṇḍala-upāyikā Ratna-pradīpa-uddyotana (fol. 294—332); 3. Bhagavac-cakra-Çaṁvara-sādhana Ratna-cintāmaṇi (fol. 271—276); 4. Maṇḍala-deva-stotra Ratna-māyā-dāna (fol. 280—282); 5. Bhagavac-Chrī-Çaṁvara-maṇḍala-vidhi (fol. 344—363); 6. Vasanta-tilaka (fol. 371—381).

[1664]) Ḳhro-phu-lo-tsa-ba Byams-paḥi-dpal.

[1664a]) Bde-chen Ral-gcig-gi-skor. Tg. RGYUD. XLIV. No.No. 31—37.

[1665]) Sems-ñid-ṅal-gso. Full title: Svacitta-viçrama-upadeça Gāthā-pañcaviṃçatika. Tg. RGYUD. XLIV. 213, 214.

[1666]) Bstan-paḥi-gru. Tg. RGYUD. XLVIII. 170—174. The work of Niṣkalanka.

[1667]) Tg. MDO. IX. 1—87. [1667a]) Rgyal-baḥi-lam-ḥjug. Cf. below.

[1668]) Thugs-rje-chen-poḥi sgrub-thabs-bgrya-rtsa-brgyad = Ārya-Avalokiteçvara-aṣṭottara-çataka-sādhana. Tg. RGYUD. LXVIII. No.No. 48—154.

[1668a]) Vajra-pada-sāra-saṁgraha-pañjikā. Tg. RGYUD. XVII. 69—169.

[1669]) Tg. MDO. LXXXIX.

The great Kashmirian Paṇḍit (Çākyaçrībhadra) ordained the Sa-kya-Paṇḍita who studied with him and with the Nepalese Sanghaçrī the science of Grammar, and, moreover, with the Great Paṇḍit and Dānaçīla, — the *Pramāṇavārtika*. Thereafter he made numerous corrections to the books that were translated before. Having become greatly learned, he refuted all who were not in possession of the pure Teaching.

Jaṅ-chub-pal and Dorje-pal were ordained by the Great Paṇḍit and kept the Observance of the Unique Seat[1670]). Thereafter a great number of scholars belonging to the spiritual descent of the Great Paṇḍit appeared.

On the Srin-po-ri the Great Paṇḍit accomplished the *Vajra-mālā-abhiṣeka*[1671]) and greatly furthered the spread of the teachings granting magical power.

Chag Ḍa-com[1672]) went to India and translated the *Jinamārga-avatāra*[1672a]) and other works. His nephew Chag Chö-rje-pal likewise went to India and, assisted by Devendra, Ratna-rakṣita and other Tantric Exorcists, translated the 9 *Uṣṇīṣa-tantras*[1763]) and made numerous corrections of (previous) translations.

Dorje-gyal-tshen of Çoṅ went to Nepal and, having invited the Paṇḍit Lakṣmīçrī[1674]), translated the *Kavyādarça*[1675]), the *Avadāna-kalpalatā*[1676]), the *Nāgānanda-nāṭaka*[1676a]), the 100

1670) *gdan-gcig-paḥi-brtul-žugs.*

1671) *rdo-rje-phreṅ-baḥi-dbaṅ-bskur.*

1672) Dgra-bcom.

1672a) Tg. MDO. XXXII. 231—271. The Work of Buddhaçrījñāna.

1673) Gtsug-dguḥi-rgyud. These are evidently the following works: — 1. Sarva-tathāgata-uṣṇīṣa-vijayā-nāma-dhāraṇī kalpasahitā, Kg. RGYUD. XIV. No. 23. 2. Sarva-durgati-pariçodhanī-uṣṇīṣa-vijayā-nāma-dhāraṇī, Ibid. No. 24. 3. Sarva-tathāgata-uṣṇīṣa-vijayā-nāma-dharaṇī kalpasahitā, Ibid. No. 25. 4. and 5. works bearing the same title, Ibid. No.No. 26 and 27. 6. Ārya-sarva-tathāgata-uṣṇīṣa sitātapatrā-nāma-aparājita-pratyangira-mahāvidyā-rājñī, Ibid. No. 28. 7. Ārya-tathāgata-uṣṇīṣa-sitātapatrā-aparājita-mahāpratyangira-parama-siddhi-nāma-dhāraṇī, Ibid. No. 29. 8. Ārya-tathāgata-uṣṇīṣa-sitātapatrā-aparājitā-nāma-dhāraṇī. Ibid. No. 30, and 9. Ārya-tathāgata-uṣṇīṣa-sitāta-patrā-nāma-aparājita-dhāraṇī. Ibid. No. 31.

1674) The Xyl. has: Lakṣiçrī.

1675) Sñan-ṅag-me-loṅ. Tg. MDO. CXVII.

1676) (Rtogs-brjod)-dpag-bsam-khri-çiṅ, Tg. MDO. XCIII. 1—361. Translators acc. to Tg. Lakṣmīkara and Dorje-gyal-tshen.

1676a) Klu-kun-tu-dgaḥ-baḥi zlos-gar. The work of Çrīharṣadeva, Tg. MDO XCII. 269—304. Translators acc. to Tg. the same.

Hymns[1676b]) etc. His younger brother Lo-ḍö-tan-pa translated the *Rakta-Yamāri-tantra*[1677]) and made corrections of previous translations.

Ḍag-pa-gyal-tshen of Yar-luṅ translated the *Acala-tantra*[1678]), the *Sādhana-sāgara*[1679]), [156 b.] the *Kriyā-saṁgraha*[1680]) etc.

My own teacher Ñi-ma-gyal-tshen-pal-s'aṅ-po studied in Nepal fourteen years and translated 14 Sūtras, the *Giryānanda*[1681]) etc. with the assistance of the Paṇḍit Anantaçrī. Above this he made many other fundamental translations and numerous corrections.

Paṅ Lo-ḍö-tan-pa translated the Commentary to the *Pramāṇa-samuccaya* of Jinendrabuddhi[1682]), the Commentary to the *Kālacakra* called *Hṛdayāloka*[1683]) and other works.

All these have greatly furthered the spread of the Doctrine. The minute details (concerning the lives of these Paṇḍits) may be known from the special biographies of each of them.

1676b) Bstod-pa-brgya-pa. Full title: Lokeçvara-çataka-stotra (Ḥjig-rten-dbaṅ-phyug-gi bstod-pa-brgya-pa). Tg. RGYUD. LXVIII. 108—121. The work of Vajradeva.

1677) Gçin-rje-gçed-dmar-gyi-rgyud. Full title: Çrī-rakta-Yamāri-tantra-rāja, Kg. RGYUD. VII, No. 13. Translators acc. to Kg. Candrakīrti and Ḍag-pa-gyal-tshen.

1678) In the Kg. we have the Acalakalpa (RGYUD. V, No. 1), translators Atulyadāsavajra and Chö-kyi-vaṅ-chug-ḍag, and the Ārya-acala-mahā-guhya-tantra (Ibid. No. 2), translators not indicated.

1679) Sgrub-thabs-rgya-mtsho. Tg. RGYUD. LXXI. 95—340.

1680) Bya-ba-bsdus-pa. Tg. RGYUD. LVII. 260—420.

1681) Riḥi-kun-dgaḥi-mdo, Kg. ÇER. (Prajñā-pāramitā) XXII, No. 20.

1682) Tg. MDO. CXV.

1683) Dus-ḥkhor-gyi-bçad-sbyar Sñiṅ-po-snaṅ-ba. Full title: Çrīmad-Vimala-prabhā-tantra-avatāraṇa-vāda Hṛdayāloka (Dpal-ldan Dri-ma-daṅ-bral-baḥi-ḥod-kyi-rgyud-la ḥjug-paḥi bçad-sbyar Sñiṅ-po-snaṅ-ba, Tg. RGYUD. III. 25—86.

Contents

Introduction 3

The Life of the Buddha according to the *Lalita-vistara* (as a part of IV Acc_1 b_2 b_3 — "The Acts of the Buddha" — in Vol. I.) 7

The Buddha's attainment of Nirvāṇa according to the *Vinaya-kṣudraka* 56

IV. Acc_1 b_2 c_3. A detailed Exposition of the Essence of the Doctrine. [88 a. 3.]

IV. Acc_1 b_2 c_3 a_4. The Rehearsals of the Kanon. [Ibid.] 73

IV. Acc_1 b_2 c_3 a_4 a_5. The Rehearsals of the Hīnayānistic Scripture:

The First Rehearsal. [88 a. 5.] 73

The Second Rehearsal. [96 b. 4.] 91

The Third Rehearsal and the 18 Sects. [99 a. 1.] 96

IV. Acc_1 b_2 c_3 a_4 b_5. The Rehearsal of the Mahāyānistic Kanon. [101 a. 3.] 101

IV. Acc_1 b_2 c_3 b_4. The Period of Existence of the Doctrine. [101 b. 1.] 102

IV. Acc_1 b_2 c_3 b_4 a_5. The Time during which the Doctrine is to exist [Ibid.] Quotations from Sūtras and Çāstras. Calculations of Atīça, of the Sa-skya Paṇḍita etc. regarding the time that has passed since the death of the Buddha. [103 a. 5.]

IV. Acc_1 b_2 c_3 b_4 b_5. The Prophecies concerning the persons who furthered the spread of Buddhism. [104 b. 3.] 108

The Prophecy of the *Mahākaruṇā-puṇḍarīka*. [104 b. 6.]. 109

The Prophecy of the *Mañjuçrī-mūla-tantra*. [105 b. 4.] .. 111

The Prophecies concerning the Tantric Ācāryas of the *Mahākāla-tantra-rāja* and the *Kālacakra-Uttaratantra*. [108 b. 4.] 120

IV. Acc_1 b_2 c_3 b_4 c_5. The Celebrated Buddhist Teachers of India. [110 a. 1.]

The Teacher Nāgārjuna. [Ibid.] 122

The Teacher Āryadeva. [112 b. 6.] 130

The Teacher Candragomin. [113 b. 3.] 132

The Teacher Candrakīrti. [114 b. 2.] 134

The Biography of the Brothers Āryāsanga and Vasubandhu. [115 a. 2.] 136

The Teacher Sthiramati. [119 a. 6.] 147

The Teacher Dignāga. [120 a. 4.] 149

The Teacher Dharmakīrti. [121 b. 6.] 152

The Teacher Haribhadra. [123 b. 3.] 156

The Teacher Guṇaprabha. [125 b. 5.] 160

The Teacher Çāntideva. [126 b. 1.] 161

The History of the Grammatical Literature. [128 b. 5.] . 166

The Lost Parts of the Kanon. [130 a. 6.] 169

IV. $Acc_1 b_2 c_3 c_4$. The Cessation of the Existence of the Doctrine. [131 b. 4.]

The Prophecy of the *Candragarbha-paripṛcchā*, etc...... 171

IV. B. The History of Buddhism in Tibet. [137 a. 1.] 181

IV. Ba. The Earlier Period of the Propagation of the Doctrine. [137 a. 2.]

The Genealogy of the early Tibetan Kings. [137 a. 4.] . 181

The Reign of Sroṅ-tsen-gam-po. [138. a 2.]........... 183

The Reign of Ṭhi-sroṅ-de-tsen. [139 b. 1.] 186

The Controversy between Kamalaçila and the Hva-çaṅ Mahāyāna. [143 a. 1.] 193

The Reign of Ral-pa-can. [144 b. 6.] 196

The Persecution of Laṅ-dar-ma. [145 b. 2.]........... 197

IV. Bb. The Subsequent Period of the Propagation of the Doctrine. [147 a. 1.]

The Activity of the 10 Monks of Ü and Tsaṅ. [Ibid.] .. 201

The Monasteries and Monastic Sections founded by them. [148 a. 6.] 203

The Arrival of Dīpaṁkaraçrījñāna (Atīça). [153 a. 4.] .. 213

The Translation of the Kanonical Texts by the Lotsavas and Paṇḍits. [153 b. 1. 214

Index

of Sanskrit Texts quoted in Part I and II

Akṣayamati-nirdeça, I. 30, 116; II. 4, 103, 143, 146.
Acala-tantra, II. 224.
Ajātaçatru-kaukṛtya-vinodana, I. 41.
Adhyāçaya-saṁcodana-sūtra, I. 12, 87 (both passages quoted in the Çikṣāsamuccaya).
Anantamukha-nirhāra-dhāraṇī, II. 68.
Anukampā-pratikaraṇa-sūtra (?), I. 108.
Abhidharmakoça, I. 15, 21, 22, 49, 50, 103 (bis); II. 105, 144, 145, 146, 148, 150.
Abhidharmakoça-bhāṣya, I. 120; II. 102.
Abidharma-samuccaya, I. 14, 22, 31, 34, 49, 56, 70, 118, 137; II. 139, 140, 148, 199.
Abhidharma-samuccaya-bhāṣya, I.118, 124, 137.
Abhidharma-sūtra, II. 102.
Abhisamayālaṁkāra, I. 43, 51, 53, 54, 105, 106, 116, 130; II. 140, 178, 222.
Abhisamayālaṁkārālokā (alias Comm. on the Aṣṭasāhasrikā or "The Great Commentary" — hgrel-chen), I. 41, 76, 80, 121, 134.
Abhisamayālaṁkāra-kārikā-çāstra, II. 139.
Abhisamayālaṁkāra-vārtika, II. 156.
Amarakoça, I. 47, 48.
Amoghapāça, II. 219.
Amoghapāça-tantra, II. 171.
Avataṁsaka, II. 169.
Arali, II. 216.
Alpākṣarī, II. 124.
Avadāna-kalpalatā, II. 223.
Aṣṭa-mahāsthāma-caitya-stotra, I.101.
Aṣṭasāhasrikā, I. 98; II. 49, 146, 158.
Aṣṭasāhasrikā-piṇḍārtha, I. 51, 53.
Aṣṭādaçasāhasrikā, II. 49.
Aṣṭānga-hṛdaya, I. 48.
Āgama-vibhanga, I. 14.
Ācāra-tantra, II. 170.
Ātmasādhana-avatāra, II. 159.
Āmnāya-mañjarī, II. 127, 219.
Āyudhopama-vacana-mukha, II. 169.
Āryasaṁcaya, I. 41.
Āryākoça, I. 44.
Ālambana-parīkṣā, II. 150.
Indravyākaraṇa, II. 166, 167.
Ugraparipṛcchā (quoted in Çiksāsamuccaya), I. 87.
Uṇādi-sūtra, II. 133.
Uttaragrantha, I. 50.
Uttaratantra, I. 16, 21, 22, 25, 42, 53, 54, 60, 134, 136, 138; II. 140, 170.
Udayana-paripṛcchā, II. 169.
Udānavarga, I. 20, 50.
Udānavarga-vivaraṇa, I. 58.
Upasarga-vṛtti, II. 133.
Upāyakauçalya, I. 134.
Uṣṇīṣa-tantra, II. 223.
Uṣṇīṣa-vijaya, II. 144.
Uṣṇīṣa-vijaya-dhāraṇī, II. 145.
Ṛgveda, I. 48.
Eka-druma-pañjikā, II. 132.
Ekottara-karma-çataka, II. 160.
Ekottarika-āgama, II. 170.
Karakāçani, II. 148.
Karaṇḍa-vyūha, II. 183, 184.
Karuṇā-puṇḍarika, I. 91, 98, 100, 108; II. 4, 97, 103, 178.
Karma-çataka, II, 186, 199.

Karma-siddhi-prakaraṇa, I. 57.
Kalāpa-sūtra, I. 47; II. 168, 169.
Kalpa-tantra, II. 170.
Kāya-traya-avatāra, II. 133.
Kāla-cakra (-garbha), II. 217, 219.
Kāla-cakra-uttara-tantra, II. 4, 121.
Kāla-cakra-tantra, I. 100; II. 108, 170, 217, 220, 221, 224.
Kāvyādarça, I. 47; II. 223.
Kriyā-tantra, II. 170.
Kriyā-saṁgraha, II. 224.
Gāyāçīrṣa-sūtra, I. 111; II. 146.
Gāthā-koça, II. 160.
Giryānanda, II. 224.
Guṇāparyanta-stotra, II. 150.
Guru-sūtra, II. 169.
Guhya-samāja, II. 159, 170.
Guhya-samāja-tantra-ṭīkā, II. 127, 134
Guhya-samāja-maṇḍala-vidhi, II. 132.
Ghanavyūha-sūtra, I. 135; II. 169.
Catuḥpīṭha-tantra-rāja-maṇḍala-upāyika-vidhi-sāra-samuccaya, II. 131.
Catuḥpīṭha-ṭīkā, II. 214.
Catuḥpīṭha-sādhana, II. 131.
Catuḥçataçāstra-kārikā, I. 80.
Catuḥçatika, II. 134.
Caturtha-avātara, II. 160.
Caturdharmaka, II. 146.
Caturmudrā-niçcaya, II. 127.
Chando-ratnākara, I. 47.
Candragarbha-paripṛcchā, II. 5, 170, 171.
Candragarbha-sūtra, II. 103.
Candrapradīpa, I. 86, 126; II. 133.
Candra-vyākaraṇa, II. 168, 169.
Caryā-melayana-pradīpa, II. 131.
Citta-āvaraṇa-viçodhana, II. 131.
Cittamātrālaṁkāra, II. 141.
Jana-poṣaṇa-bindu, I. 44; II. 126.
Jātakas (Jātaka-mālā), I. 14, 83 (bis).
Jinamārga-avatāra, II. 222, 223.
Jñāna-ḍākinī-sādhana, II. 131.
Jñāna-prasthāna, I. 49.
Jñāna-vajra-samuccaya, II. 170.
Jñāna-vaipulya-sūtra, I. 97.
Jñāna-sāra-samuccaya, II. 131.
Tathāgata-acintya-guhya-nirdeça, II. 101.
Tathāgata-guhya-nirdeça (Tathāgata-acintya-guhya-nirdeça), I. 15, 29, 30, 84, 91, 94.
Tattva-viniçcaya, II. 140.
Tantra-samuccaya, II. 126.
Tarkajvālā, II. 4.
Tārā-abhyudaya-tantra, II. 171.
Triṁçaka (Triṁçaka-kārikā-prakaraṇa), I. 48, 56.
Triçata-kārikā, I. 50, 58, 62; II. 161.
Tricaraṇa-saptati, I. 113, 130.
Traiskandhaka, I. 108.
Daçacakra-kṣitigarbha, I. 67.
Daçabhūmaka-sūtra, I. 41; II. 143, 146.
Daçabhūmaka-sūtra, Comm. on the, I. 57.
Daçasāhasrikā, II. 49.
Duḥkha-skandha-sūtra, II. 169.
Devātiçaya-stotra, II. 179.
Doha, II. 221.
Dohakoça, II. 221.
Dharma-dharmatā-vibhanga, I. 53, 54; II. 146.
Dharmasaṁgīti-sūtra, I. 41.
Dharma-skandha, I. 49.
Dhātu-kāya, I. 49.
Dhātu-sūtra, II. 133.
Dhūpa-yoga-ratna-mālā, II. 126.
Dhyāna-svapna-cakra, II. 192.
Nandamitra-avadāna, II. 179.
Naya-traya-pradīpa, I. 40.
Nāgānanda-nāṭaka, II. 223.
Nātha-abhyudaya-tantra, II. 120.
Nikāya-bheda-upadarçana-saṁgraha (Samaya-bheda-uparacana-cakra), I. 122; II. 4.
Nirnaya-saṁgraha, I. 43, 55, 56 (bis), 106, 117, 118 (bis), 124.
Nirvāṇa-sūtra, I. 23; II. 170.
Niṣpannayogāvalī, II. 219.
Nyāyabindu, I. 44.
Nyāyabindu-ṭīkā (abridged treatise of Dharmottara), I. 61.
Nyāyālaṁkāra, II. 124.
Pañcakrama, II. 126.

Pañcakrama-ṭīkā, II. 132.
Pañcarakṣā, II. 219.
Pañcaviṁçatisāhasrikā, II. 49, 155, 158.
Pañcaviṁcatisāhasrikā-ālokā, I. 29 (27—29), 99; II. 155.
Pañca-skandha-prakaraṇa, I. 57.
Paryāya-saṁgraha, I. 56 (bis).
Pāṇinīya-vyākaraṇa, II. 167.
Piṇḍīkṛta-sādhana, II. 126.
Pitṛ-putra-samāgama-sūtra, I. 134.
Prakaraṇas, II. 146.
Puṣpamālā, I. 50.
Prakaraṇa-pāda, I. 49.
Prajñapti-çāstra, I. 49; II. 178.
Prajñāpāramitā (quoted in Çikṣāsamuccaya), I. 16.
Prajñāpāramitā-bhāvanā, II. 158.
Prajñāpāramitā-sūtra, II. 4, 49, 50, 51, 101, 140, 146, 156, 170.
Prajñā-pradīpa, II. 222.
Prajñā-mūla, I. 51.
Prajñā-çataka, I. 44; II. 126.
Prajñā-hṛdaya, I. 41; II. 49.
Pratimokṣa-sūtra, I. 59.
Pratimokṣa-sūtra-ṭīkā, I. 57.
Pratītya-samutpāda-ādi-vibhanga-nirdeça (Comm. on the Pratītya-samutpāda-sūtra), I. 57.
Pratītya-samutpāda-ādi-vibhanga-nirdeça-ṭīkā, I. 24.
Pratītya-samutpāda-cakra, II. 126.
Pradīpa-uddyotana, II. 134.
Pradīpa-uddyotana-abhisaṁdhi-prakāçika-vyākhyā-ṭīkā, II. 132,
Prabhāvatī, I. 59; II. 4, 97, 142, 161. 199.
Pramāṇa-vārtika, II. 154, 155, 223.
Pramāṇa-vārtika-alaṁkāra, II. 155, 215.
Pramāṇa-viniçcaya, I. 44, 45; II. 151, 215.
Pramāṇa-samuccaya, I. 44, 45, 46; II. 150, 152, 153, 215, 221, 224.
Prasannapadā, II. 128, 134, 135.
Prasphuṭa-padā (Mādhyamika Dharmamitra), I. 124, 130, 132; II. 140.
Bahubhūmika-vastu, II. 55 (bis), 56.
Buddha-kapāla, II. 218.
Buddhabhūmi-sūtra, I. 127.
Bodhigaṇa, II. 126.
Bodhicaryāvatāra, I. 49, 53, 87; II. 127, 163, 166, 216, 219.
Bodhicitta-tilaka, II. 160.
Bodhicitta-vivaraṇa, II. 126.
Bodhisattva-piṭaka, I. 9, 82, 125; II. 179.
Bodhisattva-bhūmi, I. 49, 113, 115, 121, 123, 124; II. 160.
Bodhisattva-saṁvara-viṁçaka, I. 57, 63 ("Candragomin").
Bhadrakalpika-sūtra, I. 91, 98, 108; II. 102.
Bhāvanā-krama, I. 53.
Bhikṣu-varṣāgra-pṛcchā, II. 4, 98.
Mangala-vyākhyā, II. 160.
Mañjuçrī-guhyāpanna, II. 214.
Mañjuçrī-nāma-saṁgīti, II. 133, 220.
Mañjuçrī-mūla-tantra, II. 4 (bis), 101, 111, 121, 130, 166, 167.
Mañjuçrī-vikurvāṇa-parivarta, I. 68.
Maṇḍala-vidhi, II. 126.
Madhyamaka-alaṁkāra, I. 48.
Madhyānta-vibhanga, I. 53, 54.
Madhyānta-vibhanga-ṭīkā (Comm. on Madhyanta-vibhanga), I. 57.
Mantra-artha-vipaçyinī, II. 215.
Marma-kaumudī, II. 139, 219.
Mahā-adhigama, II. 170.
Mahā-anuttara-yoga-tantra, II. 170.
Mahā-karuṇā-puṇḍarīka, I. 97; II. 4, 109.
Mahā-kāla-tantra-rāja, II. 4, 221.
Mahā-tathāgata-uṣṇiṣa, II. 170.
Mahābhāṣya, II. 167.
Mahābherī-sūtra, II. 130.
Mahāmāyā, II. 170.
Mahā-mudrā-siddhi, II. 220.
Mahā-mūla-jñāna, II. 159.
Mahāmegha, II. 129, 169.
Mahāyāna-lakṣaṇa-samuccaya, I. 48.
Mahāyāna-saṁgraha, I. 38, 56, 123.
Mahāyāna-saṁgraha-upanibandhana, I. 112, 123.
Mahavibhāṣā, I. 50; II. 142.
Mahā-yoga-tantra, II. 170.

Mahā-vyavadāna-bhūmi, II. 170.
Mahā-Çaṁvara-abhidhāna, II. 170.
Mahāsamaya, II. 169.
Mādhyamika-alaṁkāra, II. 141.
Mādhyamika-avatāra, II. 134, 220.
Mādhyamika-catuḥçatika, II. 131.
Mādhyamika-hastavāla-prakaraṇa, II. 131.
Māyājālā, II. 170.
Mukti-tilaka, II. 160.
Mukhāgama, II. 159.
Munimatālaṁkāra, I. 116 (bis), 120; II. 103, 105, 219.
Mūla-mādhyamika, II. 134.
Maitreya-siṁhanāda-sūtra, I. 12.
Yajurveda, I. 48.
Yukti-ṣaṣṭikā, I. 51, 111.
Yoga-anuvidyā, II. 170.
Yogacaryābhūmi, I. 29, 43 (Nirnayasaṁgraha), 54 (bis), 56 (bis), 57; II. 139, 141, 145.
Yoga-çataka, II. 126.
Raktayamāri-tantra, II. 171, 224.
Ratnakūṭa (quoted in Çikṣā-samuccaya), I. 87; II. 148, 169.
Ratna-guṇa-saṁcaya, II. 49.
Ratnacūḍa-sūtra, II. 115.
Ratnajvālā, II. 159.
Ratnamegha-sūtra, I. 122; II. 184.
Ratnāvalī, I. 12, 110, 112 (bis), 130; II. 125, 126.
Rali, II. 216.
Rājāvavādaka (?), *I. 39.*
Rājaçrī-vyākaraṇa, II. 169.
Lankāvatāra, I. 131, 135; II. 4, 54, 110, 166, 169.
Lalita-vistara, I. 84, 122; II. 3, 7 *ff.*, 51.
Vacanamukha, I. 47; II. 215.
Vajra-amṛta, II. 218.
Vajracchedikā, II. 4, 103, 105.
Vajrapāṇi-tantra, II. 220.
Vajrapāṇy-abhiṣeka-tantra, II. 101.
Vajramālā, II. 222.
Vajramālā-abhiṣeka, II. 223.
Vajra-çikhara-tantra, II. 215.
Varāhy-abhibhāva, II. 221.
Varṇa-sūtra, II. 133.
Varṣāgra-pṛcchā, II. 99.
Vastu-saṁgraha, I. 55, 56.
Vāda-nyāya, I. 45.
Viṁçaka-kārikā-prakaraṇa, I. 56.
Vigraha-vyāvartanī, I. 51.
Vijaya-vidāraṇī, II. 220.
Vijñāna-kāya, I. 49.
Vinaya-kṣudraka, I. 50; II. 56 *ff.*
Vinaya-puṣpa-mālā, II. 222.
Vinaya-vastu, II. 142.
Vinaya-vibhanga, I. 50 (bis).
Vinaya-sūtra, I. 43, 50, 58; II. 160, 161.
Vibhāṣā, II. 143.
Vimalaprabhā, II. 101.
Vivaraṇa-saṁgraha, I. 56; 61; II. 141.
Vīradatta-paripṛcchā, I. 106.
Vaidalya-sūtra, I. 51.
Vyavahāra-siddhi (= Tha-sñad-grub-pa), I. 51.
Vyākhyā-yukti, I. 9 (bis), 13, 17, 18, 25, 29, 32, 42, 45, 57, 65, 71, 72, 77, 78, 80, 81, 82, 84, 136; II. 169.
Vyākhyā-yukti-ṭīkā (Guṇamati), I. 136.
Çatasāhasrikā, II. 49, 50, 124, 145, 147, 170, 192.
Çatasāhasrikā, Pañcaviṁçatisāhasrikā, and Aṣṭādaçasāhasrikā, Comm. on the, I. 52.
Çatasāhasrikā-bṛhaṭ-ṭīkā, I. 29.
Çālistambhaka-kārikā, II. 127.
Çikṣā-samuccaya, I. 13, 43, 53, 58, 86 ("Çāntideva"); *II.* 163, 166.
Çiṣya-lekha, II. 133, 171.
Çiṣya-hita, II. 168.
Çuddhimatī, I. 105, 115, 116.
Çūnyatā-saptati, I. 51.
Çūraṁgama-sūtra, II. 170.
Çramaṇera-kārikā, cf. Triçata-kārika.
Çrāvaka-bhūmi, I. 49.
Çrīparamādi-ṭīkā, II. 214.
Ṣaṇmukha-dhāraṇī, II. 146.
Saṁvara-udaya, II. 221.
Saṁgīti-paryāya, I. 49.
Saṁcaya (cf. Āryasaṁcaya), II. 51, 158, 159.
Saṁcaya, Commentaries on, I. 58.
Satya-dvaya-viniçcaya, I. 48.

Satya-dvaya-vibhanga, I. 129.
Saddharma-puṇḍarīka, I. 32, 74, 135; II. 68.
Saṁtānāntara-siddhi, I. 45.
Saṁdhinirmocana-sūtra, I. 30, 69, 134; II. 53, 54, 112, 140, 192.
Samantabhadra, II. 133, 159.
Samantabhadra-caryā-nirdeça, I. 41.
Samantabhadra-sādhana, II. 159.
Samādhirāja, I. 73, 85; II. 169. (Cf. Candrapradīpa).
Saṁpuṭa, II. 216.
Saṁbandha-parīkṣā, I. 45.
Sāgara-nāgarāja-paripṛcchā, I. 12.
Sāgaramati-paripṛcchā, I. 15, 75.
Sādhana-çataka, II. 220.
Sādhana-sāgara, II. 224.
Sāmaveda, I. 48.
Sāmudrika, I. 44.
Sārottamā (Comm. on the Aṣṭasāhasrikā), I. 31.
Siṁha-paripṛcchā, I. 12.
Subodhinī, II. 158.
Suvarṇa-prabhāsa, I. 131, 134; II. 68, 186 (-prabhāsottama).
Suhṛllekha, I. 58; II. 126.
Sūtra-melāpaka, II. 126.
Sūtra-samuccaya, I. 53; II. 125, 163, 166.
Sūtrālaṁkāra, I. 17, 36 (bis), 37, 38 (bis) 39, 43, 44, 46, 53 (bis), 58, 60, 61 (bis), 63, 65, 68, 69, 86, 104, 105, 106, 109 (bis), 110, 111, 112, 114, (bis), 119, 128 (bis), 129 (bis), 130, 131, 133; II. 142, 216.
Sūtrālaṁkāra-bhāṣya (Comm. on Sūtrālāṁkāra), I. 29, 57, 116, 134.
Skhalita-pramathana-yukti-hetu-siddhi, II. 131.
Sphuṭārthā, II. 158.
Smṛtyupasthāna-sūtra, II. 170.
Hayagrīva-kalpa, II. 171.
Hṛdaya-siddhi, II. 220.
Hṛdayāloka, II. 224.
Hetubindu, I. 45.
Heruka-abhyudaya, II. 221.
Hevajra, II. 170.
Hevajra-tantra, II. 220.
Hevajra-pañjara, II. 216.

Bibliography

Bimala Churn Law, Buddhistic Studies. Calcutta, 1931.

B. Ch. Law, Geography of early Buddhism. London, 1932.

Mrs. Rhys Davids, D. Litt., Sakya or Buddhist Origins. London, 1931.

Brahmacāri Govinda, Abhidhammattha-Sangaha, ein Compendium Buddhistischer Philosophie und Psychologie. Munchen, 1931.

Nalinaksha Dutt, Aspects of Mahāyāna Buddhism and its relation to Hīnayāna (Calc.Or.Ser. No. 23). Calcutta, 1930.

Mrs. Rhys Davids, D. Litt., The Milinda-Questions. London, 1930.

Mrs. Rhys Davids, D. Litt., Kindred Sayings on Buddhism. Calcutta, 1930.

G. Tucci, On some Aspects of the Doctrines of Maitreya(nātha) and Asanga. Calcutta, 1930.

G. Tucci, Pre-Dignāga Buddhist Texts an Logic from Chinese Sources (Gaekwad Or.Ser. No. 49), Baroda, 1929.

G. Tucci, The Nyāyamukha of Dignāga, the oldest Buddhist Text on Logic (Mat. z. K. d. Buddh. No. 15), Heidelberg (Leipzig, Harrassowitz) 1930.

Vidhushekara Bhattacharya, Mahāyāna-viṁçaka of Nāgārjuna. Reconstructed Sanskrit Text, the Tibetan and the Chinese Versions, with an English Translation. (Viçvabharati-Studies No. 1) Calcutta, 1931.

V. Bhattacharya, Catuḥçataka of Āryadeva, Part II, reconstructed, with Sanskrit and Tibetan Texts and Extracts from the Commentary of Candrakīrti (Viçvabharati-Studies No. 2), Calcutta, 1931.

Dignāga's Pramāṇa-samuccaya, Chapter I, ed. and restored into Sanskrit by H. R. R. Iyengar. Mysore, 1930.

Vijñapti-mātratā-siddhi, traduite et annotée par L. de La Vallée Poussin. 2 vols. (Buddhica, Tomes I, V.) Paris, 1928/9.

R. Grousset, Les Philosophies Indiennes, Les Systèmes, 2 vols. Paris, 1931.

A comparative analytical Catalogue of the Kanjur Division of the Tibetan Tripitaka, published by the Otani Daigaku Library. Kioto, 1930.

E. Obermiller, History of Buddhism (Chos-ḥbyung) Part I: The Jewelry of Scripture, by Bu-ston, translated from Tibetan (Mat. z. K. d. Bddh. No. 18). Heidelberg (Leipzig, Harrassowitz) 1931.

E. Obermiller, The Sublime Science of the Great Vehicle to Salvation (Uttaratantra), a work of Ārya Maitreya, with a commentary by Āryāsanga. (Acta Orient. vol. X), 1931.

T. Matsumoto, Die Prajñāpāramitā-Litteratur nebst einem Spezimen der Suvikrāntavikramī-Prajñāpāramitā. Stuttgart, 1932.

Sujitkumar Mukhopadhyaya, Nairātmya-paripṛcchā (Viçvabharati-Studies No. 4). Calcutta, 1931.

Th. Stcherbatsky, Buddhist Logic, 2 vols (Bibl. Buddh. XXVI). Leningrad, 1931/2.